Linguistics: The Cambridge Survey

Volume II
Linguistic Theory: Extensions and Implications

Linguistics: The Cambridge Survey

Linguistics: The Cambridge Survey

Edited by Frederick J. Newmeyer
University of Washington

Volume II
Linguistic Theory: Extensions
and Implications

The right of the
University of Cambridge
to print and sell
all manner of books
was granted by
Henry VIII in 1534.
The University has printed
and published continuously
since 1584

Cambridge University Press

Cambridge

New York   Port Chester   Melbourne   Sydney

Published by the Press Syndicate of the University of Cambridge
The Pitt Building, Trumpington Street, Cambridge CB2 1RP
40 West 20th Street, New York, NY 10011, USA
10 Stamford Road, Oakleigh, Melbourne 3166, Australia

First published 1988
First paperback edition 1989

Printed in Great Britain at The Bath Press, Avon

British Library cataloguing in publication data

Linguistics: the Cambridge survey.
Vol. 2: Linguistic theory: extensions and
implications.
1. Linguistics
I. Newmeyer, Frederick J.
410   P121

Library of Congress cataloguing in publication data

Linguistic theory.
(Linguistics, the Cambridge survey; v. 2)
Includes indexes.
1. Linguistics. I. Newmeyer, Frederick J.
II. Series.
P121. L567 vol. 2 410s [410] 87 18386

ISBN 0 521 30833 X   hard covers
ISBN 0 521 37581 9   paperback

Contents

Contributors to Volume II

Derek Bickerton Department of Linguistics, University of Hawaii, Manoa
Susan Curtiss Department of Linguistics, University of California, Los Angeles
Suzanne Flynn Department of Foreign Languages and Literature, Massachusetts Institute of Technology
Lyn Frazier Department of Linguistics, University of Massachusetts
Victoria A. Fromkin Department of Linguistics, University of California, Los Angeles
Per-Kristian Halvorsen Xerox Palo Alto Research Center
Bruce Hayes Department of Linguistics, University of California, Los Angeles
Mary-Louise Kean Program in Cognitive Science, University of California, Irvine
Ruth Kempson Department of Linguistics, School of Oriental and African Studies, University of London
Pieter Muysken Department of Linguistics, University of Amsterdam
Frederick J. Newmeyer Department of Linguistics, University of Washington
Carol A. Padden Department of Communication, University of California, San Diego
Ellen F. Prince Department of Linguistics, University of Pennsylvania
Thomas Roeper Department of Linguistics, University of Massachusetts
Jerrold M. Sadock Department of Linguistics, University of Chicago

Preface

Linguistic theory: extensions and implications is the second of four volumes comprising the work, *Linguistics: the Cambridge survey*. The first volume, *Linguistic theory: foundations*, presents an overview of the state of grammatical research today, focussing on particular components of the grammar and their interactions (e.g. 'syntactic theory,' 'morphological change,' 'the phonology–phonetics interface,' and so on). This second volume, like the first, addresses the motivation for, and adequacy of, the reigning conceptions in theoretical linguistics. However, unlike the first, it is devoted to probing the *independent* evidence for these conceptions, that is, evidence that can be adduced beyond the introspective data about grammatical patterning upon which theorizing has traditionally relied so heavily. The chapters in this volume also show how the theory lends itself to natural extensions that help provide answers to questions raised in diverse branches of linguistics and allied fields.

The first chapter, in addition to introducing the following ones in some detail, provides an historical sketch of the attempt to motivate the concepts of generative grammar externally and to apply them to practical goals. The point is stressed that the history of this enterprise has been a very uneven one. There was a widespread consensus in the 1960s that generative grammar was both motivated and applicable, a consensus that had collapsed by the mid 1970s. But now the pendulum has swung back again, for reasons that the authors of the following chapters will make abundantly clear, and the prestige of generative grammar among psychologists, neurologists, computer scientists, and so on has reached an all-time high.

The second through the fifth chapters treat the interplay of generative grammar with the four areas that linguistic theory has traditionally been in closest touch with: language processing (Frazier), first language acquisition (Roeper), second language acquisition (Flynn), and neurolinguistics (Kean). Each demonstrates that the basic constructs of the theory are relevant to the understanding of the particular area and, in turn, that research in that particular area has deepened our understanding of the workings of the grammar.

The sixth and seventh chapters treat 'abnormal' language. Curtiss's discussion of the acquisition of abnormal language and Fromkin's analysis of speech errors demonstrate the degree to which 'nontraditional' data can be invoked to test the foundations of grammatical theory.

The eighth, ninth and tenth chapters explore, in rather different ways, the boundaries between grammatical competence and pragmatic abilities. Kempson's chapter on conversational principles, Prince's on discourse analysis, and Sadock's on speech acts each present views on 'where the grammar stops' and where abilities and faculties derived from general principles of communication and cooperation begin.

'Applied linguistics', in two very different senses of the term, is the subject of the eleventh and twelfth chapters. Halvorsen discusses computer applications of linguistic theory, while Hayes shows how the constructs of generative phonology can be applied to an understanding of metrical patterning in verse.

The final chapters deal with language varieties that possess (or, at least have been claimed to possess) properties that are rather different from those typically studied by grammarians. Padden examines the signed languages of the deaf from the viewpoint of attempting to understand their grammatical structure and Bickerton and Muysken present sharply counterposed views on the nature of creole languages.

Frederick J. Newmeyer

1 Extension and implications of linguistic theory: an overview

Frederick J. Newmeyer

Noam Chomsky's *Syntactic structures* (1957), which introduced the theory of transformational generative grammar, did not suggest any possible extensions of the theory or point to any of its broader implications. As Chomsky wrote later, he felt that it would have been 'too audacious' for him at that time to have raised the 'psychological analogue' to the problem of constructing a linguistic theory (1975:35). But Robert B. Lees, in a review that appeared simultaneously, did not shrink from this task. He closed the review with a frontal attack on the predominant behaviorist learning theory, arguing that the complexity and abstractness of natural language grammars leads irrevocably to the conclusion that they must literally be 'in the head' of the speaker. But if so, he asked, then how could they possibly be learned inductively? 'It would seem,' he concluded, 'that our notions of human learning are due for some considerable sophistication' (1957:408).

It was Chomsky's 1959 review of B. F. Skinner's *Verbal behavior* that drove home the fact that his theory of language, far from being a mere clever manipulation of arcane symbols, was a psychological model of an aspect of human knowledge. Chomsky's review represents, even after the passage of almost 30 years, the basic refutation of behaviorist psychology. The review takes in turn each basic construct of behaviorism, and concludes that 'a critical account of his book must show that . . . with a literal reading . . . the book covers almost no aspect of linguistic behavior, and that with a metaphoric reading, it is no more scientific than the traditional approaches to this subject matter, and rarely as clear and careful' (Chomsky 1959:31).

How then is verbal behavior to be explained? While acknowledging that its complexities defy any simplistic treatment, Chomsky wrote (1959:57):

> . . . the actual observed ability of a speaker to distinguish sentences fron nonsentences, detect ambiguities, etc., apparently forces us to the conclusion that this grammar is of an extremely complex and abstract character, and that the young child has succeeded in carrying out what from the formal point of view, at least, seems to be a remarkable type of theory construction.

1

Chomsky went on to argue (p. 57) that this ability indicates that rather than being born 'blank slates,' children have a genetic predisposition to structure the acquisition of linguistic knowledge in a highly specific way, bringing to the language acquisition process a 'data-handling or "hypothesis-formulating" ability of unknown character and complexity.'

Since Chomsky's review was published in a linguistics journal, its immediate impact on the field of psychology was minor. However, it did attract the attention of George A. Miller, Eugene Galanter, and Karl Pribram, three researchers at the forefront of the young discipline of cognitive psychology, who immediately realized the relevance of Chomsky's work to their interests. Miller, Galanter, and Pribram made extensive reference to generative grammar in their ensuing book *Plans and the structure of behavior* (1960). They saw in Chomsky's approach to syntax a model example of their claim that behavior must be organized simultaneously at several levels and require a complex planning device to coordinate the interplay between the various levels. As a result of their book (and the Skinner review, which by the mid 1960s had become well-known among psychologists), Chomsky was soon regarded as a leading figure in American psychology. As Judith Greene put it (1972:15): 'Chomsky's theory of generative transformational grammar was the first to force psychologists to reconsider their whole approach to the study of language behavior, and so heralded the psycholinguistic "revolution".'

At the same time, evidence began to accumulate from neurological studies that language did indeed have a biological basis, thus providing an underlying plausibility to the nativist claims that had been made primarily on the basis of the nature of the grammar that had to be acquired (see especially Lenneberg 1964, 1967). Not surprisingly, then, the two major psycholinguistic research topics of the early 1960s were acquisition of phrase structure and transformational rules by the child (Braine 1963; Menyuk 1963; Miller & Ervin-Tripp 1964; McNeill 1966), and the relationship between those rules and a model of language processing (Miller 1962; Miller & Isard 1963).

Language teachers as well found transformational generative grammar relevant to their concerns. Disillusioned with behaviorist-inspired teaching methods like the audiolingual method and programmed instruction, many welcomed Chomsky's theory, whose emphasis on the creative aspect of language and its freedom from stimulus control seemed to encourage a more active role for the learner. By 1965, Owen Thomas could write (p. 1) that 'transformational grammar has significant application to the teaching of all languages, including English, at all grade levels and to both native and nonnative speakers.' In this period, the journals of applied linguistics routinely discussed the application of the theory for some pedagogical purpose (for an historical overview of this period of second language learning research, see Newmeyer & Weinberger in press).

2

Finally, Chomsky's early work had an impact on philosophy, particularly the philosophy of science, even before the publication of his *Cartesian linguistics* in 1966. While the success of generative grammar benefited from the retreat of empiricist philosophy, it helped contribute to that retreat as well. Indeed, Israel Scheffler's book *The anatomy of inquiry* (1963), a classic in the philosophy of science, cited Chomsky's results in *Syntactic structures* to bolster his case against empiricism. He pointed out that since Chomsky had demonstrated the need to define such theoretical notions as 'noun' and 'morpheme' independently of particular languages, so philosophers should concern themselves with the *general* nature of scientific laws, rather than take an atomistic empiricist approach.

The 1960s, then, were heady years for generative grammar, as it quickly surpassed the once-hegemonic post-Bloomfieldian approach in importance and triggered new research programs in fields as diverse as philosophy, psychology, language pedagogy, poetics, anthropology, and computer science. But the next decade saw a decline in its relative importance, both within linguistics as a whole and among those outside the field who wished to apply its conceptions and results to their own concerns. For example, the hoped for payoffs in improved methods of language teaching did not materialize, leading some to the conclusion that the generativist view of language was seriously flawed; naturally a misconceived theory could not be expected to lead to fruitful applications. John Lamendella (1969) offered a popular explanation for the failure of the attempted applications: transformational generative grammar was simply 'irrelevant' to pedagogy.

Just as applied linguists deplored the theory's seeming inability to abet language teaching, psycholinguists began to express increasing dissatisfaction with the claim that grammar is innately based. Alternative hypotheses were formulated which, it was hoped, could deal with the same range of facts without the need for the innate syntactic principles that many found jarring to common sense. In the early 1970s, more and more psycholinguists abandoned Chomsky's conception of innate grammatical universals, and turned to the Piagetian idea that language acquisition results from the interaction of all-purpose cognitive skills with external environmental stimuli. The focus of acquisition studies in this period thus shifted from the acquisition of grammatical competence to that of pragmatic abilities and to probing the cognitive basis for language development.

This rejection of a nativist basis for grammar went hand-in-hand with the conclusion by most psycholinguists that language processing proceeds without drawing on a formal grammar. This negative conclusion was arrived at for two types of reasons. First, the competence model assumed by generative grammarians at the time seemed to be inconsistent with the dominant contemporary view of the grammar–processor interface. This

3

view, the 'derivational theory of complexity' (DTC), posits an isomorphic relation between the grammatical steps involved in generating a sentence and the real time steps of the processing mechanism. According to the DTC, if a certain sequence of operations (say, transformations) applies in the grammar in a particular order, then the processor's operations will mirror those steps. It was pointed out by a number of investigators that, given current assumptions about the way that the grammar was organized, this isomorphic relationship did not exist. For example, all generative grammarians before the late 1970s assumed the existence of a transformational rule of passive, which functioned (roughly) to map sentences like *John threw the ball* onto those like *The ball was thrown by John*. Since the derivation of passives involved the application of one more rule than the derivation of actives, the DTC predicts that passive sentences should take longer to process than actives. However, Slobin (1966) found this not to be the case, and thereby called into question the idea that the grammar was utilized by the processor and, by extension, that there was any need at all for an autonomous competence grammar. Second, experimental evidence seemed to disconfirm the idea that the process of sentence comprehension involves drawing on an autonomously stored grammatical representation. For example, in one experiment, Bransford & Franks (1971) presented subjects with sentences such as (1):

(1)   Three turtles rested on a log and the fish swam beneath them

In a subsequent recognition task, subjects believed that they heard (2a) as often as (2b):

(2)   a. The fish swam beneath the log
       b. The fish swam beneath the turtles

Since the deep structure of (2a) is not represented in the deep structure of (1), Bransford & Franks concluded that meaning was inferred by the use of extralinguistic knowledge such as real-world spatial relations, rather than being based on a stored grammatical representation. Such results led many psycholinguists to reject the notion of an autonomous level of grammatical competence in their construction of parsing algorithms.

As a result of the combined weight of the above factors, the prestige of generative grammar had fallen to an all-time low around 1975. Since then, it has gradually reasserted itself and there is now widespread (though by no means universal) agreement, both within the field of linguistics itself and outside the field as well, that it forms the basis of a psychologically realistic model of human language. Much of the explanation for this must be credited to the massive evidence that has accumulated in the past decade for the idea of an autonomous linguistic competence, that is, for the existence of a

4

grammatical system whose primitive terms and principles are not artifacts of a system that encompasses both human language and other human faculties or abilities.

The most direct evidence for the reality of grammatical competence comes from the complex relationship between grammatical form and communicative function. Put simply, there is no possibility of deriving the particular shape that a grammatical construction may take from the function that the construction serves in discourse. An example might prove helpful. Consider the following three common syntactic devices in English: the occurrence of the auxiliary verb before the subject, the omission of an understood *you* subject, and the occurrence of a '*wh*-word' (*what, who, how, when*, etc.) in sentence-initial position. These devices are illustrated in (3a), (3b), and (3c) respectively:

(3) a. Are you having a good time?
     b. Go home now
     c. What are you eating?

Now consider four common discourse functions in human language: making a command, expressing conditionality, asking a question, and making an exclamation. As Figure 1 demonstrates, each of the three syntactic devices mentioned above can serve three or four of these discourse functions (see Williams 1980 for more discussion of this point):

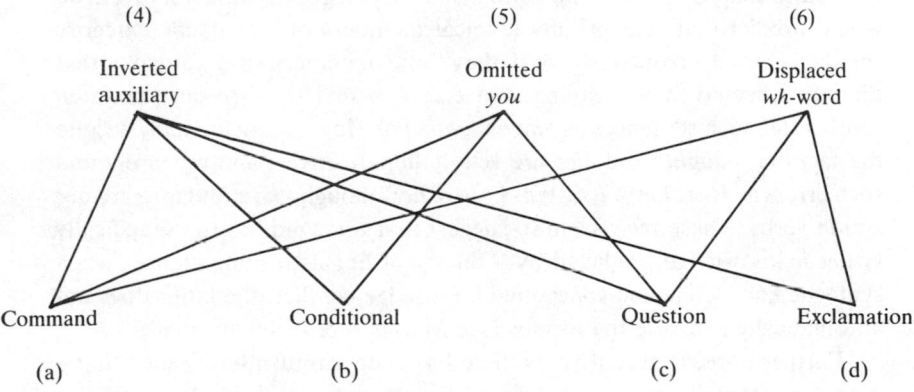

Figure 1.

(4) a. Don't you leave!
     b. Had John left (I would have taken his seat)
     c. Did he leave?
     d. Was he (ever) big!

(5) a. Leave now!
     b. Leave (and you'll regret it)
     c. Leaving now?

(6) a. How about leaving!
     c. What is it?
     d. How big he is!

This great disparity between form and function appears to be the general rule rather than the exception, a fact which strongly suggests that there are principles governing structural regularity in language that cannot be considered by-products of principles external to language. In other words, competence demands a characterization on its own terms.

The case for an autonomous linguistic competence has received support from the fact that (in extraordinary cases) linguistic abilities may be dissociated developmentally from other cognitive abilities. For example, there are cases on record of children whose syntax is completely fluent, yet who are unable to use language communicatively; conversely, cases are attested in which a child's communicative intent is obvious, yet that intent cannot be phrased according to the grammatical patterns of the language being acquired (for more discussion, see Chapter 6 in this volume). Children's errors, as well, point to the fact that the acquisition of grammar is not merely a by-product of other development, in particular conceptual development. If it were the case, for example, that the child learned concepts first and then learned to map those concepts onto syntactic categories and structures, we would predict that semantically atypical members of a syntactic category should be used erroneously as if they were members of a category that directly reflected their meaning. But errors of that sort are rare: children rarely utter such sentences as *She naughtied* or *He is nicing to them*, despite the fact that *naughty* and *nice* are actionlike adjectives, and we rarely find such errors as *He is know it* or *Was he love her*, though *know* and *love* are not action verbs. These facts seem to suggest that the child has the specifically *syntactic* knowledge predicted by a theory of linguistic competence; when syntactic knowledge and conceptual knowledge conflict, the latter does not automatically override the former (see Maratsos & Chalkley 1980).

Furthermore, in recent years there has been a return to the idea that a model of mentally represented linguistic competence *does* play a role in language processing. This change of view came about for several reasons. First, generative grammarians have (for theory-internal reasons) modified the competence model so that many once-popular grammatical analyses that were incompatible with the DTC have been abandoned for those consistent with it. Second, the DTC itself has been called into question, thereby undermining any attempt to refute the existence of linguistic competence on the grounds that it is inconsistent with that theory. And finally, the experimental evidence which challenged the utilization of a competence grammar in processing has itself been challenged. For example, the Bransford & Franks conclusions have been called into question by the demonstration that the contribution of formal grammar to sentence comprehension is manifest only during online tasks, i.e. those performed simultaneously with sentence processing; after a certain (short) period, nongrammatical factors predominate. Hence, it seems that Bransford & Franks' offline experiment does not undercut the idea that speakers utilize grammatical representations when processing a sentence (for discussion, see Carlson & Tanenhaus 1982 and Chapter 2 in this volume).

At the same time, other experimental evidence has borne out the idea that processing does draw on competence. One study shows that when subjects are presented with a class of sentence pairs that differ in some minimal way, their response times in determining that the sentences are different show a significant effect of grammaticality, but not of plausibility. Thus there is evidence for distinct syntactic and semantic components in processing. Another study finds that sentences with syntactic violations take longer to read than well-formed sentences, even when perceivers do not consciously detect the violation – a finding that would be unexpected on the view that syntax is used in a haphazard manner or only when other sources of information yield no unique analysis of an input sentence. Yet another study shows that readers are temporarily 'garden-pathed' (i.e. they initially pursue an incorrect analysis) in syntactically ambiguous structures even when preceding sentences provide disambiguating information which in principle could guide the processor's choice of an appropriate syntactic analysis (for discussion, see Frazier, in Chapter 2 of this volume).

The discovery (and increased acceptance) of the idea of the autonomy of formal grammar is of profound importance in and of itself. The broader implications of this concept follow from the current conception of the relationship between the grammar and the other faculties and abilities involved in giving language its overall character. It is now well-accepted that complex linguistic phenomena are best explained in terms of the *interaction* of these diverse systems. This so-called *modular* approach to linguistic complexity can be represented schematically (following Anderson 1981:494) as in Figure 2.

Even though it is only in the last decade that modular explanations have come into their own, they were invoked in the earliest days of generative grammar. For example, Miller & Chomsky (1963) noted that sentences with multiple center-embeddings are invariably unacceptable, as in example (7):

(7)   the rat [$_s$the cat [$_s$the dog chased] ate] died

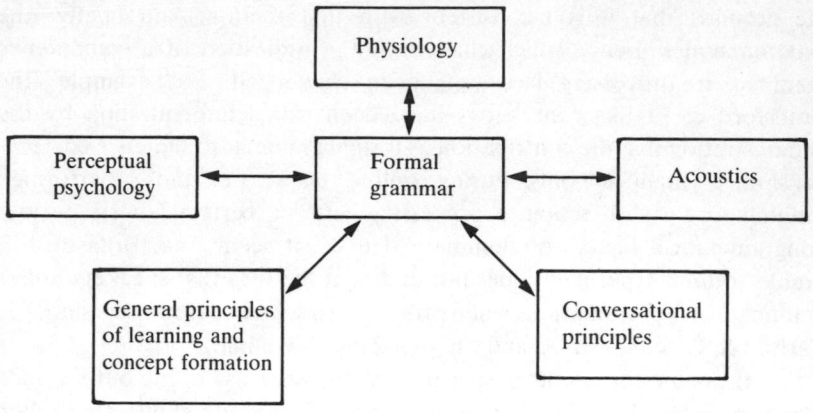

Figure 2.

They demonstrated the implausibility of a strictly grammatical explanation of the unacceptability. For one thing, the deviance of (7) could hardly be due to a deep structure or semantic ill-formedness, since it is interpretable (if one is given time to work out its intricacies) and other sentences plausibly derived from the same deep structure are acceptable:

(8)   The rat died that was eaten by the cat that the dog chased

Nor could the unacceptability be a consequence of the filtering function of the transformational rules – no (relevant) transformations apply in the derivation of (7). And the only way to block (7) at the level of surface structure would be to incorporate into grammatical theory a device that would literally 'count' the embeddings in the surface string – a device unlike any ever proposed to govern grammatical processes.

But there is an obvious reason, Miller & Chomsky argued, for the unacceptability of (7). Quite simply, the sentence is unacceptable because it is confusing. Without special aids (e.g. paper and pencil) it is difficult to figure out which subjects are paired with which predicates. They proposed a principle of sentence comprehension that states (essentially) that sentences are processed from 'left to right' and that the processing mechanism cannot be interrupted more than once. Since the comprehension of (7) demands a double interruption of the process of subject–verb assignment, the sentence is difficult to process.

In other words, sentence (7) is generated by the grammar, i.e. it is grammatical. Its unacceptability follows from the modular interaction of the grammatical principle of unlimited center-embedding with the perceptual principle sketched above. Neither principle alone is sufficient to account for the unacceptability of (7) and the concomitant acceptability of (8).

The appeal of modular explanations is, in essence, that they allow order to be extracted from chaos. If one system alone (whether linguistic or perceptual) had been forced to deal with the facts of multiple center-embeddings, no elegant account of the facts would have emerged. But such an account is the natural result of regarding this superficial complexity as the product of two simple principles, each from a distinct domain. Modular explanations have been invoked to handle a wide variety of disparate data in recent years, and in many cases dramatic results have been obtained. Such results have been instrumental in kindling the resurgence of interest in generative grammar after its eclipse in the 1970s.

By 1980, the idea that the complexity of language could be explained by recourse to the modular interaction of formal grammar with principles from physiology, cognition, sociology, and so on had become well accepted. The central guiding principle of much current work *within* grammatical theory (in particular, within the 'government–binding' (GB) framework) is that the *internal structure of the grammar* is modular as well. That is, syntactic complexity results from the interaction of grammatical subsystems, each characterizable in terms of its own set of general principles (for discussion, see Chomsky 1981 and Volume I, Chapter 2 in this series, on 'Syntactic theory'). The central goal of syntactic theory thus becomes to identify such systems and characterize the degree to which they may vary from language to language.

Most early work in generative grammar was rather nonmodular in character. Essentially, each construction had its own associated rule: passives were derived by the passive transformation, subject-raised sentences by the raising transformation, and so on. It seems fair to say that a great deal of the ultimate failure of the generative grammar-based conceptions in psycholinguistics in the 1960s was a direct result of their carrying over to their research this view of grammatical organization. But as the work on constraints on rules accelerated throughout the 1970s, it became clear that at least some of the complexities of particular constructions could be attributed to general principles, rather than having to be stated *ad hoc* as particular rules. In GB, grammar-internal modularity is carried as far as it can go; with some minor exceptions, syntactic complexity results from the interaction of the set of grammatical subsystems. What many have found most appealing about a modular approach to the internal structure of the grammar is that it provides a theoretical foundation for linguistic typology (for discussion, see Volume I, Chapter 17 on 'Linguistic typology'). In this modular view, what appear on the surface to be major structural differences among languages result from each language setting slightly different values ('parameters') for each of the various grammatical subsystems. Thus, just as we have seen to be the case with a modular approach to language as a whole, a modular approach to grammar allows, to a significant degree, apparently complex and recalcitrant data to be derived from an elegant set of basic principles – principles that vary, but within circumscribed limits, from language to language.

All of the chapters in this volume share the assumption that linguistic competence is best characterized by an autonomously functioning grammar that interacts in modular function with other faculties involved in language. Some provide further evidence for this idea; others assume its correctness and show how it can be applied to the explanation of some particular set of phenomena. Some, but not all, adopt as well the notion of grammar-internal modularity and show how it can help provide an account of linguistic data from diverse areas of investigation.

Chapter 2, 'Grammar and language processing' by Lyn Frazier, discusses experimental evidence that supports a modular approach to language. As she points out, the processor fails to take advantage of information at particular stages in processing that a nonmodular account would predict to be available to it. For example, context is not used in identifying candidate lexical representations, even though *a priori* one might assume that such information would be helpful to it. Furthermore, lexical and syntactic processing follow radically different strategies. Frazier provides pages of support for the view that generative grammars do indeed characterize the linguistic knowledge used during language comprehension, and remarks on the interesting convergences in recent developments in linguistics and psycholinguistics.

Chapter 3, Thomas Roeper's 'Grammatical principles of first language acquisition: theory and evidence,' reviews the evidence from child language studies for innately-determined linguistic principles. Roeper notes that one can argue indirectly that such principles must exist given the (uncontroversial) assumption that the child receives only positive evidence during acquisition. It can be shown experimentally as well that principles well-known from studies of adult language – c-command, subjacency, and control, for example – also guide first language acquisition. Others however, such as the subset principle, appear to be unique to child language. Roeper argues that there is good reason to conclude from acquisition studies that the grammar is organized into distinct modules subject to parametric variation, and he discusses an important ongoing debate in the field, namely whether the principles of universal grammar (UG) are available to the child from birth, or whether they emerge maturationally.

Chapter 4, Suzanne Flynn's 'Second language acquisition and grammatical theory,' defends the controversial position that UG guides second language acquisition as well as first. As Flynn shows, adult language learners are sensitive to such abstract notions as the subjacency constraint, binding principles, and phrase structural branching direction. Flynn provides a model of acquisition based on a parameterized modular view of grammar that incorporates the best features of the *contrastive analysis* (CA) model of the 1950s and the *creative construction* (CC) approach of the 1970s.

Chapter 5, 'Brain structures and linguistic capacity' by Mary-Louise Kean, documents the evidence that human linguistic capacity is biologically specified. Kean raises the question of how the biological substrate supports language knowledge and use, but points out that we are only just beginning to understand this process. She does believe, however, that there are sufficient data to support the idea that linguistic capacity matures and changes as a consequence of neural development and that UG is a theory of an emergent property of the system and not a theory of the functional acquisition device *per se*. The chapter also discusses the evidence that dyslexia and Down's Syndrome can provide for the degree of variation possible in linguistic capacity.

Chapter 6, Susan Curtiss's 'Abnormal language acquisition and the modularity of language,' provides strong evidence for modularity: in extraordinary cases of acquisition, the syntactic, semantic and pragmatic dimensions of language can literally become dissociated from each other. Curtiss reviews the well-known case of 'Genie,' who, over eight years after her release, had acquired relatively normal nonlinguistic cognitive functions but only a rudimentary syntax. Other case studies revealed different dissociations: 'Antony' had a well-developed syntax, but no coherent semantics or pragmatics; 'Rick' demonstrated syntactic and pragmatic abilities, but was deficient in propositional semantics.

In Chapter 7, 'Grammatical aspects of speech errors,' Victoria A. Fromkin shows that such errors provide insights both into the organization of the grammar itself, and into its utilization in language production. In fact, speech error evidence reveals that linguistic units are discrete, that phonological segments must be analyzed as distinctive features, and that autosegmental representations of stress and tones are correct. Fromkin discusses many other ways in which speech errors can be drawn upon to test the predictions of linguistic theory.

The next three chapters explore the boundaries of grammatical competence, in particular as it relates to principles of language use. Chapter 8, 'Grammar and conversational principles' by Ruth Kempson, defends the idea that the propositional content of a sentence cannot be determined by the semantic component of a grammar alone, as has been commonly believed. In her view, the grammar underdetermines the truth-value of the sentence; it is only through the interaction of grammatical and pragmatic principles that

11

propositional content can be determined. Kempson argues further that basing one's pragmatic theory on the principle of 'relevance' allows for a treatment of the phenomena at the interface between semantics and pragmatics that dovetails nicely with evidence from general studies of cognition.

The thrust of Chapter 9, Ellen F. Prince's 'Discourse analysis: a part of the study of linguistic competence,' is, in a sense, the opposite from that of the preceding chapter. Prince argues that many discourse-related phenomena that one might intuitively suppose to fall under a theory of discourse, communication, pragmatics, or whatever, in reality need to be subsumed under linguistic competence. The conclusion that competence encompasses, to a considerable degree, a speaker's knowledge of how linguistic forms are used in discourse follows from the arbitrariness (i.e. non-iconicity) of many discourse functions and their great degree of variation from language to language.

Chapter 10, 'Speech act distinctions in grammar' by Jerrold M. Sadock, reviews the diverse treatments of illocutionary acts, from wholly grammatical treatments to wholly pragmatic ones, and including every point of view in between. Sadock leans toward the pragmatic side of the spectrum, but points out problems that are likely to ensue in attempting to subsume many of the well-known syntactic and semantic properties of performatives wholly within a theory of language use.

Chapter 11, 'Computer applications of linguistic theory' by Per-Kristian Halvorsen, documents the way in which the conceptions of formal linguistics have been put to practical use in computer applications. For example, programs have now been written that process written English well enough to understand questions of some degree of complexity, to search for an answer to them in a computerized database, and to respond in written English. The most successful of these programs incorporate a generative grammar. Likewise, linguistic conceptions have been put to use in the development of machines that synthesize and recognize human speech.

Chapter 12, Bruce Hayes' 'Metrics and phonological theory,' discusses the field of metrical theory, which, drawing on phonological theory, studies how conventionalized rhythmic patterns are manifested by phonological material in verse. Evidence from metrical data has been drawn upon to support the 'rhyme' constituent and the nonlinear stress analysis of metrical phonology, the prosodic hierarchy, and a number of particular analyses of segmental phenomena.

The final two chapters deal with two varieties of human language whose precise status with respect to the principles of UG has engendered considerable debate: the signed languages of the deaf and creole languages. The former is the subject of Chapter 13, Carol A. Padden's 'Grammatical theory and signed languages.' Padden defends the position that American Sign

Language (ASL) embodies structures and constraints that are quite similar to those of spoken language, including ordered rules, parallel constraints on morpheme order, and autosegmental submorphemic structure. The precise degree to which the modality influences sign structure is still open to question and will form an important research topic in coming years.

Chapter 14 is devoted to an ongoing controversy about the nature of creoles, and contains three subchapters: 14.I, Derek Bickerton's 'Creole languages and the bioprogram,' 14.II, Pieter Muysken's sharply counterposed 'Are creoles a special type of language?,' and 14.III, an exchange between the two authors entitled 'A dialog concerning the linguistic status of creole languages.' For Bickerton, such languages represent, as a result of massive pruning of lexical properties from the original target language, UG in its most basic state: they are a manifestation of unparameterized principles of syntax and an unmarked set of grammatical options by which these principles can be realized. If so, it would seem that the human species comes equipped with a means for creating new languages in situations where doing so becomes a necessity.

Muysken, on the other hand, questions whether the status of creoles with respect to UG is different from that of any other human languages. While he does not deny that creoles tend to share a number of properties in common, he feels that this commonality is not sufficient, nor profound enough, to demand that UG treat them as having a unique status. Indeed, he concludes from a careful examination of the serial verb construction, which occurs in many, but not all, creoles, that as much variation exists in this construction as in noncreoles.

The final subchapter contains replies by Muysken and Bickerton to each other's contributions.

REFERENCES

Anderson, S. 1981. Why phonology isn't natural. *Linguistic Inquiry* 12: 493–540.
Braine, M. 1963. The ontogeny of English phrase structure: the first phase. *Language* 39: 1–13.
Bransford, J. D. & Franks, J. J. 1971. The abstraction of linguistic ideas. *Cognitive Psychology* 2: 331–50.
Carlson, G. & Tanenhaus, M. 1982. Some preliminaries to psycholinguistics. *CLS* 18: 46–60.
Chomsky, N. 1957. *Syntactic structures*. The Hague: Mouton.
Chomsky, N. 1959. Review of *Verbal behavior* by B. F. Skinner. *Language* 35: 26–57.
Chomsky, N. 1966. *Cartesian linguistics*. New York: Harper & Row.
Chomsky, N. 1975. *The logical structure of linguistic theory (with a new introduction)*. New York: Plenum.
Chomsky, N. 1981. *Lectures on government and binding*. Dordrecht: Foris.
Greene, J. 1972. *Psycholinguistics*. Harmondsworth: Penguin.
Lamendella, J. 1969. On the irrelevance of transformational grammar to second language pedagogy. *Language Learning* 19: 255–70.
Lees, R. B. 1957. Review of *Syntactic structures* by N. Chomsky. *Language* 33: 375–408.

Lenneberg, E. 1964. The capacity for language acquisition. In J. A. Fodor & J. Katz (eds.) *The structure of language*. Englewood Cliffs: Prentice-Hall.

Lenneberg, E. 1967. *Biological foundations of language*. New York: Wiley.

Maratsos, M. & Chalkley, M. A. 1980. The internal language of children's syntax. In K. Nelson (ed.) *Children's language*, vol. 2. New York: Gardner.

McNeill, D. 1966. Developmental psycholinguistics. In F. Smith & G. Miller (eds.) *The genesis of language*. Cambridge, MA: MIT Press.

Menyuk, P. 1963. Syntactic structures in the language of children. *Child Development* 34: 407–22.

Miller, G. 1962. Some psychological studies of grammar. *American Psychologist* 17: 748–62.

Miller, G. & Chomsky, N. 1963. Finitary models of language users. In R. Luce, R. Bush & E. Galanter (eds.) *Handbook of mathematical psychology*, vol. II. New York: Wiley.

Miller, G., Galanter, E. & Pribram, K. 1960. *Plans and the structure of behavior*. New York: Holt, Rinehart & Winston.

Miller, G. & Isard, S. 1963. Some perceptual consequences of linguistic rules. *Journal of Verbal Learning and Verbal Behavior* 2: 217–28.

Miller, W. & Ervin-Tripp, S. 1964. The development of grammar in child language. In U. Bellugi & R. Brown (eds.) *The acquisition of language*. Monograph of the Society for Research in Child Development 29.

Newmeyer, F. & Weinberger, S. In press. The ontogenesis of the field of second language learning research. In S. Flynn & W. O'Neil (eds.) *Linguistic theory in second language acquisition*. Dordrecht: Reidel.

Scheffler, I. 1963. *The anatomy of inquiry*. New York: Knopf.

Slobin, D. 1966. Grammatical transformations and sentence comprehension in childhood and adulthood. *Journal of Verbal Learning and Verbal Behavior* 5: 219–27.

Thomas, O. 1965. *Transformational grammar and the teacher of English*. New York: Holt, Reinhart & Winston.

Williams, E. 1980. Abstract triggers. *Journal of Linguistic Research* 1: 71–82.

2 Grammar and language processing*

Lyn Frazier

2.1. Grammars

Do generative grammars characterize the linguistic knowledge used in language comprehension? This question has received several distinct answers in the psycholinguistic literature. In the early 1960s attempts were made to test transformational grammars directly, without embedding them in an explicit processing model (see Fodor, Bever & Garrett 1974: ch. 5 for an excellent review). The failure of these attempts presented a serious problem for psycholinguists. Considerable psychological evidence showed that the structures the grammar attributes to sentences are psychologically real, even if the transformational rules of the 1960-style grammar were not. Since the only known characterization of surface structures was the one provided by transformational grammar, this state of affairs presented an apparent contradiction. In response to this situation, several models of comprehension were developed in which grammatical information was either not used, used haphazardly, along with sundry heuristics and heavy reliance on lexical and world knowledge, or the grammar (specifically syntax) was used only as a last resort when other routes to comprehension failed (Bever 1970; Riesbeck & Schank 1978; see Frazier 1979: ch. 2 for a critical review).

Nevertheless, substantial evidence has accumulated showing that syntactic information is exploited in language comprehension. For example, Forster & Olbrei (1973) show that passives (presented in isolation) take longer to process than corresponding actives regardless of whether the semantic relations are reversible or nonreversible. Flores d'Arcais (1982) found that sentences with syntactic violations take longer to read than well-formed sentences, even when perceivers do not consciously detect the violation. Both of these findings are totally unexpected on the view that syntax is used in a haphazard manner and/or only when other sources of information yield no unique analysis of an input sentence.

* This work was supported by the Max Planck Institute for Psycholinguistics and Grant HD 18708. I would like to thank the staff at the Institute for the various ways they helped to make Nijmegen a pleasant place to work. I am also grateful to Chuck Clifton and Fritz Newmeyer for comments on an earlier draft.

15

Further evidence about the role of syntax derives from studies of eye movements during reading. Frazier & Rayner (1982) show that readers assign the minimal grammatically permissible syntactic structure to an input sentence as the words of a sentence are encountered. Hence, readers assign (1) the structure appropriate for (1a), since this structure requires the postulation of fewer syntactic nodes than does the competing analysis which is appropriate for (1b):

(1) Rita knew the answer to the difficult problem . . .
     a. Rita knew [NPthe answer to the difficult problem by heart
     b. Rita knew [S[NPthe answer to the difficult problem was wrong

The conflict between the preferred 'minimal attachment' analysis of (1) and the continuation in (1b) is immediately apparent in the record of subjects' eye movements. For example, the fixations in the disambiguating region of a sentence like (1b), but not (1a), are significantly longer than the duration of preceding fixations. The preference for the minimal attachment analysis of a temporarily ambiguous sentence can be observed in a large range of disparate structures. It appears that these structures are only open to a syntactic characterization (see Frazier 1979, 1985 and references therein). Hence, the empirical evidence supporting the minimal attachment strategy argues strongly for immediate and systematic use of syntactic information during language comprehension.

As noted above, the question of whether grammars are psychologically real has received all possible answers by psycholinguists: predominantly 'yes' in the early 1960s, 'no' in the late 1960s, 'not really' in the 1970s, and 'yes' in the 1980s. Why? What changes in linguistic and psycholinguistic assumptions have permitted the grammar to (re)assume a central role in theories of language performance?

Two, perhaps obvious but important, factors seem to have eased the apparent tension between linguistics and cognitive psychology. The fact that grammars are neutral between the production, comprehension, and acquisition systems entails that the grammar does not by itself constitute a theory of any of these systems. This in turn implies that a processing model must be specified in order to account for the abilities of speakers, hearers, and language learners. It is, of course, an interesting question whether the properties of the processing model may themselves be explained entirely in terms of general perceptual and cognitive principles (in interaction with the grammar); whether the properties of this system are unique to language; or perhaps some mixture of the two. In any case, it is now quite clear that specifying the details of the mechanisms and architecture of the language processing system is not merely a matter of trivial execution or implementation of a generative grammar. Thus, while it has been recognized for several

decades that grammars only make clear predictions about language performance once they are interpreted in a theory of language processing,[1] by and
large it is only recently that linguists have concerned themselves seriously
with the properties of the processing system itself.

Theories of grammar have also changed. Compared with earlier transformational grammars, current grammars are easier to interpret as a set of
structure well-formedness conditions that may be applied essentially
simultaneously during the ongoing processing of a sentence. There are two
reasons for this. Transformational grammars of the *Aspects* variety
(Chomsky 1965) implied the imposition of processing delays because large
portions of an input sentence needed to be available to the processor before
substantial syntactic analysis of the input could begin. In part, this was due to
explicit rule ordering in the grammar and to problems arising because certain
transformations (e.g. *wh*-movement or question formation) were not well-
defined 'in reverse' (which would be necessary in order to analyze an input by
de-transforming it). But, even setting aside these problems, processing
delays would be imposed by the derivational characterization of well-formed
surface structures. Whether rules are ordered explicitly or not, a well-formed
derivation is defined by the well-formedness of each individual step in the
derivation (i.e. the pairwise mapping between two representations). This
necessarily results in successive rather than simultaneous rule application.
For the comprehension device to determine that, say, each of five transformations could apply to one particular structural description of an input would
thus involve essentially wasted computational effort. This would amount to
discovering one step in five *separate* derivations, not five steps in a single
derivation.

Sequential application of rules *per se* is not necessarily problematic for a
processing device. However, given a limited capacity processor, it would be
risky to apply each of several rules successively to an input if the probability of

---

[1] Following Miller & Chomsky (1963), I would argue that even the relation between the grammar and
the speaker's well-formedness intuitions is complex and indirect. It is perhaps easy to overlook this
point when dealing with intuitions about strings that are easy to process. In such cases, the theoretical
distinction between grammaticality and acceptability is unlikely to be at issue, regardless of the
particular model of language processing that one adopts. However, even in this case, it is the grammar
taken jointly with implicit assumptions about language processing which permit native speakers' well-
formedness intuitions to be interpreted as constraining the theory of grammar rather than theories of
processing.
   In practice (though not in principle), theories of language acquisition still tend to ignore the
contribution of grammatical principles or the influence of processing factors in accounts of language
development. Though the importance of both factors has been explicitly recognized in the literature
(e.g. de Villiers & de Villiers 1978), with few exceptions (e.g. Goodluck & Tavakolian 1982), studies of
acquisition have focussed on either grammatical questions or performance questions, treating
'intrusions' from the other system as noise in the data, rather than important information constraining
the overall theory of language competence and performance. It is still not unusual, for example, to hear
claims about grammatical markedness translated directly into predictions about relative order of
acquisition (without serious attention directed to the implicit '*ceteris paribus*').

17

the current derivation being the correct one (or leading to the correct one) is extremely low. The processor might easily exhaust its limited resources without getting any closer to the actual syntactic description of the input. Thus, constructing possible derivations online, as each word of a sentence is encountered, would be computationally expensive. Further, without the benefit of the constraints imposed by 'right' context (i.e. subsequent items), this computational effort is likely to be wasted. (Imagine, for example, the number of derivations consistent with a sentence beginning with the word *The*.) Thus derivational characterization of well-formedness necessarily imposes delays of analysis on a limited capacity processor, unless it is assumed (counterfactually) that the derivations are extremely shallow (i.e. involve very few steps) and/or the actual applicability of each rule can be determined immediately and unambiguously from information contained in left context. Current grammars are essentially nonderivational (e.g. Chomsky 1981; Gazdar 1981; Bresnan 1983). This removes one serious obstacle to the direct exploitation of grammatical rules or principles in the online processing of language.

The recent move towards modular grammars (Chomsky 1981) removes yet another obstacle to the assumption that grammar is used in the immediate analysis of an incoming string. To see this, consider first the case of a monolithic grammar with no differentiation between subsystems of rules or principles. Given this undifferentiated grammar, the analysis of some word will be complete only once the processor's hypothesis about the analysis of this word has been checked against *all* of the well-formedness conditions of the grammar, since there is no other way for the processor to determine the legitimacy of its analysis of this word. Assuming this process takes some non-negligible amount of time, the analysis of the following word will be delayed. By contrast, if the grammar is modular and thus consists of several distinct subsystems, it may be determined rapidly whether the analysis of the current word is well-formed at some particular level of structure, e.g. with respect to the conditions of one grammatical subsystem. The analysis of the following word may then immediately begin at this same level of structure, regardless of whether the analysis of preceding words has been completed at other levels of structure.

For example, imagine that there is a processing module or subsystem which utilizes phrase structure rules and Case theory to assign constituent structure relations to an input string. As soon as the constituent structure analysis of $word_n$ has been checked against principles of phrase structure and Case theory, the constituent structure analysis of $word_{n+1}$ may begin regardless of whether the analysis of $word_n$ (perhaps a bound anaphor) has already been checked against the principles of binding theory, control theory, etc. And, when the sentence-final word is checked against principles of phrase structure and Case theory and incorporated into a constituent structure representation of the sentence, no *post hoc* check will be required to assure the well-formedness of this representation with respect to the principles consulted during its formation.

In a monolithic grammar, if processing of word$_{n+1}$ were to proceed before the processing of word$_n$ had been completed (i.e. checked against *all* grammatical conditions) then the processor would risk ultimately accepting an inappropriate (ungrammatical) analysis of well-formed sentences. To avoid this situation, the processor would need to do an extraordinary amount of 'book-keeping' to keep track of which parsing decisions had already been checked against which particular grammatical conditions. So, a processor utilizing a monolithic grammar might enjoy the advantages of automatic 'book-keeping' if it required each word to be checked against all well-formedness conditions before analysis of the following item began. But this would entail that a delayed decision at one level of analysis result in delayed analysis at all levels. Alternatively, the processor might proceed with the analysis of new items regardless of whether the analysis of the current items were completed; but then, without extensive 'book-keeping,' having arrived at the end of an input sentence would have no guarantee of the well-formedness of the analysis assigned to the sentence.

In short, nonderivational grammars do not impose the processing lags resulting from successive application of rules in a representation subsuming large portions of the input string. Also, modular grammars further diminish the delays imposed by monolithic or nonmodular grammars, because subsystems of grammatical principles can be applied independently of each other by processing subsystems that operate concurrently (provided, of course, that grammatical subsystems can be organized into processing modules with coherent tasks).[2] Though it would be a serious mistake to interpret generative grammars as constituting theories of language processing, current gener-

---

[2] The principles underlying the organization of grammatical subsystems into some (presumably smaller) number of processing modules are, I think, of considerable interest. Two or more sets of grammatical principles are likely to form the representational basis for a single processing module only if they have at least some of their vocabulary in common and if they heavily constrain the same natural class of processing decisions.

Of course, we would expect some set of principles to be excluded from this processing module if their exclusion would drastically reduce the amount of information to be consulted in executing some tasks, without introducing errors of analysis that would be undetected by the normal operation of other processing modules. (See discussion of the 'grammatical signature hypothesis' in Frazier 1985.) Clearly, the notion of a 'natural class of processing decisions' being exploited here is closely related to the notion of 'level of representation' in the grammar. However, at present I think it is far from obvious which of these notions has, if you will, causal priority. The grammatical notion of distinct levels of representation may be basic and thus define natural classes of processing operations; alternatively, functionally distinct processing tasks (e.g. determining the relations between lexical items vs. determining the relations between phrases that have already been analyzed or identified) may eventually provide insights into the organization of the grammar and the distinct levels of representations it contains.

ative grammars do seem to have essentially the right kinds of properties to permit the grammar to be used directly in the immediate analysis of an input.[3] Obviously this observation is encouraging, given the empirical evidence showing that normal rapid ongoing language processing is guided by the grammar; the grammar is not called in just under exceptional circumstances when attempts to solve the comprehension task by alternative means have failed.

We turn now to more detailed proposals concerning the use of the grammar in comprehension. We will begin with the issue of autonomous vs. interactive use of information, which has dominated psycholinguistic research for the last decade. We will then turn to 'modular' accounts of the language system in section 2.3.

2.2. Autonomy vs. interaction

Forster (1979) proposed an extremely important model of language comprehension, illustrated in Figure 1. On this view, the language processing system consists of three linearly ordered processing systems (or stages of processing). Each of these processors accepts as input the output of the immediately preceding processor. In all other respects, the operation of each processor is autonomous in that it can neither benefit from nor influence, the operation of other processors. Because no interaction is permitted, the only natural way for the model to handle ambiguities of analysis is to assign all grammatically possible representations to an input, at each level of analysis. Representations can later be discarded if they prove to be ill-formed or inappropriate at some subsequent stage of analysis. Thus, well-formed phonological representations that happen to be syntactically ill-formed may be discarded by the syntactic processor. Anomalous syntactic analyses can be rejected by the message processor. And, the pragmatically most plausible semantic representation of an input can be determined by the 'general problem solver,' which has access to real-world knowledge.

---

[3] The discussion here has focussed on the role of grammar in the syntactic processing of sentences. The role of phonology in language processing has been almost entirely ignored in the psycholinguistic literature (though see *Cognition* 25 (1–2) on auditory word recognition). However, the issues are very similar to those involved in syntactic processing. Superficially, it might appear that there is a principled distinction between phonological and syntactic processing. After all, phonological forms are stored in the lexicon. Nevertheless, phonologically interpreting some portion of the incoming string is not unlike syntactically structuring some input item. In both cases the possible analysis of new material will depend on the structure assigned to already encountered material. Thus focussing exclusively on the prestored nature of phonological representations (as most work on word recognition has done) is likely, in my opinion, to have been a serious mistake. Further, just like the syntax, the phonology of current grammars is not characterized in derivational terms, nor in terms of an undifferentiated set of principles. Rather, it is increasingly common to find phonological principles stated as sets of constraints on well-formed phonological representations. (For example, compare the treatment of stress in Prince 1983 and in Selkirk 1984 to that in Chomsky & Halle 1968.)

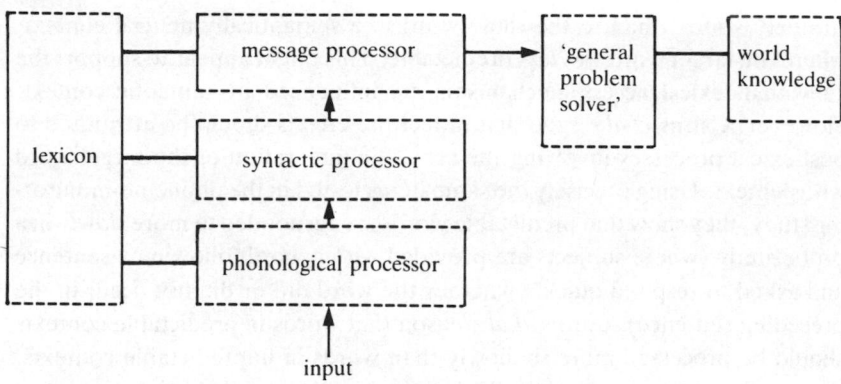

Figure 1

Experimental evidence supports several predictions of this model. The architecture of the model leads us to expect the identification of prestored lexical representation for an input to be accomplished on the basis of information about the phonological form of this input, regardless of the nature of preceding syntactic and semantic context.[4] Studies of lexical ambiguities involving two or more roughly equiprobable meanings confirm this prediction. For example, results from cross-modal priming studies[5] (e.g. Swinney 1979; Seidenberg *et al.* 1982) show that there is activation of both meanings of ambiguous words even in strongly biased or disambiguating contexts. Within a few hundred milliseconds, evidence for the activation of inappropriate meanings is no longer observable, indicating that appropriate lexical representations are selected and inappropriate ones are discarded within a very short time period.

Cairns, Cowart & Jablon (1981) provide another impressive demonstration of the independence of the lexical access mechanisms from information derived from computing the semantic relations in a sentence. Subjects were asked to monitor a sentence for a word that began with a particular sound (e.g. /t/). They responded more quickly to a word in a semantically con-

[4] There is a truly extensive literature on lexical access mechanisms and I could not possibly do justice here to the issues it raises concerning the interpretation of context effects in word recognition. Apparent context effects in lexical access typically fall into one of two classes: effects observed with degraded stimuli (which might result from subjects' adopting a guessing strategy), and effects due to prestored semantic associations between words (which are irrelevant to the issue at hand, since these effects are intralexical).

[5] In cross-modal priming studies, subjects are typically asked to make a lexical decision or to name a visually presented word which occurs in the middle of an auditorily presented sentence. If the target word is semantically associated with the preceding word, response times are shorter than if the target word is semantically unrelated to the preceding word. Thus, the technique may be used as a litmus for determining which lexical representations have been activated during language processing. See Seidenberg *et al.* (1982) for discussion of the technique.

21

strained context than to the same word in a semantically neutral context, where the target word was less predictable. This might appear to support the view that lexical access mechanisms *are* influenced by semantic context. However, Cairns *et al.* argue that in fact the effects should be attributed to postlexical processes involving the semantic integration of the target word with context. Using precisely the same items tested in the phoneme-monitoring study, they show that predictable words are responded to more *slowly* in a probe study (where subjects are provided with a word following a sentence and asked to respond quickly whether the word did or did not occur in the preceding sentence). Cairns *et al.* reason that words in predictable contexts should be processed more shallowly than words in unpredictable contexts, due to the ease of semantically integrating the word with surrounding material. Predictable items should then be more difficult to recognize, since less processing will have been devoted to these items in the initial stage of sentence processing. In short, in the case of lexical processing there seems to be a growing consensus that the access mechanisms are not influenced by syntactic and semantic context if one is careful to distinguish between tasks and experiments that are sensitive to postlexical processing (e.g. phoneme monitoring as above, lexical decision task) and those that are not, or that at least are less sensitive to such effects.

The model in Figure 1 also predicts that semantic and pragmatic knowledge will not influence the syntactic processing of a sentence. As mentioned above, Forster & Olbrei (1973) examined processing times for active and passive sentences. In this study, passives took longer to process than actives in all three conditions, suggesting that whatever syntactic processing complexity is associated with passives (presented in isolation), it is not alleviated by the presence of semantic constraints.

Frazier & Rayner (to appear) show that sentences with sentential subjects take longer to read than their extraposed counterparts. The reading time differences between the two sentence forms remains constant regardless of whether the sentences are presented in isolation or in contexts introducing the referents and relations expressed by the sentential subject. This finding is expected on the view that syntactic processing is unaffected by nonsyntactic information.

Perhaps the most impressive demonstration of the independence of syntactic analysis derives from a study of Ferreira & Clifton (1986). They show that readers are temporarily 'garden-pathed' (i.e. pursue an initially incorrect analysis) in syntactically ambiguous structures even when preceding sentences provided disambiguating information which in principle could guide the processor's choice of an appropriate syntactic analysis. In sum, there arc several studies indicating that the particular option selected at a syntactic choice point is not affected by the presence of biasing or disambiguating semantic information. Further, the complexity relations between various syntactic structures remain constant even when semantic information in the current or preceding sentence could in principle have altered those relations. The studies thus support the autonomy claim in so far as they suggest principled limitations on the use of potentially helpful semantic and discourse information in the initial syntactic analysis of a sentence.

In direct opposition to the autonomy hypothesis, many psycholinguists have argued for interaction of information types (phonological, syntactic, semantic, real-world knowledge) during ongoing sentence processing. The model is difficult to illustrate in a diagram, because the basic hypothesis concerns the *absence* of processing constraints resulting from or coinciding with distinctions recognized in grammatical theory. The most extreme version of interactionist models could perhaps be illustrated as in Figure 2.

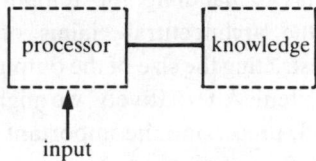

Figure 2

In his early work, Marslen-Wilson (1975, but also Marslen-Wilson & Tyler 1980) was a particularly strong advocate of interactive processing, with no principled limitations on the interaction of distinct knowledge sources. The criticisms he and others have leveled at autonomous theories of processing can be traced to a single problem, namely, the temporal predictions of the models. If the output of each processor in Figure 1 is not continuously available to the next higher processor, long delays of analysis are predicted, due to the linear arrangement of the processors. For example, imagine that the unit of language processing is the syntactic clause and, thus, the output of each processor in Figure 1 corresponds, at least roughly, to a clause-sized unit. This would predict that constraining the semantic relations within a clause could have had absolutely no effect whatsoever on the processing of a sentence until the end of the clause had been received and identified by the processor. Numerous studies show that increasing the semantic predictability of words in a sentence (as assessed by the Cloze procedure) influences some stages of language processing long before the end of a clause. Of course, this sort of data is problematic for the model in Figure 1 only if the model is construed in terms of processing units larger than a single lexical item. If the autonomy claims implicit in Figure 1 are stated over some very small-sized

23

unit, e.g. the individual lexical item, then the empirical data on rapid use of information of all types pose no difficulty for the model.

Here it is crucial, I think, to separate out two aspects of Forster's model. One important claim of the model is that information is *used* autonomously – for example, that syntactic information is processed in precisely the same manner regardless of the amount or type of semantic and pragmatic information or constraints present in the sentence. As indicated above, this claim has received considerable experimental confirmation (e.g. in Forster & Olbrei 1973; Rayner *et al.* 1983; Ferreira & Clifton 1986; Frazier & Rayner to appear). Further, the evidence supporting interactive models does not show interactive (non-independent) use of syntactic information, but merely rapid use of all information types at some stage or other in processing. Notice that it is the architecture of the model in Figure 1 (i.e. the relation between processors), not the autonomous use of information, that underlies the difficulties the model has in handling the temporal aspects of sentence processing. In short, the architectural claims of the model could be preserved, but only by restricting the size of the output unit to some small unit like the individual lexical item. Alternatively, we might abandon the architectural claims of the model, preserving the important claim concerning autonomous use of distinct information types.

There are several reasons for thinking this latter option is the more fruitful one to pursue. In the case of syntactic ambiguities (though not lexical ambiguities), the evidence strongly suggests that the processor initially computes just one analysis of an input (Bever 1970; Kimball 1973; Fodor 1978; Frazier & Fodor 1978; Frazier & Rayner 1982; Rayner *et al.* 1983; Frazier, Clifton & Randall 1983; Engdahl 1981; Crain & Fodor 1985). This, of course, conflicts with the view that multiple syntactic analyses are assigned to an input. Thus, the only natural ambiguity resolution mechanism available to the model in Figure 1, multiple analysis with later selection, conflicts with the empirical evidence.

If we give up the multiple analysis aspect of the model, there is little motivation for maintaining the architectural claims in Figure 1. Feedback loops allowing 'downward' communication of information would need to be introduced into the model to permit analysis of a sentence to continue in those cases where the initial analysis proves untenable. This would weaken the model enormously. Further, the hypothesized relation between grammatical knowledge and real-world knowledge becomes unworkable, because there is no guarantee that the grammatical processing system will have computed the particular linguistic representation that corresponds to the pragmatically most plausible reading of a sentence. In other words, real-world knowledge must be attributed some role in processing other than that of simply selecting the pragmatically most expected representation of fully ambiguous strings.[6] We will return to this issue below.

2.3. **Modularity**

Like autonomous theories of language processing, modular theories claim that the language comprehension system consists of several distinct processing subsystems, each with its own properties and its own characteristic information sources. Unlike autonomous models, there is no commitment to a serial arrangement of processing subsystems, nor to an architecturally imposed restriction on the *availability* of information that has been assigned to some linguistic input. The autonomous *use* of information may be preserved in a modular system if each of its component subsystems simply cannot utilize information stated in terms which fall outside the vocabulary of its own knowledge sources. For example, a syntactic processing module might operate on a representation which contains phonological, semantic, or even world knowledge, but this information will simply have no consequences for syntactic analysis unless the vocabulary for representing the syntactic principles available to this module overlaps with that of the representational systems for phonological, semantic, or real-world knowledge.

We have already seen two important types of evidence supporting a modular account of language processing: evidence showing that specific classes of information are not exploited at some particular stage in processing even though the information would be helpful in certain cases (e.g. context is not used in identifying candidate lexical representations for an input); and evidence that lexical processing and syntactic processing are not accomplished by the same mechanism (lexical access follows a multiple analysis strategy whereas syntactic analysis follows a single analysis strategy). Note that this difference is not logically required by the nature of the task or the representations involved. The principled distinction between lexical access and syntactic analysis may well be the difference between prestored representations and representations that must be computed using rules or principles. Nevertheless, the co-occurrence of those properties is not logically necessary: in principle, access procedures may be self-terminating (permitting a single analysis strategy to be pursued for prestored representations) and computational devices may construct several novel representations at once. Thus,

---

[6] Of course, giving up the model in Figure 1 does not resolve the conflict between evidence that initially only a single syntactic analysis of a sentence is constructed (not necessarily the most plausible one in terms of world knowledge), but ultimately it is the pragmatically most plausible analysis which people become consciously aware of. See the discussion in section 2.2.

the evidence reviewed above argues strongly against a nonmodular or monolithic processing system with some fixed set of uniform properties. If the language processor were monolithic, we would expect it to follow either a multiple analysis strategy or a single analysis strategy, but not both. In addition, either this processor would have access to some information source, for *all* aspects of language processing, or it would not. Instead, what we find are clusters of distinct properties associated with different aspects of language processing. The information sources exploited and the mode of operation of the processor are not fixed but depend on the particular processing subtask involved. This is precisely what we expect if language comprehension results from the interaction of several distinct subsystems, each making autonomous use of its own information sources, abiding by its own principles, etc.

The distinction drawn here between autonomous and modular theories of processing is also evident in the development of linguistic theory. The earlier focus on autonomy in theories of grammar emphasized the hypothesis that one component of grammar had access only to the information contained in that component and whatever representation formed the interface between that component and other components. In principle, though typically not in practice, two components could contain precisely the same principle or rule, or there could be complete identity in the vocabulary each had available for stating grammatical generalizations (see van Riemsdijk 1981). By contrast, the recent emphasis on modularity is concerned with natural classes of grammatical principles, not with restrictions on the availability of information *per se*. A set of grammatical principles that deals with some phenomenon, e.g. binding theory, may (indeed, in some cases must) make reference to the relations in structures defined by other sets of principles. Thus, the developments in linguistics and psycholinguistics seem to be converging. (If the arguments for modular parsing given immediately above are examined, this convergence is even more striking. The convergence has resulted from independent considerations in linguistics and in psycholinguistics; it is not merely a reflection of the dependence of psycholinguistic theories on theories of grammar.)

2.4. The architecture of the language processing system

We turn now to questions concerning the architecture of the language processor, beginning with the relation between linguistic and nonlinguistic systems. Fodor (1983) has developed an interesting theory of mind, extending the basic insights of faculty psychology (for an overview of this theory, see Volume III of this series, Chapter 2 on 'Language and cognition'). The central idea is that the mind is made up of qualitatively distinct subsystems. The 'vertical' or 'input' systems (e.g. the visual system, the language system) are domain-specific. They autonomously use only the information concerning some particular natural domain,[7] thereby permitting fast, mandatory operation of each self-contained module or input system. The operation of these systems is not accessible to conscious awareness. Rather, each may be considered on a par with a simple reflex. (Indeed, in the dedication, Fodor comments that the book is essentially a reflection on Merrill Garrett's comment that 'What you have to remember about parsing is that it's basically a reflex.') Unlike the input systems, the 'horizontal' or central processing system is concerned with the propositional knowledge underlying an individual's beliefs about the world. It is essentially a commonsense reasoning system that deals with propositional knowledge of all sorts, e.g. real-world knowledge. The input systems are information-encapsulated, meaning that they have access to domain-specific information relevant to their (specialized) task but not to information contained in the central processing system.

The architecture Fodor proposes for the human mind is plausibly related to biological factors. He comments that input systems typically exhibit characteristic acquisition and breakdown patterns. Further, the properties he attributes to the input systems are clearly advantageous from an evolutionary perspective. They permit rapid automatic processing of information crucial to the well-being of the organism. Thus, in addition to a bold and interesting hypothesis about the architecture of the mind, Fodor's conception offers some insight into why the mind should be organized in this particular way.

Though Fodor discussed many aspects of language processing, his central concern is with the overall architecture of the vertical and horizontal faculties, not the internal architecture of the language system. We will briefly examine the issues concerning the structure within the language system. We will then return to the hypothesis that the language system is an informationally encapsulated input system, and examine some relevant empirical evidence.

Earlier, we discussed the reasons for believing that the processing modules implicated in language comprehension operate concurrently, rather than being arranged in a linear sequence. If we accept this as given, then the relation between linguistic processing modules will follow from two facts: the nature of the modules (including the task and information sources characterizing each module) and the *inherent* temporal properties of each module

---

[7] There is an important issue here concerning whether one input system may exploit the representation computed by some 'parallel' system. For example, consider the relation between a visual input system and whatever motor system(s) are implicated in overt practiced actions like catching a ball and/or reflexive behavior like blinking. While it is clear that there must be some interface between certain vertical input systems (e.g. between the auditory system and the speech perception system) that is not necessarily mediated by the central processing system, it is unclear what constraints are intended on the relation between two distinct 'vertically' oriented input systems such as the visual and motor systems, or the visual and linguistic systems.

(which will determine what structure or representation has been assigned to an input at any given moment).

There is currently no clear consensus concerning the number and nature of the modules contributing to language comprehension. It is relatively uncontroversial to assume the existence of a lexical module, concerned with the lexical identification of an input. However, there is certainly no definite evidence about the nature of lexical representations (e.g. whether they contain detailed phonetic information and/or systematic phonological information), nor about what particular units are stored (see references in Henderson 1985, for example). It is also unclear whether lexical representations are (Connine & Clifton 1984) or are not (Frauenfelder & Marcus 1984) available to the speech perception mechanisms. Whether speech perception mechanisms and lexical access mechanisms comprise a single module or two separate ones, many diverse types of evidence indicate that these mechanisms must be separate from the other processes involved in language comprehension. Lexical ambiguity studies (reviewed above) indicate that these mechanisms are not influenced by semantic or syntactic context. Phoneme restoration studies strengthen this conclusion. Samuels (1981) shows that semantic context influences the response bias of subjects in phoneme restoration studies but does not influence the actual perception processes (see discussion in Fodor 1983). That the operation of these mechanisms is automatic (rapid and mandatory) is indicated by studies showing that perception and access occur even under circumstances when they may only interfere with, or inhibit, subjects' performance on some task, and even when subjects have been explicitly instructed not to attend to the linguistically relevant aspects of an input (Lackner & Garrett 1972; Conrad 1974; Oden & Spira 1983).

With respect to syntactic analysis, there is again disagreement concerning the number and nature of the modules involved. Crain & Steedman (1985) suggest that the syntactic analysis initially adopted for an input is determined by the relative complexity of constructing the appropriate discourse model for the alternative possible analyses, given whatever model of discourse has already been constructed for preceding context.

This would seem to imply no separation of the processing mechanism involved in the syntactic and semantic analysis of the sentences. However, Ferreira & Clifton (1986) argue that the technique Crain & Steedman employed was not sensitive to the initial syntactic analysis assigned to sentences. Using immediate online measures (self-paced reading, and eye movement recording), they find evidence that the first analysis assigned to an input is governed by purely structural principles even in strongly biased contexts, suggesting that the distinction between syntactic and semantic/discourse mechanisms must be maintained.

Ford, Bresnan & Kaplan (1983) propose that initial syntactic analysis is governed by the strongest (momentarily dominant) lexical form of input items, e.g. the strongest lexical form of the word *position* includes two internal arguments, the strongest form of *want* includes only one (though see also Frazier 1983). Presumably it is the most frequently occurring lexical form of an item that is the 'strongest' lexical form in neutral contexts. However, Ford *et al.* suggest that the strongest lexical form of an item may be altered by the pragmatic content of proceding context, though they do not indicate how this might be accomplished. Thus, while it is clear that they intend for information about lexical forms to be directly available to the syntactic processing system, it is unclear whether the effects of semantic and pragmatic context are to be handled directly by the system responsible for syntactic analysis, or mediated by some separate system.

Working within the general framework of GPSG (Gazdar 1981), Crain & Fodor (1985) propose that there exists a single syntactic processing module. Indeed, they stress that the uniformity in the format for stating all syntactic well-formedness conditions in this framework is advantageous from the perspective of sentence processing. Stating long-distance dependencies in the same form as traditional phrase structure rules permits the same parsing mechanisms to be used for both. So, they argue, long-distance or filler-gap dependencies can be handled just like traditional phrase structure dependencies. This is advantageous, since we already know more-or-less how these are parsed. By contrast, Frazier, Clifton & Randall (1983; also Frazier 1985; Frazier & Clifton in progress) propose the existence of two distinct syntactic subsystems: one concerned with the constituent structure analysis of sentences, and one concerned with evaluating the (binding, bounding and obligatory control) relations between phrases in this structure. In this system, context and pragmatic plausibility effects are handled in yet a third, nonsyntactic subsystem (the 'thematic processor', to be described below).

With the possible exception of Crain & Steedman,[8] all of these accounts propose the existence of (at least one) syntactic processing system which abides by a single analysis strategy (as do most of the computer models based on linguistic theory, e.g. Wanner & Maratsos 1978; Marcus 1980; Berwick & Weinberg 1984). It is worth emphasizing this fact, because it is at the heart of the issue concerning whether the language processing system is information-encapsulated in the particular way Fodor (1983) suggests. Any 'single analysis' syntactic processing system must account for how it is that people ultimately arrive at the semantically and pragmatically most plausible

---

[8] Crain & Steedman seem to have considered both a single analysis and a multiple analysis version of their proposal. The evidence presented in Ferreira & Clifton (1984) is incompatible with either version of the specific processing account Crain & Steedman offer. However, the general point that they are making – that null contexts are not presuppositionally neutral and that discourse context biases the interpretations (ultimately) assigned to sentences – is surely correct.

analysis of an input. There is, of course, no guarantee in any of these systems that the initially adopted syntactic analysis will correspond to the most plausible analysis on nonsyntactic grounds. So, the problem is how the existence of an alternative (more plausible) analysis is detected by the processor. Further identifying pragmatically plausible analyses obviously requires access to world knowledge. Thus, once we eliminate Forster's solution to the plausibility problem (i.e. computing multiple linguistic analyses in the language processing system proper, with subsequent selection of the most plausible analysis by a general cognitive processor), it appears that world knowledge must be used in the language input system, in violation of Fodor's information encapsulation constraint.

The most serious problem for information encapsulation[9] is the means by which the existence of a pragmatically more plausible analysis of a sentence may be identified in cases where the originally computed analysis is perfectly coherent on semantic and pragmatic grounds. Either the syntactic processor must benefit from information about the likely or expected states of affair in the real world to alert it to the possibility of a more plausible alternative analysis, or the central processing system must be attributed the grammatical knowledge and ability necessary to construct alternative well-formed syntactic structures. It would appear that each of these solutions is incompatible with an information-encapsulated language system. Apparently, real world knowledge does in some way influence the ongoing operation of the grammatical processing system.

Rayner *et al.* (1983) suggest that world knowledge is available during language processing to a subsystem responsible for assessing discourse representations and selecting the pragmatically most plausible thematic frame for the head of each syntactic phrase identified by the constituent structure processor. Since the selection of a particular frame has direct consequences for the constituent structure of a sentence,[10] this mechanism would permit plausible alternative analyses to be identified as a result of the mismatch between the thematic frame chosen on plausibility grounds (by the 'thematic processor') and the initial constituent structure chosen on purely structural grounds (by a 'syntactic processor'). If anything along these lines is

[9] Recovery from garden paths would not pose any problems for information encapsulation if all garden paths were consciously detected by perceivers. In this case, one might simply assume that all syntactic processing beyond assignment of an initial analysis takes place outside the language system proper. However, many minor, temporary, unconscious errors of analysis seem to occur in sentences which perceivers understand without any conscious difficulty (see references in the text). *If* world knowledge contributes to the recovery from such error, this poses a potential problem for encapsulation of the language system, since it is unlikely that reanalysis of these sorts of errors is accomplished by a central processing system.

[10] I am assuming here that every strictly subcategorized phrase must be associated with a slot or position in a corresponding thematic frame. Thus, selection of a thematic frame with, say, only one thematic role assigned to a subcategorized phrase would be inconsistent with a constituent structure in which the head of the phrase had two sisters, i.e. two internal arguments.

the correct solution to the above problem, then it appears that either the thematic processor is not part of the language input system, or the language system is not information-encapsulated.

Alternatively, we might consider the possibility that a functionally identified input system may include a subsystem which serves as an interface between the truly encapsulated system and the central processing system. Regardless of which of these options proves to be superior, it should be emphasized that the spirit of Fodor's proposal actually remains intact, given the thematic processor hypothesis. World knowledge is not readily or directly available to any of the grammatical processing subsystems; they may be influenced by such knowledge (more accurately, by the consequences world knowledge has for linguistic analysis) only indirectly, once it has been translated into the vocabulary of linguistic theory. By hypothesis, it is the vocabulary of thematic relations which is shared by the linguistic and nonlinguistic systems (permitting the translation to be accomplished through thematic frame selection).

2.5. Summary and conclusions

Empirical evidence supports the view that generative grammars do indeed characterize the linguistic knowledge used during language comprehension. For example, perceivers seem systematically to use syntactic well-formedness conditions in processing sentences. They apparently do not rely on a collection of probabilistic heuristics derived from the grammar, nor do they apply syntactic analysis only as a last resort, when other routes to comprehension fail.

The rules or principles of grammar may now be assumed to participate directly in language comprehension. Two changes in recent approaches to language have made this possible. Unlike early psycholinguistic theories, recent theories recognize in practice the need to specify the details of the processing mechanism, avoiding the pitfalls of attempts to interpret the grammar as a theory of processing. Further, due to changes in linguistic theory, the assumption that grammatical well-formedness conditions are exploited directly by the processor no longer entails delays of analysis in language processing. Current grammars are essentially nonderivational. A single grammatical module or subsystem does not assign contradictory relations to a phrase or sentence (as was possible in derivational grammars), and thus simultaneous rather than successive application of rules is possible. Further, modularity within the grammar means that distinct subsystems of principles may be applied concurrently. Delays of analysis with one subsystem need not result in delayed operation of all subsystems.

Experimental evidence on language processing seems to support the central claim of the autonomy model: independence in the processor's use of distinct information types. However, the rallying point for interactionist models, namely the claim that all types of information are used rapidly during language comprehension, is also empirically supported. These observations were used above to argue against the serial arrangement of processing subsystems which was implied in the autonomy model, in favor of a modular model in which processing subsystems operate concurrently.

A review of several current hypotheses about the details of the comprehension mechanism reveals continued debate concerning the precise characterization of the structure internal to the grammatical processing system and its relation to a general cognitive processor with access to real-world knowledge. Current evidence does, however, clearly argue against the existence of a monolithic language comprehension system in which some powerful general purpose processor with unlimited access to knowledge of all types operates in some fixed or uniform manner for all aspects of language comprehension. Rather, the nature of the processor – the information sources available to it, the strategies employed and the mode of operation (single vs. multiple analysis of an input) – seems to depend crucially on the particular 'domain' investigated. 'Domains' in the above sense may be characterized either representationally, in terms of the grammatical subsystem implicated in processing, or functionally, in terms of the comprehension subtask involved. That the representational and functional characterizations of domains (or modules) are highly interrelated may provide an important key to understanding the efficiency and robustness of the human language comprehension systems.

REFERENCES

Berwick B. & Weinberg, A. 1984. *The grammatical basis of linguistic performance*. Cambridge, MA: MIT Press.
Bever, T. G. 1970. The cognitive basis for linguistic structures. In J. R. Hayes (ed.) *Cognition and the development of language*. New York: Wiley.
Bresnan, J. 1983. *The mental representation of grammatical relations*. Cambridge, MA: MIT Press.
Cairns, H. S., Cowart, W. & Jablon, A. D. 1981. Effects of prior context upon the integration of lexical information during sentence processing. *Journal of Verbal Language and Verbal Behavior* 20: 445–53.
Chomsky, N. 1965. *Aspects of the theory of syntax*. Cambridge, MA: MIT Press.
Chomsky, N. 1981. Lectures on government and binding. Dordrecht: Foris.
Chomsky, N. & Halle, M. 1968. *The sound pattern of English*. New York: Harper & Row.
Connine, C. & Clifton, C. 1984. Evidence for the interactive nature of Ganong's lexical effect. University of Massachusetts. MS.
Conrad, C. 1974. Context in language comprehension: a study of the subjective lexicon. *Memory & Cognition* 2: 130–8.
Crain, S. & Fodor, J. D. 1985. How can grammars help parsing? In D. Dowty, L. Karttunen &

A. Zwicky (eds.) *Theoretical perspectives on natural language parsing*. Cambridge: Cambridge University Press.

Crain, S. & Steedman, M. 1985. On not being led up the garden-path: the use of context by the psychological parser. *Natural language parsing: psychological, computational and theoretical perspectives*. Cambridge: Cambridge University Press.

deVilliers, J. G. & deVilliers, P. A. 1978. *Language acquisition*. Cambridge, MA: Harvard University Press.

Engdahl, E. 1981. Interpreting sentences with multiple filler-gap dependencies. Max-Planck-Institut für Psycholinguistik, Nijmegen. MS.

Ferreira, F. & Clifton, C. 1986. The independence of syntactic processing. *Journal of Memory and Language* 25: 348–68.

Flores d'Arcais, F. B. 1982. Automatic syntactic computation in sentence comprehension. *Psychological Research* 44: 231–42.

Fodor, J. A. 1983. *Modularity of mind*. Cambridge, MA: MIT Press.

Fodor, J. A., Bever, T. G. & Garrett, M. F. 1974. *The psychology of language: an introduction to psycholinguistics and generative grammar*. New York: McGraw-Hill.

Fodor, J. D. 1978. Parsing strategies and constraints on transformations. *Linguistic Inquiry* 9: 427–74.

Ford, M., Bresnan, J. & Kaplan, R. 1983. A competence-based theory of syntactic closure. In Bresnan (1983).

Forster, K. 1979. Levels of processing and the structure of the language processor. In W. E. Cooper & E. C. T. Walker (eds.) *Sentence processing*. Hillsdale: Erlbaum.

Forster, K. I. & Olbrei, I. 1973. Semantic heuristics and syntactic analysis. *Cognition* 2: 319–47.

Frauenfelder, U. & Marcus, S. M. 1984. Phonetic decisions and lexical constraints in the real-time process of speech perception. Ms no. 488, Institute for Perception Research, Eindhoven.

Frazier, L. 1979. On comprehending sentences: syntactic parsing strategies. Doctoral dissertation, University of Connecticut.

Frazier, L. 1983. Review of Bresnan's *The mental representation of grammatical relations*. *Natural Language and Linguistic Theory* 1: 281–310.

Frazier, L. 1985. Modularity in sentence processing. In *NELS* XII.

Frazier, L. & Clifton, C. In progress. Island constraints in parsing.

Frazier, L., Clifton, C. & Randall, J. 1983. Filling gaps: decision principles and structure in sentence comprehension. *Cognition* 13: 187–222.

Frazier, L. & Fodor, J. D. 1978. The sausage machine: a new two-stage parsing model. *Cognition* 6: 291–326.

Frazier, L. & Rayner, D. 1982. Making and correcting errors during sentence comprehension: eye movements in the analysis of structurally ambiguous sentences. *Cognitive Psychology* 14: 178–210.

Frazier, L. & Rayner, K. To appear. Parameterizing the language processing system: left- vs. right-branching within and across languages. In J. Hawkins (ed.) *Explaining linguistic universals*. Oxford: Blackwell.

Gazdar, G. 1981. Unbounded dependencies and coordinate structure. *Linguistic Inquiry* 12: 155–84.

Goodluck, H. & Tavakolian, S. 1982. Competence and processing in children's grammar of relative clauses. *Cognition* 11: 1–28.

Henderson, L. 1985. Toward a psychology of morphemes. To appear in A. W. Ellis (ed.) *Progress in the psychology of language*, vol. 1. London: Erlbaum.

Kimball, J. 1973. Seven principles of surface structure parsing in natural language. *Cognition* 2: 15–47.

Lackner, J. R. & Garrett, M. F. 1972. Resolving ambiguity: effects of biasing contexts in the unattended ear. *Cognition* 1: 359–72.

Marcus, S. M. 1980. *A theory of syntactic recognition for natural language*. Cambridge, MA: MIT Press.

Marcus, M. & Frauenfelder, U. 1985. Word recognition – uniqueness of derivation? Instituut voor Perceptic Onderzoek, Eindhoven. MS.

Marslen-Wilson, W. D. 1975. Sentence perception as an interactive parallel process. *Science* 189: 226–8.

Marslen-Wilson, W. D. & Tyler, L. 1980. The temporal structure of spoken language understanding. *Cognition* 8: 1–72.

Miller, G. A. & Chomsky, N. 1963. Finitary models of language users. In R. D. Luce, R. R. Bush & E. Galanter (eds.) *Handbook of mathematical psychology*, vol. II. New York: Wiley.

Oden, G. C. & Spira, I. L. 1983. Influence of context on the activation and selection of ambiguous word senses. *Quarterly Journal of Experimental Psychology* 35A: 61–4.

Prince, A. 1983. Relating to the grid. *Linguistic Inquiry* 14: 19–100.

Rayner, L., Carlson, M. & Frazier, L. 1983. The interaction of syntax and semantics during sentence processing: eye movement in the analysis of semantically biased sentences. *Journal of Verbal Language and Verbal Behavior* 22: 358–74.

Riemsdijk, H. van 1981. On 'adjacency' in phonology and syntax. In *NELS* XI: 399–413.

Riesbeck, C. & Schank, R. 1978. Comprehension by computer: expectation based analysis of sentences in context. In W. I. M. Levelt & G. B. Flores d'Arcais (eds.) *Studies in the perception of language*. Chichester: Wiley.

Samuels, A. C. 1981. Phoneme restoration. *Journal of Experimental Psychology: General* 110: 474–94.

Seidenberg, M., Tanenhaus, M., Leiman, J. & Bienkowski, M. 1982. Automatic access of the meaning of ambiguous words in context: some limitations of knowledge-based processing. *Cognitive Psychology* 14: 489–537.

Selkirk, E. 1984. *Psychology and syntax: the relation between sound and structure*. Cambridge: MIT Press.

Swinney, D. 1979. Lexical access during sentence comprehension: (re) considerations of context effects. *Journal of Verbal Language and Verbal Behavior* 18: 646–59.

Wanner, E. & Maratsos, M. 1978. An ATN model of relative clause comprehensions. In M. Halle, J. Bresnan & G. A. Miller (eds.) *Linguistic theory and psychological reality*. Cambridge, MA: MIT Press.

3 Grammatical principles of first language acquisition: theory and evidence

Thomas Roeper

3.0. Introduction

The field of first language acquisition research came to life as a major branch of linguistics in response to Chomsky's (1959) claim that much of grammar is innate and that therefore all languages are, in some fundamental sense, the same. The initial goal of many researchers was devoted, perhaps simplistically, to either proving or disproving this proposition, particularly those who have sought to undermine the idea of grammatical universals. They attempt instead to ground language acquisition in general principles governing pragmatics and cognition.[1] Others have been motivated by strictly non-theoretical aims; their work has been confined to the collection and cataloging of the undeniably fascinating data from child language. Indeed, as in most sciences, the data are, in a sense, ahead of the theory. A good deal of intriguing acquisition data lack an explanatory theoretical apparatus.

The hypothesis that underlies this chapter is that universal grammar (UG) will eventually explain all of the significant structural and semantic aspects of child grammar. The role of pragmatics and cognition, though intimately connected to language, will be seen to be external to the grammatical heart of language. The essence of language is a system of grammatical rules that interact with other aspects of mind in deceptively subtle ways. Our focus in this chapter, however, will not be on the interactions themselves, but rather on the more narrow goal of articulating how a grammar develops.

We will review acquisition research that sheds light on the precise sequence of hypotheses that a child entertains and on the acquisition path followed in grammar construction. We believe that such hypotheses will provide the springboard into a unified theory of language: a theory which is the input to a neurological theory, a theory of mental concepts, and a theory accounting for the coordination of diverse mental abilities. Grammar, one hopes, will work like a theoretical laser to locate specific abilities in a brain of

---

[1] The idea that language might be a by-product of general cognition is an old one. See, for example, the writings of Wundt (1912) and Stern & Stern (1928). Blumenthal (1970) reviews the issue.

overwhelming intricacy. Once grammar is isolated, the questions of how cognition, pragmatics, and other brain functions relate to language will become central. These questions, from the perspective of theoretical psycholinguistics, are not yet coherently approachable, though they are certainly not, intrinsically, more or less interesting than the question of how a grammar is acquired.[2]

We begin with an historical review of work whose primary aim was to do battle with various empiricist views of language. We can summarize the results of such work as follows:

(a)   A child's grammar refers to *abstract* structures.

(b)   A child's grammar is *rule-governed*.

(c)   A child's grammar is constructivist and non-imitative.

The presence of abstract structures is evident from the fact that children will treat phrases as units from an early stage (see Read & Schreiber 1982; Crain & Nakayama 1984; Otsu to appear). A straightforward example from Otsu's work involves 3-year-old children's differential responses to sentences like (1a) and (1b):

(1)   a. I hit the boy with my hand
        b. I hit the boy with a hat

If one asks *Who did you hit?*, the answer corresponding to (1a) is *the boy*, not *the boy with my hand*; for (1b) the answer is *the boy with a hat*. The difference lies in the fact that *with my hand* is not part of the noun phrase containing *the boy*, while *with a hat* can be. Thus even 3-year-old children show clear knowledge of abstract structure above word level, i.e. that *the boy with a hat* should be analyzed as a noun phrase: $[_{NP}$the boy $[_{PP}$with a hat$]]$.

Evidence that children's language is non-imitative comes from regularly produced overgeneralizations like *comed* or double negatives like *No I am not a nothing boy*. Some children are highly consistent in their creative grammars and allow auxiliaries to be repeated (*Can I can sing?, Is John is busy?*) or consistently use a single auxiliary as a question word (*Are you can come?, Are you did go?*). Children's creativity is evidenced whenever they say something grammatically novel. Interestingly, their novelty may involve their creative use of formal distinctions in universal grammar. For example, at one stage, children might say both *That a my house* and *My house* (Brown & Bellugi 1964). At a later stage, they learn that possessive *my* and article *a*

---

[2] While theoretical goals are paramount, applied fields need not wait for theoreticians to come up with the ultimately correct theories before they can begin their work. Workers in second language teaching, reading, aphasia, and so on can and should acquire a basic handle on how pragmatics and cognition interact with language. In this vein, we can make an analogy: health concerns need not wait for a full biology of nutrition before it is decided, in rough terms, what a good diet is.

are disjunctive in English. In other words, children have the equivalent of both braces notation, which gives alternatives:

$$\begin{Bmatrix} \text{Dem} \\ \text{Art} \end{Bmatrix} \text{N}$$

and parentheses notation, which gives compatible options:

(Dem) (Art) N

as available methods to represent input information.

These examples are a few among many. To cite another, the process of negation reveals creative, rule-governed, consistent behaviors among children. First, they make negation sentence-initial (*No I want milk*); then we find negatives in second position (*That no fish school*); then in several positions (*No I am not a nothing boy*); and then without appropriate scope sensitivity (*I want anything* to mean *I want nothing*) (for discussion, see Bellugi 1967; Phinney 1981). Child grammar is systematically different from adult grammar in other ways. For example, children allow the form *What I can do?* where adults must obligatorily invert the auxiliary in such structures, and we find forms like *Was this is the boat I saw?*, where the auxiliary is moved from one clause and the past tense from the other (see Cromer 1968; Valian, Winzemer & Erreich 1981), although this does not occur in the adult language.

The semantics of child language are subject to formal originality in a similar vein. Children regularly produce causatives in a fashion not found in English, such as *Don't giggle me*, *Don't uncomfortable the cat*, and *She combed me baldheaded* (see Bowerman 1982). Children overgeneralize other semantic relations as well: *Feel it to me* is not an adult locution, but it is a natural use of the preposition *to* to express the idea of putting something next to someone.

In sum, the paradigm established by Chomsky has received very clear *general* support, and the notion that children follow rules and that their behavior adheres to certain principles is now widely accepted.

It is worth reflecting for a moment on what the true goals of linguistic theory should be. There are three possible extremes:

(1) establish the principles of mind; or

(2) write a complete grammar for every human language; or

(3) provide a sufficiently detailed description of human linguistic
    abilities to make connections to other sciences.

The first goal is the traditional goal of philosophy, while the second is a natural prerequisite for all applied linguistic work. The third, I believe, is the natural goal of linguistics. We would like a map of linguistic abilities that does not specify every detail of every language, but one which is sufficiently specific that one could begin to do neurological research and one could see how ancillary abilities feed into language. In sum, the goal of linguistics should be to become a part of biology. It is, once again, not enough to establish general truths.

3.1. A problem for acquisition theory and a solution

3.1.1. Non-occurring errors among children; non-occurring structures in human language

As we have seen, novel formations in children's speech point to their grammars being abstract, rule-governed, and non-imitative. Yet paradoxically, from the point of view of the linguistic theory of the 1970s, there seem to be errors that children *never* make, despite the fact that one would be led to predict that they would do so. For example, children do not produce such sentences as *What did you buy a Ford?*, despite the standard analysis that allows for an NP position after the verb *buy*. In terms of trace theory, it is not clear why a child should not postulate the possibility of a *Wh*-node without a corresponding trace. Moreover, a natural semantics is possible. The sentence could mean 'What kind of Ford did you buy?' Likewise, what prevents children from overgeneralizing the noun phrase *the city's destruction* to the impossible *the play's enjoyment*? The theory of grammar current in the 1970s provided no answer to this question.

In addition, it was unclear why children *stopped* making certain errors (Randall 1982). Why should a child who says *shirter* or *mistaker* or *I'll be the listener and you be the storier* ever cease to use these locutions? Since similar exceptional examples of this sort (*New Yorker, Detroiter*) exist in the adult language, the child would seem to have enough input to invite a false generalization. How does the child come to know that some forms are exceptions and should not be generalized, particularly after having initially begun to generalize them?

The linguistic theory of the 1970s was, in a sense, faced with the same problem. Just as it invited the incorrect conclusion that certain non-existent errors should occur in children's speech, it also predicted that certain linguistic *structures* should occur which, nevertheless, were unattested in any human language. Put simply, languages were found to be much more similar to each other than the theory would lead one to predict.

3.1.2. A modular solution to the problem

As in most sciences, many of the assumptions of TG were overthrown by detailed analysis, in both theory and acquisition work. In response a new vision of grammar emerged, one that is exact, particularistic, and quite surprising in its predictions. The concept articulated by Chomsky (1981) was that grammar was composed of a group of modules, each with its own simple principles, which interact mechanically to produce sentences. The theory began to resemble other sciences in the presence of intricate mechanisms whose role was opaque to common sense.

We can now see a grammar as a set of *modules*, each governed by a set of general principles. The complex interaction of these principles results in the sentences of the language. To give one example, a language-specific rule of passivization has ceased to exist. The surface facts of the passive construction now result from the interaction of several modules, including a syntactic one (the principle of 'Move α,' which allows free optional movement of any element to any position); a morphological one (the theory of abstract Case, which demands that every NP be assigned Case); and a semantic one (the θ-criterion, which disallows any NP from bearing two semantic roles).

This approach, while attractive in its elegance, did not lead in and of itself to a solution to the problems outlined above. These diverse modules, if allowed to combine freely and without constraint, would seemingly lead to as many possible grammars as any 1970s model. If the child had to juggle every possible combination of every possible manifestation of every module, it is not clear how acquisition could proceed at all.

Chomsky's answer to this problem was an extension of the nativist approach that had long characterized his work. He posited that the nature of the modules and their general principles of interaction are part of innate knowledge. Yet, obviously, languages exhibit extensive variation. This problem was solved by allowing language-particular *parameters* of variation in the modules. The child would, on the basis of particular data, set the values for particular parameters. The setting of a value for one module triggers a series of obligatory consequences in other modules. The child's discovery, for example, that the language is SVO rather than SOV, that it has obligatory rather than optional subjects, or that it allows clitics, would have far-reaching consequences for the grammar as a whole. In other words, every language-particular feature of a grammar does not require separate learning. Thus it follows that languages will exhibit a smaller range of grammars (and children exhibit fewer incorrect grammars) than the premodular approach to grammar would predict.

Under this model, until encountering misleading data, the child will make no errors in grammar at all. The ways in which the child's grammar diverges from the adult's lie not in a series of wrong grammars that are replaced by better grammars, but rather in the presence of *incomplete* grammars in which some particular module has not been established or some information simply has not registered. This perspective (which is articulated in Lebeaux forth-

39

coming, and developed further in Pinker 1984) both fits the grammaticality facts, whose subtlety and diversity have mushroomed over the last decade, and provides, as we shall illustrate, an empirically supported account of the route to acquisition.

3.2. Background concepts for substantive theories

The idea that acquiring a language involves setting parameters implies that acquisition can be linked to certain explicit pieces of information, or 'triggers' that have irrevocable consequences once encountered. Perhaps some triggers lead straightforwardly from one generalization to the next, as the property of a language having a rich inflectional system seems to lead to the possession of optional subjects. Or perhaps triggers act as 'bootstraps' by which the child induces a higher-order generalization from overt information. For example, perhaps the child's association of subjects with agents in some way bootstraps the child into a purely structural definition of 'subject', which then applies to non-agents;[3] others argue that bootstrapping is unnecessary.

One fact is now well-known, namely that triggering factors are all positive ones. The fact that correction is not a significant factor in acquisition means that the child is exposed only to positive evidence. If so, then the child must deduce what is ungrammatical simply from knowledge of UG and exposure to good sentences. In fact, the child has an even more difficult task – he or she must be able to disregard certain pieces of positive evidence and label them as exceptional, and hence not the basis for generalization. For example, though children will overgeneralize past tense formation to produce *comed*, they will not overgeneralize *sit* and *sat* to *fit* and *fat* or *think* and *thank*.[4] How the child manages to accomplish the feat of acquisition given sometimes misleadingly positive evidence will be the subject of the following sections.

3.2.1. The subset principle

The fact that a child is exposed only to positive evidence leads to what has been called the *subset principle* which has been extensively developed in Berwick (1985; see also Williams 1981; Wexler & Manzini 1987; Roeper to appear). According to this principle, if one grammar is a proper subset of another, acquisition can proceed only from smaller to larger; this follows from the fact that positive evidence might force a revision to a larger grammar, but cannot force a larger grammar to be smaller.

The subset principle has an important implication: in a case where a child

---

[3] This idea is proposed in Pinker (1984). See Chomsky (1981), Grimshaw (1981), Marantz (1984), Roeper (to appear), and Nishigauchi & Roeper (1987) for relevant discussion.

[4] A few examples are reported in the literature, but there is no evidence of systematic generalization.

might be in a position to posit an obligatory or an optional rule, he or she will take the obligatory rule. Suppose that the contrary were true. If so, the child would hear the sentence (a) *What can I do?* and thus hypothesize an optional inversion rule, thereby admitting both (a) and (b) *What I can do?* But, then, how could the child ever learn that (b) is ill-formed? Nothing could lead to this conclusion, if the child is sensitive only to positive examples.

In other words, since sentences with obligatory inversion are a subset of those with optional inversion, the child, assuming the grammar with the former, will be right from the outset. Only positive evidence (in this specific case non-existent) could prompt the child to revise the rule to make it optional.

For the sake of contrast, let us approach the issue from another perspective. What is the opposite hypothesis to the subset principle and why is it untenable? The opposite hypothesis is that a child begins with a grammar broad enough to accommodate any sentence in any language in the world. Such a grammar, for example, would allow both SVO and SOV constructions and allow questions to be formed in a number of different ways. Then upon exposure to real sentences, the child would narrow his or her grammar to the correct one. Such a process, while seemingly commonsensical, is nevertheless untenable. It fails because the existence of one construction in a language does not *ipso facto* rule out the existence of another. For example, the existence of one formal device to form questions (say, *wh*-fronting) does not eliminate another form (say, that formed in yes/no questions). In a word, the assumption that the child begins with all possibilities fails because it demands that certain forms be excluded. But how and when could the child decide that something was 'not heard'? The subset principle is superior because it allows new information to be added, rather than demanding the deletion of incorrect information.

Subset theory applies just when one grammar lies entirely within another. Where grammars are not in a subset relation, then, in fact, a new piece of data *could* parametrically trigger the discarding of a formerly acceptable construction. So an important question is this: how often is it the case that grammars form a subset? In the following section we illustrate the issues at stake.

3.2.2. Optional subject languages

The obligatory/optional relation from subset theory has several applications. One arises in a well-known case of crosslinguistic variation, namely the contrast between English and some Romance languages, like Italian, with respect to the obligatoriness of subjects. In English, we must say *he went*, while in Italian one can optionally say *went* with subject omitted (but with verbal morphology indicating the number and gender of the subject). Rizzi (1986) has made the straightforward prediction that English and Italian children should both begin with the hypothesis that the subject is obligatory. The Italian child, upon hearing a sentence with an absent subject, will revise his or her grammar to make subjects optional. The English-speaking child never hears such a sentence and therefore retains obligatory subjects.

Hyams (1986) has explored the acquisition data and found Rizzi's prediction to be incorrect. Both English and Italian children begin with optional subjects; they both begin, as it were, speaking Italian. In English, children utter sentences like *Yes, is toys in the kitchen*, *Want to get it*, *Crawl downstairs*, and *Want Kathryn a put in tank*. These occur together with sentences that have subjects: *I want kiss it*; *Kathryn want build another house*. Why should such subjectless sentences exist? Their presence, in the past, had always been treated as a phenomenon rooted in performance rather than competence.

Hyams provides a subtle explanation based upon a second difference between English and Italian: English has expletive subjects, while Italian does not. That is, English speakers say *It appears to be rainy*, where *it* has no reference, but fills the (obligatory) subject position.[5] Italian has no expletives, and allows in their place an empty subject. Hyams argues that the expletive in English *triggers* a reanalysis based on the following substantive universal: subjects are obligatory if expletives are present. Interestingly, she found that just when expletive subjects appear in children's grammars, the subjectless sentences disappear.

To conclude, English and Italian are not in a subset relation, but, rather, overlap. Since the crucial sentences that trigger obligatory subjects lie outside the shared set, a parametric explanation is called for. It is important to note that there is no *logical* necessity for expletives to be linked to obligatory subjects. Logically speaking, some verbs might allow expletive subjects and some verbs empty subjects. But a careful examination of the facts has shown that it is parametric theory, not an *a priori* appeal to 'logic,' that points the way to the correct approach. Child language is full of incomplete sentences and deletions. It was only once the hypothesis of a null subject parameter was on the agenda that the issue was even visible. Once visible, Hyams was able to show that absent subjects are systematic in ways that other deletions are not. Thus, her work provides good support for the parametric approach to language variation.

---

[5] Hyams cites two other possibly relevant differences between Italian and English: that of the relationship between the auxiliary system and the subject position and the possibility (for English) of unstressed pronouns in subject position.

3.3. **Universal grammar and growth**

Many interesting questions arise when we study the child's grammar. What do the final steps of acquisition look like? Do they follow the universal principles that we expect them to follow? How do these universal principles emerge? It is obvious that a principle that applies to a complete syntax cannot emerge until a complete syntax is present, but less obvious how UG is invoked. Several hypotheses pertaining to UG and growth have been put forward. The first is the *continuity hypothesis*, which states that universal principles are instantly present when needed. A second is maturationally based: linguistic principles apply when biological maturation enables them to.[6] For example, children might lack recursive structures until a certain stage. If so, then they must ignore complex sentences from input data until they are biologically ready to absorb them. A third hypothesis is that extraneous cognitive factors prevent children from using knowledge that they in fact have. For example, children might not exhibit the 'raising' construction until their consciousness of possible worlds enables them to understand the meaning of the word *seem*. Borer & Wexler (1987) make the interestingly specific proposal that one transformational type, NP-movement, requires maturation, which would explain the putative delayed acquisition of both raising with 'seem' and passive. A fourth hypothesis is that children represent language in partially nonlinguistic terms before they trigger the acquisition system. These hypotheses constitute the domain of much current research and it is premature, in my estimation, to claim that one must be true. In fact, they all could be true for different portions of the grammar.

3.3.1. **C-command and its effects**

What evidence is there for the use of linguistic principles at an early stage of acquisition? What principles of linguistic theory are preconditions for a child's grammatical analysis? One seems particularly important, namely that of *c-command*. The c-command relation is stated as follows: one node c-commands another if the first branching node dominating the former, dominates the latter. Thus in (2) below, Y c-commands Z, W, and Q.

(2)

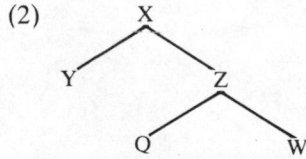

---

[6] For a maturational account in the Piagetian tradition, see Sinclair-de-Zwart (1969). Other maturational accounts are discussed in Slobin (1973), Gleitman (1981), and Borer & Wexler (1987).

However, in (3), N and M c-command no nodes (except each other), since the first branching node dominating them dominates no other node:

(3)

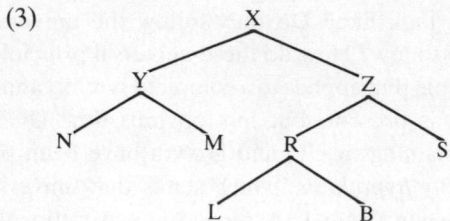

This is true despite the fact that N and M are 'higher' in the tree than L and B.

Interestingly, c-command is at work in a variety of grammatical processes. Since there is no logical necessity for this to be true, it provides interesting evidence that purely linguistic processes exist independent of other cognitive ones.

Recent work by Solan (1983) bears out the idea that c-command is brought by the child into the acquisition process. Solan did a simple experiment utilizing the uncommon phenomenon of 'backward pronominalization.' He called attention to the following sentences:

(4)   The sheep hit him_i after the dog_i ran around

(5)   *The horse told him_i that the $sheep_i$ would run around

Why is (5) ungrammatical but not (4)? Linguistic theory provides a well-established principle of coreference, namely that a pronoun cannot c-command a regular noun phrase. This formulation allows backward co-reference where the pronoun is lower than the noun it refers to, whether the pronoun precedes or follows its antecedent. Thus in (4), represented as (6), the attachment of the PP to the topmost S prevents the pronoun from c-commanding its antecedent. Hence (4) is grammatical. However, in (5), represented as (7), *him* c-commands *sheep*, resulting in the impossibility of coreference between them:

(6)

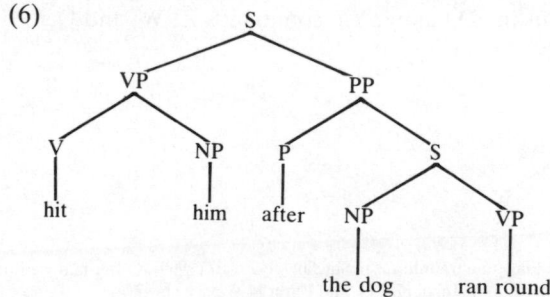

(7)

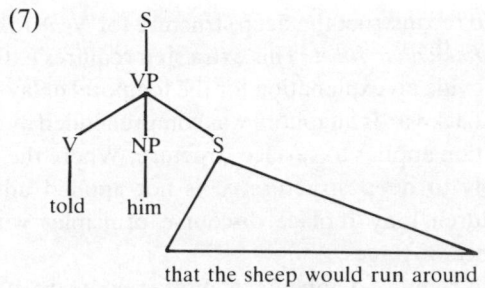

that the sheep would run around

Solan carried out an act-out experiment with 4- to 6-year-old children and showed that they were three times as likely to assign coreference in (4) as in (5). The role of c-command received further support in experiments by Goodluck (1978), Hsu (1981), Crain & McKee (1986), and Lust (1986a, b), showing that the c-command effect can be detected even among 3-year-olds. Such results illustrate dramatically the necessity of assuming that c-command is literally brought forward by the child into the acquisition process. Since backward pronominalization is rare even in adult speech, the children's judgements could not have been based primarily on experience. Furthermore, these facts refute the idea that the children might have no assumptions at all about how to interpret pronouns or that they simply use context to determine antecedents (just as adults do to determine the antecedent of *he* in *John thinks he is big*). One is forced to the conclusion that there exists a structural constraint on anaphora, and this constraint is essentially preprogrammed into the child.

3.3.2. Blocked forward coreference

The facts acquire intriguing new complexity when we consider that the same principle will exclude *forward* coreference in some environments: c-command predicts that forward coreference is impossible in a sentence of the form *Near Bill, he put a hat*. The same logic predicts that children will not allow coreference here. Eventually they do not, but there is a period of time (roughly between age 4 and 7) when they do allow incorrect forward coreference to a significant degree. It seems that they are then using a general discourse principle, known from grammar books, that a pronoun has an antecedent. The antecedent may occur anywhere in the previous discourse, i.e. their strategy tells them that coreference is only forward.[7] At some point the child hears evidence which invites a reconstruction of deep structure, for instance, *Himself John likes* is the same as *John likes himself*. From such

---

[7] Though there is disagreement in the experimental literature on the details (see Ingram & Shaw 1981; Carden 1986; O'Grady 1987). There is no question that children allow more coreference on sentences of the form: *Near Bill he put a hat* than on *He put a hat near Bill*.

sentences, the child can learn to reconstruct the deep structure for *Near John he put the snake* as *He put the snake near John*. This extra step requires extra evidence and therefore may provide an explanation for the temporal delay in acquisition. In the cases where backwards anaphora was comprehended by 3-year-olds, the c-command relation applies to surface structure. Where the c-command principle must apply to deep structure, it is not applied until children are older. Thus children may replace discourse principles with sentence grammar in a sequence of stages.

The structural principle of c-command appears in another context – it is involved in the subtle difference between discourse coreference and bound variable coreference (i.e. coreference involving quantifier binding). The latter, as (8) shows, is restricted by sentence boundaries; it does not apply in the domain of a discourse:

(8) *Everyone$_i$ talked. He$_i$ knew that it was a mistake

(9) John$_i$ talked. He$_i$ knew that it was a mistake

(10) Everyone$_i$ said he$_i$ knew that it was a mistake

In (8) we automatically assign *he* to an unknown but specific outside observer, not to *everyone*. In (9), where coreference but not bound variables are involved, coreference across a sentence boundary is fine, and *he* can be *John*. In (10), where *he* is c-commanded by *everyone*, the two are linked as bound variables and the *he* refers to each one of everyone. This kind of knowledge is far too subtle to be acquired via instruction. It must therefore be deducible from principle. The relevant principle in this case is that bound variables can be linked only if one c-commands the other.

An important question is whether children allow coreference in sentences like (8). The answer to this question will provide more insight into how c-command helps to shape emergent grammars. For preliminary discussion, see Roeper *et al.* (1985).

3.4. **Parametric interactions**

Manzini & Wexler (1987) and Matthews (to appear) propose an interesting acquisition principle, namely that parameters are independent. Let us examine this principle with respect to the state of the developing organism. After all, interactions may exist for an incomplete grammar that do not exist for an adult or *vice versa*. Their hypothesis can be tested by reference to the claim that children will assume that English is a pro-drop language until they learn expletives (see section 3.2.2.). Expletives, as it turns out, are relevant to binding theory: if an expletive intervenes, an anaphor may be bound outside of its clause. Note:

(11) They think it is a good idea for each other to drink

For adults, the *it* must be an expletive and could not refer, say, to a particular glass of chocolate milk. For a child, however, who has not acquired expletives, *it* must be referential and refer to a specific drink. Consequently, the child would be forced to the assumption that positive evidence allows *each other* to refer outside of its clause, even when the clause contains a referential subject. The child would thus mis-set the binding parameter. Moreover, once mis-set, it would be very difficult to obtain information leading to correction. How can this problem be solved? Only, it seems, by appealing to an acquisition theory in which the parameters interact and are ordered in the following manner:[8]

> 1st: Determine the presence of expletives.
> 2nd: Fix the pro-drop parameter.
> 3rd: Fix binding theory.

What is the status of this hypothesis? Since ordered parameters are not found in (atemporal) linguistic theory, this ordering belongs to an acquisition theory. Nonetheless the acquisition theory (like linguistic theory) remains contingent: our knowledge of linguistic theory might find a different means to guarantee that children do not mis-set the binding relation. (See Pica 1985 for suggestions.) Since ordered parameters in child acquisition are among a raft of contingent hypotheses that are subject to rearrangement as our knowledge of language and acquisition deepens, this idea might have to be revised if a more adequate theory of the role of expletives in acquisition is put forward.

We might next ask logically what the evidence shows about when binding is acquired. Though complex, it points to the later appearance of this phenomenon. For example, Matthei (1981) showed that children to the age of 4 years allowed anaphors to refer outside their clause, pointing to their interpretation of sentences like *The chickens told the rats to hit each other*. On the other hand, Otsu (to appear) obtained evidence suggesting that they *do* obey constraints on binding at a better than random rate at the age of 3 years.

Jacubowicz (1984), Wexler & Manzini (1987), and Otsu (to appear) have shown that children make errors in pronominal reference, allowing pronouns to refer within clauses (see also Deutsch & Koster 1982), by interpreting sentences like *John likes him* to mean *John likes himself*. Yet at the same time, their rate of correct answers is better than random. In addition, Roeper *et al.* (1985) provide evidence from a group of 20 3-year-old children that these young children do obey the clause-mate restriction when *wh*-movement is involved. They never allow coreference in *Whose hat did he lift?*, while a

---

[8] These decisions could occur (virtually) simultaneously in real time acquisition, so long as the logic of the sequence is observed.

significant number do allow it in *Who lifted his hat?* Furthermore, the errors in pronominal reference persist after reflexives are correctly analyzed.

These results can be analyzed from several perspectives. One is that whenever children show knowledge of universals, then any counterevidence is simply attributable to experimental noise. A second possibility is that constraints are absolutes, and thus one must hypothesize a motivation for any violation of them. A third is that micro-steps are involved of a sort we have not yet discovered.

Nevertheless, with respect to the hypothesis that parameter fixing is ordered, the data are compatible with the view that binding is fixed later than expletives. Children seem not to have all of the constraints of binding theory completely fixed until they are age 6 or older.

3.4.1. Subjacency and control

There are other structural principles that the child brings forward innately to the process of language acquisition. Otsu (to appear), for example, has shown that children as young as 3 years have the *subjacency* principle (for thorough discussion of subjacency, see Chomsky 1986 and Volume I, Chapter 2 of this series; see also Goodluck & Hakansson (to appear) for Swedish data supporting Otsu). Subjacency predicts that it is impossible to question a noun phrase contained within another noun phrase. Thus subjacency predicts that, given structures (13a) and (13b) for sentences (12a) and (12b) respectively, the answer to the question *What did John hit the dog with?* can only be *a broom*, not *a bandage*. As (13b) reveals, the noun phrase *a bandage* is contained within a prepositional phrase, itself within a noun phrase:

(12) a. John hit the dog with a broom
     b. John hit the dog with a bandage

(13) a.

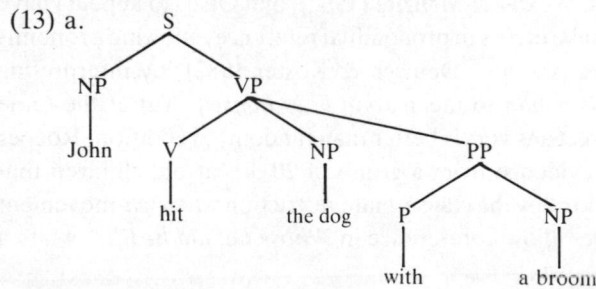

b.

Otsu tested 72 children from ages 3 to 8 years. After determining in a pretest that in sentences like (12b) the children did exhibit awareness that the PP fell within the NP, he found that 62 of the 72 children had grammars that obeyed the subjacency principle. These children rejected interpretations which involved extracting one NP from another NP. His results argue for the innateness of structural constraints, since they are evident at a very early point in acquisition. Indeed, as soon as syntactic structure is evident, the constraints are evident as well, thereby providing the strongest argument, short of neurological evidence itself, that can be made for innateness.

Another topic central to linguistic theory besides pro-drop, anaphora, and subjacency has produced results from acquisition research, namely that of *control*. In a study by Roeper (1982), it was shown that 3-year-old children grasp the differences between the control properties of noun phrases and verb phrases. It is a universal feature of grammar that deverbal nouns do not have obligatory subjects. If one says *Mom likes not singing*, then *Mom* is the singer, whereas if one says *Mom likes no singing*, then anyone can be the singer. In experiments centered around conversation, 4- and 5-year-old children demonstrated clear awareness of this distinction. Also, in a toy-moving experiment, 19 3- and 4-year-old children showed awareness of the control differences between *Can you show Mary jumping?* and *Can you show Mary the jumping?* It was found that 97% of the children correctly identified *Mary* as the controller in the former, but only 49% did so (incorrectly) in the latter.[9]

---

[9] Similarly, Phinney (1981) demonstrated a sensitivity among 4-year-olds to a very subtle constraint on complementizers, namely that one can extract a subject from a complement clause except when it is contiguous to *that*.

3.5. **The future**

What does the future hold? The basic course of the acquisition of even one single language remains uncharted. Take English, for example. In English, there are at least 20 different forms of *wh*-movement, but we have no sense of when they arrive or how. Do they appear at once, or in terms of sequence of exposure, or haphazardly? Do children learn subject and object extraction equally well? Such questions deserve investigation and need to be tied to subtle aspects of theoretical formulations.

In addition, there need to be many new detailed studies tying acquisition to parametric variation. Such will shift the focus of research away from English (just as has been the case in linguistic theory itself) and toward a comparative perspective (for example, see Lust 1986 for crosslinguistic acquisition studies of coreference). Moreover, the research focus will shift from attention to the child's syntax itself to the means by which children *interpret* sentences. To cite one example of this, children learn that in *John wants to lift a tractor*, *John* is interpreted as the agent of the lower clause, while in *John wants a tractor to be lifted*, anyone can do the lifting.[10] If early rules of control are inferential, then one would expect that children could not make this distinction. But then, how do they learn that a certain interpretation is not correct? Questions of this kind call for subtle experimentation, probably involving conversational feedback.

Linguistic theory and acquisition research work in concert. Theory and data from many quarters may seem at first to bear little relation to each other, but over time, principles are uncovered that unify the two. As the principles of linguistic theory become more refined, they should point to patterns in language growth that in turn could provide a key to genetic structure.

Linguistic theory is often said to confront a dual challenge. It must account for adult knowledge of language and for the problem of how a child acquires one language among a large number of possible languages. It is a mark of progress that these goals are becoming increasingly inseparable.

REFERENCES

Bellugi, U. 1967. The acquisition of negation. Doctoral dissertation, Harvard University.
Berwick, R. 1985. *The acquisition of syntactic knowledge.* Cambridge, MA: MIT Press.
Blumenthal, A. 1970. *Language and psychology: historical aspects of psycholinguistics.* New York: Wiley.
Borer, H. & Wexler, K. 1987. The maturation of syntax. In Roeper & Williams (1987).
Bowerman, M. 1982. Reorganizational processes in lexical and syntactic development. In Wanner & Gleitman (1982).

[10] The first steps in this direction have been taken in the study of morphology by Randall (1982, 1984), who has explored the issue of how underlying verbal arguments are expressed in derived environments.

Brown, R. & Bellugi, U. 1964. Three processes in the child's acquisition of syntax. *Harvard Educational Review* 34: 133–51.

Carden, G. 1986. Blocked forwards anaphora: theoretical implications of the data. In Lust (1986b).

Chomsky, N. 1959. Review of B. F. Skinner, *Verbal behavior*. *Language* 35: 26–57.

Chomsky, N. 1981. *Lectures on government and binding*. Dordrecht: Foris.

Chomsky, N. 1986. *Barriers*. Cambridge, MA: MIT Press.

Crain, S. & McKee, C. 1986. Acquisition of structural restrictions on anaphora. *NELS* 16.

Crain S. & Nakayama, M. 1984. Structure dependence in grammar formation. University of Connecticut. MS.

Cromer, R. 1968. The development of temporal reference during the acquisition of language. Doctoral dissertation, Harvard University.

Deutsch, W. & Koster, J. 1982. Children's interpretation of sentence internal anaphora. *Papers and Reports on Child Language Development* 21.

Gleitman, L. 1981. Maturational determinants of language growth. *Cognition* 10: 103–14.

Goodluck, H. & Hakansson, To appear. Children's syntax: grammar and experimental evidence. In R. Söderbergh (ed.) *Proceedings of the symposium on child language*, Lund University.

Grimshaw, J. 1981. Form, function, and the language acquisition device. In C. L. Baker & J. McCarthy (eds.) *The logical problem of language acquisition*. Cambridge, MA: MIT Press.

Hyams, N. 1986. *The acquisition of parameterized grammars*. Dordrecht: Reidel.

Hsu, J. 1981. The development of structural principles in children's grammar of complement subject interpretation. Doctoral dissertation, City University of New York.

Jacubowicz, C. 1984. On markedness and binding principles. *NELS* 14: 154–82.

Lebeaux, D. Forthcoming. Levels of representation. Doctoral dissertation, University of Massachusetts.

Lust, B. 1986a. Introduction to Lust (1986b).

Lust, B. (ed.) 1986b. *Studies in the acquisition of anaphora*. Dordrecht: Reidel.

Manzini, M. & Wexler, K. 1987. Parameters and learnability in binding theory. In Roeper & Williams (1987).

Marantz, A. 1984. *On the nature of grammatical relations*. Cambridge, MA: MIT Press.

Matthei, E. 1981. Children's interpretation of sentences containing reciprocals. In Tavakolian (1981).

Matthews, R. To appear. Formal learning approach to linguistic theory. In R. Matthews & R. May (eds.) *Learnability and linguistic theory*. Dordrecht: Reidel.

Nishigauchi, T. & Roeper, T. 1987. Deductive parameters and the growth of empty categories. In Roeper & Williams (1987).

O'Grady, W. 1987. *Principles of grammar and learning*. Chicago: Chicago University Press.

Otsu, Y. To appear. *Universal grammar and syntactic development in children*. Dordrecht: Reidel.

Phinney, M. 1981. The acquisition of embedded sentential complements. Doctoral dissertation, University of Massachusetts.

Pica, P. 1985. Subject, tense, and truth: toward a modular approach to binding. In J. Guéron, J. V. Pollack & H. Obenauer (eds.) *Grammatical representation*. Dordrecht: Foris.

Pinker, S. 1984. *Language learnability and language development*. Cambridge, MA: Harvard University Press.

Randall, J. 1982. Morphological structure and language acquisition. Doctoral dissertation, University of Massachusetts.

Randall, J. 1984. Thematic structure and inheritance. *Quaderni di Semantica*.

Read, C. & Schreiber, P. 1982. Why short subjects are harder to find than long ones. In Wanner & Gleitman (1982).

Rizzi, L. 1986. Null objects in Italian and the theory of *pro*. *Linguistic Inquiry* 17: 501–58.

Roeper, T. 1982. Linguistic universals and the acquisition of gerunds. In Wanner & Gleitman (1982).

Roeper, T. To appear. The acquisition of implicit arguments and the role of theory, process, and mechanism. In B. MacWhinney (ed.) *Mechanisms of language acquisition*. Hillside: Erlbaum.

Roeper, T. & Williams, E. (eds.) 1987. *Parameter setting*. Dordrecht: Reidel.

Roeper, T., Rooth, M., Akiyama, S. & Mallis, L. 1985. The problem of empty categories and the acquisition of binding. University of Massachusetts. MS.

Sinclair-de-Zwart, H. 1969. Developmental psycholinguistics. In D. Elkind & J. H. Flavell (eds.) *Studies in cognitive development.* New York: Oxford University Press.

Slobin, D. 1973. Cognitive prerequisites for the acquisition of grammar. In D. Slobin & C. Ferguson (eds.) *Studies in child language development.* New York: Holt, Rinehart & Winston.

Solan, L. 1983. *Pronominal reference: child language and the theory of grammar.* Dordrecht: Reidel.

Stern, C. & Stern, W. 1928. *Die Kindersprache: eine psychologische und sprachtheoretische Untersuchung.* Rev. 4th edn. Leipzig: Barth.

Tavakolian, S. (ed.) 1981. *Language acquisition and linguistic theory.* Cambridge, MA: MIT Press.

Valian, V., Winzemer, J. & Erreich, A. 1981. A 'little linguist' model of syntax learning. In Tavakolian (1981).

Wanner, E. & Gleitman, L. (eds.) 1982. *Language acquisition: the state of the art.* Cambridge: Cambridge University Press.

Wexler, K. & Manzini, R. 1987. Parameters and learnability in binding theory. In Roeper & Williams (1987).

Williams, E. 1981. Language acquisition, markedness, and phrase-structure. In Tavakolian (1981).

Wundt, W. 1912. *Die Sprache.* Rev. 3rd edn. Leipzig: Wilhelm Engelmann.

4 Second language acquisition and grammatical theory*

Suzanne Flynn

4.0. Introduction

The goal of developing a theory of second language (L2) acquisition based on a principled theory of language is not new. Two of the most well-developed approaches to the study of L2 acquisition contrastive analysis (CA) (Fries 1945; Lado 1957) and creative construction (CC) (Dulay & Burt 1974) were each based upon a version of an available theory of language. A traditional CA model, in which L2 acquisition is thought to consist of the learning of a fixed set of linguistic habits, was based upon a structuralist approach to language. A CC model of L2 learning, in which L2 acquisition is thought to be a creative rule-governed process, was based upon a version of a generative theory of language. Though CA and CC were each able to capture the sense of one important component of the L2 acquisition process – CA the role of the first language (L1) experience, and CC the role of principles of acquisition independent of the L1 experience – neither succeeded in providing a principled framework within which a full account of the L2 learning process could be developed. The reasons for this failure, in the case of CA, had to do, in large part, with the nature of the linguistic theory upon which it was developed. Structuralist theories, with their behaviorist grounding, focussed on language as behavior. Such theories are known to have problems explaining how knowledge is acquired or put to use (Chomsky 1959, 1986).[1]

Even though CC was articulated within a framework more consistent with current goals of linguistic theory, the imprecise formulation of the L2 model within this paradigm left it empirically untestable (see the review in Flynn 1985a). When empirical work did emerge, it often focussed on language in the manner dictated by structuralism, that is, in terms of surface structure features.

The failure of CA and CC unfortunately left us without an explanatory

* The author wishes to thank Jack Carroll and Fritz Newmeyer for helpful discussion, comments and suggestions for revisions throughout the preparation of this chapter.

[1] It should be pointed out that DiPietro (1971) did attempt to construct a CA account of L2 acquisition based on a 1960s transformational model of language.

theory of L2 acquisition and unable to accommodate the important new insights which the study of L2 acquisition could provide. Because L2 acquisition involves speakers who have already reached a mature steady state in terms of their L1s, and in many cases in terms of their overall development,[2] L2 acquisition provides a potentially rich source of data essential for the development of linguistic theory and for theories of the mind. Results which might emerge from such a study could confront a theory of language in new and important ways. This is especially true when establishing the role of experience in acquisition.

The challenge, then, is to develop a theory of L2 acquisition which is built on fundamental principles that are both linguistically and psychologically sound. Such a theory must also integrate the contrastive and constructive properties of language, captured by the two earlier theories within one principled account. Not surprisingly, then, many have addressed the need for such an integration (for example: Wode 1976, 1981; Eckman 1977; Sheldon 1978; Gass 1980; Zobl 1980; Andersen 1983; Gundel & Tarone 1983; Rutherford 1983; White 1983; Selinker 1984; Felix 1985).

One of the most promising recent developments in pursuit of such a principled characterization of the adult L2 acquisition process has been work articulated within a generative framework. This work has focussed on several different aspects of a theory of universal grammar (UG), e.g. phonology (Broselow 1983), syntax (Ritchie 1978; Flynn 1983a; Liceras 1983; Sharwood Smith 1983; Mazurkewich 1984a; Muysken & Clahsen 1984; Felix 1985; White 1985a), morphology (Adjémian 1983), and semantics (Haegeman 1985).

Empirical results provide strong initial support for the role of UG in L2 acquisition (cf. Wode 1981; Schachter 1983; Muysken & Clahsen 1984) while also providing the basis for the development of a principled theory of L2 acquisition. They also provide initial empirical support for the development of a unified theory of language acquisition in general.

One purpose of this chapter is to consider these findings in light of the development of a theory of L2 acquisition and in terms of their relevance for linguistic theory. Specifically, these results will be used to illustrate how L2 acquisition follows from the same set of deep principles of acquisition as L1. They will also be used to suggest how, without invoking traditional empiricist accounts of the role of the L1 experience in L2 learning, systematic dif-

---

[2] When discussing L2 acquisition in this chapter, I am for the most part referring to the adult acquisition of an L2. Most of the work conducted within a generative framework of UG has been with adults. A reasonable assumption to make, therefore, is that these learners have reached full cognitive development. However, even when talking about child L2 acquisition, we are still discussing acquisition by learners who are at a more advanced stage of development than young children learning an L1, albeit they might be at slightly less mature stages than their adult counterparts.

ferences can be accounted for among different L1 language groups learning a common L2. In so doing, this chapter will outline the issues and the debates which are emerging within this area of L2 acquisition research. It is important to note at the outset that development of work within this framework is still relatively new – fundamental questions are still being formulated and methodologies are still being worked out. Nonetheless, these preliminary findings suggest that this pairing of a generative theory of UG and L2 acquisition is a productive, and potentially a very important, one.

4.1. Universal grammar and L2 acquisition

In a highly idealized picture of language acquisition, Universal Grammar is taken to be a characterization of the child's pre-linguistic state. (Chomsky 1981:7)
[And principles of Universal Grammar] sharply restrict the class of grammars and narrowly constrain their form, but with parameters that have to be fixed by experience. (Chomsky 1981:4)

As suggested in the quotations above, a theory of UG specifies that there are abstract and linguistically significant principles that underlie all natural languages. These principles are argued to define the 'initial state' of the L1 learner's mind and constrain the L1 acquisition process. Essentially, UG predicts, as Lust (1986:3) states, that children's early hypotheses about language will be structure-dependent:

Structure dependence in this case means that experienced language will be analyzed in terms of an abstract representation of sentence stimuli. Early hypotheses about possible grammatical components are defined on sentences of words analyzed into abstract phrases.

The principle of structure dependence is not learned but forms a part of the conditions for language learning (Aitchison 1976; Chomsky 1977; Lust 1986). That is to say, the composition and production of utterances is not a question of simply stringing together words. Instead, every sentence has an inaudible internal structure which must be understood by the learner. In addition to this prediction, UG also proposes that there is a significant deductive component to L1 learning 'that is determined by the application of biologically determined principles and parameters to the structure-dependent experience of primary data' (Lust 1986:4).

While the theory of UG directly endeavors to characterize L1 acquisition, it makes no statements concerning L2 acquisition. One might expect that L2 learners approach language acquisition in a manner very different from L1 learners and that the nature of the acquisition principles that characterize

L2 acquisition might differ in many ways from those which characterize L1 acquisition. There are a number of reasons why this might be so. For example, differences in general cognitive development alone between the L1 and the L2 learner might lead us to expect very basic dissimilarities in the two language acquisition processes. In addition, L2 learners already have a full set of L1 principles available to them; there may be no need to develop structure-dependent hypotheses about the L2 they are learning in the manner that L1 learners have been observed to do. If this were the case, then we might expect L2 learners to apply astructural processing strategies to the learning of the L2, for example, by consulting linear order alone or by simply translating words, one item at a time, from the L1 to the L2 in the acquisition of the new target language.

On the other hand, it might be reasoned that if UG provides for a language faculty that is biologically determined and that is necessary to explain how language acquisition is possible, then UG should underlie L2 acquisition in some way, assuming that the language faculty does not change substantially over time. If this is the case, we would expect to find evidence that L2 learners approach acquisition in much the same manner as L1 learners do (for support for this idea, see Jenkins 1976; Flynn 1983a, b, 1984, 1987, in press; Liceras 1983; Comrie 1984; Cook 1984; White 1985b).

4.2. L2 Acquisition findings

Two fundamental problems concerning the role of UG in L2 acquisition follow from the above discussion. First, there is a need to demonstrate that L2 learners apply structure-dependent hypotheses to the L2. Second, there is an equally important need to demonstrate that principles and parameters isolated in L1 acquisition and argued to constitute UG also emerge in L2 acquisition.

One way that the structure dependence of L2 acquisition can be demonstrated is by showing that L2 learners do not simply translate between the L1 and the L2 but, like L1 learners, apply hypotheses to the L2 which are defined on sentences analyzed into abstract phrases. Such findings have already been frequently isolated in the L2 literature. Most of this evidence can be culled from work which does not directly test the efficacy of a model of UG for L2 acquisition (see the studies in Hatch 1978 for a comprehensive collection of this early work).

Ravem (1968), for example, reports that the patterns of acquisition of the negative in English by his two Norwegian-speaking children closely paralleled that for children learning English as their L1 (Brown 1973). Importantly, the developmental patterns isolated by Ravem sharply contrast with those which we would expect if these children had simply translated from their L1, Norwegian, to English, their L2. If language were not acquired in a structure-dependent manner, we would expect, as Ravem points out, that the speech of these children would have evidenced such structures as *I like that not* which reflect a direct translation from Norwegian to English. Instead, Ravem notes that the stages of development of the negative for his children were comparable to those for children learning English as their L1.

Milon (1974), investigating the acquisition of English by a Japanese-speaking child, similarly demonstrated that patterns of acquisition for this learner closely paralleled those isolated by Brown for L1 acquisition of English and those isolated by Ravem for L2 acquisition of English. Examples of similar patterns of development for adults can be found in the work of Cancino, Rosansky & Schumann (1978).

Another interesting example of this type which emerges from the early literature is one reported by Huang & Hatch (1978) in their investigation of a young Chinese speaker learning English. They report utterances of the following form in the speech of this learner:

'This####kite.'
'Yeah, that ####bus.'
'This ####car.'

[In these utterances] there is a pause between the two words
and each is equally stressed so that it sounds neither like 'this kite'
in the sentence 'This kite is bigger than that one' nor 'I bought this
kite yesterday.' There is a distinct juncture between the two words
with falling intonation on each word. (Huang & Hatch 1978:123)

Huang & Hatch suggest that these utterances are not the result of faulty imitations on the part of the learner. In other speech productions, the young speaker did not omit the copula or the article in such imitations as *If you have a nickel* or *All the birds sing up the tree*, or *That's all right*. Huang & Hatch claim that this child was clearly capable of reproducing word-final consonant clusters and unstressed words. They also argue that the pause between the NPs above could not be an error of transfer, since omission of the copula in the dialect of the child's L1 is not allowed in sentence of this type (p. 124). Rather, Huang & Hatch claim that these examples indicate how the child is developing syntax in English. Consistent with other findings, this child seems to be aware of the constituent structure of English. He uses the pause as a constituent placeholder in much the same way attested in the literature for early L1 acquisition of English (Bloom 1970).

Results of work from later studies also indicate several other ways that L2 learners, like L1 learners, apply structure-dependent hypotheses to learning. In a well-known example, Ritchie (1978) empirically documents that adult Japanese-speaking learners of English are sensitive to the right roof constraint[3] (Ross 1968; Grosu 1973) of English. This constraint prevents surface structure strings from being formed in which an element has been moved to the right out of a sentence in which the element originated. For example, the right roof constraint accounts for the fact that the derivation of sentence (1b) from (1a) is impossible:

(1)   a.   [s that it surprised Mary that John had left] amused Alice
      b.   *[s that it surprised Mary] amused Alice that John had left

Japanese does not have any rightward movement rules; yet, these L2 learners found sentences like (1b) to be ungrammatical. This finding cannot be attributed to transfer but rather to the application of deep structural principles in L2 acquisition (see also the discussion in Newmeyer 1983). Gass (1980) and Gass & Ard (1984) have shown that adults differentiate the grammatical positions specified on the accessibility hierarchy (AH) (Keenan & Comrie 1977). Leaving aside for the moment any theoretical debate concerning the AH, different grammatical positions on the hierarchy, e.g. *subject*, *object*, *indirect object*, etc., correspond to distinct structural configurations in a sentence. For example, the *subject* can be defined structurally as being the NP most directly dominated by the S node. Thus, to the extent that we find L2 learners, regardless of L1 background, responding to each of these positions in distinct ways, we are demonstrating differential sensitivities to these structural configurations. Gass, and Gass & Ard report the results of a sentence combining test used to elicit restrictive relative clauses in English in which frequency of production followed the AH. *Subject* relatives were the most frequently produced followed by *direct object* relatives, etc. (cf. Ioup & Kruse 1977). These findings hold regardless of L1 background. Frawley (1981) demonstrates a similar pattern for the acquisition of complement clauses in English by various groups of L2 learners. Such sensitivities are also suggested in the work of Kellerman (1979) with adult L2 learners who have been shown to differentiate structurally between *that* complement clauses and infinitive complement clauses.

Flynn (1983a, 1984, 1985b, 1987), in work which has more directly tested the efficacy of a UG paradigm in L2 acquisition, reports results from both elicited imitation and comprehension tasks in which learners discriminate stimulus sentences based on structural differences. In these tests, the stimulus items were all controlled in terms of the pragmatics of the lexical items used, length of utterance, and number of syllables; however, these stimulus sentences varied systematically in terms of certain structural factors, e.g. the presence or absence of a pronoun anaphor in the subordinate clause, and pre- or postposing of a subordinate clause. In one test, Spanish speakers were

---

[3] Currently reformulated as the 'subjacency principle' (Chomsky 1973, 1977).

asked to imitate complex sentences which involved *subject* pronouns in subordinate adverbial clauses and which varied in terms of pre- and postposing of this subordinate clause. Preposed clauses in (2) corresponded to head-final structures in which the complement preceded the head; postponed clauses corresponded to head-initial structures in which the head preceded a complement (see Flynn & Espinal 1985 for a detailed discussion of this correspondence). In addition, pre- and postposing of the subordinate clauses varied the direction of anaphora. In sentence (2) the pronoun precedes the antecedent and in sentence (3), the antecedent precedes the pronoun:

(2)   When he walked down the street, the man ate the ice cream

(3)   The man ate the ice cream when he walked down the street

Results of this test demonstrated that Spanish speakers at an intermediate level of English competence imitated sentences with postposed (head-initial) clauses with forward anaphora (sentence (3)) significantly better than sentences with preposed clauses (head-final) with backward anaphora (sentence (2)).[4] This is an important result, given the fact that these adult speakers already productively control both types of structures in their L1. One might have expected these speakers to imitate both sentence structures with equal ease if they were simply translating from their L1 and were not responding to the differences in structural configurations specified by each stimulus sentence. This replicates an early L1 English preference for forward pronoun anaphora in postposed clauses (Solan 1983; Tavakolian 1977; Lust 1977, 1981, 1983) which will be discussed below.

In addition, the nature of the errors that these Spanish speakers made on these two sentence structures systematically differed. For example, there were significantly more one-clause repetitions on sentences with preposed clauses than on sentences with postposed clauses. There were also significantly more anaphora errors made on sentences with preposed clauses than on sentences with postposed clauses. For example, as illustrated in sentence (4b), the original anaphora relation shown in sentence (4a) is changed. In this case, a learner converted the pronoun anaphor to a full NP, suggesting a difficulty with the backward anaphora in this sentence that did not occur when the sentence involved forward anaphora:

(4) a. *Stimulus*: When he entered the room, the man talked to the engineer
    b. *Response*: When the man entered the room, the engineer spoke to the director

---

[4] 'Significantly better' refers to the fact that there were statistically significant differences in patterns of amount correct in elicited production between these two sentence structures (see Flynn 1983a, 1987).

Other examples in the literature of errors which suggest structural sensitivities on the part of the L2 learner emerge in terms of the systematic changes L2 learners make on the stimulus sentences. For example, Flynn (1983a, 1987) and Flynn & Espinal (1985) report that Spanish, Japanese and Chinese speakers in an imitation task will often spontaneously convert a null anaphor as in sentence (5a) to a pronoun anaphor as in sentence (5b):

(5) a. *Stimulus*: When eating the cake, the man talked to the doctor
     b. *Response*: When he ate cake, the man talked to the doctor

These L2 learners do not, however, reduce pronouns in the same position to a null anaphor. Results such as these have been used in the L1 literature to argue that learners are sensitive to structurally defined binding options which are allowed in their L1 grammar (Lust *et al.* 1986). A similar conclusion is currently under investigation for L2 acquisition (Flynn, Mitze & Mitze in preparation).

Other examples of errors which point out structural sensitivities on the part of the L2 learners include systematic reductions that they, like L1 learners, make on complex sentences in imitation. Flynn (1983a, 1987) has reported that reduction to coordination of complex sentences such as in (6a) and (6b) accounts for a significant amount of error made on these sentences in imitation by Japanese speakers at all levels of English competence:

(6) a. *Stimulus*: When the man ate the cake, he saw the janitor
     b. *Response*: The man ate the cake and the man saw the janitor

White (1985a) also reports that when corrections were made by adult French and Spanish L2 learners on sentences that were ungrammatical, 'the majority were relevant' (p. 12), suggesting that, as discussed above, L2 learners were applying structure-dependent hypotheses to the language they were learning.

With regard to evidence for the role in L2 acquisition of principles of UG isolated in L1 acquisition, several bodies of data are emerging which suggest that these principles also serve as a basis of organization for the L2 grammar. For example, Felix (1985) reports results of a study which investigated German speakers' intuitions about grammatical contrasts in constructions involving different principles hypothesized to be a part of UG. These sentences involved grammatical contrasts which do not have any direct parallels in German (see discussion in Felix and references cited therein). Examples are sentences with superiority effects (Chomsky 1977, 1981), parasitic gaps (Taraldsen 1981; Chomsky 1982; Engdahl 1983), control vs. exceptional case-marking verbs (Chomsky 1981), *that-t* effects (Chomsky & Lasnik 1977), etc. Results of this study strongly suggest that these learners were able to make the correct grammatical judgements on these sentences. Felix argues:

> it seems that adult second language learners do have access to principles of Universal Grammar, that is, they do use, at least in part, the same cognitive module that mediates the learning process in first language acquisition. Otherwise, it would be impossible to explain how our adult learners had attained grammatical knowledge that can neither be directly induced from available speech data nor is in general explicitly taught in the foreign language classroom. (Felix 1985:15)

Similarly, White (1983, 1985a, b) reports data which suggest the relevance of the pro-drop parameter (Jaeggli 1980; Torrego 1981a, b, 1984; Rizzi 1982) in adult L2 acquisition. Liceras (1981, 1983, 1985), in work on the acquisition of Spanish relative clause structures by English speakers and the acquisition of English relative clauses by Spanish speakers, has shown that abstract properties of Comp determined by a theory of UG significantly determine patterns of acquisition in these two groups of learners.

Results of related work by Flynn (1983a, b, 1984, 1985b) and Flynn & Espinal (1985) with Spanish, Japanese, and Chinese speakers' acquisition of complex sentences in English has suggested that the abstract property of head-direction of the L2 serves as a central pole around which the adult learners organize the L2 grammar. Haegeman (1985) suggests a similar pattern for Dutch speakers learning English with regard to the Comp–INFL parameter.

It is not enough, however, to demonstrate that L2 acquisition follows from a comparable set of principles isolated in L1 acquisition; early CC approaches could also accommodate these findings. Instead, it is important for the claims we are making here for L2 acquisition that we demonstrate how the role of experience isolated by CA accounts can be successfully integrated into this framework. Parameters within a theory of UG provide such a means. As suggested above, parameters within a theory of grammar allow one both to account for variation among languages and to account for the role of experience in L1 acquisition. The particular value of a parameter will vary from one language to another and, depending upon its value, will have a set of deductive consequences for the rest of the grammar. If principles which determine and explain L1 acquisition also hold in L2 acquisition, the values of those L1 principles associated with parameters may in some cases match values for the L2 and in other cases differ in value. We might, thus, expect two different patterns of acquisition to emerge in L2 learning, one for the case in which the L1 matches the L2 and one for the case in which the L1 does not match the L2. In the former case, we might expect facilitation in learning, as no 'revision' of the L1 value would be necessary. In the latter case, we might expect some disruption in learning when compared to the case in which the L1 matches the L2, as L1 values would need to be 'revised' to cohere with the L2 in this case. Several bodies of data are emerging which support this initial formulation. Flynn (1983a, 1987) and Flynn & Espinal (1985) have shown that significant differences emerge between the case in which the L1 and the L2 match in head-direction (Spanish speakers learning English) and the case in which they do not (Japanese and Chinese speakers learning English). Spanish is head-initial like English; Japanese and Chinese are both head-final.

White (1985a), similarly, reports data which suggest two distinct patterns of acquisition with regard to the role of the pro-drop parameter in acquisition. One pattern corresponds to the case in which the L1 and the L2 match in values for this parameter – French speakers learning English. The other pattern corresponds to cases in which the L1 and the L2 do not match in values for this parameter – Spanish speakers learning English. Spanish is a pro-drop language and French and English are not. Similar patterns of acquisition also emerge in the work of Haegeman (1985) and Liceras (1985), as outlined above.

It should be stressed, however, that this model differs from a traditional CA model in several important ways. First, a CA model assumes that L2 acquisition proceeds in terms of an astructural matching of surface structure properties, one by one, between the L1 and the L2. Where features match, L2 acquisition is facilitated; where features do not match, acquisition is disrupted. The model discussed in this chapter assumes that L2 acquisition does not consist of an astructural matching of the L1 to the L2; rather, it is argued that L2 acquisition is guided by deep principles of acquisition in the manner described above. One way that this can be seen is in the patterns of elicited imitation results reported by Flynn (1983a,b, 1985a,b, 1987) and Flynn & Espinal (1985) with adult speakers of Japanese and Chinese learning English as a second language. Results from these studies suggest that these adult speakers do not find structures which match their L1s in surface structure properties significantly easier to produce than structures which do not. Such a finding would be predicted by a CA account if L2 learners simply mapped their L1s onto the L2s they were acquiring. For example, given the predominant head-final structure of both Chinese and Japanese, one might expect, consistent with a CA account of L2 learning, that these L2 learners would prefer those sentence structures in English which were head-final. Results from these studies, however, indicate two important findings. First, the Japanese and Chinese learners of English do not significantly prefer structures which match the L1; that is, they do not, for example, correctly imitate sentences which instantiate a head-final structure, such as in (2) above, significantly more often than they do sentences with head-initial structures as in (3). Instead, there is an overall depression in terms of amount correct on both types of sentence structures. Secondly, the nature of the errors made on these structures in production indicate that this statistically nonsignificant result for amount correct does not reflect the fact that these learners are incapable of distinguishing these sentences structurally. As noted above, there are significant differences in the types of errors made on these structures from early stages. The nature of these errors also importantly isolates the fact that these learners are working out the head-initial properties of the L2.

Results of other work articulated within a UG framework have suggested, consistent with the role of parameters in a theory of grammar, that the setting of a parameter in one way or the other will have a set of deductive consequences for the rest of the grammar.[5] For example, languages which are pro-drop allow ungoverned null subjects (7), subject-preposing (8), and *that-t* violations (9) (cf. Chao 1981 for Portuguese).

Italian

(7) $[_{NP}e]$ verra
'(He) will come'

(8) $[_{NP}e]$ verra Giovanni
'Will come Giovanni'

(9)   Chi credi $[_{S'}$che$[_S[_{NP}e]$verra?$]]$
'Who do you believe $[_{S'}$that$[_S[_{NP}$ e$]$will come?$]]$'

Data from White's work on the pro-drop parameter suggest that Spanish (+pro-drop) speakers learning English (−pro-drop), in contrast to French (−pro-drop) speakers learning English, display discordant acquisition patterns at points in the L2 grammar where the L1 would allow different options based on the setting of this pro-drop parameter − specifically phenomena having to do with missing subjects. Such constructions are allowed in Spanish as a pro-drop language; they are not allowed in English and French as non-pro-drop languages. If L2 acquisition, as predicted by CA, consisted of the matching of L1 and L2 structures, one by one, and was not instead guided by general principles of acquisition, we would not expect such patterns to emerge.

In a different manner, Flynn (1987) has demonstrated the role of the head-initial/head-final parameter in the acquisition of grammatical anaphora in adult L2 acquisition. This finding coheres with what has been found in L1

---

[5] As noted by Grimshaw (p.c.), parameters cannot be invoked to account merely for differences in languages. Setting of a parameter for a particular value involves a set of deductive consequences that one would expect to hold in L2 learning.

acquisition (see Lust 1986 for a review of these data). Young learners at early stages of acquisition set up the direction of grammatical anaphora to cohere with the general head–complement configuration of their L1 as determined by the head-initial/head-final parameter.[6] In L2 acquisition, in the case in which the L1 does not match the L2 (for example, Japanese and Chinese speakers learning English), results indicate that a principal source of difficulty for these speakers has to do with setting up of head–complement relations. The Spanish speakers, in contrast, do not experience such difficulties. In fact, results indicate that the Chinese and Japanese speakers must first set up the head-initial structure of the grammar before they can consult this configuration in acquisition of anaphora. Spanish speakers, on the other hand, already have the configuration established for their L1. Thus, results indicate that these speakers are able to access this structure in working out the sentence-level anaphora for the L2.

Results such as those briefly summarized here provide a new way to account for the role of the L1 in L2 acquisition – a sense captured by early CA accounts. Parameters in a theory of UG, in contrast to the global hypotheses formulated in CA and CC accounts, allow us to explain a wide range of specific linguistic facts. In addition, this theory begins to allow us to understand differences in patterns of acquisition as a function of the need to reset L1 values to cohere with L2 values where the L1 and the L2 differ.

Associated with the formulation of a model of L2 acquisition in this way are a number of interesting issues, for example, what does it mean to 'revise' a parameter?, and how do L2 learners do this? For Flynn (1985b, 1987) revision involves the assignment of a new value to the parameter in question, and for Liceras (1981, 1983, 1985) it means establishing a new parametric value for the non-native grammar which does not match the L1. In the model proposed by White (1983), which draws heavily upon a theory of markedness, revision means that the L2 learner must 'lose' the L1 setting. Each proposal involves development in acquisition of some kind – the nature of the development varies from model to model.

Flynn (1983a, 1987) proposes a parameter-setting model in which all L2 learners, regardless of the match/mismatch in parametric values, use the same principles of syntactic organization isolated in L1 acquisition in the construction of the L2 grammar. All learners are sensitive to the match or mismatch of structural properties between the L1 and the L2 from early stages of acquisition. However, in the case in which values do not match, L2 learners assign a new value to cohere with the L2. Since these principles

---

[6] Lust (1981, 1983) refers to this parameter as 'principal branching direction parameter.' See discussion in Flynn (1987) and Flynn & Espinal (1985) with regard to convergences between these two formulations and others in the literature. Also see discussion in Lust (1986) with regard to the relationship between this parameter and principles of binding theory.

determine fundamental properties of grammatical organization for the language to be learned, L2 learners in this case must establish this basic grammatical organization for the L2 they are learning. In the case in which values match there is no need to re-establish this basic grammatical structure, as it matches the L1. Different patterns emerge between the two cases – in one case we observe L2 learners (Chinese and Japanese speakers) working out these fundamental properties for the L2 in much the same way that early L1 learners do. In the second case we observe that L2 learners (Spanish speakers in this case) do not need to assign a new value to this principle; they already have the correct value set for the L1, and as a result, these speakers can consult the structure established by this value in working out the sentence-level properties of grammatical anaphora. Both developmental patterns, in some sense, match L1 patterns of acquisition for this language; however, each corresponds to a distinct stage in L1 acquisition in this developmental sequence (see Flynn 1985a, 1987, for a more detailed discussion).

In the work currently being developed by White (1983, 1985a,b), there are three possible courses of development. The first two do not involve any revisions of parametric values; the third does. The first involves the case in which the L1 and the L2 match in terms of an unmarked setting for a particular value; in this instance L2 learners will correctly assume the unmarked setting for the L2 grammar. In a second case, L2 acquisition involves the setting of a parameter for which the L1 has not had a particular parameter set at all. In this instance, the L2 learner will correctly establish the new L2 value. In the third case, in which the L1 has the unmarked setting and the L2 the marked setting, revision of the L1 value is necessary. In this instance, White claims that the L2 learner will first assume the unmarked L1 setting and eventually establish the L2 value. She claims that this is so, not because this is necessarily dictated by a theory of markedness but because this is what is familiar from the L1 (1983: 5–6). She claims that predictions for patterns of acquisition at initial stages in this third case are indistinguishable from those predicted by a CA model.

Liceras argues that three factors interact in establishing a new parametric value for the non-native grammar:

(1)   Attained linguistic knowledge: the grammatical knowledge of the native language and of any other language(s) familiar to the learner.

(2)   Metalinguistic abilities: the learner's capacities to reflect on and to perceive (perhaps surface) regularities in incoming linguistic data.

(3)   The theory of markedness which imposes preference structures upon

65

the properties of universal grammar may also play a role at the level of intake. (Liceras 1983:359–60)

A precise interaction of these three components is still under investigation.

Using a slightly different approach, i.e. a nonparametric approach to language acquisition, Mazurkewich (1984a,b, 1985) has focussed on the acquisition of the dative alternation, and more recently, the acquisition of gerunds and infinitives, in the L2 acquisition of English by French and Iniktitut speakers. Mazurkewich argues that regardless of the L1, L2 learners will opt for the unmarked case in L2 learning, i.e. the case that reflects historical development and that corresponds to what we know to be true about L1 patterns of acquisition. For example, Mazurkewich has found that there is uniform L2 acquisition of English (unmarked) dative prepositional phrase complements (*give* NP$_1$ *to* NP$_2$) before double NP complements (*give* NP$_1$ NP$_2$) irrespective of the status or existence of such constructions in the L2 learner's L1.

Is there any principled way that we can choose among these various formulations? There are a number of factors to consider. At the most general level, more data from language learners whose L1s and L2s vary systematically along the dimensions investigated must be collected. Amassing such data will help us decide, for example, whether match/mismatch in structural properties independent of markedness considerations can explain observed patterns of acquisition.

Second, the nature of the data must be more precisely collected and controlled. That is, some of the differences in the claims made by each model reflect differences in the experimental methodologies employed in eliciting data from the various language learners tested. As in L1 acquisition, many differences in the results reported can be accounted for in terms of either a lack of methodological control imposed on the experimental design, or in terms of a lack of knowledge of how different experimental task requirements relate to each other. For example, with regard to experimental tasks, differences in the test requirements often result in differences in the manner in which linguistic competence is accessed and in what aspects of linguistic competence are tapped. Elicited imitation, in L1 acquisition, for example, has been found to tap language competence more directly than comprehension tasks. This has also been shown to be the case for L2 learning (Flynn 1986). In addition, because tests of comprehension demand and often involve nonlinguistic strategies (i.e. solving the experimental task by by-passing any structural decomposition of the sentence), there is a great need to exercise caution when interpreting results from these tests. These differences which emerge between results of comprehension-type tests and imitation tests seem to be greater than those differences which emerge in L1 learning. This suggests one way in which the adult, in contrast to the child, is able to draw upon advanced cognitive skills. Tests of grammatical judgements present problems in this regard, both in terms of being able to evaluate exactly what the learner is responding to and of presenting ungrammatical sentences to the learner. Ideally, we need converging evidence from a variety of tasks in order to establish the nature of this development.

In addition, in L2 acquisition there is a further burden involved in controlling for factors of age and knowledge of the L2. Age can be used to establish fairly comparable levels of linguistic ability in L1 acquisition. However, this is not the case in L2 learning. General groupings into low, mid and high levels of, for example, English ability, are often not enough to capture the subtle differences involved in language development in these learners. The use of standardized tests, though an important first step in establishing comparable levels among language groups, is also problematic in that these tests often only test surface-type properties of language, e.g. control of *who* or *whom*; they do not, however, evaluate whether language learners can yet control embedding or are sensitive to subtle effects due to movement of a noun phrase. Placement into comparable levels of language ability for testing demands multiple, and more sophisticated, controls for comparisons among language levels and across language groups. The use of a covariate, and pretesting in the design are often useful in this regard (see Flynn 1983a, 1987).

Other issues which must be addressed in L2 acquisition concern a definition and an understanding of what it means to 'transfer'. This term is invoked in many ways, as suggested in the work outlined in this chapter. For example, it has been used as a metaphor for the role of the L1 experience in L2 learning, and it has been used literally to mean a blind astructural mapping of the L1 onto the L2 without first consulting the structure of the L2. If used in the latter sense, we must be cautious. While it might be the case that L2 learners, in contrast to L1 learners, use nonlinguistic strategies or respond to negative evidence in acquisition to a significant degree, preliminary findings in this domain suggest that this is not the case (see discussion in Hatch 1983). In addition, results reported here do not support such a claim. If this, however, turns out to be the case, we would need to develop a model which is not inherently self-contradictory; that is, we would need to explain how and why in some cases L2 learners apply structural principles isolated in L1 acquisition to L2 development and how and why in other cases they do not. At the present time, differences between L1 and L2 acquisition which do emerge in this regard might be accounted for in terms of differences in the task requirements, as discussed above.

Other topics which must be addressed concern the definition of markedness invoked in the various models. This problem is not unique to L2 acquisition; however, caution must be exercised when developing models or making claims concerning the status of certain grammatical structures (see Kean 1984; Rutherford 1984).

More work within domains such as phonology, morphology, and semantics is also needed in order to help clarify the issues. Broselow (1983), for example, is one of the few to investigate phonological problems within this framework. Her work, which draws upon a metrical theory of phonology, allows one to make precise predictions concerning patterns of acquisition of English phonology by Arabic speakers.

These problems notwithstanding, this first set of results provides a potentially viable framework within which we can reconcile the two previously isolated components of L2 learning. Results also provide the framework within which we can develop unified theories of language acquisition in general. In brief, consistent with early CC accounts, L2 acquisition seems to be guided by a set of principles comparable to those isolated in L1 acquisition. In spite of all the range of possibilities of strategies one might think that L2 learners are capable of invoking, they approach the L2 learning in fundamentally the same way that L1 learners do *vis à vis* structure-dependent hypotheses and constraints by principles and parameters of UG. Properties of configurations important in L1 acquisition also emerge as important in L2 acquisition. We saw this in a number of ways. Options that could have been taken were not exercised. For example, the L2 acquisition literature demonstrates that L2 learners do not simply translate between the L1 and the L2. If they were applying nonstructural hypotheses to the acquisition of the L2 we would expect translation to emerge as an important strategy in acquisition.

And, importantly, consistent with the sense captured by CA theories of acquisition, L2 learning seems to diverge from L1 acquisition in an interesting manner. That is, resetting a parameter in L2 acquisition differs from the setting of a parameter in L1 acquisition, in that while both sets of learners are capable of deducing the value for parameters in a non-inductive manner, L2 learners are able to consult L1 principles and structures not yet available to the L1 learner. Where values match, these L2 learners appear to be able to use the structural configuration established by these principles in L2 acquisition. Where they differ, L2 learners appear to assign new values to these principles. Again, much more empirical research is needed to elucidate precisely this developmental process.

Now that we have established the role of principles of acquisition in L2 learning, we can proceed to ask: what does this preliminary set of results have to say for a theory of language? First, it satisfies the fundamental prediction of UG – that L2 acquisition like L1 acquisition is structure-dependent. Moreover, principles and parameters isolated in L1 acquisition also emerge as important in L2 acquisition. Second, these findings provide converging evidence for the relevance of the properties of language delineated by these hypothesized principles and parameters of UG, since they emerge as important in the construction of both the L1 and L2 grammar. Third, these results suggest that development observed in L1 acquisition is not due to constraints which hold independently of the language faculty. Comparable patterns of development which emerge in both child L1 acquisition and adult L2 acquisition suggest that language acquisition follows from properties which hold of the language faculty as an independent domain of human cognition. Specifically, these L2 results suggest that language development is not instantaneous but involves the working out of the grammar of the language to be learned under the constraint of principles of UG.

4.3. Conclusions and discussion

The point of this chapter was to demonstrate that by developing a theory of L2 acquisition within a principled linguistic paradigm, i.e. a generative theory of UG, an explanatory framework for the construction of a full theory of L2 acquisition can be developed. Central to this development was the observation that previous investigations looked at language in a manner dictated by structuralist theories of language. When we formulate questions in light of a UG approach, we find that we are able to move beyond these early accounts and to reconcile two previously isolated components of L2 learning – the role of the L1 experience and the role of principles independent of this experience. Both of these aspects naturally fall out within this new framework.

There is much left to do. In this chapter a number of ways have been outlined in which this work needs to be developed. Specifically, there is a need for more precise formulation of the questions asked and methodologies used to seek answers to these questions. Many issues still exist and many are left unexplained by current versions of a theory of UG. For example, given the claims about current formulations of the head-direction parameter, one might expect problems in the case in which the L1 and L2 did not match in all domains within which headedness is arguably relevant. Examples of other questions this body of research bears on include whether or not a theory of markedness must be invoked in the grammar generally, or more specifically with regard to a parameter-setting formulation.

Furthermore, if parameters are part of the universal competence for language, is it possible to have parameters set in two different ways at the same time? With continued work, answers to such questions can be found. At the same time, these results will confront a theory of UG with a body of data which, up until this time, has been overlooked and not integrated into such a framework.

REFERENCES

Adjémian, C. 1983. Universal grammar, parsing and the structure of intake. In Gass & Selinker (1983).

Aitchison, J. 1976. *The articulate mammal*. New York: McGraw-Hill.

Andersen, R. 1983. Transfer to somewhere. In Gass & Selinker (1983).

Bloom, L. 1970. *Language development*. Cambridge, MA: MIT Press.

Broselow, E. 1983. Nonobvious transfer: on predicting epenthesis errors. In Gass & Selinker (1983).

Brown, R. 1973. *A first language, the early stages*. Cambridge, MA: Harvard University Press.

Cancino, H., Rosansky, E. J. & Schumann, J. H. 1978. The acquisition of English negatives and interrogatives by native Spanish speakers. In Hatch (1978).

Chao, W. 1981. Pro drop languages and non-obligatory control. In W. Chao & D. Wheeler (eds.) *UMASS Occasional Papers in Linguistics*, vol. 7. University of Massachusetts/Amherst.

Chomsky, N. 1959. Review of Skinner's *Verbal behavior*. *Language* 35: 26–58.

Chomsky, N. 1973. Conditions on transformations. In S. R. Andersen & P. Kiparsky (eds.) *A festschrift for Morris Halle*. New York: Holt, Rinehart & Winston.

Chomsky, N. 1977. *Essays on form and interpretation*. Amsterdam: North-Holland.

Chomsky, N. 1981. *Lectures on government and binding: the Pisa lectures*. Dordrecht: Foris.

Chomsky, N. 1982. *Some concepts and consequences of the theory of government and binding*. Cambridge, MA: MIT Press.

Chomsky, N. 1986. *Knowledge of language: its nature, origins, and use*. New York: Praeger.

Chomsky, N. & Lasnik, H. 1977. Filters and control. *Linguistic Inquiry* 8: 425–504.

Comrie, B. 1984. Why linguistics need language acquirers. In W. Rutherford (ed.) *Language universals and second language acquisition*. Amsterdam: Benjamins.

Cook, V. 1984. Chomsky's universal grammar and second language learning. *Applied Linguistics* 6: 1–18.

DiPietro, R. 1971. *Language structure in contrast*. Rowley: Newbury House.

Dulay, H. & Burt, M. 1974. A new perspective on the creative construction process in child second language acquisition. *Language Learning* 24: 253–78.

Eckman, F. 1977. Markedness and the contrastive analysis hypothesis. *Language Learning* 27: 315–30.

Engdahl, E. 1983. Parasitic gaps. *Linguistics and Philosophy* 6: 5–34.

Felix, S. 1985. UG-generated knowledge in adult second language acquisition. University of Passua. MS.

Flynn, S. 1983a. A study of the effects of principal branching direction in second language acquisition: the generalization of a parameter of universal grammar from first to second language acquisition. Doctoral dissertation, Cornell University.

Flynn, S. 1983b. Differences between first and second language acquisition: setting the parameters of Universal Grammar. In D. Rogers & J. Sloboda (eds.) *Acquisition of symbolic skills*. London and New York: Plenum.

Flynn, S. 1984. A universal in L2 acquisition based on a PBD typology. In F. Eckman (ed.) *Universals in second language acquisition*. Rowley: Newbury House.

Flynn, S. 1985a. Principled theories of second language acquisition. *Studies in Second Language Acquisition* 7: 99–107.

Flynn, S. 1985b. Nature of development in L2 acquisition and implications for theories of language acquisition in general. Paper presented at Linguistic Theory at Second Language Acquisition Working Conference, MIT.

Flynn, S. 1986. Comprehension vs. production in a parameter setting model of L2 acquisition. *Studies in Second Language Acquisition* 8: 135–64.

Flynn, S. 1987. *Parameter-setting models of L2 language acquisition: experimental studies in anaphora*. Dordrecht: Reidel.

Flynn, S. In press. L2 Acquisition in pronoun anaphora: resetting the parameter. In B. Lust (ed.) *Studies in the acquisition of anaphora: defining the constraints*, vol. II. Dordrecht: Reidel.

Flynn, S. & Espinal, I. 1985. Head-initial/head-final parameter in adult Chinese L2 acquisition of English. *Second Language Acquisition Research* 1: 93–117.

Flynn, S., Mitze, C. & Mitze, K. In preparation. The interaction of syntax and semantics in adult L2 acquisition of English.

Frawley, W. 1981. The complement hierarchy: evidence for language universals from L2. Paper presented at the Winter LSA meeting, New York.

Fries, C. 1945. *Teaching and learning English as a foreign language*. Ann Arbor: University of Michigan Press.

Gass, S. 1980. An investigation of syntactic transfer in adult second language learners. In S. Krashen & R. Scarcella (eds.) *Issues in second language research*. Rowley: Newbury House.

Gass, S. & Ard, J. 1984. Second language acquisition and the ontology of language universals. In W. Rutherford (ed.) *Language universals and second language acquisition*. Amsterdam: Benjamins.

Gass, S. & Selinker L. (eds.) 1983. *Language transfer in language learning*. Rowley: Newbury House.

Grosu, A. 1973. On the status of the right-roof constraint. *Language* 49: 294–311.

Gundel, J. & Tarone, E. 1983. Language transfer in the acquisition of pronominal anaphora. In Gass & Selinker (1983).

Haegeman, L. 1985. Scope phenomena in English and Dutch and L2 acquisition. University of Geneva. MS.

Hatch, E. 1978. *Readings in second language acquisition*. Rowley: Newbury House.

Hatch, E. 1983. *Psycholinguistics: a second language perspective*. Rowley: Newbury House.

Huang, J. & Hatch, E. 1978. A Chinese child's acquisition of English. In Hatch (1978).

Ioup, G. & Kruse, M. 1977. Interference versus structural complexity as a predictor of second language relative clause acquisition. In H. Brown, C. Yorio & R. Crymes (eds.) *On tesol 77*. Washington: Georgetown University.

Jaeggli, O. 1980. On some phonologically null elements in syntax, Doctoral dissertation, MIT.

Jenkins, L. 1976. Chomsky and second language learning: the extended standard theory. Paper presented at the First annual Boston University Conference on Language Development, October.

Kean, M.-L. 1979. On a theory of markedness: some general considerations and a case in point. *Social Sciences, Research Report no. 41*. University of California, Irvine.

Keenan, E. & Comrie, B. 1977. Noun phrase accessibility and universal grammar. *Linguistic Inquiry* 8: 63–100.

Kellerman, E. 1979. The problem with difficulty. *Interlanguage Studies Bulletin* 4: 27–48.

Lado, R. 1957. *Linguistics across cultures*. Ann Arbor: University of Michigan Press.

Liceras, J. 1981. Markedness and permeability in interlanguage systems. *Working Papers in Linguistics* 2, University of Toronto.

Liceras, J. 1983. Markedness, contrastive analysis and the acquisition of Spanish syntax by English speakers. Doctoral dissertation, University of Toronto.

Liceras, J. 1985. The role of intake in the determination of learners' competence. In S. Gass & C. Madden (eds.) *Input in second language acquisition*. Rowley: Newbury House.

Lust, B. 1981. Constraints on anaphora in child language: a prediction for a universal. In S. Tavakolian (ed.) *Language acquisition and linguistic theory*. Cambridge, MA: MIT Press.

Lust, B. 1983. On the notion 'principal branching direction': a parameter of universal grammar. In Y. Otsu, H. van Riemsdijk, K. Inoue, A. Kamio & N. Kawasaki (eds.) *Studies in generative grammar and language acquisition*. Tokyo: Monbusho Grant for Scientific Research.

Lust, B. 1986. Introduction. In B. Lust (ed.) *Studies in the acquisition of anaphora*. Vol. 1: *Defining the constraints*. Dordrecht: Reidel.

Lust, B., Solan, L., Flynn, S., Cross, C. & Schuetz, E. 1986. A comparison of null and pronoun anaphora in first language acquisition. In B. Lust (ed.) *Studies in the acquisition of anaphora*. Vol. 1: *Defining the constraints*. Dordrecht: Reidel.

Mazurkewich, I. 1984a. Dative questions and markedness. In F. Eckman, L. Bell & D. Nelson (eds.) *Universals of second language acquisition*. Rowley: Newbury House.

Mazurkewich, I. 1984b. The acquisition of the dative alternation by second language learners and linguistic theory. *Language Learning* 34: 91–110.

Mazurkewich, I. 1985. The acquisition of infinitive and gerund complements by L2 learners. Paper presented at Linguistic Theory and Second Language Acquisition Conference, MIT.

Milon, J. P. 1974. The development of negation in English by a second language learner. *TESOL Quarterly* 8, 2: 137–43.

Muysken, P. & Clahsen, H. 1984. The accessibility of move α and the acquisition of German word order by children and adults. Paper presented at Glow, Spring.

Newmeyer, F. 1983. *Grammatical theory: its limits and possibilities*. Chicago: University of Chicago Press.

Ravem, R. 1968. Language acquisition in a second language environment. *International Review of Applied Linguistics* 6: 175–85.

Ritchie, W. 1978. The right-roof constraint in adult second language. In W. Ritchie (ed.) *Second language acquisition research*. New York: Academic Press.

Rizzi, L. 1982. *Issues in Italian syntax*. Dordrecht: Foris.

Ross, J. R. 1968. Constraints on variables in syntax. Bloomington: Indiana University Linguistics Club.

Rutherford, W. 1983. Language typology and language transfer. In Gass & Selinker (1983).

Rutherford, W. 1984. Description and explanation in interlanguage syntax: state of the art. *Language Learning* 32, 1: 85–108.

Schachter, J. 1983. A new account of transfer. In Gass & Selinker (1983).

Selinker, L. 1984. The current state of interlanguage studies: an attempted critical study. In A. Davies, C. Criper & H. P. Howatt (eds.) *Interlanguage*. Edinburgh: Edinburgh University Press.

Sharwood Smith, M. 1983. Crosslinguistic aspects of second language acquisition. *Applied Linguistics*, 3: 192–9.

Sheldon, A. 1978. Assumptions, methods, and goals in language acquisition research. In F. Eckman & A. Hastings (eds.) *First and second language learning*. Rowley: Newbury House.

Solan, L. 1977. On the interpretation of missing NP's. *Occasional Papers in Linguistics 3*. University of Massachusetts/Amherst.

Solan, L. 1983. *Pronominal reference: child language and the theory of grammar*. Dordrecht: Reidel.

Taraldsen, T. 1981. The theoretical interpretation of a class of marked extractions. In A. Belletti, L. Brandi & L. Rizzi (eds.) *Theory of markedness in generative grammar. Proceedings of the 1979 Glow Conference*. Pisa: Scuola Normale Superiore.

Tavakolian, S. 1977. Structural principles in the acquisition of complex sentences. Doctoral dissertation, University of Massachusetts/Amherst.

Torrego, E. 1981a. On the non-evidence for a special comp structure in Spanish. University of Massachusetts/Boston. MS.

Torrego, E. 1981b. Spanish as a pro-drop language. University of Massachusetts/Boston. MS.

Torrego, E. 1984. On inversion in Spanish and some of its effects. *Linguistic Inquiry* 15: 103–29.

White, L. 1983. Markedness and parameter setting: some implications for a theory of adult second language acquisition. Paper presented at the 12th Annual University of Wisconsin-Milwaukee Linguistic Symposium on Markedness.

White, L. 1985a. The 'Pro-drop' parameter in adult second language acquisition. *Language Learning* 35: 47–63.

White, L. 1985b. Universal grammar as a source of explanation in second language acquisition. In B. Wheatley *et al.* (eds.) *Current approaches to second language acquisition*. Bloomington: Indiana University Linguistics Club.

Wode, H. 1976. Developmental sequences in naturalistic L2 acquisition. *Working Papers on Bilingualism* 11: 1–31.

Wode, H. 1981. *Learning a second language*. Amsterdam: Benjamins.

Zobl, H. 1980. The formal and developmental selectivity of L1 influence on L2 acquisition. *Language Learning* 30: 43–57.

5 Brain structures and linguistic capacity

Mary-Louise Kean

5.0. Introduction

The linguistic capacity of human beings is a biological endowment. The normal child placed in a typical speech community will acquire the language of that community in a consistent fashion. While the specific language a child acquires is a function of the linguistic environment, how any child acquires any language is, in fundamental respects, the same. Acquisition can be impaired either by deprivation of linguistic experience or by various forms of anomaly in the central nervous system. Observation of the everyday experience of human language acquisition provides, then, compelling evidence of a biological foundation for language. Linguistic capacity is, in fact, not unlike a host of other biological capacities: the organism encounters experience with a physical system poised to engage with that experience and develop in consequence of it. It is therefore of consequence to explore the biological foundations of language if we are to gain a clear understanding of the structure of human linguistic capacity.

It is impossible to study the functional structure of any biological system in the absence of some concept of the function being subserved. Little follows directly for the analysis of particular behavioral systems from simply looking at neurons, collections of neurons, their physiological properties, or their chemistry. Thus, consideration of the biological foundations of language requires that we have at the outset some behavioral conception of human linguistic capacity. Led by the extensive work of Chomsky, over the last quarter century, considerable research on the theory of grammar has been dedicated to providing a formal account of the endowment which a child brings to the task of language acquisition (Chomsky 1965, 1985). Any theory of grammar which attempts to characterize the linguistic endowment of children is, of necessity, a biological model, a model of the functional endowment humans bring to the task of language acquisition. As such, it provides the necessary conceptual framework for studying the biological foundations of language.

The standard linguistic conception of language acquisition has assumed

74

that the child encounters experience with a fully developed theory of grammar, *universal grammar* (UG), which characterizes the domain of learning and guides the learner in the construction of tacit hypotheses in the development of the particular grammar of the language being acquired (Hyams 1987). From a biological perspective, this view is not *a priori* plausible. There is extensive postnatal development of the nervous system (Conel 1939–59); the youngest language user is endowed with a nervous system which is radically different from that of a 4-year-old, 6-year-old, 10-year-old, or adult.

Development of the nervous system is under the control of two basic variables: maturation and experience. As was first demonstrated by Wiesel & Hubel (1965), for example, the functional architecture of the visual system changes in consequence of specific visual experience at particular points in time. It therefore seems most biologically plausible at the outset to take the theory of grammar, UG, to be a characterization of an emergent property of the nervous system.

It should be clear that this conception of grammar is in no way a denial of its 'reality' either biologically or psychologically. It would make little sense to assume that the neural representation of language of a speaker of Finnish is identical to that of a speaker of French; if they were identical that could only mean that Finnish and French are identical, and that is surely not so. At the same time, the basic principles of grammar and the principles of nervous system development must be taken to be equivalent for all individuals independent of their particular linguistic community. This follows from three related behavioral observations: (a) language variation is not arbitrary; (b) language acquisition follows a consistent developmental course; (c) we have no selective capacity to acquire just the language of our forebears. The singular consequence of viewing the theory of grammar as an emergent property of the nervous system is that it requires one to take account of maturation. The importance of maturation for any account of the biological foundations of language was first emphasized by Lenneberg (1967).

No study of development can proceed without some conception of the mature state. Therefore, to understand the biology of language acquisition it is necessary to consider the final product. This means that we must investigate as best we can the organization of language in the mature adult brain through the study of adults, both those without any neurological impairment and those with congenital anomalies or later acquired disorders, and then through the study of children, including those with disorders of neural ontogeny and acquired lesions, and look to how that organization develops. At this point, research on both the biology of mature linguistic capacity and the biology of language acquisition is in its relative infancy. However, from the comparative study of neurologically normal and neurologically impaired individuals, as

75

well as from the broader study of the neurobiology of learning and memory, a rich collection of provocative data is emerging, and it is possible to characterize in general the components of the biological foundations of language.

5.1. **Gross anatomy and linguistic capacity: aphasia**

Broca (1861) presented the first recognized paper in which autopsy evidence was provided demonstrating that a restricted left hemisphere lesion was responsible for an acquired loss of language in an adult, an *aphasia*. On the basis of Broca's and subsequent reports on language impairments following left hemisphere lesions, Wernicke (1874) put forward an analysis of the representation of language in the mature brain. The original model noted two anatomical language areas, one Broca's area located in the frontal cortex and the other, now designated Wernicke's area, in the temporal lobe. Based on the fact that patients with Broca lesions have restricted speech output, but relatively intact comprehension, Wernicke hypothesized that Broca's area was the seat of the motor image of words. As patients with Wernicke lesions are severely impaired in comprehension, he hypothesized that Wernicke's area was the seat of the sensory image of words. Wernicke patients also show a significant problem in production: while their speech is fluent, it is *paragrammatic*, and lexical selection is strikingly distorted. The lexical distortions include substitutions of both semantically related and unrelated words and neologisms (Lecours 1982). To account for this, Wernicke hypothesized that the two areas were linked by a pathway, and proposed that a critical component of speech production was a covert monitoring of intended forms by the sensory language area. He argued for this not only on the basis of aphasiological data, but also on the basis of consideration of language acquisition, which he reasoned must have its foundation in sensory experience. Thus, from the origins of behavioral neurology, issues of language acquisition have played a significant role in our understanding of the biological bases of language, even in the adult.

While Wernicke's work set the tone for an exceedingly productive and expansive period in neurology, it was not the case that his work went without detractors (Lecours, Lhermitte & Bryans 1983). Objections were raised to both localizationism and connectionism (e.g. Marie 1906; Freud 1953; Jackson 1958), and by the early twentieth century, Wernicke's approach had fallen from grace if not been totally abandoned (but see, e.g. Dejerine 1906). In its place came a theory of equipotentiality of function, at least equipotentiality across the perisylvian region of the left hemisphere, that is, the area surrounding the lateral fissure. To the extent there were differences in the aphasias and these systematically correlated with lesion loci, such observations tended to be ignored, denied, or attributed to the fact that Broca's area lies close to the motor strip, the cortical area which controls articulatory implementation, and Wernicke's area lies close to the primary auditory cortex. If one considers the work of such eminent aphasiologists as Head (1963) and Goldstein (1948), one discovers the presentation of theories at odds with Wernicke's basic framework in works in which cases of patients are presented which fall systematically along the behavioral–anatomical dimensions which Wernicke laid out. The tradition of behavioral neurology which Wernicke put forth was resurrected by Geschwind (1965), who reviewed the old literature and, at the same time, presented new cases and their analyses in the connectionist framework.

Localization and connectionist research, both from the nineteenth and early twentieth century and from the work carried out since Geschwind's seminal paper, can provide at least a partial map of the gross behavioral anatomy of linguistic capacity. The map provides a taxonomy of areas of the brain which are known to be specifically correlated with particular behavioral deficits involving language use.

Two basic classes of disorders must be distinguished. On the one hand there are the true aphasias, which are specific linguistic disorders in which all modalities of language use are compromised. On the other hand there are disconnection syndromes, disorders which involve the severing of connections between language areas or between some language area(s) and some other functional system(s). The true aphasiological disorders all involve damage to the left cerebral hemisphere in the average adult. These include both Broca's aphasia and Wernicke's aphasia, as well as anomic aphasia (associated with a temporo-parietal lesion) and global aphasia (associated with extensive perisylvian damage). There is one syndrome which involves a disconnection of two language areas, conduction aphasia, in which the pathway between Broca's area and Wernicke's area (the arcuate fasciculus) is lesioned; other disconnection syndromes involve disconnection of the language areas from either the motor system, *apraxia* (Geschwind 1967) or some sensory system, as in pure *alexia* without *agraphia* (Geschwind 1962).

When damage to a specific area of the brain results in a functional impairment, one cannot with justification immediately draw the inference that the locus of damage is the locus of the manifestly impaired function(s). This follows from both any analysis of the structure of linguistic capacity and from properties of the functional architecture of the brain. Human linguistic capacity may be viewed as a partially ordered set of components – lexical entries, morphology, syntax, phonology, logical form, articulatory phonetics, acoustic phonetics, and so on. A schematic representation of such a system is given in Figure 1. In such a system, were component C to be disrupted, then in consequence of its deviance it would not only distort well-formed inputs from A and B, but it would also provide an ill-formed input to

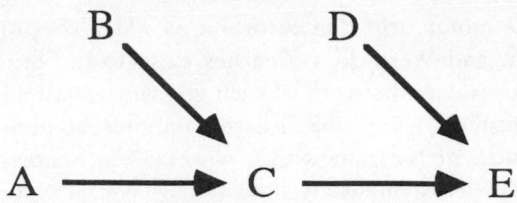

Figure 1

E, where, through interaction, it would distort the well-formed input from D. Thus, what is underlyingly a discreet functional impairment can massively distort the functional appearance of the system as a whole. The anatomical substrate also is a complex interactive system – areas, including the language areas, both projecting to, and receiving inputs from, diverse areas (Galaburda 1984; Kemper 1984).

Although drawing direct inferences of a relation between behavior and specific areas of the brain is logically unwarranted, it is, nonetheless, necessary in some degree at least (Kean 1984a). We must assume that areas such as Broca's and Wernicke's do have some specific functional commitment to linguistic capacity. The problem arises in determining just what the nature of that functional commitment is. This is, in significant degree, a task for linguistics and psycholinguistics. What is required are detailed grammatical and processing analyses of the deficits of people with specific focal lesions. Over the last two decades there has been considerable psycholinguistic research done on the aphasias in attempts to characterize the central deficits which underlie each. In no case has there been more extensive research than on Broca's aphasia, a disorder in which nearly every component of linguistic capacity shows some compromise in the behavioral manifestation. Despite the extensive research that has been carried out, there is as yet no clearly agreed upon processing analysis; plausible accounts have been put forward placing the underlying behavioral deficit in phonology, syntax, and the lexicon (see the papers in Kean 1985 for a review).

With a few isolated exceptions (Kean 1977), until recently there has been little work on the linguistic analysis of aphasic syndromes. Grodzinsky (1984) has argued that data from aphasic patients may be used to decide among competing linguistic theories. Evidence in support of one grammatical theory over another is provided when a grammatical theory provides a parsimonious account for aphasic deficits while some other does not. Grodzinsky has presented data on syntactic processing in Broca's aphasia and argued that the government–binding framework (Chomsky 1981) allows for a systematic analysis of those data. Theories of morphology and the lexicon have also come to play a role in the analysis of aphasic deficits, notably in the work of de Bleser & Bayer (in press).

Recently, a 'new' approach to the study of grammatical capacity in aphasia has emerged, the use of linguistic field methods. Under this approach, aphasics are systematically interviewed, asked to make judgements about the grammaticality of sentences and are probed as to the basis of those judgements. The promise of this technique is that it provides data which can be both quantitatively and qualitatively analyzed. In a recent study of Dutch-speaking Broca, Wernicke, and global aphasics, Koster *et al.* (1985) found that all aphasic populations showed quantitatively anomalous responses as compared to control subjects, with the globals being significantly more impaired than the Broca's. An item analysis indicates domains of similarity and domains of difference among the groups.

One domain of similarity involves the pattern of responses to sentences with sentential complements. In Dutch, verbs subcategorized for finite complements are subcategorized for one of two complementizers, *dat* or *of*:

(1) a. Zij zegt dat hij met haar naar het strand wil gaan
          'She says that he will go to the beach with her'
     b. *Zij zegt of hij met haar naar het strand wil gaan
     c. *Zij zegt   hij met haar naar het strand wil gaan

(2) a. Hij vroeg of ik met hem naar de bioscoop wilde gaan
          'He asks that I will go to the movies with him'
     b. *Hij vroeg dat ik met hem naar de bioscoop wilde gaan
     c. *Hij vroeg   ik met hem naar de bioscoop wilde gaan

Nonfinite sentential complements have no overt complementizer (with the exception of, for example, purpose clauses). Ungrammatical sentences can, therefore, be of the following types: (a) the sentential complement is well-formed but inappropriate to the verb (e.g. a finite complement with a verb that takes nonfinite complements); (b) the finite complement may be well-formed, but the specific complementizer inappropriate for the verb; (c) the complement may be ill-formed (e.g. a finite complement with no overt complementizer or a nonfinite complement with *dat* or *of*). In an analysis of the responses to these types of ungrammatical sentences as well as grammatical ones, the same three groups of aphasics emerged in both the Broca and Wernicke populations. One group seemingly adopts the approach that if a verb may take a sentential complement then it may take any complement, well-formed or ill-formed. The second group adopts a more conservative position: if a verb subcategorizes for a sentential complement then it may take any complement with a phonologically specified complementizer; this group makes consistently 'correct' responses to well-formed and ill-formed sentential complements with phonologically empty complementizers. The third group gives a normal pattern of responses except in one case; these subjects accept any sentence with a well-formed finite complement even if the complementizer is wrong (e.g. *dat* instead of *of*) or the verb subcategorizes only for nonfinite complements. The sensitivity of an aphasic to grammatical structure is not an index of ability to effectively (if ungrammatically) verbally communicate. Thus, for example, the Broca patient with the best (most normal) performance in the sentence judgement task had the worst performance in a test of everyday language use (Blomert *et al.* 1987), and the Wernicke patient who showed almost no communicatively usable language abilities was in the second group in terms of assessment of complement structures.

A domain where Broca and Wernicke patients show distinct patterns of performance is in *one* pronominalization:

(3) a. Ik zag een hond en zij zag er een
'I saw a dog and she saw one'
b. *Ik zag de vogel en hij zag er een
*'I saw the bird and he saw one'
c. *Ik zag Men. Smit en jij zag er een
*'I saw Mr. Smit and you saw one'

Broca patients are frequently *agrammatic*, that is, show a tendency to omit function words, including articles, in their speech. They have also been shown to have an insensitivity to articles in sentence comprehension (Goodenough, Zurif, & Weintraub 1977). The Broca patients, in contrast to the Wernicke patients only rejected as ungrammatical sentences such as (3c) and not sentences such as (3b). This pattern of response was found not only in agrammatic Broca patients but also in those who do not show a pattern of omission of articles in their spontaneous speech. The performance of the Wernicke patients on these sentences was basically normal.

The absence of any accepted and detailed grammatical analysis of aphasic disorders at this time is in some measure due to an absence of a sufficiently rich corpus of data. As experimental research is increasingly approached from the perspective of specific grammatical theories and more extensive field research is carried out, detailed grammatical analyses will become viable. Because one finds subpopulations within specific diagnostic groups, it remains to be seen whether or not there will be such a thing as the linguistic analysis of Broca's or Wernicke's aphasia; rather, it may turn out that clinical classification is not coextensive with linguistic classification. Given that clinical classifications are not based on linguistically systematic parameters, such a result is quite conceivable.

The fact that there is no overwhelmingly compelling analysis of any of the aphasias could arise from a variety of circumstances, independent of the current availability of relevant data. Three possibilities suggest themselves. (1) Brain lesions in humans are messy, and, as no two patients have the same lesion, there may be subtle but significant differences in their behavior. If one studies groups of patients, these differences will be lost in statistical analysis and the picture which is derived may be systematically misleading. (2) Aphasiological research has traditionally assumed that all human beings have equivalent linguistic capacity, at the level of biological representation and at the levels of grammatical representation and processing. There is, however, variation in the physical substrate (Galaburda *et al.* 1978) and there are variations in linguistic capacity (Kean 1984b). (3) Given that there is variation in the physical substrate, it may well prove to be the case that the gross anatomy of aphasiology is not the appropriate level for any detailed description relating brain to linguistic capacity.

5.2. Anatomical asymmetries and linguistic capacity

Superficially, the two cerebral hemispheres seem strikingly similar, so similar that it was thought that their differences were not of sufficient magnitude to account for any putative functional differences; until relatively recently, it was widely accepted, evidence from aphasia for left hemisphere speech dominance notwithstanding, that linguistic capacity was not associated with significant anatomical differences between the two hemispheres (von Bonin 1962, cited in Geschwind & Levitsky 1968). Geschwind & Levitsky (1968) carried out an analysis of 100 human brains in which they measured the right and left plana temporale and found that in 65% of the cases the left planum was significantly larger than the right, in 11% of the cases the right was larger than the left, and in the remaining 24% the two sides were of essentially equivalent size. The magnitude of the asymmetry found was impressive. Significantly, the area studied by Geschwind & Levitsky lies immediately behind the primary auditory cortex and, on the left, includes Wernicke's area; cortical stimulation studies further implicate it in language function (Penfield & Roberts 1959; see Ojemann 1983). In subsequent measurement research, the technique used by Geschwind & Levitsky was refined, but the basic findings of asymmetry have not been altered, even in studies of fetal brains (Wittleson & Pallie 1973; Chi *et al.* 1977). Related to the planal asymmetry is an asymmetry in the Sylvian fissure; the left fissure is both longer and more horizontally placed in adult and fetal brains (LeMay & Culebras 1972).

The asymmetry of the plana temporale is not the only gross anatomical asymmetry to be observed in the human brain. Heschl's gyrus, primary auditory cortex, is often accompanied by additional transverse gyri on the right (Pfeifer, 1936, cited in Galaburda *et al.* 1978), in both fetal (Chi, Dooling, & Gilles 1977) and adult brains (Campain & Minckler 1976). The right frontal lobe is typically wider than the left, while the left occipital lobe is typically wider than the right (LeMay 1976). In right-handed subjects, the left occipital horn of the lateral ventrical has been found to be longer in 60% of cases, with the right longer in only 10% of cases; only 38% of left-handed and ambidexterous subjects show greater length of the left occipital horn, while 31% show greater length on the right (McRae, Branch, & Milner 1968). The pyramidal tracts, which project from the left and right hemispheres to the spinal cord for the control of movement, cross in the medulla, the one from the left hemisphere ultimately controlling movement on the right side of the body and the one from the right controlling the left. Kertesz & Geschwind (1971) showed that the decussation of the left pyramid was rostral to that of the right in 82% of the 158 adult medullas studied. Gross asymmetries are, then, a characteristic of the organization of the human brain; it is plausible to speculate that such asymmetries are of functional significance.

Measures of gross brain areas, as in the case of the studies of the temporal plane, are consistent with observations of functional asymmetry and, in particular, lend credence to the phrenological notion that 'bigger is better,' *ceteris paribus*. In all these measures there exists a considerable range of individual differences. If it is taken that human linguistic capacity is essentially uniform across the species, then the degree of apparent anatomical variation among individuals in language-related areas such as the temporal plane is not obviously explicable functionally. Indeed, if the range of individual differences observed is not of functional significance, that would raise a serious question for the plausibility of any claim that linguistic theory is a functional biological model. In order to address this question a more detailed analyses of the brain areas associated with specific functions is required.

The cortex of the human brain is organized in six layers, each layer having distinctive properties in terms of both the packing density and type of nerve cells found. The structure of the cortical layers is not uniform across the brain; rather, the cortex is composed of a large number of architectonically distinctive areas, areas which are delimitable on the basis of the constitution of their lamina. It is reasonable to assume that the variation in structure observed in architectonic parcels is related to their functions; distinctive cortical areas carrying out distinctive functions. It is certainly the case that where there is a detailed functional physiology of particular architectonic parcels, specific functions are attested (e.g. Hubel & Wiesel 1962, 1965). Areas such as the planum temporale are not architectonically uniform; it therefore becomes relevant to ask whether observed gross asymmetries are a function of the size of some specific architectonic area(s) or simply global observations. Galaburda & Sanides (1980) carried out just such a study, distinguishing three cytoarchitectonic areas in the temporal plane and measuring their volumes on the left and right. As can be seen in Table 1, temporo-parietal cortex (area Tpt, located in the posterior portion of

Table 1

(a) Right–left measurements

Case	Planum temporale planimetric units		Area Tpt volumetric units	
	Right	Left	Right	Left
1	55	171	35	254
2	68	153	69	151
3	114	156	73	101
4	136	118	95	108

(b) Left–right ratios (based on (a))

Case	Planum temporale	Rank	Area Tpt	Rank
1	3.11	1	7.26	1
2	2.25	2	2.19	2
3	1.37	3	1.38	3
4	0.87	4	1.14	4

Brodmann area 22, Figure 2) has a significantly larger volume on the left than on the right. Amaducci *et al.* (1981) report an asymmetry in a neurotransmitter substance which seemingly parallels the anatomical asymmetry of the temporal lobe language area. They found that Brodmann area 22 contains greater choline acetyltransferase activity on the left; significantly, the degree of asymmetry increases in the posterior portion. The posterior portion of the superior temporal gyrus is implicated in language by Wernicke's aphasia and is the locus of area Tpt. The data from aphasia in conjunction with the observation of this asymmetry suggest that area Tpt may have a distinctive linguistic function.

The inferior parietal lobule is implicated in language function by aphasia; lesions to this area in adults may result in anomic aphasias (Benson 1979). Animal studies provide evidence that the area is involved in trimodal sensory integration (Hyvarinen & Shelepin 1979; Lynch 1980), and it is not then surprising that inferior parietal lesions in humans are also associated with agraphia and alexia (Benson 1979). Within the inferior parietal lobule, Eidelberg & Galaburda (1984) found area PG (Figure 2) to be significantly larger on the left than on the right in those brains with a larger left Tpt, the magnitude and direction of asymmetry in PG correlating with that of Tpt. It is of significance to note that there are specific afferents from Tpt to PG (Mesulam *et al.* 1977; Pandya & Seltzer 1982).

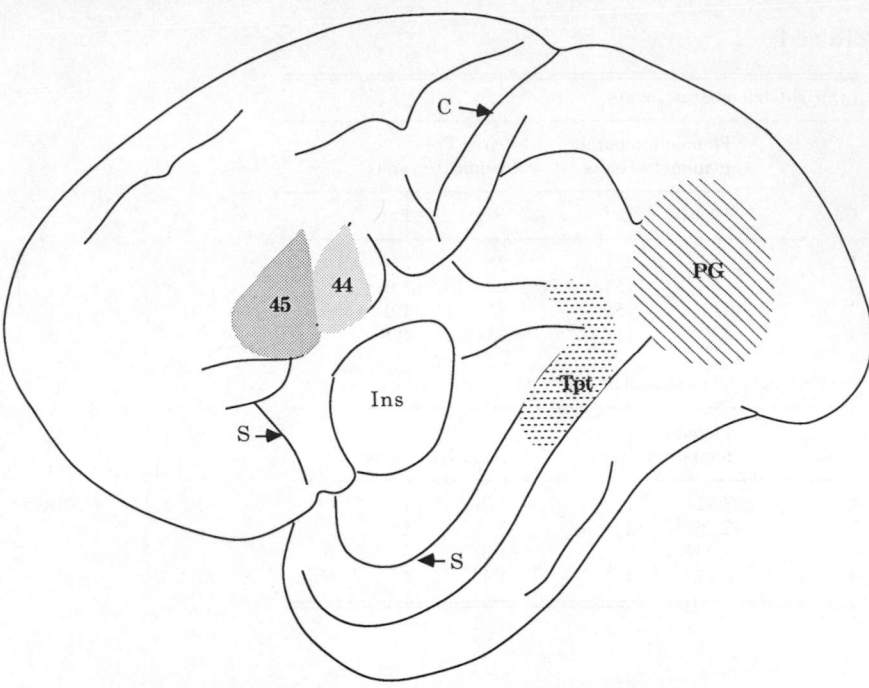

Figure 2. Schematic representation of the human brain left cerebral hemisphere. The Sylvian fossa, which is bordered by the Sylvian fissure (S), has been opened up to show the opercular portions and the insula (Ins). The anterior speech region is generally characterized as roughly occupying the pars opercularis (area 44), the posterior portion of pars triangularis (area 45) and the anterior portion of the subcentral region lying below the central sulcus (C). The posterior speech region notably includes the posterior portion of the planum temporale of which Area Tpt is a prominent feature. The supramarginal and angular regions of the parietal lobe also contain areas which have language function, including area PG of the angular gyrus.

Area PG is tightly connected to another language-related area of the brain, the lateral posterior nucleus (LP) of the thalamus, a subcortical structure (Trojanowski & Jacobson 1976; Maguiere, Baleydier, & Garde 1978). Aphasiological data, again, provide basic data for the association of linguistic function with LP (Mohr, Watters, & Duncan 1975; Ojemann 1977). Eidelberg & Galaburda (1982) report that LP is typically significantly larger on the left than on the right. Another thalamic nucleus which has been implicated in language function is the pulvinar, which lies posterior to LP. Oke *et al.* (1978) showed an asymmetry in the content of the neurotransmitter norepinepherine in the pulvinar; the left pulvinar contains more of this transmitter than the right.

Broca's area as conventionally represented spreads across the frontal operculum, including pars orbitalis, pars triangularis (area 45), and pars opercularis (area 44) (Figure 2). Galaburda (1980) reports asymmetries in favor of the magnopyramidal zone of the left frontal operculum. Of the divisions of the frontal operculum, pars opercularis shows the greatest number of specialized features (Galaburda 1982). Significantly, in a study of the homologous areas in the rhesus monkey, this area alone was found to receive projections from the posterior auditory fields (Galaburda & Sanides 1980; Galaburda & Pandya 1982); it will be recalled that dating back to Wernicke (1874) the importance of such a projection in the analysis of the neuroanatomical basis of linguistic capacity has been claimed. Lipofucsin, a substance which results from oxydative cellular metabolism, accumulates in area 44 in a manner not found in the same measure in the other frontal opercular regions (Braak 1979). The part of 44 which shows the unusual accumulation of lipofucsin is the magnopyramidal zone. Whitaker & Ojemann (1977) report that this same region is particularly vulnerable to aphasic responses after electrical stimulation. Galaburda (1980) notes that a distinctive build up of lipofucsin in area 44 is echoed in other language-related areas: the posterior superior temporal gyrus, the inferior parietal lobule, the medial surface of the hemisphere surrounding the cingulate gyrus, and the preoccipital temporal regions of the second and third temporal gyrus (Braak 1980).

Detailed microscopic study of the brain reveals, then, that the gross anatomical asymmetries reflect architectonically significant asymmetries between the left and right hemispheres. Given the scope of the asymmetries and, in particular, the correlation which exists between areas grossly implicated in language function through aphasiological and stimulation studies and the specific architectonic asymmetries found in those gross areas, it would be implausible to assume that there is not a concrete and distinctive functional neural architecture which subserves human linguistic capacity. Furthermore, the correlation of asymmetries within individual brains, and the evidence from the distribution of lipofucsin of a neurochemical communality among the language-related cortical areas, suggest that these areas are components of a functionally integrated system.

There is considerable general consistency across individuals in studies of asymmetry, but, at the same time, there is always a considerable range of individual differences. The anatomical evidence suggests that roughly 35% of the population has anomalies of cerebral dominance (Galaburda 1984). While some of the these differences are likely to be indicative of significant variations in linguistic capacity, as with other biological systems it is reasonable to assume that in some cases the differences are not of a magnitude to yield notable functional variation. Even in this 'normal' range, however, variation may be such that pooling populations of aphasics, whose precise lesions do vary, may be misleading. In order to determine to what extent variation in the substrate may influence the structure of linguistic capacity, it is necessary to consider populations who vary from the norm with respect to specific properties of the neural substrate.

5.3. **Variation in cortical structure**

Current linguistic theories such as the government–binding framework (Chomsky 1981) acknowledge one source of linguistic variation: UG constrains both the range of possible grammars a child will entertain in the course of acquisition and, by extension, the range of experience a child will encounter. The assumption that linguistic capacity is biologically specified admits variation in the neural substrate as a source of variation in linguistic capacity. In all quantitative studies of anatomical asymmetry a range of variation is observed, including at the architectonic level. This inevitably raises the question of whether there might not be significant differences in the structure of linguistic capacity. Certainly, if structure and function are related, then variation in form must reflect in some manner variation in function. Two basic domains of variation require consideration: qualitative structure and quantitative structure.

5.3.1. **Qualitative variation in cortical structure**

The cortex of the brain is formed through the migration of neuroblasts (which will ultimately be differentiated as specific types of neurons) from the zone of proliferation outward to form the cortical mantle (Sidman & Rakic 1973, 1982). If, for any area, there is some disorder in the timing of the migration, then there will be qualitative anomalies in cortical organization; cells might 'overshoot' their appropriate laminal landing site or 'undershoot' it, in the extreme not even reaching cortex. Such misplaced or atypically located neurons are known as ectopia. When the cortex is not laid down in its typical fashion then the pattern of gyri, which is a function of the pattern of growth, will be atypical as well (Goldman-Rakic & Rakic 1984). The study of any population with anomalies of neural migration in the left hemisphere, specifically in the language areas, would provide critical evidence of the functional significance of the specific organization of those areas. Such research would also provide critical evidence as to the content of claims that UG is biologically specified. If a population with anomalies of neural ontogeny involving language-related brain areas were shown to exhibit deviation from the pattern of linguistic capacity characterized by UG, that would provide critical data for determining the appropriate level at which it can be claimed that UG is a functional biological theory.

In a series of cytoarchitectonic studies of the brains of developmental dyslexics, Galaburda and his colleagues have reported qualitative anomalies of neural ontogeny (Galaburda & Kemper 1979; Galaburda & Eidelberg 1982; Geschwind & Galaburda 1987; see also Drake 1968). The anomalies observed are diffuse in the left hemisphere and in some cases are found in the right hemisphere as well. Due to anomalous neural migration during fetal development, the cortex of dyslexics exhibits anomalies in lamination with striking ectopic clusters of neurons in cortex as well as subcortical dysplasia (cortical cells which failed to reach cortex in the course of migration and are stranded in white matter) and atypical gyral patterning. In a CAT scan study of individuals with dyslexia, Heir *et al*. (1978) found that contrary to the typical pattern of gross asymmetries, a disproportionately large number of dyslexic brains showed a wider right than left parieto-occipital region. Duffy, McAnulty, & Schacter (1984) report physiological differences between dyslexic and nondyslexic subjects over the left posterior quadrant (including the temporo-parietal area) and the medial frontal lobes. Developmental dyslexics provide, then, a test case for considering the biological foundations of linguistic capacity at the level of neural architecture.

Developmental dyslexia is diagnosed when an individual fails to develop normal reading skills despite normal (or superior) intelligence, the absence of any clinical pathology (neurologic or psychiatric), and ample opportunity to learn to read; dyslexia is then by definition a specific reading disorder. As in all reported studies of dyslexic brains, anomalies involving the language areas (as well as other areas) have been found; if the diagnostic definition of dyslexia is taken at face value that would suggest that the details of cortical organization are of little consequence for normal vocal–auditory language acquisition and use. The linguistic capacity of dyslexics provides then a test of the significance of qualitative organization for the development of 'normal' linguistic capacity. As the Public Health Service estimates that 15% of American students have dyslexia (US Department of Health, Education and Welfare 1980), dyslexics constitute a significant subset of the population; any systematic anomalies of linguistic capacity found in this group would represent a major variant of UG.

In terms of everyday language use, dyslexics show intuitively the same range of verbal abilities as non-dyslexic 'normals'; some are highly verbal while others are not, with many seemingly falling at neither extreme. In a sentence judgement study involving a wide variety of syntactic constructions, Kean (1984b) found that the performance of adult developmental dyslexics was, on the whole, not quantitatively significantly different from that of either college students or adults from the community. Research studies of dyslexic language processing have, however, consistently reported anomalies in linguistic capacity (Kean 1984b; Mann 1984; Vellutino, 1979; Vogel, 1975). The range of linguistic anomalies reported covers a broad spectrum of the domains of UG. Mann (1984) provides data from longitudinal research indicating that poor readers have problems in phonological processing. Vellutino (1979) and Vogel (1975) both offer evidence of problems with inflectional morphology and syntax in developmental dyslexia. Kean (1984b) reports evidence that a subset of dyslexics encounter specific 'problems' with referential dependencies. Presented with sentences such as those in (4), read with neutral intonation, the subjects were asked first to judge the acceptability of the sentence and then, if they judged the sentence as grammatical, they were asked 'Who did the dishes?' When a sentence was judged ungrammatical, the subject was asked what was wrong.

(4)   a.   John asked Mary to do the dishes, and she did them
       b.   John promised Mary to do the dishes, and he did them
       c.   *John asked Mary to do the dishes, and he did them
       d.   *John promised Mary to do the dishes, and she did them
       e.   John asked Bill to do the dishes, and he did them
       f.   Mary promised Sally to do the dishes, and she did them

In contrast to adult and college student controls, the adult developmental dyslexics accepted all the sentence type in (4) as grammatical, selecting the gender appropriate antecedent for 'Who?' in (4a–d) and claiming that (4e, f) were ambiguous. These responses are not a result of a global anomaly in the interpretation of pronouns. This is demonstrated by the dyslexic's systematic rejection of sentences such as (5) with ill-formed tag questions and their ability to appropriately correct the error.

(5)   *Mary asked Sally if she had gone to the movies with John, didn't he/they?

While dyslexics exhibit essentially normal performance at the grossest levels of analysis, on inspection their linguistic capacity is anomalous. Critically, the data from these studies support the view that the linguistic capacity of dyslexics, their effective 'UG', is distinctive. The task remains to provide a detailed linguistic analysis of the structure of linguistic capacity in dyslexia. From such an analysis it will begin to be possible to begin to consider in detail how the structure of the neural substrate determines the functional structure of linguistic capacity.

5.3.2. **Quantitative variation in cortical structure**

The neural substrate may vary quantitatively as well as qualitatively. Quantitative variation arises when some population(s) of neurons fail to develop as would be expected; it is an inevitable consequence of the curtailment of any neuronal population(s) that there will also be qualitative anomalies in structure. Down's Syndrome (DS) provides an example of an instance of quantitative variation in the substrate. In DS the brain is smaller, has a convolution simplicity, and is grossly anatomically malformed. Architectonic analysis provides evidence of a significant quantitative curtailment of neurons; this quantitative poverty is particularly prominent in a specific class of neuronal cells, granular cells (Ross, Galaburda & Kemper 1984). The curtailment in granular cells is striking and is encountered in both motor and sensory areas of the brain. The dramatic neuronal poverty exhibited in DS provides a context for considering an extreme of limiting conditions on the emergence of linguistic capacity.

In an early study of language acquisition in a DS population, Lenneberg (1967) found that language development was delayed in its onset and its progress froze by age 12 to 13 at a level comparable to an early stage in language acquisition. In a detailed longitudinal study, Fowler (1984) also found a delay in the onset of language acquisition, but, strikingly, she found that over its active course acquisition proceeded at the same rate as in normal children. Such data are highly suggestive. There is considerable postnatal development and shaping of connections among neurons; given the poverty of the neuronal substrate in DS, it is plausible to speculate that behavioral development is delayed because it simply takes longer in DS for sufficiently articulated neuronal networks to emerge, *ceteris paribus*. Once, however, that threshold is reached, development can take off in a normal fashion; if succeeding thresholds of development in the nervous system are not achieved, then behavioral development will plateau.

Fowler's (1984) data include three additional findings of particular note for any consideration of brain and linguistic capacity. She observed that the course of normal linguistic development in DS reached that of a normal $2\frac{1}{2}$-year-old (mean length of utterance 3.0–3.5). Thus, as Gleitman (1981) observed, the data from DS provide evidence that linguistic capacity, UG, matures and is not available in full form from the onset of acquisition. Studies by Borer & Wexler (1987) of normal language acquisition support that view. The evidence from DS suggests that the earliest stages of language acquisition proceed with relative insensitivity to the detailed architecture of the brain. The data are consistent with the view that the earliest stages of language development may not be guided by (some subcomponent of) UG but rather more general mechanisms; they are also consistent with the view that UG is, from a biological perspective, an emergent property of the system. Also of note in Fowler's finding is that, in some cases, after the plateauing of the normal developmental sequence there is later linguistic development; significantly, this later development is quite anomalous in character. Given the profound anomalies of cortical structure in DS, such a finding would be expected under any assumption of a biological substrate of linguistic capacity. Third, Fowler found no correlation between language acquisition and the development of quantitative skills in her subjects. This finding is further evidence in support of the contention that linguistic capacity is biologically distinct from other cognitive capacities.

5.3.3. **Age-dependent variation in the substrate of linguistic capacity**

The brain of a child is not a miniature adult brain, and there is considerable evidence for there being a relation between the development of the brain and the emergence of linguistic capacity. As the brain develops, the functional capacities of its components change; the (dominant) functional substrate of a capacity may, therefore, shift in locus with maturation. One of the clearest cases of such a shift is provided by the study of the development of face recognition in children (Carey & Diamond 1982). Prior to the onset of puberty, a child's capacity to recognize faces is bilaterally represented; recognition is based on striking features (e.g. glasses and beards) and is relatively insensitive to the orientation of the face (right side up or upside down). With the onset of puberty, the right hemisphere becomes dominant; the normal mature right hemisphere recognition system is based not on striking features but, rather, keyed on planes and angles and is sensitive to rotation. The earlier system is not lost, but rather ceases to be functionally dominant. There is evidence that the substrate of linguistic capacity similarly shifts as the system functionally matures.

In the average adult, right- or left-handed, aphasia typically arises only in consequence of damage to the left hemisphere perisylvian region. In young children, at least below the age of 2 or 3 years, and possibly older, damage to either the left or right hemisphere may cause an aphasia (Lenneberg 1967). A variety of indirect evidence suggests that as linguistic capacity matures and the left hemisphere systems become functionally dominant, the right hemisphere maintains a significant (if not readily accessible to inspection) linguistic capacity. In studies of split brain patients, Zaidel (1976) has found that while right hemisphere grammatical capacity is quite curtailed, vocabularies may reach the level of a normal 10- or 11-year-old. As would be expected on the assumption that variation in asymmetries reflect variations in functional capacity, Gazzaniga *et al.* (1979) reports that the range of right hemisphere linguistic capacity in split brain patients ranges from being exceedingly limited to being effectively fully developed. Related data are provided by studies of individuals who have had the left hemisphere surgically excised in infancy. Dennis (1976) reports that while such children have significant grammatical limitations, their linguistic capacity is sufficiently robust that in elementary school they can maintain age-appropriate grade level.

Functional substrates not only shift in development, they also shift in aging (Finger & Stein 1982). There is little evidence bearing on the question of whether linguistic capacity may shift in normal aging. It is the anecdotal experience of people working with aphasics that there are seeming age-dependent changes in the quality of aphasia. It is an open empirical question if the representation and processing of language change in any significant fashion in aging. To understand the parameters of neural structure which circumscribe and support normal mature linguistic capacity, it is essential that this question be investigated with the same intensity as other domains bearing on the elucidation of the biological foundations of language.

The focus of current research on brain and language is on relating specific anatomical systems to aspects of linguistic capacity. The development, mature functioning, and aging of the nervous system is a function not only of its anatomy but also of neuralhumoral circumstance. Sex hormones exert considerable influence over fetal development of the brain (Nordeen & Yahr 1983; Diamond 1984). Geschwind & Galaburda (1987) have argued that sensitivity to testosterone plays a critical role in the anomalies of neural ontogeny found in dyslexia. With the onset of puberty the hormonal milieu of the nervous system undergoes a radical change. The work on face recognition indicates that there is a qualitative shift in the functional substrate at this time. A wealth of anecdotal evidence suggests that with the onset of puberty the capacity to acquire a language undergoes radical change. The data from acquisition of second languages by children, as opposed to adults, are consistent with the view that linguistic capacity is altered with the onset of puberty; work with Genie, who was linguistically deprived from age 2 to 13, is also consistent with this view (Curtiss 1977). Pituitary and adrenergic hormones play a significant role in the modulation of memory (McGaugh *et al.* 1984); whether there exist hormones which play any sort of distinctive or selective role in language acquisition or verbal memory is unknown. The extent to which the hormonal environment influences linguistic capacity through life is an area which has yet to be examined.

5.4. **Brain systems and linguistic capacity**

There is a host of compelling data which show that human linguistic capacity is biologically specified. Current research is only beginning to address in detail questions of how the biological substrate supports language knowledge and use. From aphasiological studies it has long been known that in maturity a restricted set of cortical areas have a privileged relation to linguistic capacity. Grammatical and psycholinguistic studies of aphasics are revealing with ever increasing refinement the organization of language in the mature brain. Recent research has begun to turn to consideration of how variation in the neural substrate influences the realization of linguistic capacity. Such research is critical to any attempt to ascribe substantive content to the claim that linguistic theory, UG, is a functional biological model. While there is still an immense poverty of research in this area, there are sufficient data to warrant proposing a variety of significant hypotheses: (1) linguistic capacity matures and changes as a consequence of neural development. (2) UG is a theory of an emergent property of the system and not a theory of the functional acquisition device *per se*. (3) Linguistic capacity varies as a function of specific qualitative variations in the neural substrate, anatomically and possibly neuralhumorally. The scope and extent of correlated variations in the substrate and linguistic capacity remain, however, to be delineated. It is the issue of systematic variation which poses the fundamental question and challenge of the study of brain structures and linguistic capacity.

REFERENCES

Amaducci, L., Sorbi, S., Albanese, A. & Gainotti, G. 1981. Choline acetyltransferase (ChAT) activity differs in right and left human temporal lobes. *Neurology* 31: 799–805.
Benson, D. F. 1979. *Aphasia, alexia, and agraphia.* New York: Churchill Livinston.
Bleser, R. de & Bayer, J. In press. German wordformation and aphasia. *The Linguistic Review.*
Blomert, L., Koster, C., van Mier, H. & Kean, M.-L. 1987. Verbal communication abilities of aphasic patients: the everyday language test. *Aphasiology* 1.
Bonin, G. von 1962. Anatomical asymmetries of the cerebral hemispheres. In Mountcastle (1962).
Borer, H. & Wexler, K. 1987. Maturation of syntax. In Roeper & Williams (1987).
Braak, H. 1979. The pigment architecture of the human frontal lobe, 1: Precentral, subcentral and frontal region. *Anatomy and Embryology* 157: 35–68.
Braak, H. 1980. *Architectonics of the human telencephalic cortex.* Berlin-Heidelberg and New York: Springer.
Broca, P. 1861. Perte de la parole. Romollissement chronique et destruction partielle du lobe antérieur gauche du cerveau. *Bulletin de la Société d'Anthropologie* 2: 235.
Bumke, O. & Forster, O. (eds.) 1936. *Handbuch der Neurologie*, vol. 6. Berlin: Springer.
Campain, J. & Minckler, J. 1976. A note on gross configurations of the human auditory cortex. *Brain and Language* 3: 318–23.
Carey, S. & Diamond, R. 1982. Maturational determination of the developmental course of face encoding. In D. Caplan (ed.) *Biological studies of mental processes.* Cambridge, MA: MIT Press.
Chi, J. G., Dooling, E. C. & Gilles, F. H. 1977. Left–right asymmetries of the temporal speech areas of the human fetus. *Archives of Neurology* 32: 239–46.
Chomsky, N. 1965. *Aspects of the theory of syntax.* Cambridge, MA: MIT Press.
Chomsky, N. 1981. *Lectures on government and binding.* Dordrecht: Foris.
Chomsky, N. 1985. *Knowledge of language: its nature, origin, and use.* New York: Praeger.
Conel, J. L. 1939–59. *The postnatal development of the human cerebral cortex*, vols I–VI. Cambridge, MA: Harvard University Press.
Curtiss, S. 1977. *Genie: A psycholinguistic study of a modern-day 'wild child'.* New York: Academic Press.
Dejerine, J. 1906. L'aphasie motrice; sa localisation et sa physiologie pathologique. *Presse Médicale* 56: 742.
Dennis, M. 1976. Language acquisition following hemidecortication: Linguistic superiority of the left over the right hemisphere. *Brain and Language* 2: 404–33.
Diamond, M. C. 1984. Age, sex, and environmental influences. In Geschwind & Galaburda (1984).
Drake, W. E. 1968. Clinical and pathological findings in a child with a developmental learning disability. *Journal of Learning Disabilities* 1: 9–25.
Duffy, F., McAnulty, G., & Schacter, S. 1984. Brain electrical activity mapping. In Geschwind & Galaburda (1984).
Eidelberg, D. & Galaburda, A. M. 1982. Symmetry and asymmetry in the human posterior thalamus. *Archives of Neurology* 39: 325–32.

Eidelberg, D. & Galaburda, A. M. 1984. Inferior parietal lobule: Divergent architectonic asymmetries in the human brain. *Archives of Neurology* 41: 843–52.

Finger, S. & Stein, D. G. 1982. *Brain damage and recovery: Research and clinical perspective.* New York: Academic Press.

Fowler, A. 1984. Language acquisition in Down's Syndrome children: production and comprehension. Doctoral dissertation, University of Pennsylvania, Department of Psychology.

Freud, S. 1953. *On aphasia: A critical study.* New York: International Universities Press.

Galaburda, A. M. 1980. La région de Broca: Observations anatomiques faites un siècle apres la mort de son découvreur. *Review Neurologique* 136: 609–16.

Galaburda, A. M. 1982. Histology, architectonics, and asymmetry of language areas. In M. A. Arbib, D. Caplan & J. C. Marshall (eds.) *Neural models of language processes.* New York: Academic Press.

Galaburda, A. M. 1984. Anatomical asymmetries. In Geschwind & Galaburda (1984).

Galaburda, A. M. & Eidelberg, D. 1982. Symmetry and asymmetry in the human posterior thalamus, II: thalamic lesions in a case of developmental dyslexia. *Archives of Neurology* 39: 333–6.

Galaburda, A. M. & Kemper, T. L. 1979. Cytoarchitectonic abnormalities in developmental dyslexia: A case study. *Annals of Neurology* 6: 94–100.

Galaburda, A. M. & Pandya, D. 1982. The role of architectonics and connections in the study of primate brain evolution. In E. Armstrong & D. Falk (eds.) *Primate brain evolution: Methods and concepts.* New York: Plenum.

Galaburda, A. M. & Sanides, F. 1980. Cytoarchitectonic organization of the human auditory cortex. *Journal of Comparative Neurology* 190: 597–610.

Galaburda, A. M., LeMay, M., Kemper, T. L. & Geschwind, N. 1978. Right–left asymmetries in the brain: Structural differences in the hemispheres may underlie cerebral dominance. *Science* 199: 852–6.

Gazzaniga, M. S., Le Doux, J. E., Smylie, C. S. & Volpe, B. T. 1979. Plasticity in speech organization following commissurotomy. *Brain* 102: 805–15.

Geschwind, N. 1962. The anatomy of acquired disorders of reading. In J. Money (ed.) *Reading disability.* Baltimore. Johns Hopkins Press.

Geschwind, N. 1965. Disconnexion syndromes in animals and man. *Brain* 88: 237–94, 585–644.

Geschwind, N. 1967. The apraxias. In E. W. Straus & R. M. Griffin (eds.) *Phenomenology of action and will.* Pittsburgh: Duquesne University Press.

Geschwind, N. & Galaburda, A. M. (eds) 1984. *Cerebral dominance: the biological foundations.* Cambridge, MA: Harvard University Press.

Geschwind, N. & Galaburda, A. M. 1987. *Cerebral lateralization: biological mechanisms, associations, and pathology.* Cambridge, MA: MIT Press.

Geschwind, N. & Levitsky, W. 1968. Asymmetries in the temporal speech region. *Science* 161: 186–7.

Gleitman, L. R. 1981. Maturational determinants of language growth. *Cognition* 10: 103–14.

Goldman-Rakic, P. S. & Rakic, P. 1984. Experimental modification of gyral patterns. In Geschwind & Galaburda (1984).

Goldstein, K. 1948. *Language and language disturbances* New York: Grune & Stratton.

Goodenough, C., Zurif, E. & Weintraub, S. 1977. Aphasics' attention to grammatical morphemes. *Language and Speech* 20: 11–19.

Grodzinsky, Y. 1984. The syntactic characterization of agrammatism. *Cognition* 16: 99–120.

Head, H. 1963. *Aphasia and kindred disorders of speech,* vols I and II. New York: Hafner.

Heir, D. B., LeMay, M., Rosenberg, P. B. & Perlo, V. P. 1978. Developmental dyslexia: evidence for a subgroup with reverse asymmetry. *Archives of Neurology* 35: 90–2.

Hubel, D. H. & Wiesel, T. N. 1962. Receptive fields, binocular interaction and functional architecture in the cat's visual cortex. *Journal of Physiology (London)* 160: 106–54.

Hubel, D. H. & Wiesel, T. N. 1965. Receptive fields and functional architecture in two non-striate visual areas (18 and 19) of the cat. *Journal of Neurophysiology* 28: 229–89.

Hyams, N. 1987. *Parameter setting and the theory of language acquisition.* Dordrecht: Reidel.

Hyvarinen, J. & Shelepin, Y. 1979. Distribution of visual and somatic functions in the parietal association area of the monkey. *Brain Research* 169: 561–4.

Jackson, J. H. 1958. *Selected writings of John Hughlings Jackson.* New York: Basic Books.

Kean, M.-L. 1977. The linguistic interpretation of aphasic syndromes: agrammatism in Broca's aphasia, an example. *Cognition* 5: 9–46.

Kean, M.-L. 1984a. Linguistic analysis of aphasic syndromes: the doing and undoing of aphasia research. In D. Caplan, A. R. Lecours & A. Smith (eds.) *Biological perspectives on language*. Cambridge, MA: MIT Press.

Kean, M.-L. 1984b. The question of linguistic anomaly in developmental dyslexia. *Annals of Dyslexia* 34: 137–51.

Kean, M.-L. (ed.) 1985. *Agrammatism*. New York: Academic Press.

Kemper, T. L. 1984. Asymmetrical lesions in dyslexia. In Geschwind & Galaburda (1984).

Kertesz, A. & Geschwind, N. 1971. Patterns of pyramidal decussation and their relationship to handedness. *Archives of Neurology* 24: 326–32.

Koster, C., Blomert, L., van Mier, H. & Kean, M.-L. 1985. Hoe goed het afatische grammaticaliteitsoordeel? Paper presented at the conference of the Nederlandse Vereniging voor Neuropsychologie, Nijmegen.

Lecours, A. R. 1982. On neologisms. In J. Mehler, E. C. T. Walker, & M. F. Garrett (eds.) *Perspectives on mental representation: experimental and theoretical studies of cognitive processes and capacities*. Hillsdale: Erlbaum.

Lecours, A. R., Lhermitte, F. & Bryans, B. 1983. *Aphasiology*. London: Bailliere Tindall.

LeMay, M. 1976. Morphological cerebral asymmetries of modern man, fossil man, and nonhuman primate. In S. R. Harnad, H. D. Steklis, & J. Lancaster (eds.) *Origins and evolution of language and speech*. New York: New York Academy of Sciences.

LeMay, M. & Culebras, A. 1972. Human brain: morphologic differences in the hemispheres demonstrated by carotid arterigraphy. *New England Journal of Medicine* 287: 168–70.

Lenneberg, E. H. 1967. *Biological foundations of language*. New York: Wiley.

Lynch, J. C. 1980. The functional organization of posterior parietal association cortex. *Behavioral and Brain Science* 3: 485–99.

Maguiere, F., Baleydier, C. & Garde, A. 1978. Functional anatomical organization of associative cortical areas 7, 21, and 72 in monkey. *Review Neurologique* 134: 93–102.

Mann, V. A. 1984. Longitudinal prediction and prevention of reading difficulty. *Annals of Dyslexia* 34: 117–36.

Marie, P. 1906. Revision de la question de l'aphasie: la troisième circonvolution frontale gauche ne joue aucun rôle spécial dans la fonction du langage. *Semaine medicale* 26: 493.

McGaugh, J. L., Liang, K., Bennett, C. & Sternberg, D. 1984. Adrenergic influences on memory storage: interaction of peripheral and central systems. In G. Lynch, J. L. McGaugh & N. M. Weinberger (eds.) *Neurobiology of learning and memory*. New York: Guilford.

McRae, D., Branch, C. & Milner, B. 1968. Occipital horns and cerebral dominance. *Neurology* 18: 95–8.

Mesulam, M.-M., Van Hoesen, G. W., Pandya, D. N. & Geschwind, N. 1977. Limbic and sensory connections of the inferior parietal lobule (area PG) in the rhesus monkey. *Brain Research* 136: 393–414.

Mohr, J. P., Watters, W. C. & Duncan, G. W. 1975. Thalamic hemorrhage and aphasia. *Brain and Language* 2: 3–17.

Mountcastle, V. (ed.) 1962. *Interhemispheric relations and cerebral dominance*. Baltimore: Johns Hopkins University Press.

Nordeen, E. J. & Yahr, P. 1983. A regional analysis of estrogen binding to hypothalamic cell nuclei in relation to masculinization and defeminization. *Journal of Neuroscience* 3: 933–41.

Ojemann, G. 1977. Asymmetric function of the thalamus in man. *Annals of the New York Academy of Sciences* 94: 380–96.

Ojemann, G. 1983. Brain organization for language from the perspective of electrical stimulation mapping. *Behavioral and Brain Sciences* 6: 189–230.

Oke, A., Keller, R., Mefford, I. & Adams, R. N. 1978. Lateralization of norepinephrine in human thalamus. *Science* 200: 1411–13.

Pandya, D. N. & Seltzer, B. 1982. Intrinsic connections and architectonics of posterior parietal cortex in the rhesus monkey. *Journal of Comparative Neurology* 204: 196–210.

Penfield, W. & Roberts, L. 1959. *Speech and brain mechanisms*. Princeton: Princeton University Press.

Pfeifer, R. A. 1936. Pathologie der Horstrahlung und der corticaler Horsphare. In Bumke & Forster (1936).

Roeper, T. & Williams, E. (eds.) 1987. *Parameter setting*. Dordrecht: Reidel.

Ross, M. H., Galaburda, A. M. & Kemper, T. L. 1984. Down's Syndrome: is there a decreased population of neurons? *Neurology* 34: 909–16.

Sidman, R. L. & Rakic, P. 1973. Neuronal migration, with specific reference to developing human brain: a review. *Brain Research* 62: 1–35.

Sidman, R. L. & Rakic, P. 1982. Development of the human central nervous system. In W. Haymaker & R. D. Adams (eds.) *Cytology and cellular neuropathology*. 2nd edn. Springfield, ILL: Charles C. Thomas.

Trojanowski, J. Q. & Jacobson, S. 1976. Areal and laminar distribution of some pulvinar cortical efferents in rhesus monkey. *Journal of Comparative Neurology* 169: 371–92.

US Department of Health and Welfare 1980. *Developmental dyslexia and related learning disorders*. Public Health Service, NIH Publication No. 80-92.

Vellutino, F. R. 1979. *Dyslexia: theory and research*. Cambridge, MA: MIT Press.

Vogel, S. A. 1975. *Syntactic abilities in normal and dyslexic children*. Baltimore: University Park Press.

Wernicke, C. 1874. *Der aphasiche Symptomenkomplex*. Breslau: Cohn & Weigert. Reprinted (1969) in English in R. S. Cohen & M. W. Wartofsky (eds.) *Boston studies in the philosophy of science*, vol. IV. Dordrecht: Reidel.

Whitaker, H. A. & Ojemann, G. 1977. Graded localization of naming from electrical stimulation of left cerebral cortex. *Nature* 270: 50–1.

Wiesel, T. N. & Hubel, D. H. 1965. Comparison of the effects of unilateral and bilateral eye closure on cortical unit responses in very young kittens. *Journal of Neurophysiology* 28: 1029–40.

Wittleson, S. F. & Pallie, W. 1973. Left hemisphere specialization for language in the newborn. *Brain* 96: 641–6.

Zaidel, E. 1976. Auditory vocabulary of the right hemisphere following brain bisection or hemideortication. *Cortex* 12: 191–211.

6 Abnormal language acquisition and the modularity of language

Susan Curtiss

6.0. Introduction

My daughter, Rebecca, was not an early talker. Over a long period of time she produced many delightful monologues of gibberish which, by the time she was close to two years of age, had evolved into soliloquies of gibberish combined with English words. 'When, oh when, will she start to acquire the *grammar*?' I wondered (sometimes aloud). 'Only a *linguist* would care about her *grammar*,' family and friends would say with some disdain. They were probably right. Many, if not most, linguists are concerned with characterizing and accounting for the grammar, as opposed to other aspects of language. Linguists are frequently called to task for having this narrow focus, rather than considering and studying language in its broader context.

Some theories of language acquisition reflect similar biases against the validity of focussing exclusively on grammar. The concurrent development of motor, social, cognitive, and linguistic abilities in the normal child is a fact which no doubt has influenced several theories of language development (e.g. social interaction theories: Bruner 1977; Bruner & Ninio 1978; Ratner & Bruner 1978; cognitive theories: Macnamara 1972, 1977; Lock 1978; Bates *et al.* 1979; Piaget 1980) to stress the interconnections between acquisition of the grammar and other areas of development. Such theories entail that nonspecific learning mechanisms underlie the changes that occur with increasing age across domains of knowledge. A linguistic theory of language acquisition, in contrast, has as its goal and single focus, an adequate account of the acquisition of steady state *grammars*.

In this chapter I will present data which argue that to achieve the objective of accounting for the acquisition of grammar linguists are correct in typically confining their area of inquiry to that of grammar, not just for reasons having to do with philosophy of science and research productivity, but because there is increasing evidence from atypical instances of language acquisition that grammar acquisition involves task-specific mechanisms and faculty-specific principles. The evidence comes from cases showing dissociations between grammar acquisition and the development of other aspects of linguistic knowledge. This dissociation in some cases reveals a selective impairment of grammar acquisition, in other instances a selective preservation of this faculty. The data support Chomsky's (1980) distinction between a computational linguistic component (essentially the grammar) and other faculties of mind, including other aspects of language; but they further subdivide these 'other' aspects of language into themselves dissociable components of communicative and conceptual linguistic knowledge.

6.1. Selectively impaired grammar acquisition

There is a variety of populations who give evidence of a selective impairment in grammar acquisition. They fall generally into three categories: (1) cases of acquisition beyond the critical period or beyond the most active years of first language acquisition in normal development; (2) cases where there is clear-cut damage to brain regions normally specialized for language; and (3) cases with less clear-cut etiologies.

6.1.1. Grammar acquisition beyond the typical age

Consideration of data bearing on a proposed critical period for language acquisition (Lenneberg 1967) suggests that it is acquisition of the *grammar* which is most sensitive to age at acquisition, not the development of linguistic skills *in toto* (Curtiss 1977, 1981a, 1985, in press). Two cases which support this conclusion are Genie and Chelsea.

Genie

Genie is, to date, the most extensively studied and widely reported case of acquisition beyond the normal acquisition years (Curtiss *et al.* 1974; Fromkin *et al.* 1974; Curtiss, 1977, 1979). Genie, found in adolescence having suffered unprecedented social isolation and experiential deprivation, faced the task of first language acquisition at the age of $13\frac{1}{2}$. The linguistic–cognitive profile that emerged during the eight-plus years Genie was studied, was one of good lexical and propositional semantic abilities alongside normal or relatively normal nonlinguistic cognitive function, contrasted with marked impairments in (1) psychosocial function, including the use of language for social purposes, and (2) acquisition of the grammar. Even after more than eight years of linguistic exposure and attempted acquisition, Genie's utterances remained largely agrammatic – they contained little and inconsistent use of inflectional morphology and other nonlexical grammatical markers, and were devoid of syntactic devices marking clausal relations or noncanonical sentence form (as in questions or topicalizations). Insensitivity to many of the same grammatical forms was evidenced in her comprehension as well. Examples (1)–(11) below illustrate the disparity between the lexical appropriateness and propositional clarity of her utterances on the one hand, and their unelaborated and ungrammatical form on the other.

Utterance	*Gloss*
(1) Applesauce buy store	'Buy applesuce at the store'
(2) Man motorcycle have	'The man has a motorcycle'
(3) Tummy water drink	'My tummy drinks (the) water'
(4) Want go ride Miss F. Car	'I want to go ride in Miss F.'s car'
(5) Genie full stomach	'I have a full stomach (I'm full)'
(6) Genie bad cold live father house	'I had a bad cold when I lived in my father's house'
(7) Very angry Mrs L. V. house	'I was very angry at Mrs L. V.'s house'
(8) Want Curtiss play piano	'I want you to play the piano'
(9) Father hit Genie cry long time ago	'When my father ('Father') hit me, I cried, a long time ago'
(10) Mama have baby grow up	'Mama has a baby who grew up'
(11) Genie have Mama have baby grow up	'I have a Mama who has a baby who grew up'

Note the inconsistent and often ungrammatical order of subject, verb, object in (1)–(5), the omission of obligatory constituents in all of the sentences, including main verbs in (5)–(7), and the lack of any syntactic device marking clausal relations in (8)–(11), all of this in contrast to the semantic clarity of these utterances, especially in context.

It should also be noted, however, that there is considerable evidence that Genie had acquired certain categorial facts of English. First, she adhered to the subcategorization constraints for many (though not all) verbs (*Boat have steering wheel, I like cat, Genie throw ball*, but never **Boat have, *I like*, or **Genie throw*). Second, she appeared sensitive to the constituent make-up and order of constituents in certain phrasal categories: NP→(Det) (Adj) N; PP→Prep NP; never NP→N (Adj); VP→(Det) V; VP→(Adj) V; or VP→Prep V or the like, and never PP→NP Prep (but VP→NP·V or V NP). Third, she never attached bound morphology to the wrong syntactic category (e.g. always V+*ing*, never N+*ing*). Thus, while much of the grammar remained unacquired, Genie did evidence knowledge of some syntactic facts.

Although Genie was a powerfully effective nonlinguistic communicator (see Curtiss 1977), Genie's linguistic communicative abilities were impaired. While she was able to establish and maintain topics, her linguistic means of doing so were quite limited. She relied extensively on repetitions – repetitions of short phrases, even single words, serving as topic 'labels', or of assertions in previous utterances, as a way of scaffolding her own contributions to a conversation. In addition, she never produced or appeared to learn any of the social conventions of discourse; e.g. rituals like *Hi, how are you?*, rejoinders like *Please* or *OK*, conversational operators like *Well* or *And then*, or even the vocative to call for someone's attention. In spite of these limitations, however, she was consistently able to initiate and maintain topics. Genie's case, therefore, involves impairments in grammar and in those aspects of pragmatic performance reflecting social function, but not in semantics. (For more details on Genie's profile, see Curtiss 1977, 1979, 1981b, 1982.)

Chelsea

Chelsea is a hearing-impaired adult whose first language acquisition began in 1980, when she was in her early thirties. This case was brought to light by P. Glusker and has not yet been the subject of much systematic linguistic study. The data on hand come largely from partial transcripts of didactic sessions with Chelsea, and as such may not be representative of her spontaneous speech in more naturalistic contexts. Nevertheless, the cognitive and linguistic profile so far emerging is one of relatively normal nonlinguistic cognitive and social function, plus good lexical abilities, alongside striking linguistic deficiencies in other areas, including, it appears, the area of constructing interpretable and well-formed propositions. In contrast to Genie's semantically clear but generally agrammatic sentences, Chelsea's utterances are filled with grammatical formatives; but their unprincipled use leads to consistently ungrammatical strings, which at times are also 'unsemantic,' as illustrated in (12)–(24) below (these sample utterances date from 12/80 to 8/84):

(12) The small a the hat
(13) Richard eat peppers hot
(14) Orange Tim car in
(15) Banana the eat
(16) I Wanda be drive come
(17) The boat sits water on
(18) Breakfast eating girl
(19) Combing hair the boy
(20) The woman is bus the going
(21) The girl is cone the ice cream shopping buying the man
(22) They are is car in the Tim
(23) Daddy are be were to the work
(24) The they

Note the ungrammatical occurrence in (12) of two different determiners of opposing semantic specificity on the same noun, and the possible occurrence of a determiner (Det) specifier on the modifer (Mod) *small*; the switch in order from Mod-N to N-Mod in (13); the separation of subconstituents of PP (and NP) in (14); and the inconsistent use of determiners in (12), (14), (17), and (18). Note also what is either the occurrence of Det with V in (15) and (20) or the unconstrained variation of Det-N order (compare (12), (15), (17), and (20)); the ungrammatical use of Det with proper names and pronouns in (22) and (24); the chaotic concatenation of NPs and VPs in (16) and (21); the unconstrained SVO order in (18)–(21); and the unprincipled occurrence of *be*, other AUX elements, and agreement phenomena in (16), (21), (22), and (23).

Chelsea's comprehension performance reflects a reliance on knowledge of vocabulary and situational pragmatics. Her performance on the Token Test (2/25/82) showed good comprehension of parts I–IV, which use a simple and unchanging syntactic structure but impose an increasing conceptual and memory load, but little comprehension of part V, which contains a variety of syntactic and semantic structures. Likewise, her performance on the Assessment of Children's Language Comprehension (ACLC) on 5/18/84, a test where most correct answers can be achieved without knowledge of the grammar, was quite good (e.g. 80% correct on part D), whereas in 3/84 Chelsea's performance on several subtests of the CYCLE (Curtiss Yamada Comprehensive Language Evaluation), specifically testing comprehension of morphology and syntax, revealed little comprehension of English grammar.

In contrast to her impairments in grammar acquisition, her acquisition of vocabulary has been rapid and steady. The organization of her lexicon along conceptual/semantic lines also appears to be normal, as exemplified by her above-12th-grade-level performance on a subtest of the CELF (Clinical Evaluation of Language Functions), which involves naming as many items as possible of a given category (foods and animals) within a one-minute time limit. She has also learned, and makes effective use of, automatic phrases and social formulas (e.g. *Be quiet, How are you?, What?*) and other discourse conventions (e.g. *OK, Well*), giving her conversations the trappings of normal linguistic interaction. Recall that Genie never learned any of the culturally determined social conventions of discourse, despite overt attempts to teach some to her. Thus, while in both Chelsea and Genie's cases the integrity of lexical semantic acquisition was dissociated from grammar acquisition, we see from the differences in the two cases the additional separability of social and communicative linguistic abilities from each of these other areas.

Other cases

The selective vulnerability of grammar to age at acquisition is also seen in a variety of studies investigating acquisition of American Sign Language (ASL). Young (1981) and McKinney (1983) report on several cases of first language acquisition in hearing-impaired adults. These cases show the same profile of impaired grammar acquisition in the context of good vocabulary acquisition, coding of semantic relations, and discourse skills. What is equally compelling, however, are reports of deficits in grammar acquisition in individuals who undertook first language acquisition *in childhood*, but after the typically most active years of language acquisition. Woodward (1973) notes deficits in the mastery of two morphological processes in ASL: negative incorporation (on verbs) and reduplication, in subjects who learned ASL after the age of 6 years. Newport (1984) found that not only did all the 'late' learners in her study (those learning sign between ages 12 and 21) show deficient comprehension and production of the complex grammatical properties of ASL verbs of motion (see Supalla in press), but even those who had started learning ASL as young as 4 to 6 years showed deficits relative to those exposed to ASL from birth. A growing number of experiments on the processing of ASL confirm these findings. Mayberry (1979), Fischer & Mayberry (1982), Tartter & Fischer (1982), and Mayberry, Fischer & Hatfield (1983) all report significant differences in efficiency and accuracy of processing structural linguistic information between those who had learned ASL early in life and those who had been exposed to ASL only later.

There is, then, growing evidence of selective impairments in grammar acquisition when acquisition takes place beyond early childhood years, in support of the view that grammar rests on distinct principles of organization, and that grammar acquisition involves faculty-specific mechanisms. These mechanisms appear to be maturationally constrained along a timetable which is different from, independent of, and more restricted than those governing the social-communicative and referential components of linguistic development.

6.1.2. Cases of early neurological damage to the 'language zones'

The cases in this category reveal the same basic pattern, wherein the grammar (phonology, morphology, syntax) is compromised relative to linguistic-pragmatic and lexical development.

Cases of left hemispherectomy (or hemidecortication) in childhood after at least early stages of language acquisition, are reported to result in severe grammatical deficits – limited comprehension and production of many morphological and syntactic structures, largely agrammatic speech, and an inability to correct syntactic errors, despite good auditory discrimination and vocabulary test scores (Zaidel 1973, 1977; Day & Ulatowska 1979). The one case of this type for which spontaneous speech has been described was characterized as relying on routinized social speech and producing otherwise telegrammatic output (Zaidel 1973), a pattern indicating greater impairment in grammar than in lexical or social linguistic function.

Even in left hemidecortication or hemispherectomy at or shortly after birth, before overt language acquisition, there appear to be selective deficits in acquisition of the computational linguistic component. The two hemispheres are reported to be equivalent in IQ and non-visuo-spatial, non-linguistic aspects of cognition. The two hemispheres are also reported to be equivalent in assessing prototypicality of names, lexical decision, size and range of vocabulary, and phonological discrimination and phoneme production (Dennis & Whitaker 1976, 1977). The left hemisphere is impaired relative to the right, however, on a variety of tasks requiring specific structural linguistic computations; for example, the manipulation of phonological structure as a cue in word retrieval, judgements of constituent relatedness, the use of structural cues for assigning topic or focus, judgements of sentence grammaticality, syntactic comprehension and sentence repetition across a variety of syntactic structures, and the assignment of negative scope in factives and implicatives (Dennis 1980a,b).

Studies of unilateral cortical lesions in childhood also instantiate the possibility of grammar being selectively impaired in acquisition (consistently as a result of left hemisphere damage) relative to nonlinguistic cognition and nongrammatical, linguistic modules (Rankin, Aram & Horwitz 1980; Aram *et al.* 1985; Aram, Ekelman & Whitaker 1986).

The data from clear-cut neurological damage in childhood thus provide additional support for the modularity of grammar view, and further, along with considerable other data, tie this module and the mechanisms for its acquisition to the left cerebral hemisphere. (For more complete discussion of these data and their implications, see Curtiss 1985, in press.)

6.1.3. Language acquisition in cases involving less clear-cut etiology

Language-impaired children

A significant number of children demonstrate developmental language problems, even in the absence of factors known to be associated with language learning impairments, such as mental retardation, hearing impairments, clear-cut neurolinguistic damage, autism, or other psychopathology. Such children have been labeled developmentally aphasic, congenitally aphasic, language-disordered, language-delayed, language-impaired, etc.

Research over the last 15 years has demonstrated that many, if not most, of these children evidence nonlinguistic as well as linguistic deficits (Tallal 1975, 1976; Johnston & Weismer 1983; Kamhi *et al.* 1984), and consequently, as a population, show a variety of language learning problems and patterns. Individual cases within this population, however, frequently reveal an acquisition pattern suggesting selective impairments in one or more aspects of the linguistic system, thereby providing additional evidence for the modularity of language. Data from three cases showing a selective impairment in morpho-syntax are presented below.[1]

As Table 1 illustrates, R.R., C.C. and A.P. are (4-year-old) language-impaired children whose spontaneous speech shows normally developing conversational abilities (e.g. pragmatic appropriateness, speech act range, topic-related skills) and normally developing lexical and propositional abilities (e.g. lexical range and appropriateness, range and use of semantic roles and relations expressed, propositional well-formedness) alongside marked deficiencies in morphological elaboration and an abnormal proportion of syntactically ill-formed or agrammatic utterances.

Sample utterances from each child, presented in (25)–(39) below, further elucidate this profile:

(25) R.R. And his nose right there
(26)   Him dead
(27)   Him bite mine head off
(28)   No can bite any head off them
(29)   Me no know why

(30) C.C. It a broken car, see?
(31)   He need more gas
(32)   It this kind
(33)   He little than me
(34)   I cheer and doing other things

(35) A.P. Try kill Superman
(36)   I go out now?
(37)   Wash plate
(38)   Want go show Papa
(39)   Bad guy put Superman way far away

These cases once again reveal the separability of grammar learning mechanisms in communicative-linguistic maturation from those underlying lexical and pragmatic development.

[1] These data were collected under the auspices of NINCDS contract NO1-NS-9-2322, 'Evaluation of the Outcomes of Preschool Language Impairment' awarded to Paula Tallal, Robert Kaplan, and myself.

Table 1

Child	Pragmatic appropriateness (%)[a]	Speech act range (%)[a]	Type/token nouns	Type/token verbs	Lexical misuse (%)[b]	Semantic ill-formedness (%)[c]	Ratio of score to no. of utterances[d]	Syntactic ill-formedness (%)[e]
R.R.	90	78.6	64	63	0.0	3.45	6.2	41
C.C.	84	71.4	69	62	3.6	3.60	10.0	45
A.P.	96	79.0	55	49	3.1	6.40	6.7	42
normals[f]	69[g]	86.5	67	52	4.0[g]	8.46[g]	16.25	18

Notes: [a] % of 50 contiguous child-utterances in a conversational dyad.
[b] % misuse out of a total number nouns, verbs, modifiers, quantifiers, pronouns, conjunctions, and prepositions.
[c] % of omitted or inappropriate semantic roles or arguments of total number expressed in 50 non-imitated utterances.
[d] Quantitative score reflecting general degree of morphological elaboration, syntactic complexity, and syntactic well-formedness in 50 non-imitated, nonritualistic or automatic utterances.
[e] % of 50 non-imitated, nonritualistic or automatic utterances.
[f] 10 IQ-, SES-, and 'language-age'-matched normals (ranging in age from 2¼ to 3½ years).
[g] Scores reflect the children's young age (2–3 years).

Developmental dyslexics

There is now growing evidence that developmental dyslexia is associated with specific neurological anomolies of the left hemisphere, most specifically, anomalies of neuronal migration (Drake 1968; Galaburda & Kemper 1979; Geschwind & Galaburda 1985). What is of interest here is that in developmental dyslexia, in addition to reading, lexical and grammar acquisition appear to be impaired. Vocabulary size and lexical processes such as retrieval and rapid naming are reported to be significantly affected (Denckla & Rudel 1976a,b; Jansky & de Hirsch 1976; Wolf 1986). Deficiencies in phonological representations and difficulties with inflectional morphology and syntax have also been reported (see Vellutino 1979 for a review). Recent linguistic research on adult dyslexics has revealed specific anomalies in pronoun– and anaphor–antecedent binding relations (in government and control structures) and deficient processing of *determiners* as opposed to other syntactic categories in this population (Kean 1984). There are no reports of impoverished pragmatic abilities in dyslexics, however. We see once again, then, the association of impaired grammar acquisition with impairments of the left cerebral hemisphere, the separability of grammar learning mechanisms from those underlying the acquisition of pragmatic competence, and the separability also of pragmatic development from lexical development.

6.2. **Selectively intact grammar acquisition**

Other cases of abnormal or atypical acquisition show a reverse profile, wherein grammar acquisition appears intact in the context of difficulties in other areas of linguistic development.

6.2.1. **Intact grammar acquisition in mentally retarded children**

One kind of case involves intact grammar learning despite impairments in other components of linguistic development and despite significant and pervasive retardation. Two of these cases have been presented at greater length elsewhere (Curtiss & Yamada 1981; Curtiss 1982, in press; Yamada 1983).

Antony

Antony was studied over a period when he was 6½ to 7 years of age (see Curtiss & Yamada 1981 and Curtiss 1982 for details). Estimates of his IQ range from 50 to 56, and professional reports of his developmental progress indicate pervasive delays in most areas: motor, social, and cognitive. Against this background of a generally problematic development are the parental reports of speech onset at 1 year and full sentences at 3 years. Consistent with these reports, Antony's linguistic ability appeared to outstrip his functioning in almost all other areas.

Samples of Antony's utterances are presented in (40)–(51):

(40) It's not Vivian's, it's mine
(41) I got two sisters; I got David and Vicky and Ann Margaret
(42) It's a choo-choo train
(43) You're gonna get pushed
(44) Jeni, what'd you touch?
(45) That girl doesn't have shoes
(46) He wants to chase the cat
(47) Why don't you fly?
(48) I don't want Bonnie coming in here
(49) A stick that we hit peoples with
(50) I don't know who he gots
(51) Could I take this home?

Note the use of noun and verb inflectional morphology throughout, the use of pronouns, determiners, particles, and AUX *be, do*, and modals; note also the use of passive morphology in (43), overt subject–verb agreement marking where required in (40), (42)–(46), and (50), moved constituents in (44), (47), and (49)–(51), and embedded sentences in (46) and (48)–(50). Though not formally examined, his phonology appeared to be adult-like and problem-free. We see, therefore, that Antony's grammar was quite mature, although not yet fully acquired – note, for example, the grammatical errors in (41), (49), and (50).

Antony's utterances were semantically deficient, however. He made frequent lexical errors (*birthday* for *cake, taking* for *dropping, horn* for *drum*, and *two* and *sister* in (41) above), errors involving the wrong preposition (*to* for *with, in* for *with*), or wrong pronoun (*he* for *it, that* for *he, he* for *she*). Interestingly, his lexical choice errors did not violate syntactic class, subcategorization features, or grammatical case. As a case in point, his pronoun errors were almost exclusively errors of gender, number, or animacy, and not of morphological form. In like fashion, he occasionally selected the wrong *wh*-word, but never substituted a different kind of pronoun instead.

More serious, however, was the fact that Antony's utterances did not appear to mean what they would be expected to mean. Deictic and anaphoric pronouns were often used erroneously, and when coupled with a limited and at times misused lexicon, frequently led to misinterpretations and communicative errors. The tense and aspect morphology he used also did not map onto meaning in a consistent way (e.g. past could mean present, past, or future and *vice versa*, progressive could mean habitual and *vice versa*).

His pragmatic skills were also markedly deficient. He evidenced considerable problems with topic maintenance and control. In dyadic discourse, for example, he inappropriately introduced new topics 30% of the time and in general seemed to be limited to very short communicative exchanges. Although he would continue to take turns when conversationally appropriate, longer exchanges appeared to place a burden on his limited communicative ability which he could meet only by introducing a new topic, or by repeating a prior utterance either of his own or of his partner.

Antony's nonlinguistic abilities placed him at approximately a 2-year-old level, reflected not only in his test performance and other indices of cognitive function (see above mentioned sources for details), but also in the fact that his 3-year-old brother treated Antony as a 'younger,' less competent child. Antony presents a clear case of grammar maturing independently of both other linguistic and nonlinguistic mental faculties.

Rick

Rick, a mentally retarded adolescent, 15 years of age at data collection time, suffered anoxia at birth and has been institutionalized in a state hospital for the severely retarded almost his entire life. He has severe and debilitating motor handicaps which leave him unable to sit erect, stand, or walk. He performs at a preschool (preoperational) level on nonlinguistic tasks involving drawing, classification, number concepts, and logical sequencing, as well as on Piagetian tests of seriation and conservation.

Rick possesses well-developed phonological and morphosyntactic knowledge coupled with a limited lexicon with numerous incompletely or incorrectly specified entries. Sample utterances are presented in (52)–(61):

(52) You already got it working
(53) They just ask for money
(54) If they get in trouble, they'd have a pillow fight
(55) She's the one that walks back and forth to school
(56) She keeps both of the ribbons on her hair
(57) It was hitten by a road, but one car stopped and the other came
(58) I find pictures that are gone
(59) She must've got me up and thrown me out of bed
(60) It's what I do
(61) I wanna hear one more just for a change

Note the full elaboration of nouns and verbs, including the extra passive morphology in (57), the rich AUX structures, the consistent adherence to subcategorization constraints and θ-structure, and the embedding of sentences as *wh-* and participial complements in (52) and (60) and as relatives in (55) and (58).

Rick's propositional semantic problems can be seen, even out of context, in examples (54), (58), and (61). Additional examples showing his lexical and propositional deficiencies can be seen in examples (62)–(65):

(62) R: (I) Played checkers [R doesn't know how.]
      S: How do you play?
      R: You just, you just put one pile in.
      S: One pile of what?
      R: One pile of cards.
      S: And then what?
      R: And then you put another tape. [R is looking at a tape recorder]

(63) S: . . . tell us what she looks like.
      R: She looks like she has blonde hair.
      S: What color is blonde?
      R: Black.

(64) S: How does she wear her hair?
      R: She wears it up in a pony tail.
      S: How long is it?
      R: It's big around her pony tail.
      S: When she takes her pony tail out, how long is it?
      R: It's wh, shorter.
      S: Shorter than what?
      R: Like whiskers.
      S: Is it as short as yours?
      R: Yes.
      S: How can she get it in a pony tail?
      R: She can get a pony tail from someone else.

(65) R: I liked the airplane.
      D: What airplane's that?
      R: The one that looks like a rocket.
      D: Which one's that? Where'd you see that?
      R: On television.
      D: What show was it on?
      R: ——

> D: Do you know?
> R: ——
> D: What was the rocket doing?
> R: Falling.
> D: Falling? Falling from where?
> R: Falling from the floor.

Rick has highly developed interactive pragmatic skills, especially with respect to the use of social formulas and other interactive conversational devices, as illustrated in (66)–(69) (note italicized phrases):

(66) D: Hi, Rick.
   R: Hi.
   D: Good to see you.
   R: *Good to see you, too.*

(67) D: Wanna turn the page?
   R: *Sure*, Dan, I'll turn.

(68) S: Is my name Marsha?
   R: No.
   S: Is my name Susie?
   R: No.
   S: What is it?
   R: It's Daniel. *Sweetheart, you're for me.*

(69) (After listening to a tape of music)
   M: How'd you like it?
   R: *I think it looks all right.*

Note that Rick sometimes uses a routinized phrase when semantically inappropriate or perhaps even pragmatically inappropriate (69).

In summary, in Rick, as in Antony, we see a profile of intact grammar acquisition relative to lexical and nonlinguistic development. However, in contrast to Antony, Rick has considerable pragmatic ability, demonstrating, therefore, the potential independence of grammatical, referential, and socio-communicative development from each other.

Marta

A third case is Marta, who was studied between the ages of 16 and 18 (see Yamada 1981, 1983; Curtiss in press, for details). Estimates of Marta's IQ range from 41 to 48. All developmental milestones, including linguistic milestones, were delayed. However, by the age of 4 or 5 years, Marta's language ability clearly outstripped her development in other areas.

The pattern of Marta's linguistic abilities is very much like Antony's and Rick's – a mature grammatical system in the context of considerable semantic and cognitive deficiencies. Marta is considerably more verbose than either Antony or Rick, however, and her verbosity combined with her age may make Marta's case illustrative of the eventual or 'steady' state linguistic system attained or attainable under such conditions.

Marta's speech is mature and well-formed phonologically, rich and complex morphosyntactically. Her lexicon is also rich, and her utterances long and propositionally complicated. She makes many lexical errors, however, and her sentences are often propositionally unclear. Samples of Marta's spontaneous speech are presented in (70)–(88):

(70) He's my third principal I've had since I've been here [untrue]
(71) I love eating meals
(72) Did you hear about me not going to this school up in [name of city]?
(73) I should have brought it back
(74) Last year at [name of school] when I first went there, 3 tickets were gave out by a police last year
(75) I don't want to get eaten by one
(76) I haven't shown you my garage yet, but my Dad would be really hard
(77) It is very soon that they asked us to fly out
(78) She does paintings, this really good friend of the kids who I went to school with last year and really loved
(79) He was saying that I lost my battery powered watch that I loved
(80) The police pulled my mother and so I said he would never remember them as long as we live!
(81) Oh, frack, we finally got that new Mexican 'cause his flights came in Wednesday month
(82) I think I was nineteen, when I changed dates
(83) And I told the head leader they're not sure if they're gonna set it for, for eight, eighth, out time which will be as [abrupt pause] our time and, the girl arrives where it's one, which is in school right now
(84) I was like 15 or 19 when I started moving out o' home, so now I'm like 15 now, and I can go
(85) It's no, the place where I get my hair cut, pays an hour if it's a woman, I think if it's a man it pays, he pays, 5 hours, I think of work he pays, 5 hours, I think of work he pays

(86) She was thinking that it's no regular school, it's just plain old no buses . . .

(87) It's 1976 because Nixon threw up [actually 1980]

(88) It was broken, desperately broken [re. her watch]

Note the consistent morphological elaboration of nouns and verbs, including passive morphology in (75); consistent marking of subject–verb agreement in (70), (74), (77), (78), (83)–(87); the rich AUX structures, e.g. in (73), (76), (84); the embedded sentences, including relative clauses in (70), (78), (79), (83), (85), *wh*-complements in (79), (80), (83), (86), gerundive and participial complements in (71), (72), and infinitival complements in (75), (77); adjunct clauses in (74), (82)–(84); and movement structures, including focus constructions (passives and clefts in (74), (75), (77)) and object gaps in (70), (78), (79). Many of these sentences involve multiple embeddings and/or multiple movement structures, e.g. (74), (78), (79), (82), (83), (85). Note in contrast, the clear lexical errors (*police* in (74), *hard* in (76), *desperately* in (88)), especially frequent with temporal, numerical, and quantitative terms as in (70), (77), (78), (81)–(86); note also the ill-formed concatenation of propositions in (76), (80), (82), (83), (84), (86).

Like Antony, however, despite Marta's lexical semantic limitations, she has productive word formation devices – see (89)–(92):

(89) I don't have a *roomer*. My roommate left

(90) Well, big *upsetness*!!

(91) We went *car-looking*

(92) And the lady, the *Bullocker*, very young, that cuts hair, . . .
      [referring to a hairdresser in Bullocks department store]

Marta's pragmatic abilities are also limited. She appropriately uses social rituals and other automatic phrases (*'Well'*, *'you know'*, *'I think'*, *'hey'*), giving her conversational turns the trappings of conventional dialog; but she often uses deictic terms and anaphoric pronouns without clear referents, making communication confusing. She also frequently fails to maintain topics, even when a response to a direct question is called for.

6.3. Summary

To summarize, in the cases presented above we find several different profiles with respect to the integrity of grammatical, semantic, and pragmatic development. In all of the cases, grammar and semantics were consistently dissociated, but the relationship between semantic and pragmatic development was more variable. Semantic development appears tied to conceptual and logical function – both relatively preserved in Genie and Chelsea's case,

111

both markedly deficient in Antony, Rick, and Marta's case. Pragmatic ability appears tied to both social and cognitive function, with topic-related abilities related to cognitive maturity, but rules and conventions of discourse more related to psychosocial integrity. Thus, on the one hand, Genie had relatively good topic-related skills, whereas Antony, Rick, and Marta had notable deficiencies in this area. On the other hand, Genie had sorely deficient knowledge of the social conventions of discourse, whereas Chelsea, Antony, Rick, and Marta appeared fairly normal in this area. Each of these areas, then, appears to constitute a distinct component of linguistic knowledge: (1) a *referential/propositional* component, which includes knowledge of semantic feature specifications and knowledge of propositional form and relations, and which appears to intersect with conceptual knowledge, the system of object-reference, and logical structure; (2) a *social-communicative* component, which includes the rules governing the use of language for communicative purposes, and which appears to intersect with the rule system governing nonlinguistic communication and social interaction; and (3) a *grammatical* component, which includes the rules of phonology, morphology, syntax, and logical form, and is an autonomous system of knowledge.

6.4. Discussion

A basic tenet of neuropsychology is the 'transparency' assumption: the assumption that one can extrapolate from the abnormal case to the normal case. On this assumption, instances of abnormal language acquisition can help to shed light on the mechanisms and principles of normal language acquisition. The cases presented above provide evidence that grammar acquisition can be dissociated from other aspects of language learning, from nonlinguistic cognitive development, and from other aspects of communicative ability, and is, therefore, an autonomous knowledge system. On the transparency assumption, this should hold true in normal language acquisition as well. While the data may be more clear-cut in abnormal cases, there are data from acquisition in normals confirming these findings.

First, in cases where the child and her language learning mechanisms are normal, but the language learning circumstances are not (as is the case in blind children, for example), one finds relatively intact grammar acquisition alongside more problematic pragmatic development (Urwin 1978; Anderson & Kekelis 1982 and personal communication; Landau & Gleitman 1985) and, some researchers argue, lexical semantic development as well (Dunlea 1982; Anderson, Dunlea, & Kekelis 1984).

Second, in cases such as acquisition of American Sign Language (ASL) as a native language, where the language learning circumstances afford an opportunity to directly examine the relationship between communicative development and acquisition of formal linguistic structures, one finds strong evidence that the two are maturationally and cognitively independent. Both Petitto (1983) and Jackson (1984) have found that the acquisition and use of isomorphically identical movements which in one instance are communicative gestures (e.g. deictic pointing, a head shake for 'no'), and in another are linguistic forms (e.g. pronouns, negative marker), are clearly distinct. Despite the iconicity of the ASL signs in question and the formational identity of the gestures and signs, Petitto and Jackson report that the signs were learned significantly later and were associated with errors which can only be explained by an analysis into their formal linguistic properties.

Third, in normal acquisition under normal circumstances there also can be a notable asynchrony between semantic and morphosyntactic development. Reilly (1982) presents clear evidence of such asynchrony in the acquisition of conditionals. Lord (1979) presents similar findings in the acquisition of causative structures.

Not only do I accept the transparency hypothesis, I find evidence for it in my own home. While my normally developing daughter, Rebecca, had the audacity not to be an early talker, she had the good sense to provide me with data confirming the independence of grammar acquisition. Sentences like (93)–(98) were not uncommon in Rebecca's speech (distressing her father a little, but pleasing her mother quite a bit):

(93)   When I was a dog, on the third day, I was a baby the third day, and I had blue pajamas [2;8]
(94)   That's a big whole baby in the south [2;8]
(95)   Be quiet and you'll never be loud enough if I be quiet [2;8]
(96)   I took it off and I put it in my ponytail [re. a rubber band that *had* been in her hair]
(97)   Now it's not gone and it's still gone [2;8]
(98)   She *was*, in a couple of hours [2;10]

Thus, even my 2-year-old daughter believes in the necessity of a theory of language acquisition that allows for the independent growth of syntax and semantics. Why, just the other day, during a game of Zoo Lotto, she argued for a modular theory of mind, wherein grammar (and its acquisition) is based on domain-specific cognitive principles. In her view the principles of UG (whatever their final version) are specific to the language faculty and are not a set of principles constraining cognitive systems more generally. She thinks the data I've presented in this chapter support this view. It's good to know I'm doing something right.

REFERENCES

Anderson, E. & Kekelis, L. 1982. Effects of visual impairment on early mother–child communication. Paper presented at the Boston University Conference on Language Development.

Anderson, E., Dunlea, A. & Kekelis, L. 1984. Blind children's language: resolving some differences. *Journal of Child Language* 11: 645–64.

Aram, D. M., Ekelman, B. L. & Whitaker, H. A. 1986. Spoken syntax in children with acquired unilateral hemispheric lesions. *Brain and Language* 27: 75–100.

Aram, D. M., Ekelman, B. L., Rose, D. F. & Whitaker, H. A. 1985. Verbal and cognitive sequelae following unilateral lesions in early childhood. *Journal of Clinical and Experimental Neuropsychology* 7: 55–78.

Bates, E., Bretherton, I., Camaoni, L. & Volterra, V. 1979. Cognition and communication from 9 to 13 months: correlational findings. In E. Bates (ed.) *The emergence of symbols: cognition and communication in infancy*. New York: Academic Press.

Bruner, J. 1977. Early social interaction and language acquisition. In H. R. Schaffer (ed.) *Studies in mother–infant interaction*. New York: Academic Press.

Bruner, J. & Ninio, A. 1978. The achievement of antecedents of labeling. *Journal of Child Language* 5: 1–19.

Chomsky, N. 1980. *Rules and representations*. New York: Columbia University Press.

Curtiss, S. 1977. *Genie: A psycholinguistic study of a modern-day 'wild-child'*. New York: Academic Press.

Curtiss, S. 1979. Genie: Language and cognition. *UCLA Working Papers in Cognitive Linguistics* 1: 15–62.

Curtiss, S. 1981a. Feral children. *Mental Retardation* 12: 129–61.

Curtiss, S. 1981b. Dissociations between language and cognition. *Journal of Autism and Developmental Disorders* 11: 15–30.

Curtiss, S. 1982. Developmental dissociations of language and cognition. In L. Obler & L. Menn (eds.) *Exceptional language and linguistic theory*. New York: Academic Press.

Curtiss, S. 1985. The development of human cerebral lateralization. In D. F. Benson & E. Zaidel (eds.) *The dual brain*. New York: Guilford.

Curtiss, S. In press. The special talent of grammar acquisition. In L. Obler & D. Fein (eds.) *The neuropsychology of talent and special abilities*. New York: Guilford.

Curtiss, S. & Yamada, J. 1981. Selectively intact grammatical development in a retarded child. *UCLA Working Papers in Cognitive Linguistics* 3: 161–75.

Curtiss, S., Fromkin, V., Krashen, S., Rigler, D. & Rigler, M. 1974. The linguistic development of Genie. *Language* 50: 528–54.

Day, P. & Ulatowska, H. 1979. Perceptual, cognitive, and linguistic development after early hemispherectomy: two case studies. *Brain and Language* 7: 17–33.

Denckla, M. B. & Rudel, R. 1976a. Naming of object drawings by dyslexic and other learning disabled children. *Brain and Language* 3: 1–16.

Denckla, M. B. & Rudel, R. 1976b. Rapid 'automatized' naming (RAN): dyslexia differentiated from other learning disabilities. *Neuropsychologia* 14: 471–9.

Dennis, M. 1980a. Capacity and strategy for syntactic comprehension after left or right hemidecortication. *Brain and Language* 10: 287–317.

Dennis, M. 1980b. Language acquisition in a single hemisphere: semantic organization. In D. Caplan (ed.) *Biological studies of mental processes*. Cambridge, MA: MIT Press.

Dennis, M. & Whitaker, H. A. 1976. Language acquisition following hemidecortication: linguistic superiority of the left over the right hemisphere. *Brain and Language* 3: 404–33.

Dennis, M. & Whitaker, H. A. 1977. Hemispheric equipotentiality and language acquisition. In S. Segalowitz & F. Gruber (eds.) *Language development and neurological theory*. New York: Academic Press.

Drake, W. 1968. Clinical and pathological findings in a child with developmental learning disability. *Journal of Learning Disabilities* 1: 9–25.

Dunlea, A. 1982. The role of visual information in the emergence of meaning: a comparison of blind and sighted children. Doctoral dissertation, University of Southern California.

Fischer, S. & Mayberry, R. 1982. Memory and shadowing of ASL: qualitative measures. Paper presented at the Annual Meeting of the Linguistic Society of America, San Diego.

Fromkin, V., Krashen, S., Curtiss, S., Rigler, D. & Rigler, M. 1974. The development of language in Genie: a case of language acquisition beyond the 'critical period.' *Brain and Language* 1: 81–107.

Galaburda, A. M. & Kemper, T. L. 1979. Cytoarchitectonic abnormalities in developmental dyslexia: a case study. *Annals of Neurology* 6: 94–100.

Geschwind, N. & Galaburda, A. M. 1985. Cerebral lateralization: biological mechanisms, associations, and pathology. I: A hypothesis and a program for research. *Archives of Neurology* 42: 428–59.

Jackson, C. 1984. Language acquisition in two modalities: person deixis and negation in American Sign Language and English. MA thesis, University of California at Los Angeles.

Jansky, J. & de Hirsch, K. 1976. Comments at Masland talk on word-finding disorders. Orton Society, New York.

Johnston, J. & Weismer, S. 1983. Mental rotation abilities in language disordered children. *Journal of Speech and Hearing Research* 26: 397–403.

Kamhi, A., Catts, H., Koenig, L. & Lewis, B. 1984. Hypothesis testing and nonlinguistic symbolic abilities in language-impaired children. *Journal of Speech and Hearing Research* 49: 162–76.

Kean, M.-L. 1984. The question of linguistic anomaly in developmental dyslexia. *Annals of Dyslexia* 34: 137–51.

Landau, B. & Gleitman, L. R. 1985. *Language and experience: evidence from the blind child.* Cambridge, MA: Harvard University Press.

Lenneberg, E. 1967. *Biological foundations of language.* New York: Wiley.

Lock, A. (ed.) 1978. *Action, gesture, and Symbol.* New York: Academic Press.

Lord, C. 1979. 'Don't you fall me down': Children's generalizations regarding cause and transitivity. *Papers and Reports in Child Language Development* 17.

MacNamara, J. 1972. The cognitive basis of language learning in infants. *Psychological Review* 79: 1–13.

Macnamara, J. 1977. From sign to language. In J. MacNamara (ed.) *Language learning and thought.* New York: Academic Press.

Mayberry, R. 1979. Facial expression and redundancy in American Sign Language. Doctoral dissertation, McGill University.

Mayberry, R., Fischer, S. & Hatfield, N. 1983. Sentence repetition in American Sign Language. In J. Kyle & B. Woll (eds.) *Language in sign: international perspectives on sign language.* London: Croom Helm.

McKinney, V. 1983. First language learning in deaf persons beyond the critical period. Doctoral dissertation, Claremont Graduate School.

Newport, E. 1984. Constraints on learning: studies in the acquisition of ASL. *Papers and Reports on Child Language Development* 23: 1–22.

Petitto, L. 1983. From gesture to symbol: the relationship between form and meaning in the acquisition of personal pronouns in American Sign Language. Doctoral dissertation, Harvard University.

Piaget, J. 1980. Schemes of action and language learning. In M. Piattelli-Palmarini (ed.) *Language and learning: the debate between Jean Piaget and Noam Chomsky.* Cambridge, MA: Harvard University Press.

Rankin, J., Aram, D. & Horwitz, S. 1980. A comparison of right and left hemiplegic children's language ability. Paper presented at the International Neuropsychological Society Annual Meeting, San Francisco.

Ratner, N. & Bruner, J. 1978. Games, social exchange, and the acquisition of language. *Journal of Child Language* 5: 391–401.

Reilly, J. 1982. Acquisition of conditionals in English. Doctoral dissertation, University of California at Los Angeles.

Supalla, T. In press. Structure and acquisition of verbs of motion and location in American Sign Language. Cambridge, MA: Bradford Books/MIT Press.

Tallal, P. 1975. Perceptual and linguistic factors in the language impairment of developmental dysphasics: an experimental investigation with the Token Test. *Cortex* 11: 196–205.

Tallal, P. 1976. Rapid auditory processing in normal and disordered language development. *Journal of Speech and Hearing Research* 19: 561–71.

Tartter, V. & Fischer, S. 1982. Perceiving minimal distinctions in ASL under normal and point-light display conditions. *Perception and Psychophysics* 32: 327–34.

Urwin, C. 1978. The development of communication between blind infants and their parents. In Lock (1978).

Vellutino, F. 1979. *Dyslexia*. Cambridge, MA: MIT Press.

Wolf, M. 1986. Rapid alternating stimulus naming in the developmental dyslexias. *Brain and Language* 27: 360–79.

Woodward, J. 1973. Inter-rule implication in American Sign Language. *Sign Language Studies* 3: 47–56.

Yamada, J. 1981. Evidence for the independence of language and cognition: case study of a 'hyperlinguistic' adolescent. *UCLA Working Papers in Cognitive Linguistics* 3: 121–60.

Yamada, J. 1983. The independence of language: A case study. Doctoral dissertation, University of California, Los Angeles.

Young, R. 1981. Sign language acquisition in a deaf adult: a test of the critical period hypothesis. Doctoral dissertation, University of Georgia.

Zaidel, E. 1973. Linguistic competence and related functions in the right cerebral hemisphere of man following commissurotomy and hemispherectomy. Doctoral dissertation, California Institute of Technology.

Zaidel, E. 1977. Unilateral auditory language comprehension on the Token Test following cerebral commissurotomy and hemispherectomy. *Neuropsychologia* 15: 1–18.

7 Grammatical aspects of speech errors
Victoria A. Fromkin

'A final word about the theory of errors. Here it is that the causes are complex and multiple . . .'

Henri Poincaré 1854–1912 (Reprinted in Newman 1956)

'Give me fruitful error any time, full of seeds, bursting with its own corrections.'

Vilfredo Pareto 1848–1923 (Quoted in Mackay 1981)

7.1. Historical background

Linguists have been collecting and analyzing slips of the tongue at least as far back as the eighth century CE when the Arab linguist Al-Ki-sa'i wrote his book *Errors of the populace* (Anwar 1979). As Anwar (1979, 1981) points out, more than a hundred books on speech errors written by Arab grammarians have been published since that seminal work, many during the important medieval period of Arabic linguistic studies.[1]

Although a number of these medieval studies have prescriptivist intent, using the term 'error' primarily in reference to wrong usage by non-native speakers of Arabic or speakers of nonstandard dialects, the grammarians also recorded, analyzed and classified a wide variety of slips of the tongue, i.e. 'unintentional linguistic innovation(s)' (Sturtevant 1947) or 'involuntary deviation(s) in performance from the speaker's current phonological, grammatical or lexical intention(s)' (Boomer & Laver 1968), as is being done by linguists today. Like Paul (1886, 1919), Sturtevant (1917), Jespersen (1922) and Meringer (1908), many of the medieval Arab studies were motivated by an interest in speech errors as a possible cause of historical change; others attempted to provide phonetic and phonological explanations in terms of assimilatory factors and/or the interface between phonological and morphological processes. Anticipations, deletions, and insertions of linguistic units were noted in studies conducted over eleven centuries ago.

Cutler's (1982a) bibliography on speech errors lists ten of these early studies including a ninth-century manuscript of As-Sikkit and a tenth-century work of Al-Jawzi. The bibliography contains references to 315 books and

---

[1] Anwar is justifiably critical of Fromkin's (1971, 1973) and Cutler & Fay's (1978) reference to Rudolf Meringer (Meringer & Mayer 1895; Meringer 1905) as 'the father of the linguistic interest in speech errors' (Fromkin 1971). It would unfortunately not be the first time that Western 'scholarship' revealed its ethnocentricity.

117

articles on slips of the tongue and related subjects (slips of the ear – hearing misperceptions, slips of the pen – writing errors, tongue twisters, slips of the hand in signing, slips of the eye – reading errors, and slips of the mind) published up to April 1982, but, as the author points out, the 'coverage falls far short of being complete' even in regard to these error types. In addition, other kinds of errors – second language errors, children's errors in acquisition, aphasic errors (except where normal errors are also discussed), tip-of-the-tongue phenomena, errors of action, and typing errors were deliberately excluded.

82% of the entries in the Cutler bibliography (258 out of 315) were published after 1950, and 223 since 1970. In the four years since the bibliography was prepared, a sizeable number of additional publications have appeared. Thus, although there has been linguistic interest in speech errors since the work of the Arabic grammarians, the last three decades show that such data are now being regarded as increasingly important by linguists and psycholinguists in the development and testing of theoretical and processing models. Since speech errors are used as evidence for hypotheses concerning the mental grammar, general linguistic interest in such data had to wait until the emergence of Chomskyan theory (Chomsky 1957) in the late 1950s which 'overthrew' the anti-mentalist behaviorism which dominated American linguistics for three decades (Newmeyer 1986). Those who agreed with Twaddell (1935:57) that 'the linguistic processes of the "mind" are . . . simply unobservable . . . we have no right to guess about the linguistic workings of an inaccessible "mind",' would clearly be uninterested in errors which can only be understood by reference to the linguistic workings of the mind which, through errors as well as through error-free language data, become accessible.

The scientific interest in speech errors is, of course, not limited to the linguistic community and, as is to be expected, the questions that are asked in the analyses of the errors, and the hypotheses that are tested, differ according to the aims of the investigator.[2]

Some psychologists, for example, are less concerned with how speech errors reflect the underlying linguistic system than with what they reveal about the psychological mechanisms which create or cause the occurrence of such errors. Freud's interest in speech errors (1901/1958, 1916/1974) lay in what they revealed about repressed thoughts. He suggested that speech errors 'arise from the concurrent action – or perhaps rather, the mutually opposing action – of two different intentions' (1916/1974), with one of these the conscious message target of the speaker and the second, which may or

---

[2] The creative use of speech errors for humor or other effects is extensive in world literature; see Fromkin (1971) for examples from Rabelais, Peacham, and Carroll, and Robins (1966) for additional literary references.

may not be conscious, revealed by the slip. This view is not too different from that expressed by Hippocrates who, in the fourth century BCE suggested that some speech errors occur 'because before a thought is expressed other thoughts arise, before words are spoken, other words are formed.'

This 'competing plan hypothesis' also underlies much of the current research of Baars and Motley (e.g. Baars 1980, Motley, Baars & Camden 1983) echoing an earlier suggestion of Hockett (1967:117): 'A single individual's share of articulatory equipment is such that two words or phrases cannot be uttered simultaneously. The attempt to do so can only result in the production of a string of sounds drawn partly from each of the two words or phrases.' Hockett thus concludes that 'a wide variety of lapses . . . can be handled in terms of two basic mechanisms, blending and editing.'

Freud was interested in determining the reason for the competing 'plan'; Baars and Motley are interested in showing that the existence of such competing plans 'explain' how errors arise in the course of speech. All three suggest the existence of an internal 'censor' or monitor or editor which may itself 'slip', causing an error, which should have been detected and blocked by the monitor, to surface. That is, a thought which arises internally or externally, unconnected to the intended message, becomes or generates the competing plan.

In addition to those who have investigated slips of the tongue because of the light they may shed on the psychology of the speaker, or the psychological causes and mechanisms which produce errors, others have been interested in how speech errors reflect more general neuromotor controls which are posited to account also for nonlinguistic behavioral errors (MacKay 1971; Norman 1981; Bierwisch 1982). Speech errors have also played an increasingly important role in psycholinguistic attempts to construct linguistic performance or processing models (e.g. Fromkin 1971, 1985; Garrett 1975; Cutler 1980a; Butterworth 1981). The focus of this chapter will be primarily on what linguistic theory can tell us about the nature of speech errors.

7.2. Speech errors and linguistic theory

A basic assumption of all linguistic speech error research is that an analysis of these data:

> . . . can give some clues to the particular mechanisms of language production, in which the abnormal case – in accordance with a general methodological principle – can lead to conclusions about the factors involved in normal functioning. . . . (T)he phenomena involved in spontaneously produced incorrect sentences can (thus) be of interest in sorting out questions of the linguistic system proper.

119

> . . . The fact is not surprising, since the essential factor in linguistic behavior is linguistic competence (i.e. the mental grammar) so that all phenomena of language production, even pathological phenomena, can be related to competence . . . (L)inguistic and psycholinguistic analyses of spontaneous error, if they are to be meaningful, can only be made against the background of significant hypotheses concerning the structure of the language in question. (Bierwisch 1982:31)

Without these linguistically 'significant hypotheses' we would be unable to reconstruct the intended utterance from which the actual utterance deviates and, more importantly, would be unable to reveal the nature of the deviance. Furthermore, the interpretation and analysis of spontaneous speech errors may help to clarify concepts, reveal inconsistencies in the theory, and lead to new hypotheses concerning the unimpaired system. However, whereas a viable interpretation of speech errors depends on the existence of grammatical theory, the reverse is not true. Speech errors may be used as evidence, but, given the accumulation of linguistic evidence *per se*, are no more necessary than any other kind of performance data.

Speech errors and other behavioral data, however, are of interest to linguists because of the implicit or explicit acceptance of the 'contention that the rules of grammar enter into the processing mechanisms' such that 'evidence concerning production, recognition, recall, and language use in general can . . . have bearing on the investigation of rules of grammar, on . . . "grammatical competence" or "knowledge of language" ' (Chomsky 1980:200–1).

It should be pointed out at the start that, to date, speech error data have not led to new grammatical concepts. They have helped to decide, in a few cases, between competing linguistic hypotheses, but not between theories of grammar, except in the most general sense. Future research may be fruitful in this direction, particularly if linguists investigate speech errors with this goal in mind. Such data have been more valuable in establishing stages and levels in processing models and in modeling the structure of the lexicon (Fromkin forthcoming; see also Chapter 5 in Volume III of this series, by Emmorey and Fromkin).

As we will see below, the attempt to understand (and explain) the kinds of speech errors that occur would not be possible without general linguistic concepts. All theories of grammar (however they may differ in detail, concepts or goals) posit a number of basic components: phonology, morphology, lexicon, syntax, semantics. Questions of interest concern the autonomy of these components, the ways in which they interact, their units and the forms of their representation, and the rules which constrain the well-formedness of structures. It is interesting that spontaneously produced speech errors reveal deviations in the units and rules of all these components, occurring at different stages of the production of an utterance (which parallel, but may not be identical to, the stages in a derivation of a sentence).

There are two major kinds of errors: those involving linguistic units, e.g. disordering, deletion, or addition of intended segments, morphemes, words; and those involving grammatical rules, e.g. application of a rule which should not apply, or failure to apply a rule which should.

Furthermore, errors occurring at one stage of production may produce what Garrett (1980a) refers to as 'accommodatory' phenomena. For example, misordering of phonological segments may result in the application or reapplication of a morphophonemic rule, showing that rules in the competence grammar may also serve as real-time processing rules. Examples of these two major classes of speech errors as occurring in all the components of the grammar are illustrated in the following lists:[3]

(Note that the intended utterance occurs on the left side of the arrow; the actual utterance containing the error on the right side.)

(1)   Phonology
      a. fish grotto   → frish gotto (segment)
      b. reasonably careful→ reasonably carepul (S) (feature)
      c. computation → ponkutation (homorganic nasal rule)
        [mp]   → [ŋk]

(2)   Morphology
      a. many ministers in our church → many churches in our minister
      b. a language acquisition problem → an anguage lacquisition . . .
        $a → an/—V$ (when a=indefinite morpheme) (G)
        [Author's note: A schwa followed by a vowel as in *American is*
        beautiful is permitted by the phonology. Therefore, the change
        from *a* to *an* is not the result of a phonetic 'fix-up' rule, but the
        application of a morphophonemic rule.]
      c. he swam in the pool → he swimmed in the pool
      d. motionless → immotionly

(3)   Syntax
      a. It's not possible that he's going → It's possible that he's not
        going (neg-shift)
      b. *She made him to do the assignment over (non-deletion of *to*)

---

[3] The source of the speech errors taken from the UCLA corpus of close to 15,000 errors collected by the author will be unmarked; those from Garrett (1975, 1980a,b) will be designated by (G) and those from Stemberger (1984) by (S).

    c. *Marcel wanted her play the sonata   (deletion of *to*)

    d. *What it is that has to be welded?   (failure to invert)

(4)   Lexicon/semantics

    a. That's a horse of another color → . . . of another race

    b. edited/annotated → editated   (blend)

    c. Three, five and eight are the worst years for wine → . . . are the worst years for beer

    d. the A over A constraint → the A over B constraint

    e. Don't burn your fingers → Don't burn your toes

    f. Some semantic facts → some syntactic facts

    g. Don't forget to return *Aspects* → . . . to return *Structures* uh – *Aspects*

    h. the four deaf children → the four blind – uh, deaf children

    i. the Razamouvsky Number 3 → the Razamouvsky Number 59 (Note: the Beethoven Razamouvsky quartets are Opus 59)

The remaining sections of this chapter will discuss the conclusions drawn from these different kinds of errors. Much of what follows will probably be uncontroversial and already known to the reader; the aim is simply to summarize the 'state of the art' in linguistic speech error research.

7.3. Competence vs. performance

Long before anyone investigated the linguistic aspect of slips of the tongue, it was commonly agreed that, underlying the semi-continuous nature of the speech signal produced by the speaker and comprehended by the listener, there was an abstract string of discrete phonological segments, grouped into a hierarchical structure composed of larger discrete phrases, words, and morphemes. Such abstract units are not normally observed in error-free utterances, although one can easily tease out such units by, for example, asking subjects (even students in introductory classes) to divide sentences into phonological, lexical, morphological, or syntactic units. Such discrete segments or structures are made transparent in speech errors, as is reported in the vast literature referred to above, and as further shown in the following examples:

(5)   Discreteness of linguistic units

    a. Cedars of Lebanon → Cedars of Lemadon (phonological feature)

    b. brake fluid → blake fruid   (consonant segment)

    c. *ad hoc* → odd hack   (vowel segment)

   d. unanimity of opinion → unamity. . .   (stress 'unit')
      [junənímət i]   [junǽmət i]
   e. easily enough → easy enoughly   (stem, affix morphemes)
   f. Are my tires touching the curb? → Are my legs touching the
      curb?   (semantic features? words)
   g. rules of word formation → words of rule formation
      (inflectional morpheme, stem)
   h. tend to turn out → turn to tend out   (word)

These errors illustrate the distinction between the discrete character of
the abstract structures of the intended utterance, and the analog nature of its
physical signal. This conclusion is hardly a contemporary one. As pointed out
by Cutler & Fay, Meringer (1908) made reference implicitly, if not explicitly,
to eight of the 11 characteristics noted by Fromkin (1971), including:

> (1) the reality of the phonetic segment . . . , (2) consonant clusters as
> sequences of segments . . . , (3) the indivisibility of diphthongs . . . ,
> (4) the reality of phonetic features . . . , (5) the reality of the syllabic
> unit . . . , (6) the phonological regularity of errors . . . , (7) the reality
> of the word, its form class, and of compound nouns . . . , and (8) the
> reality of semantic features. (Cutler & Fay 1978: xvii)

None of these characteristics could have been understood without reference
to the linguistic competence grammar. It is thus strange to note that the
distinction between linguistic competence and performance should remain
controversial.

The errors cited above also show grammatical rules 'at work' in performance. That they can be violated does not negate their existence as rules of
grammar. Derwing (1973:310) suggested that we replace the notion of a
grammar as 'a system of rules' which express the basic regularities of a
language, with a notion of 'linguistic rule which can be directly elicited from
surface structures.' But the very existence of speech errors shows that such
rules can not be so elicited. He further proposes:

> that we replace Chomsky's abstract notion of a rule with a
> reconceptualization specifically designed to represent part of a model
> of linguistic behavior (a performance model), that is, a model in which
> 'putting rules to use' means simply behaving according to the rules.
> This decision has the important immediate consequence of implying
> that one kind of evidence is necessary if we are to justify the formation
> of any particular rule: we must demonstrate that the linguistic
> behavior of the speaker, at least is 'regular' in the manner stated by
> the rule . . . We must demonstrate, in short, that the speaker does

behave according to the rule . . . We may then postulate that the rule in question is a general surface-structure constraint (or 'output condition') on the form of utterances, and the language user has learned he must conform to it.

Derwing concludes: 'Under a direct behavioral interpretation, . . . it will no longer be possible to hide behind a competence/performance distinction.'

But positing a competence/performance distinction is not hiding behind anything; it is, rather, recognizing a traditional distinction between knowledge and behavior. Without such a distinction we could not possibly understand speech errors. In addition, speech errors invalidate any rule viewed as a surface structure constraint or output condition. Without the notion of a rule which represents stored knowledge, rather than behavior, we would be unable to recognize a violation of a rule, and would therefore be unable to recognize that an error had occurred. Output conditions must be competence conditions, because actual speech violates such conditions. It is only by recognizing the competence/performance, or grammar/processing distinction that speech error research is possible.

7.4. **Phonological errors**

7.4.1. **Features**

There are a number of phonological errors included in Meringer's published corpus that involve features rather than entire segments. Celce-Murcia (1973) groups these according to the following features: umlaut, ablaut, vowel length, voicing, affrication, nasality. Fromkin (1973) lists 55 feature errors. Many phonological errors are ambiguous as to whether they involve whole segments or segmental features:

(6)   feèd the póoch → Foòd the péach
       (/i/ ↔ /u/ or [−back] ↔ [+back])
       (Note: Since [−low, +back] vowels are redundantly [+round], the roundness switch is 'automatic'.)

(7)   keèp a tápe → teèp a cápe (/k/ ↔ /t/ or [−coronal] ↔ [+coronal])

(8)   baked macaroons → maked bacaroons
       (/m/ ↔ /b/ or [+nasal] ↔ [−nasal])

A number of researchers report that the relation between the consonants in anticipatory, perseverating, or reversal segmental errors is not a random one, but is dependent to a great extent on their phonological similarity, i.e.

the number of features they have in common. As summarized by van den Broecke & Goldstein (1980): 'Typically, one-feature errors occur more often than two-feature errors, which again occur more often than three-feature errors etc.' (p. 48).

While errors such as those cited in (6)–(8) may not clearly show the independence of phonological features, those in (9)–(13) can only be interpreted as feature errors:

(9) metaphor → menaphor

(10) Is Pat a girl → Is bat a curl

(11) He's a vile person → He's a file person

(12) clear blue sky → glear plue sky

(13) big and fat → pig and vat

In (9) (and in (5a)) only the nasality feature is reversed (with the redundant voicing accommodation); all other segmental features remain as intended; in (10)–(13) only the voicing value is switched.

It may well be that Klatt (1979) is correct in his claim, based on a statistical analysis of consonantal errors, that there is 'little evidence in the speech error corpus to support independently movable distinctive features as psychologically real representational units of utterances.' One would then need some plausible explanation for how such errors arise in spontaneous speech. Furthermore, features must be clearly 'psychologically real' in the mental grammar to account for language change, phonological rules which pertain to classes of sounds based on single features, child language acquisition, morphophonemic patterns etc. Furthermore, there would be no explanation for these errors without a theory of distinctive features: they would appear to be accidental and random.

Roberts (1975) goes so far as to argue that all phonological errors should be viewed as feature errors. Stemberger (1982) counters this opposition to segments by reference to word blends, pointing to the fact that there appear to be no word blends in which a 'new' segment arises containing features from the two blended words, where the segment does not occur totally in one of the words, and therefore that blends appear to occur at the level of segments.

(14) a. smart/clever → smever
     b. frown/scowl → frowl
     c. flavor/taste → flaste (not *tazor) (S)

In (14c) Stemberger points out that *tazor* should be possible as a blend if segments are not the blended elements, since /z/ combines some features of the /s/ in 'taste' and the /v/ in *flavor*. He also uses this fact to argue for

125

separation feature and segmental levels in phonological representation. Although such a blend as *tazor* does not occur in Stemberger's corpus, one cannot be sure that it is an impossible word blend. Whether or not further evidence supports Stemberger's claim that word blends occur only at the level of segments, it is clear that some blends do occur at this level, further supporting the segmental unit. Segment deletion and addition errors such as those illustrated in (5), above seem sufficient to counter Roberts' claim.

Linguistic theory which posits phonetically based features as the most basic phonological element is thus able to account for single feature errors and for the phonological similarity of segments involved in errors (Nooteboom 1969; MacKay 1970; Fromkin 1971; Shattuck-Hufnagel 1979; Shattuck-Hufnagel & Klatt 1979; Soderpalm 1979; Stemberger 1982). Stemberger (1982) found that 88.3% of simple substitution errors, i.e. where one sound is substituted for another with apparently no contextual influence, involved consonants differing by only one feature. Furthermore, 69.3% of the consonants misordered in between-word errors differed only by one feature. He points out that these are far more frequent than would be expected by chance. Only a feature theory can account for such findings.

7.4.2. The abstractness of phonemic segments

Certain controversies in linguistics seem to persist despite mounting evidence to support one among several hypotheses. One such controversy concerns the nature of phonological representation, centering around the question, 'How abstract is phonology?' (Kiparsky 1968). As part of this ongoing controversy, speech errors have been used to support phonological representations of lexical entries which do not constitute a subset of their phonetic representations, and which are more 'abstract' than any phonetic representation (Bond 1969; Fromkin 1972, 1973). Simple segmental errors reveal that the targeted allophonic segments do not occur as such when disordered, but surface as the segment predicted by the new phonological environment:

(15) a. rank order   → rand orker
        [ræŋk ɔrdər] → [rænd ɔrkər]
     b. Bing Crosby   → Big Cronsby
        [bɪŋ krɔzbi] → [bɪg krɔ̃nzbi]
     c. Stan Kenton   → Skan Tenton
        [stæn kʰɛ̃ntən] → [sk . . . tʰ . . .]

It might be that the disordered elements are the targeted phonetic segments which are changed by the phonological rules which are applied to prevent a violation of phonotactic constraints. By this account, the [ŋ] in *rank* would become a homorganic [n] when the [d] replaces the [k], denasalization of a vowel would occur when a following nasal is deleted, and deaspiration of a voiceless stop would occur when the stop is moved to a position following an initial [s]. The speech error data are not conclusive on this question. What is clear from these errors is that phonological rules function as processing rules in addition to stating grammatical constraints on phonetic phonological sequences. Such rules are therefore shown to be used in speech production as well as providing an explicit statement of phonological generalizations.

In addition, speech errors which involve velar nasals are cited (Fromkin 1971) to support an analysis in which /n/ is represented as /ng/.

(16) a. swing and sway → swin and sweyg
   [swɪ̄ŋ] and [swe] → [swɪ̄n] and [sweg]
   (cf: /swɪŋ . . . swe/ → /swɪn . . . sweg/)
   b. Chuck Young → Chunck Yug
   [čʌk jʌ̃ŋg] → [cʌ̃ŋk jʌg]

Stemberger (1983) argues that there are other possible analyses for the nasal errors cited by Fromkin. For example, in an autosegmental analysis, (16b) might be represented as in (17):

(17)   [+nas]   [+nas]
   č ʌ k   j ʌ̂ G → č ʌ k   j ʌ̂ G

The error would then consist of the anticipatory shift of the autosegment [+nas] to the first word. The archisegment /G/ would, according to Stemberger, show up either as /g/ or /n/ 'with /g/ being most likely because of its frequency.' This is an interesting argument which also provides support for archisegments and autosegmental phonology. It is not, however, evident how such an analysis would work for (16a) except by a most complicated process, which is not required with the /ng/ analysis. Example (18) illustrates how the error given in (16a) might be analyzed using an autosegmental nasal representation rather than an /ng/ representation:

(18)   [+nas]   [+nas]
   sw i Ĝ . . . swe → sw i n̂ . . . sw e G

Given this representation, the error may consist of a shift of the archisegment to a later word, which is realized as /g/ for the same frequency reason as given above, and the insertion of an /n/ to replace the moved archisegments because a nasal autosegment must be associated with a consonant as well as a vowel. This may be the case, but it does not seem to be a better solution than the /ng/ solution.

Some stress shift errors also suggest non-surfacing phonological segments:

(19) a. treméndously   → trémenly
     [ə]   [ɛ́]
    b. San Vicente Blvd → San Vinte Blvd
     [vəsénti]   →   [vínti]
    c. specificity   → spec[í]fity

In these errors, a syllable is deleted, resulting in a movement of the primary word stress in accordance with English stress rules (Chomsky & Halle 1968). When the stress has moved, the emerging stressed vowel is given a full vowel articulation, substituting for the reduced schwa target, even if there is no word in the paradigm in which this vowel surfaces, as in (19a) and (19b). The form in (19c) may be the result of the intrusion of another word of the same lexical paradigm, e.g. *specific*. Cutler (1980a,b) suggests that all such stress shifts may be explained in this way; if so, errors such as (19a) and (19b) are unexplained by any of the mechanisms used to account for other errors.

In addition to invoking archisegments to account for the velar nasal errors, Stemberger (1982) presents other speech errors in support of archisegmental representation of lexical items. Fromkin (1973) had argued that at least in the case of stop consonants, speech errors provide evidence against archisegments. If stops after initial /s/ were represented as archisegments, one might expect that when the initial cluster was split in speech errors, voiced and voiceless segments would occur initially with equal probability. In the UCLA corpus, this is not the case:

(20) a. long and strong   → trong and slong   (not *drong)
    b. stick in the mud   → smuck in the tid   (not *did)
    c. speech production → peach seduction (not *beach)

Davidsen-Nielsen (1975), however, in a tongue twister task found that /s/ was added to both voiced and voiceless stops, and conversely, both voiced and voiceless stops surfaced when an /s/ was deleted. This would support an archisegmental solution, and, as already pointed out, the homorganic nasal accommodations that surface in speech errors (see above) might be used as support for the representation of preconsonantal nasals as archisegments. Since alternative hypotheses can be used to account for all these errors, we are dependent on the kinds of linguistic arguments such as those now being raised in support of archisegments in autosegmental phonology (Goldsmith 1979; Halle & Vergnaud 1980; Clements & Keyser 1983).

7.4.3. **Suprasegmentals, autosegmentals, and CV phonology**

Stress, intonation, length, and tone had traditionally been considered qualitatively different from segmental features like voicing, nasality, aspiration, rounding, etc. (Lehiste 1970). With developments in generative phonology (Chomsky & Halle 1968), all phonological features, including the 'suprasegmentals' became features of segments, e.g. [±stress], [±HI TONE]. Leben (1978) broke with this new 'tradition' by arguing for a suprasegmental representation of tone, a position which was then supported by Goldsmith (1979) in his autosegmental approach.

Simultaneously with these developments, Liberman (1975) proposed a metrical theory (further developed by Liberman & Prince 1977), in which stress is shown by the relative prominence among syllables represented by binary branching tree structures, with the stronger node of a pair of syllables labelled 's' and the weaker node, 'w'.

Further developments along these lines have continued in metrical theory, autosegmental phonology, and CV phonology (cf. Halle & Vergnaud 1980; Hayes 1980, 1986; McCarthy 1981; Clements and Keyser 1983). Since these theories posit separate tiers, matrices, or levels for a given class of suprasegmental features:

> one of the strongest predictions made is that (they) will be relatively independent of the segments with which (they are) . . . associated . . . Segments may be deleted or moved without any effect on the suprasegmental, which will simply become associated with some nearby segments. (Stemberger 1984:895)

Such a prediction is upheld by speech error data. Becker (1979) specifically argues in favor of an autosegmental representation of stress on the basis of speech errors. Fromkin (1971, 1977, 1980) and Garrett (1975) both argue that phrasal stress must be independent of segments or even words, since they are determined by syntactic structure, and do not move with disordering of target units. That is, when words are disordered or interchanged, primary stress occurs in the place as intended in the target utterance; it must therefore be independent of the particular segment or lexical item on which it was intended to fall, as is illustrated in the following:

(21) a. What do people have if they first learn a language and then lose it? → What do people have if they first lose a language and then learn it?
   b. There's a small restaurant on the island → There's an island on the small restaurant
   c. In linguistics there are two kinds of people → In linguistics there are kind of two peoples
   d. I would like you to read that letter – I mean – I would like to read that letter to you
   e. They made seven runs in one inning → They made seven innings in one run

129

Other kinds of errors also show that phrasal stress is 'suprasegmental' when the syntactically determined primary stress is shifted to accommodate the new structures created, as shown in (22):

(22) a. I'm páying for it all → I'm pay fóring it . . .
   b. Doès Jàck smóke? → Dòes smòke Jáck?
   c. Saul said 5000 marines were covered up by lánding nèts → . . . by lànding néts, uh I mean by lánding nèts
   d. the Jèrry Wést Nìght gàme → the Jèrry Wèst Níght gàme (then corrected)
   e. Làrry Hỳman's páper → Làrry's Hýman pàper

The stress errors in (22c,d,e) might not be stress errors at all, but rather syntactic structure errors. That is, 'landing nets' might have been wrongly labeled (in short-term memory) as a VP rather than a noun compound. Similarly (22d) can be explained as:

(23) $_{NP}[_N[_N[\text{Jerry West}]_N[\text{night}]]_N[\text{game}] \rightarrow$
   $_{NP}[_N[\text{Jerry West}]_N[_N[\text{night}]_N[\text{game}]]$

And in (22e), when the possessive morpheme was anticipated, the syntactic structure of the phrase was changed, thus causing a stress change in keeping with the new structure.

It is of course the case that phrasal primary stress falls on the stressed syllable in the word and the above errors do not show that lexical stress is independent of segments. This is, however, revealed in simple vowel errors:

(24) a. féet mòving   → fúte mèeving
   b. fish and táckle   → fàsh and tíckle
   c. prèváiling   → praìvéeling . . .
   d. annotáted bibliography → annotóted . . .
   e. bràin résearch   → brèen ráisearch
   f. dèep phráse màrker   → dèep fréeze màrker

Gandour (1977) has also shown that tones in Siamese can be anticipated, can persevere, and can occur in tonal 'spoonerisms' independently of the vowels on which they would normally fall, thus supporting a suprasegmental or autosegmental representation of tones, as well as stress.

In addition to the autosegmental analysis of the stress phenomena in errors, Stemberger (1984) presents a strong case for the autosegmental treatment of length, again using speech error data. In a large majority of errors occurring in German (Meringer & Mayer 1895) and Swedish (Soderpalm 1979) which involve long and short segments, 'the misordered vowel does not retain its original length, but takes on the length of the vowel it replaces.'

7.5. Morphology

Rules of inflectional and derivational morphology 'surface' in speech errors through accommodation mechanisms, production of non-occurring morphologically complex forms, and errors in morphological rule application (non-application when a rule applies, application when it should not), as shown in the following examples:

(25) *Inflectional morphology*
    a. the last I knew about it → the last I knowed about it
    b. he had to have it → he haved to have it
    c. if he swam in the pool nude → if he swimmed . . .
    d. I meant to say → I meaned to say
    e. I don't know that I'd know one if I heard it → . . . that I'd hear one if I knew it (G)
    f. I already took a bath → I already tooken a bath (G)
    g. I thought I was finishing your beer! → I thought you were finishing my beer! (G)
    h. cow tracks [/. . . ks] → track cows [/. . . wz]
      (Cf. mouse /maws/ to show that this is a morphological 'rewrite', not simply a phonological rule.)

(26) *Derivational morphology*
    a. a New Yorker → a New Yorkan
    b. with motion (?) → motionly
    c. counter indicator → counter indicant
    d. untactful → distactful
    e. I regard this as imprecise → I disregard this as precise
    f. Tibetan → Tibeter

There has been much discussion in linguistics and psycholinguistics regarding lexical representation of morphologically complex words (cf. Chapter 5, by Emmorey and Fromkin, in Volume III of this series). The question asked is whether the entire paradigm of full words is entered in the lexicon, or whether stems and affixes are stored and combined by rule. Jackendoff (1975), Halle (1973) and others support the 'full entry' hypothesis (Jackendoff 1975). Fromkin (1980) does not argue against this view but points out, on the basis of speech errors such as those above, that speakers can and do access word formation rules. If this were not the case, one could not account for the accommodations that occur, or the non-occurring derived forms produced in speech errors that are cited above.

7.6. **Lexical errors and semantics**

Lexical errors, i.e. word substitutions and word blends, are no more random or inexplicable than the other errors already discussed. The substituted words, or words blended together, may reflect phonological similarity, as shown in (27) and (28):

(27) a. George's wife → George's life
      b. Did you see the rock garden → . . . the lock garden
      c. making headlines → making hairlines
      d. What is the phone number of Del Amo fashion square? → . . . of Del Amo passion square?
      e. They'll all be worrying → wondering about that
      f. prohibition against incest → . . . against insects
      g. At 4:30 we're adjourning the meeting → . . . adjoining . . .
      h. There are ways to organize programs → . . . pronouns
      i. sufficiently ambiguous → sufficiently ambitious
      j. I'm studying linguistics → I'm stuttering linguistics

(28) a. trying/striving   → strying
      b. grizzly/ghastly   → grastly
      c. terrible/horrible   → herrible
      d. slick/slippery   → slickery
      e. mainly/mostly   → maistly

The effect of phonological similarity of words in lexical substitutions and blends has important consequences for processing models, and possibly for the organization of the lexicon. Equally important, and possibly a more frequent phenomenon than phonological similarity, is the effect of semantic relatedness of the words involved. This, of course, is seen in the blend errors in (28). It is also shown in the blends in (29), in which the blended words are not easily interpreted as being phonologically similar, and in the substitution errors in (30):

(29) a. minor/trivial   → minal
      b. edited/annotated   → editated
      c. instantaneous/momentary   → momentaneous

(30) a. Don't forget! → Don't remember
      b. He's going up town → . . . down town
      c. I called my Uncle Sam → . . . my aunt, I mean, my uncle Sam
      d. 'Jack' is the subject of the sentence → . . . is the president of the sentence

   e. He has to pay her alimony → . . . pay her rent
   f. hot under the collar → hot under the belt
   g. The Mafia moved into Boston → The Mafia moved into Italy
   h. I'm going to England in May → I'm going to April in May
   i. I thought Westerns were where people ride horses instead of
       cars → . . . instead of cows
   j. You have too many irons in the fire → in the smoke
   k. I hope you won't do anything behind my back → . . . behind my
       face

Note that (30j) and (30k) involve word substitutions in idioms, showing that such complex semantic units are decomposable into words with their own semantic representation even if the meaning of the idiom can not be determined by the individual lexical items.

All such errors show that semantic representations must be included in lexical storage. They do not argue for any particular hypothesized form of representation, e.g. semantic features as opposed to meaning postulates. Blends reflect lexical indecision – the selecting of two semantically related words – supporting, at least in these cases, the Motley–Baars 'competing plan hypothesis'.

Semantically determined word substitutions may be accounted for by a separate semantic sub-lexicon; the error results from selecting a closely related word which is listed 'close to' the intended word. This lexical structure is also supported by aphasic word substitution errors (Fromkin 1985, forthcoming), in which lexical items are entered according to semantic class or properties. Examples (30g)–(30i) suggest that just as features, segments, syllables, words may be anticipated or persevere, so also may semantic features or properties. That is, in (30g) the substitution of the place word *Italy* for *Boston* may be due to the perseveration of a [+Italian] element in the semantic representation of *Mafia*. Similarly, the word *May* is not anticipated in (30h); only the [+month] feature. And in (30i) the substitution of *cows* for *cars* may be due to the phonological similarity plus the semantic interference of *horses*.

Antonym substitutions also reflect semantic influences and possibly feature value reversals.

Semantic similarity (and structural/syntactic similarity) may be responsible for idiom blends such as those in (31):

(31) a. In one ear and out the other/Here today and gone tomorrow →
        In one ear and gone tomorrow
      b. Give him an inch and he'll take a yard/Give him a rope and he'll
        hang himself → Give him an inch and he'll hang himself
      c. It's either feast or famine/It's either all or nothing → It's either

feast or nothing – uh, I mean – all or famine – no – feast or famine

One also finds semantic errors, that is, utterances which do not represent the intended meaning of the speaker (as in the phonologically similar word substitutions), as a result of word or morpheme disordering, and in syntactic errors. Examples of the last two categories are given in (32):

(32) a. Turkish and German don't have the 3rd dimension; so does Swedish
     b. Does it sound different? → Does it hear different?
     c. I really hate to correct exams → I hate to really correct exams
     d. I don't say that because I want to go → I say that because I don't want to go
     e. The electric blanket that we have right now isn't working → The electric blanket that we don't have right now is working (corrected)
     f. People agree that it is not well-formed → People don't agree that it's well-formed   (corrected)

If errors such as (32d,e,f) were not corrected, we might not know that the negative element or node was disordered or that the intended meaning was changed.

7.7. Syntax

Probably the most commonly occurring speech errors are those which produce grammatically ill-formed sentences. These may result from sentence blends, or, more interesting for our purposes, wrong rule application, i.e. non-application of a rule which should apply or application of a rule which should not apply. Some ungrammatical utterances also arise as the result of inflectional errors. Examples are given in (33):

(33) a. *The last I know about that
    b. *She was so drank when she called him
    c. *I don't know whether anyone has saw the review
    d. *It would be of interesting to see
    e. *I (John) would be easy to prove that
    f. *She made him to do the assignment over
    g. *The rule agrees that segments in voicing
    h. *John is going, isn't it?
    i. *I wouldn't be surprised if he failed, do you?
    j. *This is something that we should discuss about
    k. *She was waiting her husband for
    l. *How he can get it done in time?

Fay (1977, 1980; see also Foss & Fay 1975) has been interested in the analysis of syntactic errors and has proposed a transformational hypothesis, which posits transformational rules as processing rules. The difficulty in trying to assess the validity of Fay's hypothesis is that his analysis refers to a model of grammar which has been dramatically changed, so that the specific transformations he refers to are no longer posited in any grammar. Further analyses of these ungrammatical utterances are required, in the manner used by Grodzinsky (1985) in his analysis of agrammatic aphasia. Grodzinsky attempted to show that certain concepts in government–binding (GB) syntactic theory (Chomsky 1981) are able to account for agrammatic aphasics' comprehension and grammaticality judgements of relative clauses and passives in a principled way whereas, he claims, two other generative theories can only do so in an *ad hoc* fashion.

The misapplication or failure to apply minor-movement rules or lexical redundancy conditions that are part of GB theory can account for the ungrammaticality of utterances in (34):

(34) a. *But when you will leave?
    b. *And what he said?
    c. *I know where they're all – all are
    d. *Can I turn off this?
    e. *He really climbed it up
    f. *Carol threw out it the window by mistake

Wrong application of syntactic rules can account for errors such as those in (34) as well as those in (33). What is not yet clear is whether one theory of grammar, say GB, can do so more insightfully than can an alternative theory, say generalized phrase structure grammar (GPSG) (Gazdar *et al.* 1985), or lexical functional grammar (LFG) (Bresnan 1982).

7.8. Conclusion

Speech error data have been examined, and have been shown to relate to all components of grammar. Linguistic units and linguistic rules are subject to disordering, substitutions, and/or misapplications, thereby creating deviations from the speaker's intended sentence. Accommodation phenomena reveal that many rules of grammar are used as production processing rules. Given the assumption that the mental grammar underlies all speech performance – production and perception – however complex the mapping mechanisms, speech errors have already proved to be valuable evidence in linguistics.

REFERENCES

Anwar, M. S. 1979. Remarks on a collection of speech errors. *International Journal of Psycholinguistics* 6, 2: 59–72.

Anwar, M. S. 1981. The legitimate fathers of speech errors. *Historiographia Linguistica* VIII: 3.

Baars, B. J. 1980. The competing plans hypothesis: an heuristic viewpoint on the causes of errors in speech. In H. W. Dechert & M. Raupach (eds.) *Temporal variables in speech*. The Hague: Mouton.

Becker, D. A. 1979. Speech error evidence for autosegmental levels. *Linguistic Inquiry* 10: 165–7.

Bierwisch, M. 1982. Linguistics and language error. In A. Cutler (1982b).

Boomer, D. & Laver, J. 1968. Slips of the tongue. In Fromkin (1973).

Bond, Z. S. 1969. Constraints on production errors. *CLS* 5: 302–5.

Bresnan, J. 1982. *The mental representation of grammatical relations*. Cambridge, MA: MIT Press.

Broecke, M. P. R. van den & Goldstein, L. 1980. Consonant features in speech errors. In Fromkin (1980).

Butterworth, B. 1980. Some constraints on models of language production. In B. Butterworth (ed.) *Language production*. Vol. 12: *Speech and talk*. London: Academic Press.

Butterworth, B. 1981. Speech errors: old data in search of new theories. *Linguistics* 19: 627–62.

Celce-Murcia, M. 1973. Meringer's corpus revisited. In Fromkin (1973).

Chomsky, N. 1957. *Syntactic structures*. The Hague: Mouton.

Chomsky, N. 1978. On the biological basis of language capacities. In G. Lenneberg & E. Lenneberg (eds.) *Psychology and biology of language and thought. Essays in honor of Eric Lenneberg*. New York: Academic Press.

Chomsky, N. 1980. *Rules and representations*. New York: Columbia University Press.

Chomsky, N. 1981. *Lectures on government and binding*. (2nd rev. edn 1982.) Dordrecht: Foris.

Chomsky, N. 1982. *On the generative enterprise: a discussion with Riny Huybregts and Henk van Riemsdijk*. Dordrecht: Foris.

Chomsky, N. & Halle, M. 1968. *The sound pattern of English*. New York: Harper & Row.

Clements, G. N. & Keyser, S. J. 1983. *CV phonology: a generative theory of the syllable*. Cambridge, MA: MIT Press.

Cutler, A. 1979. The psychological reality of word formation and lexical stress rules. In *Proceedings of the 9th International Congress of Phonetic Sciences*, vol. 2. Copenhagen: Institute of Phonetics.

Cutler, A. 1980a. Syllable omission errors and isochrony. In H. W. Dechert & M. Raupach (eds.) *Temporal variables in speech*. The Hague: Mouton.

Cutler, A. 1980b. Errors of stress and intonation. In Fromkin (1980).

Cutler, A. 1982a. *Speech errors: a classified bibliography*. Bloomington: Indiana University Linguistics Club.

Cutler, A. 1982b (ed.) *Slips of the tongue and language production*. Amsterdam: Mouton.

Cutler, A. & Fay, D. 1978. Introduction. In R. Meringer & C. Mayer, *Versprechen und Verlesen*. Amsterdam: Benjamins.

Davidsen-Nielsen, N. 1975. A phonological analysis of English sp, st, sk, with special reference to speech error evidence. *Journal of the IPA* 5: 3–25.

Derwing, B. 1973. Transformational grammar as a theory of language acquisition. Cambridge: Cambridge University Press.

Emmorey, K. & Fromkin, V. A. 1987. The mental lexicon. In F. Newmeyer (ed.) *Linguistics: the Cambridge survey*, vol. III. Cambridge: Cambridge University Press.

Fay, D. 1977. Surface structure and the production of speech. Paper presented at the 49th Annual Meeting of the Midwestern Psychological Association, Chicago.

Fay, D. 1980. Transformational errors. In Fromkin (1980).

Fay, D. 1982. Substitutions and splices: a study of sentence blends. In Cutler (1982b).

Fay, D. & Cutler, A. 1977. Malapropisms and the structure of the mental lexicon. *Linguistic Inquiry* 8: 505–20.

Foss, D. & Fay, D. 1975. Linguistic theory and performance models. In D. Cohen & J. Wirth (eds.) *Testing linguistic hypotheses*. New York: Halstead.

Freud, S. 1901/1958. *Psychopathology of everyday life*. Translated by A. A. Brill. New York: New American Library, Mentor.
Freud, S. 1916/1974. *Introductory lectures on psychoanalysis*. Translated by J. Strachey. Harmondsworth, England: Penguin Books.
Fromkin, V. A. 1968. Speculations on performance models. *Journal of Linguistics* 4: 47–68.
Fromkin, V. A. 1971. The non-anomalous nature of anomalous utterances. *Language* 47: 27–52.
Fromkin, V. A. 1972. On the reality of linguistic constructs: evidence from speech errors. *Proceedings of the VIIth International Congress of Phonetic Sciences*. The Hague: Mouton.
Fromkin, V. A. 1973 (ed.) *Speech errors as linguistic evidence*. The Hague: Mouton.
Fromkin, V. A. 1977. Putting the emPHAsis on the wrong sylLAble. In L. M. Hyman (ed.) *Studies in stress and accent*. Southern California Occasional Papers in Linguistics. No. 4.
Fromkin, V. A. 1980 (ed.) *Errors in linguistic performance: slips of the tongue, ear, pen, and hand*. New York: Academic Press.
Fromkin, V. A. 1985. Evidence in Linguistics. In R. H. Robins & V. A. Fromkin (eds.) *Linguistics and linguistic evidence*. Newcastle upon Tyne: Grevatt & Grevatt.
Fromkin, V. A. Forthcoming. The lexicon: evidence from acquired dyslexia. *Language*.
Gandour, J. 1977. Counterfeit tones in the speech of Southern Thai bidialectals. *Lingua* 41: 125–43.
Garrett, M. 1975. The analysis of sentence production. In G. Bower (ed.) *Psychology of learning and motivation*, vol. 9. New York: Academic Press.
Garrett, M. 1976. Syntactic processes in sentence production. In R. Wales & E. Walker (eds.) *New approaches to language mechanisms*. Amsterdam: North-Holland.
Garrett, M. 1980a. The limits of accommodation. In Fromkin (1980).
Garrett, M. 1980b. Levels of processing in sentence production. In B. Butterworth (ed.) *Language production*, vol. 1. New York: Academic Press.
Gazdar, G. 1981. Phrase structure grammar. In P. Jacobson & G. Pullum (eds.) *The nature of syntactic representation*. Dordrecht: Reidel.
Gazdar, G., Klein, E., Pullum, G. K. & Sag, I. 1985. *Generalized phrase structure grammar*. Cambridge, MA: Harvard University Press.
Goldsmith, J. 1979. The aims of autosegmental phonology. In D. A. Dinnsen (ed.) *Current approaches to phonological theory*. Bloomington: Indiana University Press.
Grodzinsky, Y. 1985. On the interaction between linguistics and neuropsychology. *Brain & Language* 26: 186–99.
Halle, M. 1973. Prolegomena to a theory of word formation. *Linguistic Inquiry* 4: 3–16.
Halle, M. & Vergnaud, J. -R. 1980. Three dimensional phonology. *Journal of Linguistic Research* 1: 83–105.
Hayes, B. 1980. A metrical theory of stress rules. Doctoral dissertation, MIT. Distributed by Indiana University Linguistics Club (1981).
Hayes, B. 1986. Assimilation as spreading in Toba Batak. *Linguistic Inquiry* 17, 3: 467–500.
Hockett, C. F. 1967. Where the tongue slips, there slip I. In *To honor Roman Jakobson*. The Hague: Mouton. Reprinted in Fromkin (1973).
Jackendoff, R. 1975. Morphological and semantic regularities in the lexicon. *Language* 51: 639–71.
Jespersen, O. 1922. *Language: its nature, development and origin*. London: Allen & Unwin.
Kiparsky, P. 1968. How abstract is phonology? In O. Fujimura (ed.) 1973. *Phonological representations in three dimensions of linguistic theory*. Tokyo Institute for Advanced Study of Language.
Klatt, D. 1979. Lexical representations for speech production. Paper presented at the International Symposium on the Cognitive Representation of Speech, Edinburgh.
Leben, W. 1978. The representation of tone. In V. A. Fromkin (ed.) *Tone: a linguistic survey*. New York: Academic Press.
Lehiste, I. 1970. *Suprasegmentals*. Cambridge, MA: MIT Press.
Liberman, M. 1975. The intonational system of English. Doctoral dissertation, MIT. Distributed by the Indiana University Linguistics Club (1978).
Liberman, M. & Prince, A. 1977. On stress and linguistic rhythm. *Linguistic Inquiry* 8: 249–336.
Mackay, A. L. 1981. *The harvest of a quiet eye*. London: The Institute of Physics.
MacKay, D. G. 1970. Spoonerisms: the structure of errors in the serial order of speech. In Fromkin (1973).

137

MacKay, D. G. 1971. Stress pre-entry in motor systems. *American Journal of Psychology* 84: 35–51.

MacKay, D. G. 1972. Lexical insertion, inflection, and derivation: creative processes in word production. *Journal of Psycholinguistic Research* 8: 477–98.

McCarthy, J. 1981. A prosodic theory of nonconcatenative morphology. *Linguistic Inquiry* 12: 373–418.

Meringer, R. 1908. *Aus dem Leben der Sprache*. Berlin: Behrs Verlag.

Meringer, R. & Mayer, K. 1895. *Versprechen und Verlesen*. Stuttgart: Goschensche Verlagsbuchhandlung. New edn 1978, ed. A. Cutler & D. Fay. Amsterdam: Benjamins.

Motley, M. T., Baars, B. J. & Camden, C. T. 1983. Experimental verbal slip studies: a review and an editing model of language encoding. *Communication Monographs* 50: 79–101.

Newmeyer, F. J. 1986. Has there been a 'Chomskyan revolution' in linguistics? *Language* 62: 1–18.

Nooteboom, S. G. 1969. The tongue slips into patterns. In A. G. Sciarone, A. J. van Essen & A. A. van Raad (eds.) *Nomen Society, Leyden studies in linguistics and phonetics*. The Hague: Mouton.

Norman, D. A. 1981. Categorization of action slips. *Psychological Review* 88: 1–15.

Paul, H. 1886. *Prinzipien der Sprachgeschichte*. Halle: Niemayer. 2nd edn trans. H. A. Strong as *Principles of the history of language*. College Park: McGrath Publishing Co.

Paul, H. 1919. Über Kontamination auf syntaktische Gebiete. *Sitzungsberichte der bayrischen Akademie der Wissenschaften: Philosphisch-philologische und historische Klasse* 2.

Poincaré, H. 1956. Chance. In J. R. Newman, (ed.) *The world of mathematics*, vol. 2. New York: Simon & Shuster.

Roberts, E. W. 1975. Speech errors as evidence for the reality of phonological units. *Lingua* 35: 263–96.

Robins, R. H. 1966. The warden's wordplay: toward a redefinition of the spoonerism. *Dalhousie Review* 46: 457–65.

Shattuck-Hufnagel, S. 1979. Speech errors as evidence for a serial ordering mechanism in sentence production. In W. E. Cooper & E. Walker (eds.) *Sentence processing*. New York: Halsted Press.

Shattuck-Hufnagel, S. 1982. Sublexical units and suprasegmental structure in speech production planning. In P. F. MacNeilage (ed.) *The production of speech*. New York: Springer.

Shattuck-Hufnagel, S. & Klatt, D. 1979. The limited use of distinctive features and markedness in speech production: evidence from speech errors. *Journal of Verbal Learning and Verbal Behavior* 18: 41–55.

Soderpalm, E. 1979. Speech errors in normal and pathological speech. *Travaux de l'institut de linguistique de Lund* 14. Lund: Gleerup.

Stemberger, J. P. 1982. The nature of segments in the lexicon: evidence from speech errors. *Lingua* 56: 235–59.

Stemberger, J. P. 1983. *Speech errors and theoretical phonology: a review*. Bloomington: Indiana University Linguistics Club.

Stemberger, J. P. 1984. Length as a suprasegmental: evidence from speech errors. *Language* 60: 895–913.

Sturtevant, E. H. 1917. *Linguistic change*. Chicago: University of Chicago Press.

Sturtevant, E. H. 1947. *An introduction to linguistic science*. New Haven: Yale University Press.

Twaddell, W. F. 1935. *On defining the phoneme*. Language Monograph no. 16.

8 Grammar and conversational principles*

Ruth Kempson

8.1. Preliminaries: truth-conditional semantics and the semantics–pragmatics distinction

In this chapter we turn to the relation between properties of grammar and principles of conversation. There are two assumptions which have formed the background to this relation; and they have been taken for granted in virtually all work on properties of meaning of natural languages during the last 20 years. They are as set out below.

I. A complete account of sentence meaning for a language is given by recursively specifying the truth conditions of the sentences of the language (see Lewis 1972):

SEMANTICS = TRUTH CONDITIONS

II. Pragmatics, which provides an account of how sentences are used in utterances to convey information in context, has to account for whatever else there is to the content of a sentence in use, apart from the specification of its truth-conditional content (Gazdar 1979):

PRAGMATICS = MEANING minus TRUTH CONDITIONS

On the truth-conditional semantics view, the central property of natural languages is that we humans use language to communicate propositions, that is to say, information about the world around us; and the concept of semantic content that we should articulate for sentences is the link between a sentence of the language and the information about the world which it succeeds in conveying – its propositional content. A specification of the propositional content associated with a sentence is a specification of the minimal set of conditions under which the particular proposition expressed by that sentence would be true. So on the view crudely expressed by the equation, SEMANTICS = TRUTH CONDITIONS, it is assumed that the semantic content of a

* Thanks to Wynn Chao, Clive Matthews and Deirdre Wilson for comments on a draft of this chapter.

sentence is exhausted by determining its propositional content. It is uncontroversial that the meaning of a sentence is made up of the meanings of the words which it contains and their syntactic arrangement in that sentence. Accordingly, the semantic component of a grammar is, on this view, assumed to be a formal algorithm which assigns propositional contents to a sentence on the basis of the meanings of expressions it contains and the syntactic configuration of the sentence, where these expressions are characterized in terms of the individuals they refer to, the properties they denote, etc. I shall call all such properties *truth-theoretic*. In addition, it is assumed that the semantics of a grammar should provide rules for predicting such relations of meaning between sentences as, for example, synonymy and entailment (see Ladusaw, Volume I of this series, Chapter 4 and references cited there).

The view that the domain of explication for semantics is that of articulating propositional contents associated with sentences has been buttressed by the central figure of early work in pragmatics – Paul Grice. Grice was the first to give an overall account of how utterances succeed in conveying far more information than is explicitly expressed by the words used (Grice 1975). Imagine for example, the following conversation in which A and B are trying to decide where to go to eat:

(1)　A:　What's the new Pizza House like?
　　　B:　All the cooks there are Italian
　　　A:　Let's go there then

A asks B what the new Pizza House is like, which B takes to be a question about the food cooked there. B replies with information about the nationality of people there, which A takes to be information about the food cooked there. The indirect information which A and B trade on for the success of their conversation is that if one is asking what a house which serves food is like, one is asking about the food served there, that people who cook a dish particularly associated with the country of their origin cook it well, and that pizza is an Italian dish. None of this information is explicitly expressed, but its manipulation is essential to the flow of information in this particular conversation.

On Grice's view, there is an underlying *conversational principle* which determines the way in which all indirect information can be conveyed in utterances. According to Grice, the propositional content of the utterance ('what the speaker said') is determined by semantics as in the truth-conditional program; and the cooperative principle comes into play solely to determine the additional information (called *implicatures*) which a hearer might deduce from an utterance over and above such truth-conditional content. This cooperative principle involves the assumptions that by and large speakers do not say what is false, or irrelevant, or too much or too little – a set of assumptions called *maxims of conversation*. It is when these assumptions are seemingly violated that indirect information is supposedly conveyed, such violations forcing the hearer to make additional assumptions in order to understand the speaker as (indirectly) conveying something true and relevant. In (1) it is the maxim of relevance which is apparently violated, which a hearer can reinstate by adding assumptions about Italians cooking pizza well.

Despite the extreme generality of these maxims, they constituted a first step in articulating an overall pragmatic framework, and Grice's work is justly influential. (For a more detailed account of Grice's theory, see Blakemore, Chapter 13, Volume IV in this series, and for a survey of the literature on implicature see Levinson 1983.) Indeed there has since been a spate of work on adopting Grice's framework more or less wholesale (some researchers made minor modifications to the maxims), all of which has argued that a wide range of phenomena which had previously been thought to be part of the linguistic meaning of the expression in question were to be explained in terms of the maxims. Given the framework, it followed that such phenomena had to be analyzed as conversational implicatures and not part of the proposition directly expressed by the utterance or part of the linguistic content of the sentence in question. And this was the general line adopted in Horn (1973), Kempson (1975), Harnish (1976), Morgan (1978), Gazdar (1979), Davison (1980), Atlas & Levinson (1981), Sadock (1981).[1]

However, the burden of this chapter is to show that this division of labor between grammar and conversational principles is incorrect – to show that principles of grammar and pragmatic principles *interact* to determine propositional content, a position precluded by both truth-conditional semantics and Gricean pragmatics. It is further intended to show that there is a well-articulated alternative framework in which all problems pertaining to the orthodox account outlined above can be resolved, while yet maintaining the separateness of grammar and general conversational principles.[2]

---

[1] These Gricean implementations in their turn led to extreme functional accounts in which the entire burden of syntactic characterization is reduced to functional explanations (cf. Givón 1978, 1979b; García 1979; Sheintuch 1980; Riddle & Sheintuch 1983).

[2] One of the few people in the mid 1970s to recognize the gap between linguistic content of a sentence and the articulation of the truth conditions of its associated propositions was Jay Atlas, who argued in a series of papers (Atlas 1975, 1977, 1979) that the linguistic concept of sentence negation was weaker than any concept sufficient to characterize the truth-theoretic properties of propositions that negative sentences express.

8.2. **Problems for truth-conditional semantics**

8.2.1. **Anaphora**

The first problem is that if we take truth-theoretic properties of expressions as the basis of linguistic content for natural language expressions, we find ourselves forced to give up the possibility of providing a unitary account of anaphora. On the contrary, we are forced to postulate ambiguities which natural languages do not recognize as discrete words. The paradigm case of an anaphoric expression is a pronoun, an expression whose value is determined by something other than itself. It either refers to some entity in the discourse situation, or relates to some other expression earlier in the discourse, which is referred to as the 'antecedent' of the pronoun.

According to a truth-theoretic account of meaning, there are up to five different types of pronoun:

(a) *Referential pronouns*, which refer directly to some nonlinguistic entity in the discourse:[3]

(2)   He's clever

(3) $Mark_i$ thinks he_j's clever   [he≠Mark]

(b) *Coreferential pronouns*, which refer to some nonlinguistic entity in virtue of their coreference with some linguistic expression elsewhere in the discourse (the antecedent):

(4) $Mark_i$ thinks he_i's clever   [he=Mark]

(5)   After his_i bath, $Johnny_i$ goes to bed   [he=Johnny]

(c) *Bound-variable pronouns*, which do not refer to a fixed entity at all but may pick out various individuals in virtue of their dependence on some quantifying expression in the sentence:

(6)   Every boy_i worries that he_i's inadequate   [he=each one of the boys]

(d) *E-type pronouns*, which for technical reasons are neither straightforward bound-variable pronouns, nor pronouns whose value is fixed by coreference (see Evans 1980):

(7)   Most people who bought a donkey have treated it well   [it=the donkey that each of the people in question bought]

(e) *Lazy pronouns*, which are so-called because they are not identical in

---

[3] The indices are a standard means of indicating whether or not an expression is intended to refer to the same entity as some other expression in the sentence.

truth-theoretic content to their antecedent; they appear rather to pick up on the linguistic form of that antecedent:

(8) My gran put her paycheck under the bed, but everyone with any sense put it in the bank   [it=their paycheck]

All these types of pronoun are quite distinct from each other, either in their truth-theoretic content (according as they are referential, bound-variable, E-type or lazy) or in the nature of the link between them and their antecedent from which that content is established (referential vs. coreferential, referential vs. bound-variable, coreferential vs. lazy). On the orthodox truth-conditional view, in which linguistic meaning is identified as truth-theoretic content, there is no way of avoiding the claim that every pronoun in every language is ambiguous, a set of discrete lexical senses. Moreover it is coincidence on this view that such uses of pronouns occur in all languages. In general, ambiguity of a word does not translate from language to language – *duck*, for example, cannot be translated into any language and preserve the ambiguity it has in English. But with pronouns, we have a case of an expression where the same range of ambiguities occur in all languages. There has been a considerable amount of research trying to reduce this ambiguity (Cooper 1979; Hausser 1979; Evans 1980; Reinhart 1983; Kempson 1986), but any analysis of the meaning of pronouns in terms of their truth-theoretic content cannot give a unitary explanation of pronominal anaphora.

Moreover, it is not just pronouns which are subject to such ambiguity. Noun phrases which are interpreted as definite, in English expressed by the use of the word *the*, are similarly ambiguous. Thus, overlapping with the pronominal types (a)–(e), we have referential definite NPs, coreferential definite NPs, bound-variable definite NPs, E-type definite NPs, plus a phenomenon specific to such NPs, bridging cross-reference:

(9)   The man in the green coat coughed   (referential)

(10) John walked in and the poor dear was crying   (coreferential)

(11) Of every house in the area that was inspected, it was subsequently reported that the house was suffering from subsidence problems   (bound-variable)

(12) Everyone who bought a house discovered too late that the house was riddled with damp   (E-type)

(13) John walked into the kitchen. The windows were filthy

In this last case, a bridging cross-reference example, the marker of definiteness is not marking coreference, but rather a link of association with some preceding expression, a link which we can establish via our knowledge that kitchens have windows. In the considerable literature on definite NPs, at least some of these uses of definite NPs are assumed to be quite separate. In particular, the truth-theoretic properties of nonreferring uses are quite distinct from all referential uses;[4] and bridging cross-reference cases are distinct in establishing the link with their antecedent only via the addition of background knowledge (see Clark & Haviland 1977). So the phenomenon of definiteness would have to be treated as heterogeneous, subject to ambiguity in all languages. No unitary explanation of definiteness is proffered.

8.2.2. **The presupposition projection problem**

The second problem emerges in attempts to give a detailed account of the properties of referential (and coreferential) definite NPs (types (a) and (b)) upon the assumption that this account should provide a basis for predicting the relations of meaning between sentences such as (14) and (15) which definite NPs give rise to:

(14) Joan went to the exhibition

(15) There was an exhibition

The relation in question is one that has been called *presupposition*. It arises with several different kinds of structure. I give here just two: definite NPs, which give rise to a presupposition of the existence of the object referred to by the definite NP – hence (14) is said to presuppose (15); and verbs such as *regret*, which give rise to a presupposition of the truth of the complement sentence – hence (16) is said to presuppose (17):

(16) Joe regrets that Bill is married

(17) Bill is married

Informally, the evidence for this relation is taken to be that any speaker of a presupposing sentence is automatically taking for granted/presupposing the truth of the presupposed sentence. There has been much argument about the nature of this relation (cf. Strawson 1950, 1964; Van Fraassen 1968; Allwood 1972; Atlas 1975, 1977; Kempson 1975; Wilson 1975; Boër & Lycan 1976; Grice 1981; Von Stechow 1981); but what is accepted as uncontroversial is that the relation between (14) and (15) and between (16) and (17) is due to the meaning of the words in question, of the definite article *the* in (14), and the verb *regret* in (16). If we then assume that the semantic component of the grammar should at least provide a basis for predicting relations of meaning between sentences, an assumption that is central to the truth-theoretic

---

[4] The philosophical debate between Russell and Strawson applied to only the first of these uses (cf. Russell 1903; Strawson 1950, 1964; Donnellan 1966; Kripke 1977).

program, we seem committed to the view that the grammar should recursively define presupposition relations of meaning between sentences.

The difficulties start with what is known as *the presupposition projection problem*, a problem which has received a great deal of attention (Karttunen 1973, 1974; Stalnaker 1974; Wilson 1975; Gazdar 1979; Karttunen & Peters 1979; Soames 1979, 1982; Landman 1981). This is the problem, that a recursive characterization of such presupposition relations has to be sensitive at least to the linguistic context in which the presupposing sentence is contained; for although sometimes the presupposition is preserved when this sentence is embedded, sometimes it is not. Thus we want our account to predict that (18) and (19) presuppose (15), in the sense that anyone uttering (18) or (19) would take the truth of (15) for granted. But we also want the account to predict that (20) and (21) do not presuppose (15):

(18) If Bill stayed at home, Joan went to the exhibition

(19) Bill stayed at home and Joan went to the exhibition

(20) If Bill has set up an exhibition, then Joan went to the exhibition

(21) Bill has set up an exhibition and Joan went to the exhibition

Similarly, (22) and (23) presuppose (17), but (24) and (25) do not:

(22) If Bill is in love with Sue, then she regrets that Bill is married

(23) Bill is in love with Sue and she regrets that Bill is married

(24) If Bill is married, then Sue regrets that Bill is married

(25) Bill is married and Sue regrets that Bill is married

It is no coincidence that (18), (20), (22), (24) contain *if* and (19), (21), (23) and (25) contain *and*, for it is generally agreed that the reason why these presupposition relations do or do not hold in the cases here is due to interaction between the meaning of *the* and *regret* and the connectives *if* and *and*. Thus, as long as we maintain that the rules of grammar must be defined so as to predict relations between sentences of this type, then these rules must be set up to make the varying predictions of (18)–(25).

We now come to the second major problem I wish to draw attention to in this chapter: the required predictions of relatedness between sentences seem to have to be sensitive not merely to information contained in the grammar, but also to real-world knowledge of a type manipulated in bridging cross-reference. There is a pair of sentences famous amongst presuppositionalists, from Gazdar (1979):

(26) If the President invites George Wallace's wife to the White House, he'll regret having invited a black militant to the White House

(27) If the President invites Angela Davis to the White House, he'll
regret having invited a black militant to the White House

Against the cultural assumptions in America in the early 1970s, (26) would
naturally be taken to be an assertion about the wife of the well-known racist
politician, George Wallace. And (27) would be taken as an assertion about
the black American militant prominent in the early 1970s, Angela Davis. But
if these assumptions are used in interpreting (26) and (27) respectively, the
presupposition projection effects in the two sentences differ. Mrs Wallace is
most certainly not a black militant if the Wallace referred to is the well-known
racist politician. So the black militant indicated in the second conjunct of (26)
cannot be taken to be Mrs Wallace. Any speaker of (26) will therefore have to
be presupposing/taking for granted the truth of the *regret* complement, that
the President has invited a black militant to the White House. However, in
(27), if the speaker is using the name *Angela Davis* to refer to the well-known
black American militant of the 1970s, she would not be taking for granted the
truth of the President having invited a black militant to the White House. On
the contrary, this is an assumption which she would be explicitly adopting in
the first conjunct of her utterance without presuming its truth.

What these sentences therefore suggest is that if we are to provide a
uniform basis for predicting both when the presuppositions associated with
parts of a sentence are preserved to be presuppositions of the sentence as a
whole, and when they are suspended and do not become presuppositions of
the whole, then it appears that we cannot restrict the explanation only to
information which is included in the grammar. For there is nothing in one's
knowledge of the language which differentiates between (26) and (27): it is
knowledge of the people described which the speaker is trading on. But the
initial premise we started from was that the relation between (14) and (15),
and between (16) and (17), was due to the meanings of the lexical items
themselves, and hence is to be characterized by rules of grammar. It is when
we extend this assumption to the entire range of presupposition phenomena
that the inconsistency arises. Some of the presupposition projection problem
is solvable by facts of grammar alone, but some of it is not.

How then can we give a unitary account of the phenomenon? None of the
major accounts of the presupposition projection problem does so adequately.
Examples such as (26)–(27) are straightforward counterexamples to Karttunen & Peters' proposed analyses, for they analyze all presuppositional
phenomena as projected from properties of (non-truth-conditional) meaning
associated with lexical items as part of their entry in the lexicon.[5] So they

---

[5] Grice had called the apparently exceptional non-truth-conditional aspects of linguistic meaning
'conventional implicatures' (Grice 1975), and Karttunen & Peters listed presupposition-inducing
effects with specific expressions under this label. See Blakemore on 'The organization of discourse'
(Volume IV in this series, Chapter 13) and her dissertation (1986) for an account of the apparently

predict that presupposition projection effects should arise only from lexically specified information.

Gazdar analyzes such presuppositional phenomena as pragmatic properties associated with lexical items, so in principle does not preclude an explanation of the phenomena in a unitary way. Indeed, he provides a formal theory of context incrementation in discourse set up specifically to recursively characterize the presupposition projection data. However, his characterization of context change in discourse is restricted to effects predictable from stipulated lexical properties, albeit pragmatic ones. So there is no basis for explaining how the suspension of presupposition in (27) can arise from general encyclopedic knowledge. (27) is thus explained not in virtue of the information assumed by the speaker to be associated with the woman Angela Davis, but in virtue of a so-called *anaphoric* property of indefinite noun phrases. The noun phrase *a black militant* is said to be anaphorically dependent on the expression *Angela Davis* by a rule of anaphora associated with indefinite NPs, the presupposition associated with the *regret* complement thereby being suspended. But this account is stipulatory, with no independent motivation.

Like Karttunen & Peters, and Gazdar, Soames provides a rule-driven characterization of the data. But unlike them, his characterization of the presupposition projection phenomena is functionally motivated. However, his explanation of examples such as (27) is little more than a promise; and moreover, as he explicitly grants (fn.53), he has no account of the principles underlying the interaction between information specified by rules of grammar and information of a more general encyclopedic sort. Indeed his account singularly lacks a theoretical framework, and amounts to little more than a formal statement of the facts.

So all three analyses correctly predict presuppositional effects (and their absence) when these arise from lexical properties of the items in question, but none of them can account successfully for parallel effects caused by general information stored in memory. They are all, therefore, at best incomplete accounts of the phenomena.[6]

8.2.3. Quantifier–pronominal binding

The third problem emerges in the predominant syntactic account of pronominal anaphora, and is a combination of the problems I have so far presented. In the current Chomskyan government and binding paradigm, definite NPs and pronominals are assumed to be ambiguous; and, as we shall see, the type of

recalcitrant data of conventional implicature which follows from general principles of pragmatic theory with no exception mechanisms.

[6] See Levinson (1983) for a survey of the presupposition literature up to 1982.

anaphoric dependency argued to be the provenance of grammar has to involve sensitivity to the addition of encyclopedic knowledge which is not itself specified by any rule of grammar. Reinhart (1983) argues within this paradigm that two types of pronoun have to be distinguished: pronouns which are construed as bound variables (type (c) above – dependent on their antecedent exclusively for their value), and referential pronouns (type (a) above – referring directly to some entity in the discourse situation without any dependence on an antecedent).[7] All other types of pronoun, she argues, can be reduced to these.[8]

What is of particular relevance here is that the characterization of an anaphoric expression as a variable bound by some quantifier – see example (6) – is argued to be subject to configurational restrictions and hence a process which must be characterized syntactically. The facts are these. In order for a pronoun to be construed as dependent on a quantifier, that quantifier must 'c-command' the pronoun (roughly, be higher up in the hierarchical configuration of the sentence). Thus in (28), the pronoun *he* can be dependent on the quantifier *every* in subject position because the subject expression, as subject, is higher in the syntactic configuration of the sentence than *he* (which is subject of the subordinate clause). If however we reverse the two NPs as in (29), the pronoun cannot be construed as dependent on the NP:

(28) Every actor thinks that he is ugly

(29) He thinks that every actor is ugly

The details of the definition of *c-command* are not essential here: suffice it to say that there is a clear configurational restriction.

Now the problems arise when we turn to the parallel phenomenon of dependency on a quantifying expression of a definite NP. Such relations are subject to a similar restriction:

(30) Every singer complained that the accompanist played too loudly

(31) The accompanist complained that every singer sang too loudly

(30) allows a dependency relation between *the accompanist* and *every singer* (on this interpretation, each singer complaining about whoever was her accompanist); but (31) does not. This only allows the interpretation in which there is just one accompanist who complained about all of the singers. So if the restriction precluding this bound-variable type of interpretation in (29) is a syntactic one, then so should the restriction precluding a bound-variable type of interpretation in (31) be a syntactic one. But in (30), whose configuration allows the bound-variable reading (in which the accompanist is

---

[7] See Cooper (1979), who argues for the same conclusion within a Montague semantics framework.
[8] She argues elsewhere (Reinhart forthcoming) that E-type pronouns are a subtype of bound-variable anaphora.

each singer's accompanist), the dependency between the expression *the accompanist* and the expression *every singer* is not made by identity between accompanist and singer but rather by the additional premise that 'Every singer had an accompanist.' But this premise is not part of the definition of the concept of 'singer'. It is something which has to be added to the interpretation of the utterance, via our knowledge that classical singers at least do, characteristically, have accompanists. This phenomenon, whereby a definite NP can be linked to some antecedent is what is called *bridging cross-reference* (see p. 143). Now it is quite uncontentious that this phenomenon is pragmatic, for the dependency between the definite expression and its antecedent involves detailed nonlinguistic knowledge of the objects described. What is particular about (30) is that we have at once a bridging cross-reference phenomenon and a quantifier–variable dependency. But how can quantifier–variable dependencies, which are characterized within the grammar, be sensitive to the accessibility of premises necessary to establish bridging cross-reference, which are not?

We appear to have only two solutions, neither of which is attractive, given the orthodox assumptions of current syntactic theory. Either we have to incorporate the premises necessary to characterize bridging cross-reference as part of the lexical specification of the words in the grammar, a conclusion which leads to the incorporation of our entire range of general encyclopedic knowledge as a subpart of our language faculty. Or we have to grant that quantifier–variable dependency has to be sensitive to information added by the process of utterance interpretation, and thus grant that it cannot be entirely implemented as a process of grammar. So from arguments of ambiguity, arguments about systematic meaning relationships, and arguments about syntactic restrictions on interpretation, we come to the same paradox: we cannot give a unitary account of the phenomena without granting that each of the phenomena both has to be characterized by principles of grammar and yet is not completely characterizable by rules of grammar.

3.2.4. The contribution of implicatures to truth conditions

I turn to one further problem. It has been known for some time by people working within the Griccan tradition that the additional information accrued to the interpretation of an utterance by a chain of reasoning involving the presumption of the maxims can sometimes be part of the propositional content of the utterance expressed. One of Grice's original examples was the contrast between (32) and (33):

(32) Rob Roy jumped on his horse and rode away

149

(33) Rob Roy rode away and jumped on his horse

Grice forcibly argued that the sequence of time implicit in (32) and violated in (33) is not due to the linguistic content of *and* but to implicatures worked out via an assumption of the speaker conforming to the conversational maxims; similarly for other additional relations construed between two sentences joined by *and* such as causality. Yet, as pointed out by Cohen (1971), Wilson (1975), and recently in detail by Carston (forthcoming), there are undeniably cases in which such uncontentiously pragmatic properties of *and* do contribute to the proposition expressed by the sentence;

(34)   He didn't steal some money and go to the bank; he went to the bank and stole some money

(35)   It's better to get married and have a baby than to have a baby and get married

(34) would be contradictory if there were no difference in the proposition expressed by *He stole some money and went to the bank* and *He went to the bank and stole some money*. (35), similarly, would be a meaningless assertion to make if the alternatives being compared were indistinguishable. Such examples are serious counterexamples to the Gricean view that the maxims operate only to determine the indirect information conveyed by an utterance and do not operate in determining the direct propositional content expressed.

Until very recently, no one had any substantial answers to any of these problems. In so far as these problems were addressed, detailed analyses were made without any attempt to articulate an alternative framework of assumptions. There have been three types of response to Grice's original ideas. People either assumed Grice's account was essentially correct, and applied it almost doctrinally (Kempson 1975; Harnish 1976; Davison 1980; Atlas & Levinson 1981; Horn 1984, 1985; Levinson 1985); or they assumed that it was so informal as to be almost contentless and hence could not be taken seriously (Gazdar 1979; Kamp 1979); or they devised their own informal small-scale explanations without any attempt to fit the specific analysis into an overall theory of utterance interpretation (cf. Prince 1978, 1981; Erteschik-Shir, 1979, 1986; Erteschik-Shir & Lappin 1979, 1983; Lappin 1982).

However, there is now an alternative overall theory of cognition with a fully articulated theory of pragmatics as a subpart, in which the phenomena outlined here as problematic for the truth-conditional approach to linguistic content or for Grice's particular proposals are all directly predicted – *relevance theory*.

8.3. **Relevance theory**

Relevance theory takes the maxim of relevance (which Grice merely phrases as the instruction 'Be relevant') as the only central concept of pragmatic theory, and constructs an entire framework of assumptions around a defined concept of relevance (Sperber & Wilson 1982, 1986). It is based on assumptions about the nature of the cognitive system made in Fodor (1982, 1983). According to Fodor's view, we process the information presented by the world around us by the construction of mental representations – i.e. propositions. More technically, the cognitive mechanism is a system of mental representations, the language of thought, and explanations of cognitive activity such as inference are characterized syntactically, operating in virtue of the form of such mental representations. What relevance theory claims to provide is a theory of the central cognitive mechanism, from which an account of how utterances are interpreted follows.

One of the chief problems for any pragmatic theory to explain, as we've already seen, is how it is that the information derived from an utterance of a sentence is far richer than the information which a given sentence will present as its linguistically specifiable meaning. It is richer in two ways, only one of which was characterized by Grice's maxims. First, a phenomenon which Grice ignored: the proposition expressed by some utterance of a sentence may be much more precise than is given by the content of the sentence itself. The most obvious examples are anaphoric expressions, for example (36):

(36) They all do

As a sentence, this merely indicates that all the members of some set are involved in some action. But in the context of a question such as (37):

(37) How many of your friends want to come to supper tonight?

(36) expresses the proposition that all of the speaker's friends want to come to supper tonight. Secondly, there is the implicature phenomenon, that a speaker may use a sentence to convey information quite independent of the content of her utterance.

The Sperber & Wilson claim is that interpreting an utterance invariably involves establishing both its explicit content and its implicit content. These two processes are: (i) establishing what proposition the utterance has actually expressed, and (ii) accessing some extra proposition or set of propositions (called *the context*), which combines with the proposition directly expressed to yield indirect information. Within Sperber & Wilson's theory, neither aspect of utterance interpretation is completely controlled by a strictly rule-governed algorithmic process (unlike the SEMANTICS=TRUTH CONDITIONS program). To the contrary, they claim that both aspects of utterance

151

interpretation involve an essential element of hypothesis formation. On their view, the content of natural language expressions considerably under-determines the proposition they can be used to assert, so the grammar cannot provide more than a partial basis for determining the proposition to be associated with a sentence. Rather, the grammar is said to assign to each sentence what they call the *logical form* of the sentence, this logical form being an incomplete representation of propositional form from which propositions can be constructed.

The processes of proposition selection and context construction are said to be controlled by the principle of relevance. An utterance is relevant to a hearer if, and only if, it combines with some context to yield new information not derivable from the utterance or the context alone. And relevance is maximized when information is made available to a hearer at minimal processing cost. The central claim of relevance theory is that the human cognitive mechanism is wired up to maximize relevance: the interpretation it extracts from its visual, aural and other input systems is that which provides the largest amount of information for the least cognitive effort. The constraint that this assumption imposes on utterance interpretation is what Sperber & Wilson call the *principle of relevance*. This is an assumption controlling utterance interpretation that the speaker believes that what she has said is optimally relevant to the hearer in the circumstances, immediately providing the hearer with a set of premises (proposition expressed plus context) with minimal processing effort. A direct consequence of this principle is that the first proposition that comes to the hearer's mind which also provides a context set of premises will be construed as the proposition the speaker intended, because the speaker could not have intended the hearer to engage in the processing effort of entertaining some hypothesis as to the proposition expressed only to reject it. So in (1) (repeated here):

(1) A: What's the new Pizza House like?
  B: The cooks are all Italian

B takes A's question, given the accessibility of the link between Pizza Houses and food, to be a question about the food at the Pizza House. Her reply, being deliberately indirect, instructs A to construct a context premise such as 'Italians cook pizza well' in order to deduce an answer to the question as the implicit content of what B said. This reply has the advantage of encouraging her hearer to derive a whole range of indirect information via her beliefs about Italian cooks ('They are likely to serve home-made pasta,' 'They will serve espresso coffee,' 'The place will be cheap and cheerful,' etc.). So in the circumstances this indirect response is more relevant than a direct answer.

8.3.1. **A relevance theory account of anaphora**

Among the data that best display the effects of these principles of relevance theory are the anaphor–antecedent relations exemplified in (2)–(30), the very data which were so problematic for the SEMANTICS = TRUTH CONDITIONS AND PRAGMATICS = WHAT'S-LEFT-OVER view. So suppose we now assume that pronominal and definite NP anaphor–antecedent relations constitute a unitary and pragmatic phenomenon, contrary to our earlier assumptions. What would relevance theory lead us to expect? The output of the grammar underdetermining propositional form does not on this view determine the value of an anaphoric expression at all. The selection of a propositional form to be assigned to some utterance then depends not merely on the logical form output of the grammar, but also on the addition of information available to the hearer at minimal processing cost. And in the case of anaphor–antecedent relations, if they are identified pragmatically, they must be available to the hearer from such immediately accessible information.

What sort of information is accessible to a hearer at low processing cost? Assumptions of relevance theory provide both a general answer to this question and a specific one. The general answer is that all that is accessible to the cognitive mechanism is a set of internal representations. So the concept of accessibility is representational. The specific answer is that a range of information is predicted to be immediately accessible, as follows:

(A) representations of information visually present to the speaker and hearer (if suitably picked out, for example by pointing);

(B) information already represented either in previous propositions or in what precedes the part of the utterance the hearer is processing;

(C) information associated with concepts used in immediately previous linguistic material;

(D) the implicit content of an utterance derived by deduction from the utterance in combination with whatever the hearer takes to be the context;

(E) the logical form of the sentence associated with the utterance being processed.

This variety is exactly what we need to give a unitary pragmatic account of anaphora. For information visually present to the hearer corresponds to the referential use of pronouns and definite NPs; information previously represented in the discourse corresponds to the coreferential use of pronouns; information associated with additional premises is how we establish bridging cross-reference; and information from the logical form of the sentence (its linguistic content) is how lazy pronominal interpretations arise.

Let's take these in somewhat more detail. According to this pragmatic analysis, the concept of definiteness controlling the interpretation of the pronouns and definite NPs in examples (2)–(13) is simply that of presumed accessibility. If a speaker uses a definite expression, she is indicating to the hearer that a representation of an NP type is accessible to her in the sense specified. In the simplest cases, the information that is easily accessible is either the hearer's perception of the scenario of the utterance itself (the directly referential use of pronouns), or the preceding utterance, or preceding parts of the same utterance (the coreferential use of pronouns).

The visual environment and the sequence of utterances in the discourse are not however all that are accessible. The words chosen by the speaker express concepts, and by claim these are stores of information associated with a particular expression of the user's language, the use of which serves to make information listed under that concept accessible. Information from such stores can be used as a context for the proposition directly expressed by the utterance to yield implicit content. And of course, when the hearer deduces further information it is accessible to her. It is from this last source of information that the bridging cross-reference cases such as (38) are straightforwardly predicted:

(38)   I walked into John's kitchen. The windows were spotless

Since the content of all anaphoric expressions is that of a guarantee that an antecedent is immediately available, we predict that where no antecedent is provided by the explicit content of the discourse, nor from the visual scene itself, it must be presumed to be provided by additional premises as part of 'the context.' This is the situation in the bridging cross-reference cases. The discourse preceding the use of *The windows were spotless* in (38) contains no mention of any windows. Yet a speaker of (38) would be using the expression *the windows* as a guarantee of such a representation being accessible. However what the hearer has accessible, in virtue of the speaker's choice of words, are the concepts 'window' and 'kitchen'. Since the concept 'window' consists in part of the information that windows are a means of looking out of a room, and the concept 'kitchen' that it is a room, the hearer deduces that the speaker must have been assuming the accessibility of the additional premise 'John's kitchen had windows.' In other words, the very use of the definite article in the second sentence indicates to the hearer that the context contains an additional premise 'Sue's kitchen had windows.' What this bridging cross-reference phenomenon provides us with is confirmation that the antecedent-identification process is dependent on relevance. For the theory imposed the prediction that any identification process solely dependent on relevance should make use of extra information derived as implicit content just as freely as explicit content, a prediction which turns out to be correct.

In the case of lazy pronouns, what is critical is the fact that the linguistic content of an anaphoric expression specified in the grammar radically underdetermines its propositional value. Among the representations accessible to a hearer, on the relevance theory view, is the logical form of what she is processing, for this is the representation which the grammar makes available. Thus the analysis forces the prediction that an anaphoric expression may pick up on the logical form of some selected antecedent. And this is precisely the phenomenon displayed by lazy pronouns such as in (39):

(39) Joan always puts her paycheck in the bank but Sue normally puts it in the post office

Here the representation that the speaker presumes is accessible to the hearer is the linguistic form of the antecedent, this being 'female's paycheck.' This value for *it* is then in its turn identified as the paycheck of some accessible individual, to wit the subject of the second conjunct, this being the representation most accessible given the position of the pronominal being identified inside the second conjunct.[9]

.3.2. Anaphora and quantifier binding

What all these cases have in common is that the anaphoric NP expression is assigned as an interpretation a representation of some individual via some information accessible to the hearer. The assumptions of relevance theory have therefore provided the basis for a unitary account of anaphora despite semantic divergences, which are indeed predicted. However we have not yet provided an account of bound-variable anaphora. The third of the problems posed earlier was that bound-variable effects could be sensitive to pragmatically provided information. In particular, in (30), bridging cross-reference effects were shown to interact with quantifier–variable dependencies. In the light of relevance theory, the problem now becomes one of how we can make use of the assumption that linguistic content underdetermines propositional content to characterize the required interaction. Though this assumption does not impose any particular analysis of quantification, it does impose a restriction on such analyses. What is required is an analysis of quantification in which the logical operator associated with the quantifying expression is

---

[9] It might be argued that in (39) the lazy pronoun identifies its value from the surface form of its antecedent. However this is not so for all lazy pronominal uses, in particular example (7). See Kempson (1986b) for detailed arguments that lazy pronouns identify their values from the logical form of their antecedent and not the surface form.

assigned in the lexicon, and yet the actual implementation of the binding of the variables associated with the quantifier has to be a pragmatic process building the propositional form associated with the sentence.

This interaction of pragmatic effects with the process of quantifier binding can be straightforwardly characterized if we assume that the output of the grammar is not merely an incomplete propositional form but that such a form has associated stores of information constraining the completion of the proposition. In particular, suppose we assume quantifying NP expressions have a variable assigned as argument as part of the structure of the logical form of the sentence, plus a stored quantifier as a restriction on the binding process to be implemented. The status of this variable *vis à vis* antecedent identification is identical to that of a name. It is a representation accessible in just the same ways as a referential expression – because antecedent identification, being a pragmatic process, is sensitive only to accessibility of representations, not to their truth-theoretic content. The only difference is that the variable is accessible only within the c-command domain of its associated quantifier. In this way the specification of linguistic content for quantifying expressions imposes restrictions on the form of proposition expressed without fully determining it, without binding the variables, and hence without the actual construction of the proposition being a process that is characterized as part of the grammar. To capture the interaction with bridging cross-reference effects, all we need to add is the assumption that quantifiers will bind any new variable introduced by additional premises. It has been argued by several people that quantifiers should bind unselectively any variables in their restrictive clause (Lewis 1975; Kratzer 1981; Heim 1982; Haik 1984; Reinhart forthcoming). What this means is that instead of assuming that a stored quantifier binds just one variable quantifying over individuals, we assume it can bind more than one, thus quantifying over, for example, ordered pairs of individuals. This is what we need for (30) (repeated here):

(30) Every singer complained that the accompanist played too loudly

for the required interpretation is that for each singer–accompanist pair, the singer complained that the accompanist played too loudly.

The detailed specification of this process remains a topic of current research (see Kempson 1986a for one account of the interaction between quantifier binding and bridging cross-reference). There is, however, nothing problematic in principle about assuming that linguistic content is in part a configurational specification of an incomplete logical form and in part a set of constraints on completing that specification. Indeed, there is independent evidence that such an approach to linguistic content is correct, though incomplete. As is argued in detail in Volume IV of this series, Chapter 13 (see also Blakemore 1981, 1986), the concept of linguistic content has to be generalized to include rule-encoded constraints on all aspects of utterance interpretation, for the meaning of discourse connectives such as *so, therefore, after all, but,* needs to be given in terms of constraints on the process of context construction. In this more general view of linguistic content as an articulation of whatever constraints on utterance interpretation are imposed as a decoding mechanism by the grammar, constraints on the proposition expressible by a sentence fall out as merely the major subpart of this set of constraints.

3.3. Presupposition projection

We have now already resolved the first and third of our earlier problems. The problem posed by the truth-theoretic ambiguity of anaphoric expressions is directly predicted. Moreover relevance theory also predicts correctly that anaphor–antecedent identification will be sensitive only to the form of representations, not their truth-theoretic content. And the problematic interaction of bridging cross-reference effects and quantifier-variable binding has reduced to the descriptive problem of specifying a recursive algorithm which characterizes the rule-governed constraints on utterance interpretation correctly.

Implicitly, we have also resolved the second problem – that of presupposition projection. The presupposition projection problem arose from the assumption that the grammar should characterize the relation between sentences such as:

(40)   John regretted that the bill was unpaid

(41)   The bill was unpaid

(42)   There was a bill

But such truth-theoretic relations are relations between propositions, and propositions are not directly and completely characterized by the grammar. So on relevance theory assumptions we predict that truth-theoretic relations between propositions may be in part dependent on nonlinguistic knowledge about the entities being described.

This was precisely the burden of the problem posed by (26) and (27) (repeated here):

(26)   If the President invites George Wallace's wife to the White House, he'll regret having invited a black militant to the White House

(27)   If the President invites Angela Davis to the White House, he'll regret having invited a black militant to the White House

(26) implies the President *has* invited a black militant to the White House, (27) does not. Within the relevance theory framework, the supposed presupposition projection problem is simply not a linguistic one. Presupposition projection is a problem of how information from one conjunct in a conjunction is used as immediately accessible information for the second conjunct, and how information presumed to be accessible is interpreted as an implicit part of the context even when it is not an explicitly stated part of that context. This we have already looked at. All we have to add is the claim that complements of *regret* are definite in the same way as anaphoric expressions, presumed to constitute information accessible independently of their present mention. All the rest follows exactly as in the case of anaphoric expressions. Thus the use of (23) would as a whole 'presuppose' that Bill is married because this information is presumed in the second conjunct to be accessible, but the first conjunct doesn't make it so.

(23) Bill is in love with Sue, and she regrets that Bill is married

(25) Bill is married and Sue regrets that Bill is married

In (25), by contrast, the first conjunct does make this information accessible so an utterance of (25) would not as a whole 'presuppose' that Bill is married. Even the Angela Davis cases are unproblematic.

(26) If the President invites George Wallace's wife to the White House, he'll regret having invited a black militant to the White House

(27) If the President invites Angela Davis to the White House, he'll regret having invited a black militant to the White House

They merely parallel bridging cross-reference cases: the use of the predicate 'black militant' in the second conjunct of some utterance of (27) represents a deliberate choice by the speaker to increase the accessibility of that information stored under the concept 'Angela Davis' to guarantee that the propositions 'Angela Davis is a black militant' and (by deduction) 'The President invites a black militant to the White House' are added as members of the context set of propositions against which the second conjunct is interpreted. Hence (27) as a whole, with these assumptions, would not presuppose that the President has invited a black militant to the White House. (26), which contains no such cross-concept linkage has no trigger for adding to the implicit content of its first conjunct, so the invitation of a black militant to the White House is not made accessible by the first conjunct. Hence this information has to be presumed to be accessible independently of (26) itself, and so an utterance of (26) itself would presuppose that the President has invited a black militant to the White House.

8.3.4. Pragmatic principles and truth conditions

Finally, consider the problem of *and* and its causal and temporal 'implicatures'. What the Cohen, Wilson and Carston examples, (35)–(36) demonstrate is merely the Sperber–Wilson and Carston point that effects induced by pragmatic principles may affect the proposition expressed. Thus even in a case such as *and* whose linguistic content appears to fully determine its propositional content (as that of '&') may underdetermine the content of the coordinate proposition expressed. More precisely, the principle of relevance determines that the hearer will process the sentence of the form *p and q* as offering her two propositions which the speaker thought relevant together for her.

Take for example (43):

(43) Joan went to the bank and stole some money

In order for the two conjuncts to be relevant together, rather than as two quite separate asserted sentences, there must be some correlation between these conjuncts in virtue of which they are together. The two principal ways in which propositions can be related to each other are temporally and causally. Thus the assumption of optimal relevance by the hearer leads her to interpret the two conjuncts as related in some such way as a part of the proposition they jointly express, unless explicitly directed not to interpret it so. The simplest strategy for fixing time specification if no explicit correlation is given is to assume that the order of events mirrors the order in which the sentences are put. Thus in this case the proposition most likely to be expressed is:

(43′) Joan went to the bank at time t_i < time of utterance &
        Joan stole money from the bank at time t_j, t_i < t_j < time of utterance

The proposition (43′) is richer than (43) in more than one respect – in particular, the linguistic content of (43) imposes no restriction on where Joan stole the money from. Again the principle of relevance predicts this enrichment. Since the first conjunct itself provides information that Joan went to the bank and since the concept of 'bank' includes the information that banks contain a lot of money, the least effortful interpretation to make is that Joan stole money from the bank.

That the enrichment of the interpretation of a sentence of the form *p and q* to its construal as 'p and then q' is due to pragmatic principles is not a source of disagreement between Griceans and relevance theory. The disagreement with Grice is merely over the status of such added effects. The Cohen and Wilson examples were problematic for Grice because they showed that effects of conversational maxims could influence truth-value judgements. They are unproblematic for relevance theory because it is an explicit claim of the theory that the linguistic content of a sentence characteristically under-determines the propositions expressible by that sentence, and that the principle of relevance controls the selection of the proposition associated with the utterance that is made on the basis of that linguistic content. Hence the linguistic content of *and* can be specified as logical '&', with pragmatic effects controlled by relevance being part of the proposition expressed.

8.4. The semantics–pragmatics boundary redrawn

We must now step back and consider the relation between grammar and conversational principles that has emerged from the details of this chapter. The identity of the linguistic content of a sentence as a specification of its truth conditions, and the consequent identification of pragmatics as whatever aspects of utterance interpretation remain unaccounted for by the truth-conditional paradigm, led, as we've seen, to paradoxes both within semantics and within pragmatics. Indeed, some people have suggested that the distinction between the semantic properties of grammar and general principles of communication is unworkable and should be more or less abandoned (see Kamp 1979, who suggested that semantics should be taken to be all aspects of utterance interpretation which could be characterized with formal rigor and pragmatics be merely that which is subject only to more informal explanation). However, the distinction between properties intrinsic to language itself and properties of the general cognitive mechanism is essential if we are to be able to give a characterization of properties specific to the language faculty. Construed in terms of relevance theory, this division is unproblematic. The notion of semantics that we want in a grammar is simply a characterization of such properties of interpretation of utterances of a sentence as are rule-governed and unvarying from context to context. Pragmatic theory then articulates the principles underlying utterance interpretation, making use of whatever input to that process that the grammar provides.

The attraction of relevance theory is twofold. First it articulates a detailed explanation of processes involved in utterance interpretation with predictions which are precise enough to bring pragmatics back into the field of serious inquiry. Secondly, the entire account of pragmatics is embedded within an overall theory of cognition. Indeed, Sperber & Wilson claim to provide an account of central cognitive processes which is singularly and explicitly absent in Fodor's own account of the cognitive system (Fodor 1983). The detailed implementation of this claim and its consequences opens up a whole new range of answers to both linguistic and psychological questions. We can now not only ask such questions as: What are the properties of the logical form of sentences? What is the best explanation of quantifier-variable binding? What is the basis for the range of truth-theoretic values available to anaphoric expressions? How can we explain presupposition phenomena?; but we can articulate answers which have the advantage of fitting into an overall psychological framework. We can also, for the first time provide precise answers to the major question: what is the link between the language faculty and general cognitive processes? And we can give new answers to questions particular to psychology: How are concepts structured? How does memory interact with processes of retrieval of information? What forms of inference does the cognitive mechanism employ? Thus relevance theory provides a new taking-off point for pragmatic, linguistic and psychological research.

REFERENCES

Allwood, J. 1972. Negation and the strength of presuppositions. Logical Grammar Report 2. Gothenburg. ms.
Atlas, J. 1975. Frege's polymorphous concept of presupposition and its role in a theory of meaning. *Semantikos* 1: 29–44.
Atlas, J. 1977. Negation, ambiguity and presupposition. *Linguistics and Philosophy* 1: 321–36.
Atlas, J. 1979. How linguistics matters to philosophy: presupposition, truth and meaning. In Oh & Dinneen (1979).
Atlas, J. & Levinson, S. 1981. *It*-clefts, informativeness and logical form. In P. Cole (ed.) *Radical pragmatics*. New York: Academic Press.
Blakemore, D. 1981. Semantic constraints on relevance. In H. Parret *et al.* (eds.) *Possibilities and limitations of pragmatics*. Amsterdam: Benjamins.
Blakemore, D. 1986. Semantic constraints on relevance. Doctoral dissertation, University of London.
Boër, S. & Lycan, W. 1976. The myth of semantic presupposition. Distributed by Indiana University Linguistics Club.
Carston, R. Forthcoming. Implicatures, explicatures and truth-theoretic content. In R. Kempson (ed.) *Mental representations: the interface between language and reality*. Cambridge: Cambridge University Press.
Chomsky, N. 1982. *Lectures on government and binding*. Dordrecht: Foris.
Clark, H. & Haviland, S. 1977. Comprehension and the given–new contract. In R. Freedle (ed.) *Discourse production and comprehension*. Hillsdale: Erlbaum.
Cohen, L. 1971. Some remarks on Grice's views about the logical particles of natural language. In Y. Bar-Hillel (ed.) *Pragmatics of natural language*. Dordrecht: Reidel.
Cole, P. (ed.) 1978. *Syntax and semantics*. Vol. 9: *Pragmatics*. New York: Academic Press.
Cole, P. & Morgan, J. (eds.) 1975. *Syntax and semantics*. Vol. 3: *Speech acts*. New York: Academic Press.
Cooper, R. 1979. The interpretation of pronouns. In Heny & Schnelle (1979).
Davison, A. 1980. Peculiar passives. *Language* 56: 42–65.
Donnellan, K. 1966. Reference and definite descriptions. *Philosophical Review* 75: 281–304.
Erteschik-Shir, N. 1979. Discourse constraints on dative movement. In Givón (1979).
Erteschik-Shir, N. 1986. *Wh*-questions and focus. *Linguistics and Philosophy* 9: 117–50.
Erteschik-Shir, N. & Lappin, S. 1979. Dominance and the functional explanation of island phenomena. *Theoretical Linguistics* 6: 41–85.
Erteschik-Shir, N. & Lappin, S. 1983. Under stress: a functional explanation of sentence stress. *Journal of Linguistics* 19: 419–53.
Evans, G. 1980. Pronouns. *Linguistic Inquiry* 11: 337–62.
Fodor, J. A. 1982. *Representations*. Cambridge, MA: MIT Press.
Fodor, J. A. 1983. *Modularity of mind*. Cambridge, MA: MIT Press.

161

García, E. 1979. Discourse without syntax. In Givón (1979).

Gazdar, G. 1979. *Pragmatics*. New York: Academic Press.

Givón, T. 1978. Negation in language: pragmatics, function, ontology. In Cole (1978).

Givón, T. (ed.) 1979a. *Syntax and semantics*. Vol. 12: *Discourse and syntax*. New York: Academic Press.

Givón, T. 1979b. From discourse to syntax: grammar as a processing strategy. In Givón (1979a).

Grice, P. 1975. Logic and conversation. In Cole & Morgan (1975).

Grice, P. 1978. Further notes on logic and conversation. In Cole (1978).

Grice, P. 1981. Presupposition and conversational implicature. In P. Cole (ed.) *Radical pragmatics*. New York: Academic Press.

Haik, I. 1984. Indirect binding. *Linguistic Inquiry* 15: 185–224.

Harnish, R. 1976. Logical form and implicature. In T. Bever, J. Katz, & T. Langendoen, (eds.) *An integrated threory of linguistic ability*. New York: Crowell.

Hausser, R. 1979. How do pronouns denote. In Heny & Schnelle (1979).

Heim, I. 1982. The semantics of definite and indefinite noun phrases. Doctoral dissertation, University of Massachusetts/Amherst.

Heny, F. & Schnelle, H. (eds.) 1979. *Syntax and semantics*. Vol. 10. New York: Academic Press.

Horn, L. 1984. Towards a new taxonomy for pragmatic inference. In D. Shiffrin (ed.) *Meaning, form and use in context*. Washington: Georgetown University Press.

Horn, L. 1985. Metalinguistic negation and pragmatic ambiguity. *Language* 61,1: 121–74.

Kamp, H. 1979. Semantics *versus* pragmatics. In F. Guenthner & S. Schmidt (eds.) *Formal semantics and pragmatics in natural language*. Dordrecht: Reidel.

Karttunen, L. 1973. Presuppositions of compound sentences *Linguistic Inquiry* 4: 116–93.

Karttunen, L. 1974. Presupposition and linguistic context. *Theoretical Linguistics* 1: 181–94.

Karttunen, L. & Peters, S. 1979. Conventional implicature. In Oh & Dinneen (1979).

Kempson, R. 1975. *Presupposition and the delimitation of semantics*. Cambridge: Cambridge University Press.

Kempson, R. 1986a. Definite noun phrases and context dependence. In T. Myers *et al.* (eds.) *Reasoning and discourse processes*. New York: Academic Press.

Kempson, R. 1986b. Logical form: the grammar–cognition interface. SOAS. ms.

Kratzer, A. 1981. The notional category of modality. In H. J. Eikmeyer & H. Rieser (eds.) *Words, worlds, and contexts*. Berlin and New York: de Gruyter.

Kripke, S. 1977. Speaker's reference and semantic reference. *Midwest Studies in Philosophy* 2: 255–76.

Landman, F. 1981. A note on the projection problem. *Linguistic Inquiry* 12: 467–71.

Lappin, S. 1982. The pragmatics of mood. *Linguistics and Philosophy* 4: 559–78.

Levinson, S. 1983. *Pragmatics*. Cambridge: Cambridge University Press.

Levinson, S. 1985. Minimization and conversational inference. Paper presented at the International Pragmatics Conference, Viareggio.

Lewis, D. 1972. General semantics. In D. Davidson & G. Harman (eds.) *Semantics of natural languages*. Dordrecht: Reidel.

Lewis, D. 1975. Adverbs of quantification. In E. Keenan (ed.) *Formal semantics of natural language*. Cambridge: Cambridge University Press.

Morgan, J. 1978. Two types of convention in indirect speech acts. In Cole (1978).

Oh, G.-K. & Dinneen, D. (eds.) 1979. *Syntax and semantics*. Vol. 11 *Presupposition*. New York: Academic Press.

Prince, E. 1978. A comparison of *wh*-clefts and *it*-clefts in discourse. *Language* 54: 883–907.

Prince, E. 1981. Toward a taxonomy of given–new information. In P. Cole (ed.) *Radical pragmatics*. New York: Academic Press.

Reinhart, T. 1983. Coreference and bound anaphora: a restatement of the anaphora question. *Linguistics and Philosophy* 6: 47–88.

Reinhart, T. Forthcoming. A surface-structure analysis of the 'donkey' anaphora. In E. Reuland & A. ter Meulen (eds.) *The representation of indefinites*. Cambridge, MA: MIT Press.

Riddle, E. & Sheintuch, G. 1983. A functional analysis of pseudo-passives. *Linguistics and Philosophy* 6: 527–63.

Russell, B. 1903. On denoting. *Mind* 14: 479–93.

Sadock, J. 1978. On testing for conversational implicature. In Cole (1978).

Sadock, J. 1981. Almost. In P. Cole (ed.) *Radical pragmatics*. New York: Academic Press.

Sheintuch, G. 1980. The *there*-insertion construction in English. *Glossa* 14: 168–87.

Soames, S. 1979. A projection problem for speaker presuppositions. *Linguistic Inquiry* 10: 623–66.

Soames, S. 1982. How presuppositions are inherited: a solution to the projection problem. *Linguistic Inquiry* 13: 483–546.

Sperber, D. & Wilson, D. 1982. Mutual knowledge and theories of comprehension. In N. Smith (ed.) *Mutual knowledge*. New York and London Academic Press.

Sperber, D. & Wilson, D. *Relevance: cognition and communication*. Oxford: Blackwell.

Stalnaker, R. 1974. Pragmatic presupposition. In M. Munitz & P. Unger (eds.) *Semantics of philosophy*. New York: New York University Press.

Strawson, P. 1950. On referring. *Mind* 59: 320–44.

Strawson, P. 1964. Identifying reference and truth values. *Theoria* 30: 96–118.

Van Fraassen, B. 1968. Presupposition, implication and self-reference. *Journal of Philosophy* 65: 136–52.

Von Stechow, A. 1981. Presupposition and context. In U. Monnich (ed.) *Aspects of philosophical logic*. Dordrecht: Reidel.

Wilson, D. 1975. *Presupposition and nontruthconditional semantics*. New York and London: Academic Press.

9 Discourse analysis: a part of the study of linguistic competence*

Ellen F. Prince

9.1. Terminological preliminaries

'Discourse analysis' is without a doubt one of the most widely used and loosely defined terms in the entire field of linguistics. At least two reasons for this come to mind, one a positive one, the other a negative one. The positive one is that discourse, in all its many aspects, is a salient and important object of study in a large number of domains: it is hard to imagine a full account of human cognition, development, language, behavior, culture, interaction, creativity, pathology, or simulation that does not attend to discourse. The negative reason for the looseness of the term is that no one theory or account of discourse has had a wide or strong enough acceptance to have an imperialistic monopoly on it.

Not surprisingly then, the term 'discourse analysis' does not denote a unitary field of inquiry. That is, on the assumption that a field is defined by a common set of beliefs, a common methodology, and a common set of goals, 'discourse analysis' denotes many fields; the term has been and no doubt will continue to be used in different ways by sociolinguists, ethnomethodologists, ethnolinguists, psycholinguists, literary theorists, and computational linguists, among others, as long as they find the study of stretches of language relevant. An overview of all these fields is truly beyond both the scope of this paper and the abilities and interests of this author; the reader is referred instead to Grimes (1975), Hobbs (1976), Bolinger (1977), Clippinger (1977), Coulthard (1977), Ervin-Tripp & Mitchell-Kernan (1977), Freedle (1977), Keenan & Bennett (1977), Labov & Fanshel (1977), Myers (1977), Dressler (1978), Morgan (1978), Givón (1979), Rochester & Martin (1979), Hinds (1980), Joshi, Webber, & Sag (1981), Werth (1981), Tannen (1982), Brady &

* I should like to thank Susumu Kuno for first impressing upon me the fact that the form of an utterance may well have something to do with the communicative intentions of the speaker and that the study of this correlation is an indispensable part of linguistics. In addition, I thank Ruzena Bajcsy, Mascha Benya, Henry Hiż, Arkady Plotnitsky, Gerald Prince, and Shiva Vakli for their help with the data, and Dominique Estival and Gregory Ward for their comments and criticisms.

Berwick (1983), Brown & Yule (1983), Klein (1983), Levinson (1983), Stubbs (1983), Wirth (1983), Schiffrin (1984), among others, and to the papers or references therein.

In what follows, the discussion will be limited to one approach to discourse analysis, which, following Kuno (1978), may be called the 'generativist.' My goal will not be to recount what has been done but to address a broader issue that is crucially relevant to all work in the field but which has not received the attention it requires: the relationship between the discourse functions of linguistic form and linguistic competence. First, however, I shall give a historical justification for the use of the term 'discourse analysis' for the study of the discourse functions of linguistic form.

9.2. Origin of the term 'discourse analysis'

So far as I know, the term 'discourse analysis' was first used by Zellig S. Harris in his 1952 papers with that title. What he meant by it was quite limited and clearly defined: the analysis of a discourse, i.e. the breaking up of a discourse into its fundamental elements or component parts, by standard distributional methods. Following Harris (1952a,b and elsewhere), these fundamental elements consist of the 'elementary' or 'kernel' sentences corresponding to the pure propositional content of the discourse, plus the operations, or 'transformations,' performed on them. The practical motivation for such 'regularizations of texts,' apparent (in retrospect) from the beginning but not made explicit until Harris (1958), was for computer information storage and retrieval of scientific texts; the methods, however, were intended to work equally well on all other types of texts. Early on, however, Harris realized that discourse analysis, as he saw it, was premature, and that more had to be known about what he referred to as his 'cavalier treatment of horizontal order' (Harris 1952a: 9), i.e. about transformations. Thus discourse analysis was postponed while he and his students, most notably Noam Chomsky, concentrated on developing the necessary tool, a theory of syntax.

9.3. Generative discourse analysis as a direct descendant

Today, 35 years later, syntacticians working in a variety of frameworks, transformational and nontransformational, are still trying to perfect that tool. One does, however, have a fairly clear sense of what sorts of generalizations the final account will have to make, and I believe we are well equipped to return to discourse analysis. In particular, a number of linguists working in the generative spirit, although not generally in any particular framework, have in the past decade begun to ask certain questions that Harris's discourse

165

analysis raises but which he himself has never posed; e.g. why *does* a naturally occurring text differ from the set of 'kernel' or canonical sentences representing its propositional content? Put differently, why do syntactic and referential options exist for conveying a proposition, and what makes a speaker select one over the others in a given discourse context? How do the particular syntactic and referential options chosen guide a hearer's understanding of the discourse? Thus the study of the functions of syntax and reference (e.g. matters of definiteness/indefiniteness) have come to represent, for certain linguists, the proper domain of discourse analysis.

9.4. Discourse analysis and linguistic competence

> Linguistic knowledge, of course, extends beyond the level of the sentence. We know how to construct discourses of various sorts, and there are no doubt principles governing discourse structure. (Chomsky 1980:225)

> Certain laws are linguistic, others belong to discourse. (M. Ronat, in Chomsky 1977:146)

One question which has unfortunately received very little explicit attention, but which lies at the heart of the generativist view of discourse analysis, is whether the kind of competence studied therein is part of *linguistic* competence. That is, on the Chomskyan assumption that humans are endowed with a special, encapsulated, species-specific competence for *language*, quite apart from their other endowments, is their discourse competence part of that linguistic competence, as Chomsky suggests above, or does it follow from something else, as Ronat assumes? If linguistic, where does it fit in our model of linguistic competence?

The latter question is perhaps the easier of the two to answer: discourse analysis has been assumed (by those who think about it at all) to fall under *pragmatic* competence, within a view of language that divides up understanding into (truth-conditional) semantics and (non-truth-conditional) pragmatics. Pragmatics, however, is itself still poorly understood and is often assumed to contain a host of diverse phenomena, some of which are not in any obvious way a part of linguistic competence.

For example, consider (1):

(1) a. It's cold in here
     b. Shut the window

If (1a) pragmatically implicates (1b) in some context, as has been claimed, then that 'pragmatic implicature' is clearly not a *linguistic* pragmatic implicature, since no linguistic competence is required beyond the ability to process the literal meaning of the sentence. On the other hand, upon hearing (1a) while seeing the speaker drenched in perspiration, one would presumably *not* infer that the window should be shut (or the heat turned up, or the air conditioner turned down, or a sweater offered, or . . .). That is, in all these situations, an individual is simply inferring some state of a co-participant and acting upon it, showing *interactive* competence but certainly not pragmatic *linguistic* competence.

Of course, the fact that some things assumed or claimed to be part of linguistic pragmatic competence are not does not entail that there is no linguistic pragmatic competence. One domain that seems, to my mind, the most likely place to find such competence is precisely discourse analysis as construed above, in the principles underlying the choice of a particular syntactic or referential option in a context and in the principles underlying the understanding of it. In what follows, I shall look more closely at some discourse phenomena in the hope of establishing their linguistic nature and therefore their relevance to a theory of linguistic competence. First, we shall consider several instances where the competence in question appears to be arbitrary and language-specific and hence linguistic. Then we shall look more closely at a related set of discourse functions to see how subtle, fine-tuned, and non-commonsensical linguistic competence at the discourse level is.

9.5. **Arbitrariness and language specificity**

In (1) above, we saw that the inference that one should shut the window is not triggered by the uttering of *It's cold in here* but rather by the inferrer's belief that the speaker is cold, which s/he may of course have acquired by hearing that sentence uttered and by presuming that the speaker is observing the Gricean maxim of quality. Obviously, whatever is going on in (1), the story to be told is not a story about English: in the same context, a Basque or Hungarian or Hebrew speaker would presumably draw the same inference upon hearing the Basque or Hungarian or Hebrew counterpart of (1a) – or upon hearing the co-participant's teeth chatter.[1] In contrast, there are a host of cases where the pragmatic competence at issue is language-specific; hence it must have been acquired with the language. And we find this both in the domain of the discourse functions of syntax and in the domain of reference.

---

[1] Of course, it may be the case that, in some culture, talk about air temperature is taboo, in which case the uttering of (1a) might have an altogether different effect. But this would be a special fact about the *culture*, not about the language.

9.5.1. Arbitrariness and language specificity: discourse and syntax

Consider, first, (2):

(2) [Whether the Israelis found Eichmann alone, or whether someone informed them, is not known. Both Wiesenthal and a second Nazi-hunter, Toviah Friedman, have claimed that . . .]

    a. . . . they found Eichmann

    b. . . . it was they who found Eichmann

Both (2a) and (2b) are felicitous in the context of (2), and they convey the same propositional content (*pace* Atlas & Levinson 1981; cf. Horn 1981). Compare these with (3) (the insertion of # indicates an infelicitous, rather than a strictly ungrammatical, sentence):

(3) [Just last week Eichmann's supporters claimed he would never be found and this morning Wiesenthal and Friedman announced that . . .]

    a. . . . they found Eichmann

    b. # . . . it was they who found Eichmann

The canonical (a) sentence is as felicitous in the context of (3) as in the context of (2) (though the stress is different); however, the *it*-cleft (b) sentence is infelicitous in the context of (3). The difference, of course, is that an *it*-cleft is a 'focus–presupposition' sentence (Chomsky 1971), whereby the proposition conveyed is structured into two parts, one an open proposition, the other its instantiation, and its felicitous use in discourse requires that the open proposition be appropriately construable as 'shared knowledge' (Prince 1978a). On the basis of (2), the speaker is warranted in taking the open proposition in (4) as 'shared knowledge' (or 'first background entailment', Wilson & Sperber 1979); on the basis of (3), however, the speaker has no such warrant:

(4) X found Eichmann

If the competence underlying these intuitions follows from some nonlinguistic 'common sense', from some 'iconic' value of the *it*-cleft construction, then we should expect to find that languages whose syntax is not strikingly different from English have fairly literal counterparts of *it*-clefts, in particular with some syntactic highlighting or isolation of the instantiating constituent *they*, with the syntactic subordination of the rest of the sentence corresponding to the 'backgrounding' or 'presuming' of the open proposition, perhaps also with some concomitant marking of the variable's position, say with a trace. However, this is not the case in at least one related – and not dramatically different – language, Yiddish:

(5)   a. . . . zey hobn gefunen aykhmanen
      '. . . they have found Eichmann'
      b. . . . *dos* hobn zey gefunen aykhmanen   (*Forward*, March 23,
      1986 p. 1)
      . . . this have they found Eichmann
      '. . . it was they who found Eichmann'

In the context of (the Yiddish counterpart of) (2), both the canonical (5a) and
the noncanonical *dos*-construction (5b) are felicitous, the latter having in fact
occurred naturally in just this context. Furthermore, (5b) is felicitous in
general if and only if the speaker is warranted in taking the open proposition
in (4) as shared knowledge, and it is predictably infelicitous in the context of
(the Yiddish counterpart of) (3). That is, (5b) is the functional equivalent of
an English *it*-cleft. However, there seems to be no iconic reason for this form
having this discourse function: the functionally focussed *zey* is not syntactically isolated or highlighted in any obvious way, there is no subordination,
and there is no trace. Instead, this one-clause construction has an invariant
dos 'this' in leftmost position, followed by the verb, followed by the subject
and complements. What marks the special function of this construction is the
presence of a sentence-initial *dos* which is not an argument of the verb.
Syntactically, the *dos*-construction is absolutely analogous to the *es*-construc-
tion exemplified in (6c); however, *es*-constructions have a totally different
discourse function, being used when the subject is 'nonthematic', in fact,
when the sentence is 'athematic', when the fewest assumptions about shared
knowledge are warranted:

(6)   [Come to me, I've been away looking for you on twisted roads. I'm
      still young, inexperienced . . .]
      a. . . . fremde mentshn kenen mikh farnarn
      . . . strange people can me entice
      'Strange people can entice me'
      b. . . . *es* kenen fremde mentshn mikh farnarn   (Shvaib: *Moyde
      ani*)
      . . . it can strange people me entice
      'Strange people can entice me', 'It can happen that strange
      people entice me'
      c. # . . . *dos* kenen fremde mentshn mikh farnarn
      . . . this can strange people me entice
      'It is strange people that can entice me'

That is, both the *es*-construction in (6b) and the *dos*-construction in (6c)
consist of a single clause, have a postverbal subject, and have a dummy NP in
first position which is not an argument of the verb; the only difference is which

dummy NP is used: *es* 'it' vs. *dos* 'this'. However, the two constructions are functionally unrelated, *es*-constructions like (6b) occurring when the fewest assumptions about shared knowledge are warranted, *dos*-constructions like (6c) occurring when very rich and specific assumptions about shared knowledge are warranted.

One may perhaps counter the above by claiming that, for Yiddish speakers, *dos*-constructions (the *it*-cleft counterparts) *are* iconic. That is, nonthematic subjects may be called 'new information', and focussed constituents in focus–presupposition constructions may likewise be called 'new information'. Thus the postverbal position of subjects in both *es*- and *dos*-constructions could be said to represent 'new information.' The problem with this line of reasoning lies in the sloppiness of the terminology. That is, the term 'new information', like 'old/given information', has been used to cover a variety of different phenomena, adding considerable confusion to an already confused field. In *es*-constructions, the subject is perhaps 'new' in that it is not what is being talked about (Gundel 1974; Reinhart 1981; Davison 1984), i.e. the information status of the entity evoked is what is relevant.[2] In *dos*-constructions, on the other hand, the subject is new insofar as it represents the instantiation of a variable in an open proposition which is taken to be already in the discourse model. Of course, the actual entity that this constituent evokes may be 'old' or 'new' in terms of its own information status in the discourse model, depending on whether it has already been evoked, is being talked about, etc. Note that, if it is, it may then be represented by a proform, as in (5b), proforms being a mark of '*old* information' in terms of the information status of an entity (Halliday 1967; cf. also Grosz 1977; Sidner 1979; Webber 1979; Prince 1981c). Thus the argument for the iconicity of *dos*-constructions remains unconvincing.

Finally, Yiddish is not unique in having such a noncleft functional counterpart of an *it*-cleft; consider the Russian counterparts of (2) in (7):

(7)   a. . . . on'i nashl'i aykhmana
       . . . they found Eichmann
    b. . . . eto on'i nashl'i aykhmana
       . . . this they found Eichmann
       'It was they who found Eichmann'

That is, the Russian functional counterpart of an *it*-cleft is, like the Yiddish, a single clause, the only difference between it and the canonical sentence being

---

[2] Parenthetically, it should be noted that *entity* is being used here in the broad sense of anything of which something may be predicated: individuals, sets, exemplars, propositions, facts, events, etc. (Webber 1979).

the addition of a sentence-initial *eto* 'this'.[3] It is most plausible that the Yiddish construction is a calque from Slavic, with the difference that Yiddish has the Germanic trait of requiring the tensed verb to occur in second position.[4]

In sum, then, the felt iconicity of some syntactic construction with respect to some discourse function is no doubt simply a metalinguistic illusion: if a syntactic construction 'feels' iconic to the speakers of its language, as *it*-clefts do to me (and very likely as their functional counterparts do to speakers of Yiddish and Russian), then it must be the case that such feelings of iconicity are acquired with the language. Of course, speakers find iconicity at all levels of linguistic form; cf. the many silly jokes about X being called *Y* because it *is* a Y, or Diderot's claim (Chomsky 1965:7) that French is better suited to scientific discourse than other languages because its syntax follows 'the train of thought.' This phenomenon is interesting in its own right, but it clearly must not be allowed to influence the linguist's preconceptions of the borders of linguistic competence.[5]

---

[3] But see Gundel (1977) for arguments that these Russian *eto*-constructions are in fact derived from cleft constructions. Thus (7b) would be derived from (i):

(i) . . . eto ∅ on'i kotorii nashl'i aykhmana
 . . . this ∅ they who found Eichmann
 'This/It is they who found Eichmann'

Such an analysis is syntactically problematic, however, in that it requires the deletion of the *wh*-word, otherwise impossible in Russian, and, in the case of a focussed nonsubject, the copying of the case features of the (deleted) *wh*-word onto the focussed constituent. Furthermore, it depends on the fact that present tense copulas do not occur overtly: hence the positing of ∅ following *eto* in (i) above. In Yiddish, such an analysis would be even more problematic. The Yiddish equivalent of (i) is (ii):

(ii) . . . dos iz zey, vos hobn gefunen aykhmanen
 . . . this is they, that have found Eichmann

Note that one would have to posit, in addition to *wh*-word deletion (otherwise ungrammatical), also copula-deletion, which is likewise ungrammatical (in main clauses) in Yiddish. Finally, one would have to account for the permutation of the (putatively subordinate) tensed verb with the focussed constituent.

[4] There is one other difference between Yiddish *dos*-constructions and Russian *eto*-constructions. *eto*-constructions can focus any constituent simply by fronting it to the position immediately after *eto*, as seen in (i):

(i) eto aykhmana on'i nashl'i
 this Eichmann they found
 'It was Eichmann that they found'

In contrast, *dos*-constructions can focus only subjects (Weinreich 1971:333); clearly the V/2 constraint is relevant to this difference.

[5] Parenthetically, it should be noted that while the demonstration that some phenomenon is an arbitrary fact of some language seems to be sufficient evidence that that phenomenon is linguistic, the converse is not true: a universal may of course be linguistic in origin as well. Now, the fact that speakers hypothesize that an open proposition may be assumed to be shared knowledge and then mark these open propositions linguistically may well be universal, since I know of no language (other than pidgins) which lack linguistic forms for such purposes. But it is not at all clear whether such hypothesizing is *linguistic*, or whether it reflects rather some prelinguistic or extralinguistic human thought processes. Of course, the same problem obtains in many other conceptual distinctions reflected in language, e.g. aspectual marking.

9.5.2. **Arbitrariness and language specificity: discourse and reference**

Now let us turn to the other domain of discourse analysis as construed here, the study of choices among referential options in discourse. Consider (8):

(8)   a. Last week I read a book and I met an author
      b. Last week I read a book and I met the author

The most usual understanding of (8a) is one in which the author met is not the author of the book read. In contrast, the most usual understanding of (8b), with no special prior context, is one in which the author met is the author of the book read. Now this difference in understanding is not a truth-conditional one, since, if (8b) is true, then (8a) is true, as argued convincingly in Kempson (1975). Rather, the difference appears to be a pragmatic one concerning the choice of definite vs. indefinite NPs, where definite NPs signal that the hearer is assumed to be already familiar with the entity in question – or to be able to have inferred it from other beliefs (here, 'A book generally has an author'), while indefinite NPs signal that the hearer is assumed not to know, and not to be able to infer, the entity in question (Christophersen 1939; Hawkins 1978; Prince 1978b, 1981a; Heim 1982; Ariel 1985; among others). That these different understandings are conveyed at all is, once again, perhaps a universal phenomenon that may follow from general nonlinguistic – here interactive – principles; but that they are conveyed by the use of two different articles is a fact of English. Consider (9–11):

(9)   *Egyptian Arabic*:
      a. aret kitab wa-shoft katib
         I-read book and-I-met author
         'I read a book and I met an author'
      b. aret kitab wa-shoft al-katib
         I-read book and-I-met the-author
         'I read a book and I met the author'

(10) *Turkish*:
      a. Bir kitap ekudum ve bir yazarinla görüçdüm
         a book I-read and an author-with I-met
         'I read a book and I met an author'
      b. Bir kitap ekudum ve onun yazarinla görüçdüm
         a book I-read and its author-GEN-with I-met
         'I read a book and I met the author'

(11) *Slovak*:
      a. Som citala knihu a som stretla spisovatela
         I read-f. book and I met-f. writer
         'I read a book and I met an author'

    b. Som citala knihu a som stretla autora
       I read-f. book and I met-f. author
       'I read a book and I met the author'
    c. Som citala khihu a som stretla jej spisovatela
       I read-f. book and I met-f. her writer
       'I read a book and I met the author'

(12) *Polish*:
    a. Przeczytałem książkę i poznałem pewnego autora
       I-read-m. book and I-met-m. certain author
       'I read a book and I met an author'
    b. Przeczytałem książę i poznałem autora
       I-read-m. book and I-met-m. author
       'I read a book and I met the author'

That is, there are languages like Arabic which have definite articles but no indefinite, there are languages like Turkish which have indefinite articles but no definite, and there are languages like Slovak and Polish which have no articles at all. Interestingly, all seem to mark the difference in understanding between (8a) and (8b), but they mark it in very different ways: by opposing whatever articles they have to the non-occurrence of an article, by adding possessives (for the definite understanding) or adjectives (for the indefinite), by lexical means, and no doubt by other means as well.[6]

Furthermore, even in languages like English which have both definite and indefinite articles, the form–understanding correlation may still be arbitrary; compare (13):

(13) a. I have flowers
    b. I love flowers
    c. There are flowers in the vase

Both (13a) and (13b) have no article, but (13a) is understood as indefinite while (13b) is understood as generic, a special case of definite (and marked as such in many languages, e.g. French *J'aime les fleurs*). That is, the hearer of (13a) is not expected to already know or to be able to infer some (set) entity for the flowers that the speaker has, but the hearer of (13b) is indeed expected to have in his/her knowledge store some entity for the class of things called flowers that the speaker loves. Note that the generic understanding is impossible in (13c), owing to the requirement for a (conceptual) indefinite in *there*-sentences. Similarly, consider (14):

---

[6] Even in Arabic, Turkish, Slovak, and Polish, it is very likely that there are other means of conveying these two understandings. I simply asked native speakers of these languages to translate the English sentences as naturally as possible.

(14) a. He offered the usual suggestions
      b. He offered the useful suggestions
      c. There were the usual suggestions offered
      d. # There were the useful suggestions offered

Although both (14a) and (14b) have object NPs containing the definite article, the object NP in (14a) is conceptually indefinite. That is, the hearer of (14a) is not already expected to be familiar with, or infer, the set of suggestions offered – they are new suggestions, both in the discourse model and presumably in the hearer's knowledge store (although it is predicated of them that they are *like* suggestions usually offered and therefore presumably known to the hearer). In contrast, (14b) is felicitous just in case the speaker is warranted in assuming that the hearer is already familiar with the suggestions offered. Note the felicity of *the usual suggestions* in the *there*-sentence in (14c), where (conceptual) indefinites are called for, as opposed to the more expected infelicity of *the useful suggestions* in the *there*-sentence in (14d) (Ziv 1981; cf. also Rando & Napoli 1978).

Thus, while it may follow from some nonlinguistic pragmatic endowment that one must make hypotheses about certain aspects of the co-participant's beliefs and reasoning, and that one must communicate the results of this hypothesizing, the ability to communicate these results in some language is clearly part of the speaker's linguistic competence in that language.

9.6. The subtlety of discourse competence

I shall now turn to several functionally related syntactic constructions to get a closer look at discourse competence, in particular, at the subtlety and complexity of the discourse functions of syntactic constructions.

Speakers choose particular syntactic options to convey a variety of non-truth-conditional understandings. (See, in addition to the works already mentioned, Chafe 1976; Kuno 1976b; Erteschik-Shir & Lappin 1979, Green 1980; Thompson 1983, 1984; Oehrle forthcoming.) These may relate to information structure, or 'packaging', topic-hood, dominance, empathy, and point of view, among other things. However, the particular understandings that a given syntactic construction triggers are often far subtler than such broad rubrics might lead one to believe. In particular, one type of 'information packaging' involves the marking of an open proposition as shared knowledge in the discourse, as discussed above. As is well-known, *wh*-questions, *it*-clefts, and *wh*-clefts have such a function.[7] What is less well-known, however, is that there are as well a number of other 'focus–presupposition' constructions in English; all share this gross function, but

[7] If affirmation/negation is admitted as a variable, then all questions have this function.

each has special features, in terms of both function and syntax. In order to appreciate how fine-tuned discourse competence is, I shall now consider three such constructions: topicalization, VP-preposing, and gapping.

9.6.1. Topicalization

As argued in Prince (1981b) and Ward (1985), the syntactic construction *topicalization*,[8] exemplified in (15a) and (16a), has a double discourse function. First, its leftmost NP is understood as bearing a particular anaphoric relation to something already in the discourse model that the co-participants are constructing – it represents either an entity already evoked in the discourse (15a) or else an entity which bears some set relation to something already in the discourse model (16a). Second, the proposition corresponding to the sentence as a whole (with the leftmost NP, when it evokes an element of a set, replaced by that set), with the tonically stressed constituent replaced by a variable, represents an open proposition that is appropriately construable as salient 'shared knowledge' (15b) and (16b):

(15) a. . . . a . . . schefflera had been cut down and seemingly disposed of. From the wreckage he cut a piece of leafless stem some 3 ft (1 m.) in length with the thought that it would make a good walking stick. *This he used ∅ daily around the nursery for nearly two months;* . . .   (Davidson & Rochford 1976:70)

b. he Xed (with respect to) this

(16) a. . . . 'What have you done with my papers?' he ranted, almost incoherent with worry. 'Everything is fine, Sir,' the maid assured him brightly. 'I only burned the papers that were already written on. *The nice clean sheets I put ∅ in your desk drawer.'*   (Spalding 1969:4)

b. I Xed elements-of-set-of-papers.[9]

It turns out, however, that a more general statement can be made, of

---

[8] The term *topicalization* is used here because it is the conventional name for the construction, since its introduction in Ross (1967). No relevance to the notion 'topic' is to be inferred.

[9] A manipulation of topicalization for humorous effect is shown in (i):

(i) [Response to a letter arguing against Miss Manners' claim that spaghetti should be eaten simply with a fork and for the practice of eating it with a fork and spoon] 'That many people use spoons to assist forks in eating spaghetti, Miss Manners is well aware ∅. That correct spaghetti eating, with fork only, is not easy, Miss Manners also knows ∅. (Why Miss Manners is suddenly writing her sentences backwards, she does not know ∅.) . . .   (Martin 1982:163)

Here, the first two topicalizations have as 'backward-looking centers' propositional entities (facts) which have just been evoked in the discourse (see below). The third, however, has as its 'backward-looking center' a fact which is salient in the situation but which has not been evoked by linguistic means. See Prince (1981c) for a discussion of textually vs. situationally evoked entities.

which topicalization is a special case. That is, there are a number of constructions in which the leftmost constituent represents a certain type of 'backward-looking center' (Grosz, Joshi & Weinstein 1983), i.e. something that looks to the already existing discourse model for its understanding, and where the replacement of the tonically stressed constituent by a variable corresponds to an open proposition which is appropriately construable as salient 'shared knowledge'.

9.6.2. **VP-preposing**

Taking topicalization to be a preposing construction, we find that a number of other preposing constructions have analogous discourse functions. They are dealt with in detail in Ward (1985); here I shall simply point out one of them, *VP-preposing*, exemplified in (17) and (18):

(17) a. As members of a Gray Panthers committee, we went to Canada to learn, and *learn we did* 0. *(Philadelphia Inquirer*, 16 June, 1985 [=Ward's 377])
      b. # As members of a Gray Panthers committee, we went to Canada and *learn we did* 0
      c. *We X learned (=We did/didn't learn)*

(18) a. It's much easier for you, Ferre, to go, and *go you will* 0! *(Newsweek*, 12 November, 1984 [=Ward's 407])
      b. # It's much easier for you, Ferre, to talk to him, and *go you will* 0
      c. You X will go (=You will/won't go)

That is, such constructions, where an untensed VP is fronted and where the tensed verb or modal is tonically stressed, are felicitous in discourse just in case the following holds. The open proposition, arrived at by replacing the affirmation carried by the tensed element with a variable, is already in the discourse model, and saliently so, but it has not yet been entailed and its negation has not yet been entailed; as such, of course, it represents something appropriately construable as salient 'shared knowledge', as in the case of topicalization. Also like topicalization, the tonically stressed constituent in a VP-preposing construction represents the instantiation of this 'affirmation' variable, here resulting in the proposition's being entailed.[10]

---

[10] When the negation of the proposition is entailed, the discourse constraints may be looser. Compare:

(i) a. He was so sick I thought he'd die, and *die he did* 0
     b. He was so sick I thought he'd die but *die he did not* 0

(ii) a. # He was so sick and *die he did* 0
     b. He was so sick but *die he did not* 0

9.6.3. **Gapping**

Preposing constructions are not, however, the only syntactic constructions in which the leftmost constituent represents such a 'backward-looking center' and which are understood as instantiating an open proposition which is appropriately construable as salient in the discourse model. Consider the following:

(19) a. Could Miss Manners resolve a problem for a confused foreigner? I
          was brought up . . . to believe that it is correct to hold one's fork in
          one's left hand, tines pointing down, and one's knife in one's right.
          The fork is used to secure the particular square inch of food on
          which one has set one's sight, and the knife 0 to sever it from its main
          body.   (Martin 1982:123)
       b. Elements-of-set-of-knife/fork are used to X

(20) a. [Discussion of new Pennsylvania drug benefits for the elderly]
          Individuals can earn $9000, married couples 0 $12,000. (KYW
          Radio, 27 October, 1983)
       b. Elements-of-set-of-elderly can earn X

Gapping, exemplified in (19) and (20), is another syntactic construction which appears to trigger the same sort of understandings with respect to the leftmost constituents, in fact always the set-membership understandings, and which appears to instantiate an open proposition by the tonically stressed constituents, the open proposition appropriately construable as salient 'shared knowledge', at least by the time the first gapped conjunct is produced. (See Kuno 1976a; Levin & Prince 1982.) Note, for example, that, if (20a) were not a gapping, it would be ambiguous: individuals could conceivably constitute married couples. Of course, stress can preclude such an understanding, but gapping does so by forcing the two leftmost NPs to be construed as disjoint elements of the set of elderly persons. This is perhaps clearer in (21):

(21) She wrote long [. . .] letters, which *she sent to her sister and she 0 to my*
      mother. (*Heat and dust*)

If the token in (21) were not gapped, the leftmost NPs of each conjunct could easily be understood as coreferential, i.e. she sent long letters to her sister and to my mother. In a gapping, however, the disjoint reference is forced.

In the negative cases, the proposition whose negation is entailed need not have been explicitly entered into the discourse model; when it is not, a scalar implicature (Horn 1972; Gazdar 1979) seems to be triggered that is otherwise absent – in (iib), for example, he was very sick but not to the point of dying. The exact details have not yet been worked out, but it is interesting that scalar implicatures are related to the set inferences discussed above (Hirschberg 1985) and are triggered by other preposing constructions as well (Ward 1983, 1985; Ward & Hirschberg 1985).

9.6.4. Comparison

Let us now briefly compare these three constructions. First, note that, functionally, VP-preposing is a special case of topicalization: the preposed constituent (the VP) represents a 'backward-looking center'; the replacement of the tonically stressed constituent by a variable produces an open proposition that can be construed as salient 'shared knowledge'; and the entire sentence instantiates that open proposition. VP-preposing is more restricted than topicalization, however, in that the preposed constituent is a VP and represents an activity, action, or state; the open proposition must have been explicitly entered into the discourse (and not simply inferrable); and the variable must represent affirmation or denial.[11]

That VP-preposing is functionally a special case of topicalization is perhaps not surprising, given that it can be seen as a special case of topicalization on syntactic grounds as well (Ward 1985). It is surprising, however, that gapping is also a special case of topicalization on functional grounds, given their syntactic dissimilarity. But in fact the leftmost constituents of gapped clauses represent backward-looking centers and the rightmost constituents represent instantiations of a variable in an open proposition taken to be shared knowledge. The difference between topicalization and gapping is that in the latter the backward-looking centers must be in a set relation, not simply evoked in the discourse; the instantiation must be different for each member of the set mentioned; and the tensed verb must not be what is instantiated. Predictably then, gapping can be combined with topicalization, as in (22):

(22) a. The former we call the linguistic meaning of the expression, the latter 0 its context of use.   (Barwise & Perry 1983:194)
   b. We call elements-of-set-of-2-mentioned-items X

However, it seems that gapping cannot be combined with VP-preposing:

(23) [They expected me to go to college and (not) get married . . .]
   a. . . . Well, go to college I did and get married I did not
   b. # . . . Well, go to college I did and get married 0 not
   c. I X-do set-of-mentioned-activities

---

[11] Interestingly, this restricted function of English VP-preposing does not seem to follow from its syntax or semantics; in Yiddish, for example, where topicalization is functionally very similar to English, the preposing of a VP is functionally identical to (other) topicalizations, as shown in the proverb in (ia):

(i) a. layen darf men mit eytses, gebn zol men on eytses
      lend must one with advice, give shall one without advice
      'One should get advice before lending, but not before giving'
   b. One must do members-of-set-of-paying-activities X-with advice

I believe the reason lies in an incompatibility between discourse functions. That is, gapping requires that the tensed item be gapped; this may be an arbitrary syntactic fact or not. In either event, the discourse reflex of this is that the tensed item must represent information which is not the variable in the open proposition. On the other hand, the discourse function of VP-preposing is such that the tensed item must represent information which instantiates the variable in the open proposition. As such, it must be present. Furthermore, it appears that, even when the clause is negative and the tonic stress falls on *not*, as in (23), the tensed item, though unstressed, is still *part* of the instantiation and, therefore, must be present.[12]

9.7. Conclusion

In sum, I have tried to show that a significant part of a speaker–hearer's competence involves knowing how linguistic forms are used in discourse, more specifically, knowing which syntactic and referential forms trigger which nonlogical inferences. At least for the cases mentioned here, the competence in question appears to be language-specific, for, while it may be the case that all languages trigger the same set of inferences, particular form–inference correlations vary from language to language. Furthermore, even a brief crosslinguistic view suggests strongly that the inferences are not due to any 'iconicity' of the forms in question but manifest the sort of arbitrariness found in other linguistic levels. Finally, I have tried to show that form–inference correlations are far more subtle and complex than one might think but that at the same time they are amenable to generalization and prediction. Each of these points provides compelling evidence that discourse competence is a part of linguistic competence – part of the endowment that an individual must have if s/he can be said to 'know a language', that discourse analysis is interesting, and that no theory that ignores such discourse phenomena can be an adequate theory of linguistic competence.

REFERENCES

Ariel, M. 1985. Givenness markers. Doctoral dissertation, Tel-Aviv University.
Atlas, J. D. & Levinson, S. 1981. It-clefts, informativeness, and logical form. In P. Cole (ed.) *Radical pragmatics*. New York: Academic Press.

[12] Note that in Yiddish, where VP-preposings are no more restricted than (other) topicalizations, gapping is as possible with a preposed VP (ia) as with (other) topicalizations (ib):

(i) a. layen darf men mit eytses un gebn Ø on eytses
       lend must one with advice and give Ø without advice
   b. far a tsap hot men moyre fun fornt,
      for a goat has one fear of front,
      far a ferd Ø fun hintn, far a nar Ø fun ale zaytn
      for a horse Ø of rear, for a fool Ø of all sides
      'Of a goat one fears the front, of a horse Ø the rear, of a fool Ø all sides' (Proverb)

Barwise, J. & Perry, J. 1983. *Situations and attitudes*. Cambridge, MA: MIT Press.
Bolinger, D. 1977. *Meaning and form*. London: Longman.
Brady, M. & Berwick, R. (eds.) 1983. *Computational models of discourse*. Cambridge, MA: MIT Press.
Brown, G. & Yule, G. 1983. *Discourse analysis*. Cambridge: Cambridge University Press.
Chafe, W. 1976. Givenness, contrastiveness, definiteness, subjects, topics, and point of view. In C. Li (ed.) *Subject and topic*. New York: Academic Press.
Chomsky, N. 1965. *Aspects of the theory of syntax*. Cambridge, MA: MIT Press.
Chomsky, N. 1971. Deep structure, surface structure, and semantic interpretation. In D. Steinberg & L. Jakobovits (eds.) *Semantics: an interdisciplinary reader in philosophy, linguistics, and philosophy*. New York: Cambridge University Press.
Chomsky, C. 1977. *Language and responsibility*. New York: Pantheon.
Chomsky, N. 1980. *Rules and representations*. New York: Columbia University Press.
Christophersen, P. 1939. *The articles: a study of their theory and use in English*. Copenhagen: Munksgaard.
Clippinger, J. H. 1977. *Meaning and discourse: a computer model of psychoanalytic speech and cognition*. Baltimore: Johns Hopkins University Press.
Coulthard, M. 1977. *An introduction to discourse analysis*. London: Longman.
Davidson, W. & Rochford, T. C. 1976. *The complete all-color guide to houseplants, cacti and succulents*. New York: Galahad.
Davison, A. 1984. Syntactic markedness and the definition of sentence topic. *Language* 60: 797–846.
Dressler, W. 1978. *Current trends in textlinguistics*. Berlin/New York: de Gruyter.
Erteschik-Shir, N. & Lappin, S. 1979. Dominance and the functional explanation of island phenomena. *Theoretical Linguistics* 6: 44–86.
Ervin-Tripp, S. & Mitchell-Kernan, C. 1977. *Child discourse*. New York: Academic Press.
Freedle, R. 1977. *Discourse production and comprehension*. Hillsdale: Erlbaum.
Gazdar, G. 1979. *Pragmatics: implicature, presupposition, and logical form*. New York: Academic Press.
Givón, T. (ed.) 1979. *Syntax and semantics*. Vol. 12: *Discourse and syntax*. New York: Academic Press.
Green, G. 1980. Some wherefores of English inversions. *Language* 56: 582–601.
Grimes, J. 1975. *The thread of discourse*. The Hague: Mouton.
Grosz, B. 1977. The representation and use of focus in dialog understanding. Doctoral dissertation, University of California, Berkeley.
Grosz, B., Joshi, A. K. & Weinstein, S. 1983. Providing a unified account of definite noun phrases in discourse. *Proceedings of the 21st ACL Meeting*.
Gundel, J. 1974. The role of topic and comment in linguistic theory. Doctoral dissertation, University of Texas.
Gundel, J. 1977. Where do cleft sentences come from? *Language* 53: 343–59.
Halliday, M. A. K. 1967. Notes on transitivity and theme in English. Part 2. *Journal of Linguistics* 3: 199–244.
Harris, Z. S. 1952a. Discourse analysis. *Language* 28: 1–30.
Harris, Z. S. 1952b. Discourse analysis: a sample text. *Language* 28: 474–94.
Harris, Z. S. 1958. Linguistic transformations for information retrieval. In *Proceedings of the International Conference on Scientific Information 2*. Washington, DC: NAS-NRC.
Hawkins, J. A. 1978. *Definiteness and indefiniteness*. Atlantic Highlands: Humanities Press.
Heim, I. 1982. The semantics of definite and indefinite noun phrases. Doctoral dissertation, University of Massachusetts.
Hinds, J. 1980. Japanese conversation, discourse structure, and ellipsis. *Discourse Processes* 3: 263–86.
Hirschberg, J. 1985. A theory of scalar implicature. Doctoral dissertation, University of Pennsylvania.
Hobbs, J. R. 1976. A computational approach to discourse analysis. Research report 76–2. Dept. of Computer Science, CCNY/CUNY.
Horn, L. 1972. On the semantic properties of logical operators in English. Doctoral dissertation, UCLA.

Horn, L. 1981. Exhaustiveness and the semantics of clefts. In V. Burke & J. Pustejovsky (eds.) *NELS* 11. Dept. of Linguistics, University of Massachusetts/Amherst.

Joshi, A. K., Webber, B. L. & Sag, I. A. (eds.) 1981. *Elements of discourse understanding*. Cambridge: Cambridge University Press.

Keenan, E. O. & Bennett, T. (eds.) 1977. Discourse across time and space. *Southern California Papers in Linguistics, No. 5*. University of Southern California.

Kempson, R. 1975. *Presupposition and the delimitation of semantics*. Cambridge: Cambridge University Press.

Klein, F. (ed.) 1983. *Discourse perspectives on syntax*. New York: Academic Press.

Kuno, S. 1976a. Gapping: a functional analysis. *Linguistic Inquiry* 7: 300–18.

Kuno, S. 1976b. Subject, theme, and the speaker's empathy – a reexamination of relativization phenomena. In C. Li (ed.) *Subject and topic*. New York: Academic Press.

Kuno, S. 1978. Generative discourse analysis in America. In W. Dressler (ed.) *Current trends in textlinguistics*. Berlin and New York: de Gruyter.

Labov, W. & Fanshel, D. 1977. *Therapeutic discourse*. New York: Academic Press.

Levin, N. S. & Prince, E. F. 1982. Gapping and causal implicature. Paper presented at the LSA Annual Meeting, San Diego.

Levinson, S. 1983. *Pragmatics*. Cambridge: Cambridge University Press.

Martin, J. 1982. *Miss Manners' guide to excruciatingly correct behavior*. New York: Warner Books.

Morgan, J. L. 1978. Toward a rational model of discourse comprehension. In D. Waltz (ed.) TINLAP-2. New York: Association for Computing Machinery.

Myers, T. (ed.) 1977. *The development of conversation and discourse*. Edinburgh: Edinburgh University Press.

Oehrle, R. Forthcoming. *The English dative constructions: form and interpretation*. Dordrecht: Reidel.

Prince, E. F. 1978a. A comparison of WH-clefts and IT-clefts in discourse. *Language* 54: 883–906.

Prince, E. F. 1978b. On the function of existential presupposition in discourse. In D. Farkas, W. Jacobsen & K. Todrys (eds.) *CLS* 14. Dept. of Linguistics, University of Chicago.

Prince, E. F. 1981a. On the inferencing of indefinite-THIS NPs. In A. K. Joshi, B. L. Webber & I. A. Sag (eds.) *Elements of discourse understanding*. Cambridge: Cambridge University Press.

Prince, E. F. 1981b. Topicalization, Focus-Movement, and Yiddish-Movement: a pragmatic differentiation. In D. Alford *et al.* (eds.) *BLS* 7: 249–64.

Prince, E. F. 1981c. Toward a taxonomy of given/new information. In P. Cole (ed.) *Radical pragmatics*. New York: Academic Press.

Rando, E. & Napoli, D. J. 1978. Definites in THERE-sentences. *Language* 54: 300–13.

Reinhart, T. 1981. Pragmatics and linguistics: an analysis of sentence topics. *Philosophica* 27: 53–94.

Rochester, S. & Martin, J. 1979. *Crazy talk. A study of the speech of the discourse of schizophrenic speakers*. New York: Plenum.

Ross, J. R. 1967. Constraints on variables in syntax. Doctoral dissertation, MIT.

Schiffrin, D. (ed.) 1984. *Meaning, form, and use in context: linguistic applications*. Washington: Georgetown University Press.

Sidner, C. 1979. Towards a computational theory of definite anaphora comprehension in English discourse. Doctoral dissertation, MIT.

Spalding, H. 1969. *Encyclopedia of Jewish humor*. Middle Village, New York: Jonathan David Publishers.

Stubbs, M. 1983. *Discourse analysis: the sociolinguistic analysis of natural language*. Oxford: Blackwell.

Tannen, D. (ed.) 1982. *Spoken and written language. Exploring orality and literacy. Advances in discourse processes*. Vol. IX. Norwood: Ablex.

Thompson, S. 1983. Grammar and discourse: the English detached participial clause. In F. Klein (ed.) *Discourse approaches to syntax*. Norwood: Ablex.

Thompson, S. 1984. 'Subordination' in formal and informal discourse. In D. Schiffrin (ed.) *GURT '84. Meaning, form, and use in context: linguistic applications*. Washington: Georgetown University Press.

Ward, G. 1983. A pragmatic analysis of epitomization: topicalization it's not. *Papers in Linguistics* 17: 145–61.

Ward, G. 1985. The semantics and pragmatics of Preposing. Doctoral dissertation, University of Pennsylvania.

Ward, G. & Hirschberg, J. 1985. Implicating uncertainty: the pragmatics of fall–rise intonation. *Language* 61: 4.

Webber, B. L. 1979. *A formal approach to discourse anaphora*. New York and London: Garland.

Weinreich, U. 1971. *College Yiddish*. 5th rev. edn. New York: YIVO Institute for Jewish Research.

Werth, P. (ed.) 1981. *Conversation and discourse*. New York: St. Martin's Press.

Wilson, D. & Sperber, D. 1979. Ordered entailments: an alternative to presuppositional theories. In C. K. Oh & D. Dinneen (eds.) *Syntax and semantics*. Vol. xi: *Presupposition*. New York: Academic Press.

Wirth, J. (ed.) 1983. *Pragmatics and syntactic form*. Ann Arbor: Karoma.

Ziv, Y. 1981. On some discourse uses of existentials in English, or, getting more mileage out of existentials in English. Paper presented at the LSA Annual Meeting, New York.

10 Speech act distinctions in grammar
Jerrold M. Sadock

10.1. Meaning, form, and function

In using natural language, a speaker may accomplish such things as warning, surprising, insulting, going on record, inquiring, commanding, conjecturing, and so on through a vast repertoire of effects that language is uniquely suited to achieving. Some of these effects are intended, some unwitting; some are more or less automatically associated with certain utterance types, and others are very loosely connected with the form or the content of the uttered token. In this chapter we will consider the extent to which acts of speaking are tied to the grammatical structure of an individual language, or language in general, and examine various views as to the nature of this connection, their benefits and drawbacks.

1.1.1. Locutions, illocutions, and perlocutions

In a work of great influence, the philosopher John Austin (1962) distinguished among three types of act that are ordinarily performed by someone who produces an utterance: *locutionary, perlocutionary,* and *illocutionary acts.* Locutionary acts are, according to Austin, those acts that form the substance of speech – they are acts of making use of the grammar of the language, its phonology, syntax, and semantics. Perlocutionary acts are the by-products (hence *per-*) of speaking certain words in a particular context. Typically, the affected party is the person spoken to, who may be embarrassed, confused, or convinced by what has been said. Though it is usual to treat the aforementioned effects as exhausting the range of perlocutions (as in Davis 1976), for completeness we must also include among perlocutions those by-product effects of speech that are not visited upon the addressee, e.g. embarrassing oneself, or divulging a secret to an eavesdropper.

The most crucial, and most debated, of the Austinian speech act types is the illocutionary act, which Austin said is an act performed *in* speaking. Illocutionary acts are so important to the linguistic study of speech acts that the term *speech act* in the linguistic literature is often treated as synonymous with *illocutionary act*. Typical illocutionary acts include asserting, demanding, inquiring, dubbing, defining, sentencing a defendant in a court of law, and pronouncing a couple husband and wife.

The illocutionary act is central to the speech event in something like the way that killing an official is central to an assassination. Performing a locutionary act is more like pulling the trigger, while performing a perlocutionary act is like causing the government to fall.

Illocutionary acts bear some affinities to locutionary acts and some affinities to perlocutionary acts and can be confused with either, particularly the latter. They resemble locutionary acts to the extent that they are, as Austin insisted, conventional acts – acts done as conforming to some convention. According to Austin, the locutionary act depends in part upon the conventional *sense* and *reference* of the uttered expression – the illocutionary act upon its conventional *force*. But illocutions are also akin to perlocutionary acts in that there is, in the case of a successful illocutionary act at least, an effect on the speech situation, in fact often an effect on the addressee. While according to Austin, perlocutionary acts succeed or fail, illocutionary acts are *felicitous* or *infelicitous*; they *secure uptake* or fail to.

These distinctions between illocutionary and perlocutionary acts suggest two quite distinct methods of pinning down illocutions, both of which Austin and his linguistic and philosophical followers have employed. The first is to seek within the grammar of the language the conventions that determine the force of an utterance, and the second is to investigate the conditions that determine the success of an illocutionary act, i.e. its felicity conditions. The grammatical reflection of *illocutionary force* is the main subject of this chapter.

10.1.2. Sentence types

The vast majority of languages, perhaps even all, formally divide main clauses into a small number of types that correlate at least partially with their typical or conventional use (see Sadock & Zwicky 1985). With rare exceptions, natural languages seem to distinguish at least between declarative sentences, ordinarily used among other things to report facts; interrogative sentences, used at least to ask yes/no questions; and imperatives, used to make requests. A language may have other types – a special type used for expressing wishes, a type used for cursing, one for making promises, and so on. It may also more finely divide the classes above. For example, instead of displaying a general form used for assertoric speech acts of all kinds, it may present one special form for stating conclusions, one for stating observations, and one for reporting hearsay. But no language has been reported to be completely without a system of grammatical distinctions among main clause types that is partially correlated with illocutionary force. Such a system we will call a system of *sentence types*.

Normally the markers of sentence type in a language are rather abstract: among the most common formal earmarks are intonation, word order, verbal mood, and particles with no other use. The English yes/no interrogative is distinguished from the declarative by subject–auxiliary inversion and the imperative by the absence of a subject and a form of the verb that is homophonous with the infinitive. The Eskimo declarative, interrogative and imperative are distinguished by verbal inflection: *Nerivutit* 'You eat,' *Nerivit* 'Do you eat?', *Nerigit* 'Eat!' (Compare *nerisutit* 'that you eat.') In Korean a system of sentence-final particles does the job: *Na ka ka kess ta* 'I will go,' *Na ka ka ma* 'I promise to go,' *Uli ka ka ca* 'Let us go,' *Ne ka ka la* 'You go!' etc. (Lee & Maxwell 1970). Often, some combination of these is employed. The yes/no interrogative of Yiddish, for example, is formed with the help of a sentence-initial particle, inverted word order, and a special intonation contour.

It is important to notice that these devices really do define a system, in that most normal sentences belong to one of the types and no sentence belongs to two. The system of sentence types can vary from language to language. What might be treated grammatically in a parallel fashion with other speech act distinctions in one language may be treated differently in another. Consider a language like Hidatsa (Matthews 1965) with an obligatory distinction between statements the speaker is unsure of, those which are matters of common knowledge, those based on reports of others, those which report feelings and beliefs, and finally, those based on the speaker's firsthand observations. In this language, exactly the same kind of formal device, a particle, distinguishes these five types. These particles are mutually exclusive with each other and with the particles used for distinguishing interrogatives, optatives, and imperatives. Thus, each of the various assertoric subtypes is on a par with the interrogative type, the optative type, and the imperative and should therefore be considered a separate type in its own right. While we can certainly make such distinctions among assertoric speech act intentions clear in English, for example by inserting a parenthetical *they say* or *I guess*, the means for doing this is neither parallel to, nor mutually exclusive with, the indicators of the other sentence types in the language. Therefore, at least at the top level of the analysis, English does not have the same system of sentence types as Hidatsa.

.1.3. Performative sentences

In some languages there are sentences that seem to convey their conventional force directly in terms of the meanings of their words and their structure: 'I

185

promise that . . .,' 'I order you to . . .,' 'I sentence you to . . .' Such sentences were dubbed *performative sentences* by Austin. They are commonly used under formal circumstances in Western languages, but appear to be lacking in some other languages, particularly those with a more developed system of sentence types or those spoken in societies that seem to have less cultural need for formulaic discourse of the kind represented by performative sentences.

It was Austin's belief that performative sentences, as well as nondeclarative sentences, were not subject to judgements of truth or falsity, but rather were felicitous or infelicitous. He therefore spent a good deal of effort trying to find grammatical criteria for recognizing performative sentences in order to distinguish them from *constatives*, sentences which can be said to be true or false. Often, performative sentences conform to the pattern in (1) referred to as the *performative formula*:

(1) I V (you) . . .; 'V' a verb in the simple present

But the performative formula is both too restrictive, excluding such indubitable performatives as *You are fired* and *The court finds you guilty as charged*, as well as too lax, giving no grounds for excluding such non-performatives as *I find you charming*. This realization caused Austin to abandon the attempt to separate performatives from constatives in favor of a program of determining the illocutionary force of an utterance – as opposed to either the locution (the meaning of the utterance), or the perlocution (the secondary effects of the utterance). The concept of illocutionary force is broad enough to include what is contributed to the force of an utterance by both its sentence type and its performative prefix, if it has one.

Though Austin gave up the quest for performativity, the role of performative sentences in Austin's theory of speech acts was by no means eliminated. Austin repeatedly asserted that illocutionary acts are conventional acts, as opposed to perlocutionary acts, which are not. In one often-cited passage, Austin claimed that performative sentences provided the convention that he thought was a necessary companion of illocutionary force, distinguishing it from perlocutionary intent. An illocutionary act, he wrote, (1962:103) '. . . may . . . be said to be *conventional*, in the sense that at least it could be made explicit by the performative formula.'

10.1.4. Conventionality

Austin's view of conventionality is extremely weak or even contradictory, as Strawson (1971) was quick to point out. First of all, the *possibility* of being made explicit is hardly a convention, but rather only the potentiality for a convention. Second, acts similar to illocutions can, as Austin himself observed, be brought off through nonconventional means. One can warn of the presence of a bull by snorting and pawing the ground, but the warning thus accomplished is not an illocutionary act. Strawson argued that Austin equivocated on the notion of conventionality. As officially described, the conventionality that Austin referred to was either the possibility of convention, or even more weakly, the adherence to the grammatical conventions of the language. But the performative sentences that Austin typically used in constructing his theory were formulas conventionally used in carrying out a conventional procedure, such as christening, sentencing, etc. In as much as acts like these are by no means typical speech acts, Strawson concluded that intention, rather than convention, should lie at the heart of speech act theory. In a similar vein, Cohen (1974), despairing of finding any grammatical reflections of illocutionary force, concluded that it was not even a topic for linguistics.

10.2. Grammatical theories of illocutionary force

.2.1. Searle's theory of speech acts

Cohen's claim notwithstanding, in the case of either a performative sentence or a sentence with a formal marker of its sentence type we have a clear reflection in grammar of illocutionary force. The grammarian cannot help but observe this connection, but the question remains as to the correct method of modeling it in a grammatical description of natural language.

In his important book, Searle (1970) divides the representation of a sentence into two parts: the propositional content and the illocutionary force indicating device (IFID). In the case of non-performative sentences, the IFID is the formal sentence type indicator: the mood of the verb, the word order, the speech act particle, etc. In the case of a performative sentence, the IFID is the performative clause itself. This division directly reflects Austin's notion that normal, nonparasitic uses of language include both a locutionary and an illocutionary aspect, the locutionary act involving conventional sense and reference, the illocutionary act involving conventional force.

2.2. The treatment of performative sentences

But performative clauses look like other clauses. They typically conform to the performative formula and contain words that otherwise have conventional sense and reference, such as a present tense verb and the 1st and 2nd person pronouns. In fact, a performative sentence can consist only of the performative clause as in *I congratulate you* or *I resign*. On Searle's theory, such sentences would be all IFID and no propositional content. Furthermore,

187

there seem to be no purely performative verbs, i.e. verbs that have only a force-indicating function and never a descriptive function, nor any purely performative pronouns usable always and only in performative sentences and not occurring elsewhere in the language as elements that refer to the speaker and hearer.

For these reasons, it would seem advisable to treat the performative prefix as having genuine content which is a function of the ordinary sense and reference of the elements it contains. Despite the fact that this loses Austin's intuition, making performatives true or false, and despite the fact that this counterintuitively renders an assertoric performative like *I swear that I didn't do it* true just in case the speaker does thereby swear that he didn't do it, regardless of his guilt or innocence, many now do advocate treating performatives as a kind of constative (Cresswell 1973; Lewis 1976; Bach & Harnish 1979; Searle & Vanderveken 1985).

10.2.3. **The performative hypothesis**

While Searle attempted to conflate all force to the apparently nonpropositional IFIDs found in non-performatives, others wished to do just the opposite: to reduce all force to ordinary sense and reference. The idea that illocutionary force can always be dealt with in terms of a performative clause, whether one is overt in the uttered sentence or not, is known as the *performative hypothesis* or *performative analysis*. It was made famous by Ross (1970) and developed by others, especially Sadock (1974), within the tradition of generative semantics.

Earlier, Katz & Postal (1964) had suggested that deep-structure differences characterized the basic sentence types of English. They proposed that interrogative and imperative sentences contained abstract, deep-structure markers in a structural position similar to that occupied by sentence adverbials, whereas declaratives contained either a sentence adverbial in that position or nothing. Katz & Postal suggested that these abstract, syntactically unanalyzed illocutionary markers were to be semantically interpreted as performative clauses, and in a footnote they even considered the possibility of replacing them in deep structure with fully fledged performative clauses. Ross's innovation was to extend this treatment to declaratives and to offer arguments in favor of this bold thesis.

The performative hypothesis made two sorts of claims simultaneously: (a) that the semantics of non-performative sentences can be understood in terms of the semantics of performative sentences; and (b) that the syntax of non-performatives resembles the syntax of the complements of performative clauses. While separable in principle, these two features of the performative hypothesis have often been linked in the linguistic and philosophical literature.

The debate over the performative hypothesis

Few ideas in recent linguistics have been more roundly criticized than the performative hypothesis. It has been attacked, almost from the time it was promulgated, on the basis of its syntactic claims (Anderson 1971; Fraser 1974), and has more recently been just as severely criticized for its semantic implications (Davis 1976; Gazdar 1979; Boër & Lycan 1980). It is fair to say that at the present time the performative hypothesis is generally considered to have been refuted. Recently, though, Davison (1983), McCawley (1985) and Sadock (1985) have answered some of the criticisms of the syntactic and semantic indictments of the performative hypothesis. It must be pointed out, though, that no fully worked out competitor to the performative theory exists at the present time.

Syntactic arguments for the performative hypothesis

Ross (1970), Lakoff (1972), Sadock (1974), and others assembled a battery of arguments purporting to demonstrate the syntactic utility of assuming performative clauses in the syntactic deep structures of sentences. The form of these arguments is invariably as follows:

(a)   There is a syntactic property P of subordinate clauses that is related to some syntactic feature F of a higher clause.
(b)   In main clauses, there is a restricted occurrence of property P.
(c)   This restriction in main clauses can be accounted for by assuming that they are actually subordinate to a clause with feature F', where F' is that special case of F that is characteristic of performative clauses.

A typical example is the following argument adapted from Ross (1970):

(a)'   A noun phrase of the form *NPs like X-self* may occur in a subordinate clause without an antecedent in that clause just in case the reflexive can be understood as referring to an argument of a higher clause:

(2)   Fred told Bill that linguists like himself/*herself were in demand

(b)'   But a 1st or 2nd person pronoun is possible where there is no overt higher clause:

189

(3)   Linguists like myself/yourself/*himself/*herself are in demand

(c)'   If there is a performative clause, with a 1st person subject and a 2nd person indirect object in the deep structure of every sentence, the same rule that accounts for the pattern in the first example also accounts for the pattern in the second.

The objections to what was considered at the time a valid argument form were of several types. Some questioned the data: Anderson (1971) points out the following as acceptable, thus calling into question the generalization that underpins Ross's argument:

(4)   The review which Jones' first book got seemed ridiculous to a man like himself

It was also pointed out that the predictions made by the performative hypothesis were not accurate. Most telling was the observation made by both Anderson and Fraser that performative clauses tend to display the same properties as non-performative clauses even though the former are supposed to be unembedded both in deep and surface structure. The following example of this is also from Anderson (1971):

(5)   Men like yourself are hereby warned to make themselves scarce

The same reasoning that was used in arguing for the performative hypothesis would seem to lead to the postulation of yet another abstract clause in which the performative, abstract or overt, is itself embedded (this possibility was actually entertained in Ross 1969 and Sadock 1969, 1974).

Finally, it was observed by many early and later critics of the performative hypothesis that the triggering environments for the motivating phenomena were often not restricted to higher clauses but could also be found in earlier stretches of discourse, as the following example, also from Anderson, shows:

(6)   If we're ever going to get Jones to give up this crazy plan, there's only one thing we've got to get across to him. A man like himself can never play the saxophone because he has only one lung.

The last class of arguments is by far the most interesting, since it suggests an alternative account of the facts rather than merely pointing out problems with the data or the theory. This alternative account, anticipated by Ross (1970) in his well-known article, would allow the pragmatic context of a sentence, including the identity of the participants in the speech situation and the fact that an illocutionary act of a certain sort is being performed, to influence the distribution of reflexive pronouns. We will return to the bearing that pragmatic theory has on speech act theory in section 10.3.4 below.

Semantic arguments

The performative hypothesis was supposed to account for the fact that the standard illocutionary act performed in uttering a sentence like *Snow is white* is similar to that accomplished in uttering *I say that snow is white*, and the act conventionally carried out in saying *Is snow white?* similar to that achieved by saying *I ask you whether snow is white*, and so on. It does so by postulating identical, or very similar, semantics for performatives and for non-performatives, or, in Lakoff's famous phrase (1972: 655), by '. . . largely . . . reducing [pragmatics] to garden-variety semantics.'

But if these pairs of sentences are identical in meaning, then under usual assumptions they should have identical truth conditions, logical entailments, and so forth. This consequence has been found disagreeable by almost every philosopher writing on the subject and by a good many linguists as well. The most straightforward of numerous semantic counter-arguments to the performative hypothesis rely solely on this intuition. A disarmingly simple version is to be found in Davis (1976). The following, slightly more complex version, is paraphrased from Boër & Lycan (1980): *I say that snow is white* entails that I exist. *Snow is white* does not. Therefore the two cannot have the same meaning.

There seems to be virtual unanimity among philosophers and philosophically minded linguists that this argument is iron-clad for simple declarative sentences, but there is much less agreement as to whether it holds for non-declaratives. Thus Lewis (1976) rejects the performative theory of declaratives on just this basis, while accepting it as a semantic theory for interrogatives and imperatives. After all, it is not clear what, if anything, a sentence such as *Is snow white?* entails, and therefore the simple argument form above does not so clearly go through.

More subtle argumentation is required where presumably semantic evidence has been offered in favor of the performative hypothesis. A large class of arguments, originally offered as syntactic arguments but still clearly relevant to the semantics of illocutions, involves the distribution and understanding of certain *speech act adverbials* (see Schreiber 1972; Davison 1973). In sentences like *Honestly, I don't know the answer*, or *Briefly, what is the problem?* the adverbials clearly do not modify the content of the surface clause; their understanding is similar to the way that they are understood in *I tell you honestly . . .*, or *Tell me briefly . . .*

The problem for the truth-conditional semanticist, as Boër & Lycan (1980) pointed out, is that if such adverbials are to be interpreted uniformly in all uses, there must be semantically interpreted performative clauses for them to have as arguments. However, if there is a semantically interpreted performative clause, the truth-conditional problems mentioned above ensue.

191

Boër & Lycan conclude that the resolution of this paradox, or *performadox*, as they call it, is to assume that just in case there is a speech act adverbial in a non-performative sentence, it has an abstract performative clause in its semantic representation, and otherwise it does not. The same dilemma caused Cresswell (1973), and independently, Bach & Harnish (1979) to declare sentences with speech act adverbials ungrammatical, despite their seeming normalcy. For more on the performadox see Davison (1983), Welsh & Chametzky (1983), Lycan (1984), and Sadock (1985).

10.3. Syntax, semantics, and pragmatics

10.3.1. Illocutionary act potential

A perplexing problem facing speech act theorists is the fact that most sentences can accomplish quite different things, when uttered in different contexts, and can do so in virtue of the addressee's recognition of the speaker's intention to accomplish those effects. Saying *I will return* can, depending on the circumstances, amount to a promise, warning, or prediction, and the speaker can intend for the utterance to be recognized as such. In so far as any of these acts could have been accomplished by uttering an explicit performative, they are ordinarily treated as genuine specific illocutionary forces of the sentence in specific contexts. Thus Alston (1964) labels the range of effects of a sentence that are describable in terms of performative verbs the *illocutionary act potential* of the sentence. Note that there is usually no obvious grammatical indication of which particular effect within the range of possible effects is intended.

10.3.2. Indirect speech acts

So labile is our use of sentences in context that the connection between the effect of a sentence and its form can be tenuous indeed. This disassociation of form and effect reaches its maximum in the case of what have been called *indirect speech acts*, a standard example of which is saying *It's cold in here* to get someone to close the window, an effect that could have been more directly achieved by saying *Close the window*, or more formally, *I request that you close the window*.

The term *indirect illocution* is often employed in such cases, but if the indirection is nonconventional, the term is a misnomer, given Austin's insistence that illocutionary acts must be conventional acts.

0.3.3. **The apparent failure of the performative hypothesis**

If the performative hypothesis requires that sentences are literally ambiguous among as many senses as there are more specific performative paraphrases that fall within their illocutionary act potential or can be accomplished indirectly by their use, then that hypothesis is reduced to absurdity. A virtually limitless range of potential effects would have to be recorded in the deep syntactic or semantic structures associated with every sentence. Though the performative hypothesis has often been taken as leading to this theoretical disaster, it does not actually follow from that theory, and in fact, no performative theorist has ever taken such a strong position.

There are two other possibilities for accounting for the force of an uttered sentence that the performative hypothesis does not exclude; first, that the meanings of sentences are general enough to include a range of more particular illocutionary forces. Just as the word *sweater* can on one occasion of use refer to a pullover and on another to a cardigan without being ambiguous, so it is possible that *I will be there* might have one very general assertoric force that can sometimes amount to a promise and at other times to an answer, since both of these can be conceived of as acts more specific than the act of going on record as believing a certain future tense proposition to be true. Second, it is possible, indeed by now undeniable, that in addition to the grammatical signaling of intended effects, such effects can be brought off nonconventionally. In particular, work in conversational theory stemming from Grice's (1975) seminal paper offers an attractive account of meaning that does not require everything that is conveyed by the utterance of a sentence in context to be conveyed directly in terms of the literal sense and reference of the uttered expression.

0.3.4. **Pragmatic accounts of illocutionary force**

Early on in the linguistic study of speech acts, Gordon & Lakoff (1971) recognized the relevance of Grice's work. Treating a broad class of indirect speech acts, including some that Sadock (1970) had treated as grammatically encoding their force, Gordon & Lakoff proposed that the indirect force was in fact calculated on the basis of conversational reasoning. They also noted a general feature of these forms, namely that they frequently involved either the assertion of a *speaker-based* felicity condition, as in *I want you to close the door*, or the calling into question of a *hearer-based* felicity condition, as in *Can you close the door?* Here 'Speaker wants addressee to do P,' and 'Addressee is able to do P' are both felicity conditions on acts of requesting an addressee to do P, as Searle (1970) had already pointed out.

Gordon & Lakoff, however, elevated the inferencing schemes that enabled the speaker's intentions to be worked out to nearly the status of rules of grammar. They labeled these *conversational postulates*. It remained for others, particularly Searle (1975) to remove this last vestige of grammaticality from the treatment of indirect speech acts. Searle argued that Gricean considerations alone were enough to account for indirect speech acts, obviating the need to postulate either undesirable ambiguities or special grammatical principles.

Pragmatic theory is powerful enough to pave the way to a nongrammatical account of the illocutionary effect of even the basic sentence types. Thus Schmerling (1982) provides imperative sentences with semantics other than those of propositions, and argues that their standard use in making requests, giving orders, and so on is to be understood as naturally inferrable from the fact that a speaker has chosen a form with these semantics rather than the semantics of a proposition. At the same time, Peters (1982) suggested a semantic theory of interrogative sentences that makes their content identical to that of embedded *wh*-clauses – which do not have the force of questions. Peters' theory thus makes the question force of interrogatives an entirely pragmatic matter; an interrogative has semantics such that the only reasonable way of understanding why a speaker has uttered such a sentence is to assume that he would like certain information. This leaves the declarative form as the unique sentence type which is semantically a function from possible worlds to truth values. As such, the assertoric force of declaratives also becomes amenable to pragmatic treatment; a reasonable explanation for the fact that a speaker has uttered a sentence whose meaning is that of a proposition is that he believes the proposition to be true. Pragmatic techniques are clearly sufficiently strong to allow for the treatment of much of the way we take utterances in context. Their principal drawback is their lack of precise formulation and concomitant excess of power. Many of the pragmatic accounts of illocutionary force assume some largely unstated pragmatic theory (e.g. Katz 1977), and even the more careful treatments fall far short of providing a theory of sentence use with real empirical content.

10.3.5. **Formal reflexes of intended force**

While a fully pragmatic account of the illocutionary force of the basic sentence types is fairly plausible in the case of a language like English, where the interrogative and imperative forms appear to contain the same pieces as do ordinary propositional forms such as complements of verbs of saying, it is much less plausible if there are forms for distinguishing among sentence types that do not otherwise appear in the language. As we have seen, some languages have special inflectional forms of the verb or distinct speech act particles that serve only to indicate illocutionary force. In as much as such functionally unique forms can't be independently argued to have ordinary propositional semantics, it is much harder to construct purely pragmatic accounts of their standard uses based on their meanings.

Consequently, even avowedly pragmatic accounts of illocutionary force such as those of Bach & Harnish (1979) or Leech (1983), or Searle & Vanderveken (1985), usually fall back on formal quasi-semantic markers of basic sentence type or mood. Bach & Harnish postulate three mutually exclusive sentence moods which they prefix to the propositional content of a sentence, a stance that is reminiscent of Stenius' (1967) earlier view. Leech, on the other hand, posits two mutually exclusive semantic operators – one for interrogative and one for imperative sentences – and two that occur in the semantic representations of declarative sentences – a positive and a negative operator. These latter two are, however, not mutually exclusive with the nondeclarative operators and are hence not specifically markers of assertoric force. Leech's treatment therefore strongly resembles the early grammatical treatment of Katz & Postal (1964).

0.3.6. The treatment of conventionalized indirection

There are sometimes even apparent grammatical idiosyncrasies of indirect forms. In arguing for a grammatical treatment of some cases of indirect force, Sadock (1970) pointed out that questions like *Could you close the door?* (1) admitted sentence-internal *please* (*Could you please close the door?*); (2) could have 3rd person vocatives (*Could you close the door, someone?* – cf. Thorne 1966); and could be conjoined with true imperatives (*Could you close the door, and while you're at it, please close the window*). In the case of other examples of indirect requests, such as the less direct, but still possibly effective, *Are you capable of opening the door?* none of these properties is to be found, allowing Sadock to conclude that there are two sorts of indirect speech acts, those that are conventionalized and those that are not.

Gordon & Lakoff (1971) noted these and several other grammatical reflexes of indirect force, but rather than give up a uniform, more or less pragmatic account of all indirect force, they proposed that grammatical rules could be directly sensitive to derived force in virtue of the powerful device of *transderivational constraints*, a mechanism which Lakoff (1970) had proposed on other grounds.

Searle avoided this quasi-grammatical treatment by claiming that the indirect forms that admitted grammatical indication of their intended force were idiomatic, though not exactly idioms. This vague notion was clarified by Morgan (1978), who suggested that there is an important distinction between conventions of language, which comprise the grammar, and conventions about the use of language defined by that grammar. By recognizing such a distinction, he was able to say both'that certain indirect forms were conventionalized and that their meaning, in the strict sense, did not directly render their standard effect. This idea is further developed by Horn & Bayer (1984) as their doctrine of *short-circuited implicature*, a term that is also used by Bach & Harnish (1979).

While coming to grips with some of the problems posed by conventionalized indirection, all of these schemes come perilously close to undercutting their own aims: they threaten to remove, or at least to weaken, the very semantic underpinnings that are crucial to their own accounts of how natural language is used in communication.

Recently, some distinct improvements in the pragmatically based accounts of the properties of indirect speech acts have been achieved through careful consideration of the reasons for indirection in natural language. Studies that investigate the natural tensions that exist among rules for proper speaking, such as those that pay attention to the role of politeness (Brown & Levinson 1978; Leech 1983) and those that concern the competing pressures of the need to be clear and the need to be concise (Horn 1984) are especially promising. They hold out hope of accounting not only for the fact that a particular form has an indirect use, but also of explaining why and under what circumstances that form might be chosen rather than a more direct one.

REFERENCES

Alston, W. P. 1964. *Philosophy of language*. Englewood Cliffs: Prentice-Hall.
Anderson, S. R. 1971. On the linguistic status of the performative/constative distinction. Distributed by Indiana University Linguistics Club, Bloomington.
Austin, J. L. 1962. *How to do things with words*. London: Oxford University Press.
Bach, K. & Harnish, R. M. 1979. *Linguistic communication and speech acts*. Cambridge, MA: MIT Press.
Boër, S. E. & Lycan, W. G. 1980. A performadox in truth-conditional semantics. *Linguistics and Philosophy* 4: 1–46.
Brown, P. & Levinson, S. 1978. Universals in language usage: politeness phenomena. In E. N. Goody (ed.) *Questions and politeness*. Cambridge: Cambridge University Press.
Cohen, L. J. 1974. Speech acts. In T. Sebeok (ed.) *Current trends in linguistics 12*. The Hague: Mouton.
Cole, P. & Morgan, J. L., (eds.) 1975. *Syntax and semantics*. Vol. 3: *Speech acts*. New York: Academic Press.
Cresswell, M. J. 1973. *Logics and languages*. London: Methuen.
Davidson, D. & Harman, G. (eds.) 1972. *Semantics of natural language*. Dordrecht: Reidel.
Davis, S. 1976. *Philosophy and language*. Indianapolis: Bobbs-Merrill.
Davison, A. 1973. Performative verbs, adverbs, and felicity conditions: an inquiry into the nature of performative verbs. Doctoral dissertation, University of Chicago.
Davison, A. 1983. Linguistic or pragmatic description in the context of the performadox. *Linguistics and Philosophy* 6: 499–526.
Fraser, B. 1974. An examination of the performative analysis. *Papers in Linguistics* 7: 1 40.
Gazdar, G. 1979. *Pragmatics: implicature, presupposition, and logical form*. New York: Academic Press.

Gordon, D. & Lakoff, G. 1971. Conversational postulates. *CLS* 7: 63–85. Reprinted in Cole & Morgan (1975).

Grice, H. P. 1975. Logic and conversation. In Cole & Morgan (1975).

Horn, L. R. 1984. Toward a new taxonomy for pragmatic inference. In D. Schiffrin (ed.) *Georgetown University Round Table on Languages and Linguistics 1984*. Washington, DC: Georgetown University Press.

Horn, L. R. & Bayer, S. 1984. Short-circuited implicature: a negative contribution. *Linguistics and Philosophy* 7: 397–414.

Katz, J. J. 1977. *Propositional structure and illocutionary force: a study of the contribution of sentence meaning to speech acts*. Cambridge, MA: Harvard University Press.

Katz, J. J. & Postal, P. M. 1964. *An integrated theory of linguistic descriptions*. Cambridge, MA: MIT Press.

Lakoff, G. 1970. Some thoughts on transderivational constraints. University of Michigan. ms.

Lakoff, G. 1972. Linguistics and natural logic. In Davidson & Harman (1972).

Lee, H. B. & Maxwell, E. R. 1970. Performatives in Korean. *CLS* 6: 363–79.

Leech, G. N. 1983. *Principles of pragmatics*. London: Longman.

Lewis, D. 1976. General semantics. In B. H. Partee (ed.) *Montague grammar*. New York: Academic Press. Originally published in Davidson & Harman (1972).

Lycan, W. G. 1984. *Logical form in natural language*. Cambridge, MA: MIT Press.

Matthews, G. H. 1965. *Hidatsa syntax*. The Hague: Mouton.

McCawley, J. D. 1985. What price the performative analysis? *University of Chicago Working Papers*. Vol. 1. Chicago: University of Chicago.

Morgan, J. L. 1978. Two types of convention in indirect speech acts. In P. Cole (ed.) *Syntax and semantics*. Vol. 9: *Pragmatics*. New York: Academic Press.

Peters, S. 1982. The situation in question. *Papers from the Parasession on Nondeclaratives*. Chicago: Chicago Linguistic Society.

Ross, J. R. 1969. Performatives from progressives? MIT. ms.

Ross, J. R. 1970. On declarative sentences. In R. A. Jacobs & P. S. Rosenbaum (eds.) *Readings in English transformational grammar*. Waltham: Ginn & Co.

Sadock, J. M. 1969. Superhypersentences. *Papers in Linguistics* 1: 1–16.

Sadock, J. M. 1970. Whimperatives. In J. M. Sadock & A. L. Vanek (eds.) *Studies presented to R. B. Lees by his students*. Edmonton: Linguistic Research.

Sadock, J. M. 1974. *Toward a linguistic theory of speech acts*. New York: Academic Press.

Sadock, J. M. 1985. On the performadox, or, A semantic defense of the performative hypothesis. In *University of Chicago Working Papers in Linguistics* 1: 160–9.

Sadock, J. M. & Zwicky, A. M. 1985. Sentence types. In T. Shopen (ed.) *Language typology and syntactic description*. Cambridge: Cambridge University Press.

Schmerling, S. 1982. How imperatives are special, and how they aren't. *Papers from the Parasession on Nondeclaratives*. Chicago: Chicago Linguistic Society.

Schreiber, P. A. 1972. Style disjuncts and the performative analysis. *Linguistic Inquiry* 3: 321–48.

Searle, J. R. 1970. *Speech acts: an essay in the philosophy of language*. Cambridge: Cambridge University Press.

Searle, J. R. 1975. Indirect speech acts. In Cole & Morgan (1975).

Searle, J. R. & Vanderveken, D. 1985. *Foundations of illocutionary logic*. Cambridge: Cambridge University Press.

Stenius, E. 1967. Mood and language-game. *Synthese* 17: 254–74.

Strawson, P. F. 1971. Intention and convention in speech acts. In J. R. Searle (ed.) *The philosophy of language*. London: Oxford University Press. Originally published (1964) in *The Philosophical Review* LXXIII: 439–60.

Thorne, J. P. 1966. English imperative sentences. *Journal of Linguistics* 2: 69–78.

Welsh, C. & Chametzky, R. 1983. Performatives as indexicals: resolving the performadox. *BLS* 9: 266–80.

11 Computer applications of linguistic theory

Per-Kristian Halvorsen

11.1. Fact and fiction

Computers that use language proficiently are commonplace in works of fiction and in people's fantasies about technology. Computers traffic in information, and language is the most powerful vehicle for the communication of information. Language is an integral part of our culture, of our psychology, and (some claim) of our genetic constitution. Therefore, when we think about communication, whether among people, among people and machines, or among machines networked together, it is difficult to not also think of language. In a sense, there is a good basis for this association. Programs are statements in a linguistic system. This is the case whether they are applications programs, or the programs that constitute the operating system controlling the shunting of information between different parts of the machine (disk, memory, processor), or the communications software that controls the exchange of information between computers connected together. But in talking about both computers and people as using language we also introduce the possibility of a confusing equivocation which invites the conclusion that the differences between these linguistic systems are superficial, while, in fact, they are profound. A computer language is not just a different language in the sense that French is a language different from English. Had that been the case, the linguistic skills of modern computers would, undoubtedly, be much closer to the fictional fantasies of Karel Čapek's RUR (Rossum's Universal Robot) (Čapek 1920) or the (in)famous HAL in '2001: A Space Odyssey'.

Natural languages and computer languages differ in a number of ways which we are just beginning to understand now that systematic investigations of the relationship between the two are getting under way.[1] But some things

---

[1] This merged perspective on computer science and linguistics got an institutional expression in the Center for the Study of Language and Information – a collaborative effort, sponsored by the Systems Development Foundation, between Stanford University, SRI International, and the Xerox Corporation. The center was founded in 1982 with the expressed purpose of investigating the relationship between language and computation in their role as information carriers.

are already clear. The syntax of both kinds of languages can be readily modeled by the same types of formal systems (i.e. context-free or context-sensitive rewrite systems, possibly augmented in some fashion with constraints or transformations). But in natural languages, efficient syntactic processing appears to depend on semantic constraints. This is due to the extremely high degree of structural ambiguity in natural language syntax. Computer languages, on the other hand, are designed to avoid this kind of structural ambiguity and context sensitivity.[2] Moreover, at present there is no single formal system capable of supporting an adequate semantic account for both computer languages and natural languages.[3]

Lack of appreciation for these differences and the complexity of natural language has contributed to some false starts in computational linguistics, and to exceedingly optimistic time schedules for the advent of computers capable of understanding natural language. In 1949, Warren Weaver launched the idea of using the code-breaking power of computers, which had been successfully demonstrated during World War II, to do natural language translation. But after a decade of work on the machine translation problem the whole enterprise fell into disrepute (National Research Council 1966; Bar-Hillel 1971).[4] The 1960s and early 1970s brought visions of machines that could understand ordinary language, obey commands in English, or respond in kind. Several systems were constructed which exhibited behavior that suggested to the casual observer that the machine indeed 'understood' or 'knew' a language (cf. SHRDLU; Winograd 1972). However, the opinion soon took hold that these systems merely created a powerful illusion of linguistic capabilities by exploiting special features of the limited domains in which they operated. A strong suspicion developed that the techniques which worked in the simple, closed, world of blocks and robot arms could not be extended to yield solutions to the general problem of natural language understanding.

Since machines with natural language communication skills are so obviously desirable and so easily imaginable, fantasy has outrun technology. The task has fallen on linguistic theory to reveal the complexity of the system which underlies even simple linguistic behavior. Rather than providing the basis for realization of the grand views of talking machines, linguistic theory has often provided the ammunition to silence these efforts. Consider again the history of machine translation. Weaver viewed translation as a code-breaking problem. The assumption was that sentences encode a message (the meaning of the sentence). A Russian sentence and its English translation

---

[2] There is context sensitivity in the interpretation of statements in computer languages (cf. variable binding). The issue here is structural ambiguity in the parsing of a statement.
[3] An important theory used in the investigation of the semantic properties of computer programs is *denotational semantics* (Scott 1976). See Gordon (1979) for a simple introduction.
[4] But see 11.8 for an account of the recent revival in interest in machine translation.

encode the same message. From this perspective, translation is decryption followed by encryption, and it seemed reasonable to apply the same techniques which had been so successful in breaking codes to the solution of this problem. However, code-breaking requires a 'key' which specifies explicitly the relationship between the encrypted and the unencrypted form of the message. Linguistic theory brings out the fact that the linguistic 'code' is extremely complex, with multiple levels of encoding and structural ambiguity. Moreover, we do not have a unique set of primitive concepts in terms of which the meaning of all lexical items and sentences in all languages can be adequately captured. There is no known key which specifies explicitly the mapping between the surface form of the sentence (the encrypted form) and a statement of the message in a universal system of concepts (its unencrypted form).

Despite these failings, the range of natural language computer applications currently available is impressive. While early natural language systems required large mainframe computers for their operation, their descendants now run on personal home computers (e.g. CLOUT, from MicroRim and Q&A, from Symantec) which allow PC users to interact with relational databases using natural language. In 1978 speech synthesis reached into schools and homes through the popular 'Speak-and-Spell' – an electronic device made by Texas Instruments which helps children learn spelling. Most home computers can now also be expanded with systems that convert unrestricted written text to highly intelligible speech. Such computers can be set up to recognize a limited number of words or phrases (~100) spoken in isolation, and special purpose computers which can recognize on the order of 1000 isolated words are now available and priced within the reach of individuals (KV3000 from Kurzweil Applied Intelligence, and announced products from Dragon Systems). Less powerful natural language computer applications, such as spelling checkers and automatic hyphenation facilities, are relied on every day by people using modern typewriters and wordprocessing systems.

11.2. The leap from linguistic theory to programs

While appreciation for the complexity of language has forced some overly ambitious schemes onto the back burner, the influence of linguistic theory on the development of natural language computer applications has, of course, not been entirely negative. But often the influence is hard to spot, since the relationship between linguistic theory and computational applications is not straightforward.

An important source of the indirectness of the connection between linguistic theory and natural language computer applications pertains to the

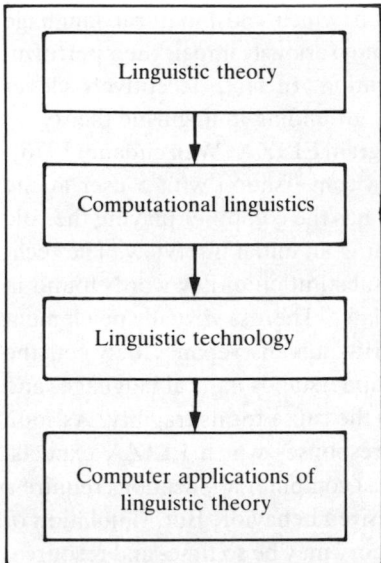

Figure 1. From linguistic theory to programs

history of generative linguistic theory. Generative linguistics has aimed to characterize the linguistic knowledge of an idealized speaker–hearer (competence) while, for the most part, remaining silent about how this knowledge is put to use in linguistic activity (performance). On the other hand, activity and processes are what computers are all about. Bridging this gap is the focal point of a separate subdiscipline of computer science and linguistics, namely computational linguistics. Computational linguistics tries to mediate between competence theory and the particular kind of linguistic performance attributable to machines by turning linguistic theory into algorithms which allow the simulation of linguistic behavior while obeying the linguistic constraints and generalizations embodied in linguistic theory and competence grammars. The honing of these algorithms gives rise to linguistic technology which provides system-builders with a library of routines that is the basis for natural language computer applications. Prime examples of linguistic technologies are grammar interpreters and parsers for various types of grammar formalisms (transformational grammars (TG), lexical-functional grammars (LFG), generalized phrase structure grammars (GPSG) etc.), and algorithms for speech synthesis.

   Duplication of a narrow range of human behavior in a machine does not imply that the machine, or the program that the machine is running, encodes the knowledge that underlies the behavior in humans. For this reason it is often the case that the loose connection which most natural language programs have with linguistic theory does not seriously impair their performance in their intended domain of application. In fact, deceptively clever language programs often do not have any grounding in linguistic theory. A good example of this is Weizenbaum's program ELIZA (Weizenbaum 1976). ELIZA appears to be able to carry on a conversation with a user at the terminal. One incarnation of the program has the computer playing the role of a nondirective psychotherapist conducting an initial interview. The technique that is used is nevertheless trivial: substitution of key words found in the users sentences into ready-made templates. There is virtually no element of linguistic knowledge in this process. But this discrepancy between the system's behavior, which suggests that it understands natural language, and the system's theoretical foundation is also the cause for its fragility. As soon as the user strays outside the range of responses which ELIZA expects, performance degrades immediately. Robust computer applications require a theoretical base which can support the desired behavior. But, simulation of the behavior according to the linguistic theory may be so time- and resource-consuming as to be impractical given existing computer technology. Shortcuts to improved performance are currently necessary.

Programs of the complexity of natural language understanding systems, while based on linguistic technology derived from linguistic theory, involve shortcuts mandated by efficiency considerations that blur the correspondences between theoretical distinctions and distinctions in the implementation. Thus, linguistic theory is only piecemeal reflected in such systems. In fact, systems are not a good place to look for signs of the impact of linguistic theory on natural language computer applications. They can be better observed in the field of computational linguistics where the bridge between theory and application is being built.

11.3. Computational linguistics

Computational linguistics is best viewed as a branch of artificial intelligence (AI). As all fields within AI, it is concerned with the investigation and modeling of a cognitive capacity. In the case of computational linguistics it is the language capacity that is in focus. However, the concern is not necessarily to construct a *psychologically realistic* model of human behavior. The goal is rather to identify and characterize the classes of processes and the types of knowledge which are implied by the ability to communicate and assimilate information using natural language regardless of their psychological status. One of the contributions of computational linguistics is a set of techniques which make it possible for linguistic knowledge to guide and constrain the

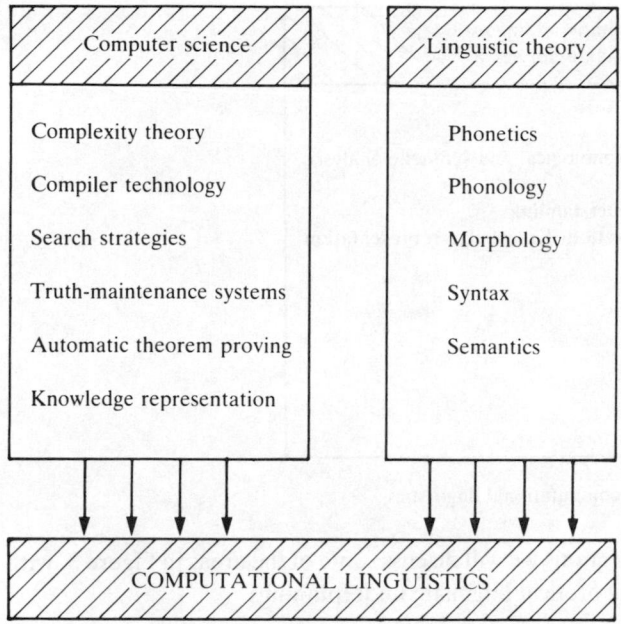

Figure 2. Influences on computational linguistics

linguistic processing performed in a natural language system. There are two fundamental problems in embedding linguistic knowledge in a computer implementation. First, conversion of a competence grammar (a specification) to a parser (a program) involves the addition of a *control structure*. The control structure specifies how to apply the knowledge embedded in the grammatical description of the competence grammar in a step by step fashion to construct an analysis for a sentence. Second is the question of how multiple linguistic knowledge sources, which are modularly represented in the linguistic theory, can be integrated in the analysis process.

In its attack on these problems, computational linguistics relies on insights from a number of disciplines within both computer science and linguistics. The most important among these are listed in Figure 2.

While computational linguistics is in some sense a derivative discipline, there are also influences flowing back from the field to its progenitors, computer science and linguistics. In particular, insights from computational linguistics regarding methods for stating structural correspondences between levels of representation and the optimal division of labor in a linguistic system have inspired developments in theoretical linguistics (e.g. LFG).

Some of the major areas of activity in computational linguistics today are listed in Figure 3.

203

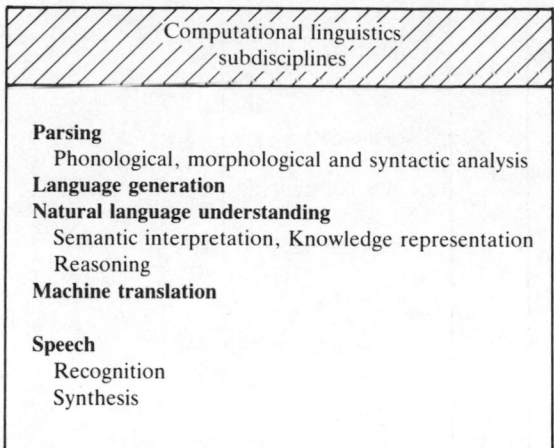

Figure 3. Sub-areas of computational linguistics

In the next few sections we will discuss some of the areas in Figure 3, with emphasis on their theoretical linguistic underpinnings.[5]

11.4. Parsing

Parsing is the recovery of structure from a signal where the structure is not apparent. It is a crucial step in any kind of natural language processing. Grammars are important for parsing since they provide an explicit definition of string membership in a language and of the association of strings with structures. The grammar provides a *knowledge base* which the parser can rely on when analyzing expressions. The use of grammars makes it possible to cleanly separate the statement of the grammatical rules from the definition of the control mechanism that governs the application of these rules in the parsing process and from the maintenance of the records of recovered constituents. This facilitates both the correction and expansion of the grammar itself and the development of new parsing algorithms.

Different types of languages require different types of grammars for their description, and different types of parsers are needed to parse them. Research in the 1950s and 1960s on formal languages and grammars resulted in a clear understanding of the relationship of the complexity of a language for the purposes of parsing and the form of the grammar which generates it (Chomsky 1959, 1963). The *Chomsky hierarchy* defines four major classes of grammars and languages of decreasing complexity: *unrestricted rewriting systems* (Type 0 grammars) corresponding to recursively enumerable sets;

---

[5] Detailed discussions of various parsing systems can be found in Winograd (1983). Bar & Feigenbaum (1981) survey a number of natural language understanding systems.

context-sensitive grammars (Type 1 grammars) corresponding to context-sensitive languages; *context-free grammars* (Type 2 grammars) corresponding to context-free languages; and *finite-state grammars* (Type 3 grammars) corresponding to finite-state languages. Upper bounds on the complexity of parsing any language in any of these classes have been established. The problem of parsing the recursively enumerable languages (i.e. those describable by Type 0 grammars) is *undecidable*: i.e. there are strings in these languages which can not be analyzed by a computer, regardless of how much time and memory resources it has at its disposal. Context-sensitive languages can be parsed in time which increases exponentially with the length of the string. Context-free languages can be parsed in time proportional to the cube of the length of the string (or slightly faster). The regular languages are simplest to parse, and it can be done in linear time, i.e. the best algorithms for parsing these languages will, in the worst case, find an analysis in time proportional to the length of the string being analyzed.

A wide variety of parsing algorithms for context-free languages was developed in the 1960s. Their intended application was the parsing of computer languages, which were intentionally restricted by their designers to be context-free languages.[6] At this time the dominant trend in linguistics was transformational generative syntax. Peters & Ritchie (1973) demonstrated that the transformational grammars of this period, with the restrictions on rules accepted at the time, allowed the generation of the full set of recursively enumerable languages – an undecidable set (though, importantly, they also pointed out that the set can be restricted to be recursive assuming bounded cycling of the rules). This created tension between what appeared to be the demands of linguistic descriptive and explanatory adequacy on the one hand, and the desiderata of computational efficiency on the other. This tension has since been a motivating force for much interesting work both in theoretical and computational linguistics. It has been the cause of much of the interest in generalized phrase structure grammar (Gazdar *et al.* 1985) and the ensuing resurgence of other context-free grammar formalisms. Computational considerations have also motivated the development of nontransformational theories of syntax such as lexical-functional grammar (Kaplan & Bresnan 1982), and nontransformational grammar formalisms such as definite clause grammar (DCG; Pereira & Warren 1980) and functional unification grammar (FUG; Kay 1978).

Another way around the problem posed by the complexity of the grammars which were commonly used for the description of natural languages is to explicitly limit the set of sentences which are admitted as input

---

[6] An early example of an algorithm for the parsing of context-free languages is given in Irons (1961). Floyd (1964) gives a survey of several early algorithms, while Aho & Ullman (1972) provides a comprehensive overview. A particularly popular algorithm can be found in Earley (1970).

to a system to a sublanguage. It is in fact quite hard to come up with examples of constructions in natural languages which definitely put them outside the bounds of the context-free languages.[7] Substantial sublanguages can therefore be constructed which are context-free. Significant improvements in the performance of machine translation systems have been achieved by the introduction of strictly defined sublanguages (Ruffino 1982), though this move is of course only possible when the creation of the source language text can be controlled, as in the writing of technical manuals.

In many applications where robustness is of the essence and the user has to have the impression that the system provides complete coverage, a different technique may be used to find a way around the ever-present lacunae of constructions (usually very large) that a grammar-based parser can not handle. A grammar-based parser can be constructed for a sublanguage and heuristically based 'parse-fitting' techniques can be invoked when input which falls outside the sublanguage is encountered (Jensen *et al.* 1983).[8]

A *rapprochement* between parsing technology and linguistic theory can also be achieved through the development of parsers that are better suited to deal with the complex grammars often used for linguistic description. This was the strategy taken by Petrick (1973), who developed techniques for parsing based on transformational grammars. This is a difficult problem, since the parsing algorithm has to be capable of reversing the effects of possibly long sequences of ordered applications of transformations. One approach is to use an analysis-by-synthesis technique. A hypothesis is made concerning the deep structure of a sentence and various sequences of transformational rules are considered with the aim to end up with a tree whose terminal elements match the original sentence. If one deep structure hypothesis fails, another one is tried. A transformational analysis of sentences can be achieved in this way, but the technique is cumbersome. A more efficient approach is based on the use of 'inverse' transformations, i.e. rules that map surface structures into deep structures rather than deep structures in surface structures.

The formulation of linguistic generalizations which has most strongly influenced the design of parsers for natural languages is the augmented transition network (ATN) grammar formalism developed by Woods (1970) and first used at Bolt Beranek and Newman Laboratories in a number of natural language understanding systems, including LUNAR (Woods *et al.* 1972). Instead of writing parsers for transformational grammars directly, Woods assimilated TG to the ATN notation, which was an extension of the already familiar transition networks or finite state grammars. A transition

---

[7] Shieber (1985), Culy (1985), Bresnan *et al.* (1982) describe such constructions in a number of different languages.
[8] Other techniques for dealing with 'ill-formed' input are discussed in Weischedel & Sondheimer (1983) and Carbonell & Hayes (1983).

network such as the one in Figure 4 can act as a recognizer for sentences, but it does not assign any structural analysis to the sentence. Transition networks can be extended to *recursive* transition networks (RTNs); see Figure 5.

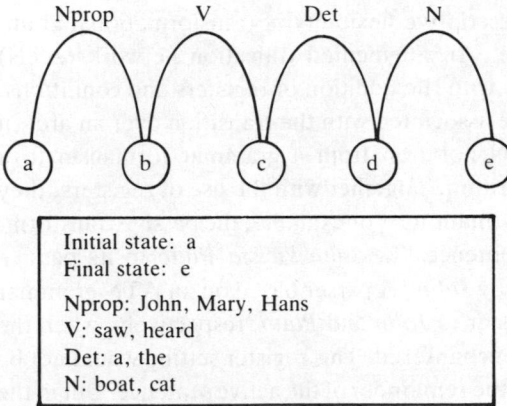

Initial state: a
Final state: e

Nprop: John, Mary, Hans
V: saw, heard
Det: a, the
N: boat, cat

Figure 4. Transition network grammars

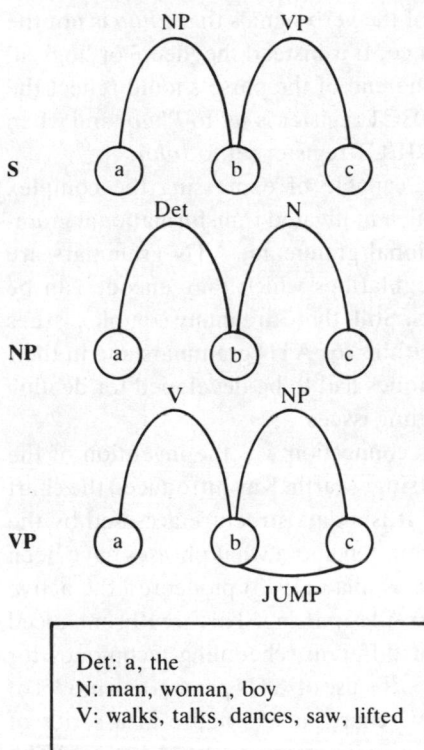

Det: a, the
N: man, woman, boy
V: walks, talks, dances, saw, lifted

Figure 5. Recursive transition network grammars

207

An RTN grammar is a hierarchy of networks. Each network describes the internal structure of a category. If there is a network corresponding to one of these categories, it is in turn invoked. In this way one can recover a hierarchical structure for the sentence.

However, to match the descriptive flexibility of transformational grammars, not even RTNs suffice. An augmented transition network (ATN) grammar is an RTN grammar with the addition of registers and conditions. Conditions allow actions to be associated with the transition over an arc. In effect, they convert the ATN notation from a grammar formalism to a specification of a parsing algorithm. Together with the use of registers, they allow the simulation of transformations. For example, the passive transformation transforms an active sentence like *John kicked Pluto* to its passive counterpart *Pluto was kicked by John*. A parser based on an ATN grammar would set the SUBJECT register to *John* and *Pluto*, respectively, when the first NP in the sentences was encountered. This register setting would not be changed during the parsing of the remainder of the active sentence. But in the case of *Pluto was kicked by John*, the setting of the SUBJECT register would be changed during the traversal of the VP network. The auxiliary in conjunction with the participial form of the verb signals that *Pluto* is not the 'deep' or 'logical' subject of the sentence. It is instead the 'deep' or 'logical' object. Since the register settings at the end of the parse should reflect the 'deep' grammatical relations, the OBJECT register is set to *Pluto*, and when the *by*-phrase is encountered the SUBJECT register set to *John*.

The ATN grammar formalism is capable of expressing the complex dependencies in linguistic structure which motivated transformational grammars, but in contrast to transformational grammars, ATN grammars are formulated in such a way that the regularities which they encode can be readily exploited in the parsing process. Still, there are many complex issues involved in the design of parsing algorithms for ATN grammars and in their implementations. In particular, techniques had to be developed for dealing both with nondeterminism and scheduling issues.

An important development in this connection was the invention of the chart and the advent of active chart parsing. Martin Kay introduced the chart in a talk in 1967 (see also Kay 1967). It is a data structure accessed by the parser during analysis. It records information about what phrases have been found and what rules are being tested. Kaplan (1973) pioneered the active chart and the application of the chart to ATN parsing. This greatly enhanced the possibility of exploring the use of different scheduling techniques for ATN parsing. It also provided a basis for the use of ATN parsers as a model of the human parsing process, and active chart parsers figure in a series of psycholinguistic investigations (Kaplan 1972; Wanner & Maratsos 1978; Ford, Bresnan, & Kaplan 1982).

Work on parsing has been moved forward by a useful shifting of emphasis between computational efforts at the improvement of parsing algorithms and linguistic attempts at finding more easily parsable grammar formalisms. Petrick focussed on the development of new parsers, while Woods with his ATNs introduced a new grammar formalism. Kaplan's chart was again a push in the direction of better parsing techniques. The pendulum has been moved back in the direction of emphasis on linguistic theory as an enabling condition for better parsing technology with the work on nontransformational grammar formalisms.

From a computational point of view, LFG is a development of the ATN theory. LFGs are in certain respects equivalent to ATNs with severe restrictions put on register setting. From a linguistic point of view LFGs are an extension of base-generated syntax. LFG strives to satisfy the needs both for linguistic adequacy and ease of utilization in parsing and psychological modeling. The system includes a sophisticated grammar interpreter which allows the linguist to use a rule format which exactly matches the familiar linguistic notation.

In LFG, the actions and conditions on arcs are replaced by a set of constraints. The use of constraints and the use of unification to enforce the satisfaction of the constraints is a significant feature of several current versions of syntactic theory which serve as the basis for computer implementations, e.g. Kay's functional unification grammar (Kay 1978), and the PATR system at SRI (Shieber *et al.* 1983).

An interesting merger of linguistic theory and parser design was accomplished by Marcus in his PARSIFAL system (Marcus 1980). Marcus takes as his point of departure the extended standard theory of transformational grammar (Chomsky 1977). He then not only builds a parser which reflects the structure of the linguistic theory, but he also attempts to explain a number of the constraints and conditions postulated in that theory (e.g. subjacency, opacity) on the basis of central properties of the parser design. The methodology pioneered by Marcus is a good indication that linguistic theory and parsing technology have matured to a point where they can be of significant mutual benefit and importance.[9]

Most of the parsing systems we have made reference to in this section are written in some dialect of the programming language LISP. But recently, a large number of natural language systems have been developed in PROLOG. Prolog parsers reconceptualize the parsing problem as a problem of theorem proving in order to utilize the built-in capabilities of the language. A whole line of grammar formalisms, collectively referred to as *logic grammars*, has

---

[9] Church (1980) adopts a similar methodology and seeks to explain linguistic constraints (e.g. limits on the acceptability of center-embedded constructions) by reference to design features of the parser.

been developed in order to make it simpler to express linguistic rules in a form that is appropriate for use with the PROLOG interpreter. One of the most prominent among these is the definite clause grammars (Pereira & Warren 1980). Logic grammars are convenient tools in the development of grammars for PROLOG parsers, but their development has, so far, had little connection with ongoing research in linguistic theory.

Syntactic parsing occupies a special position, since the development of different grammar formalisms has to a large extent been motivated by work in syntax and the development of parsing algorithms for computers has its roots in the need to automatically analyze the syntactic structure of programs. But there are as many different kinds of parsing as there are different aspects of linguistic structure. Explicit grammars can be written for the morphology and phonology of a language, and corresponding morphological and phonological parsers can be constructed. Morphological parsers recover the morphemes which constitute a complex word and their hierarchical structure. A phonological parser may indicate the syllabic and metrical structure of a word. Efforts have also been made to write grammars capturing the rules of allophonic variation and to develop parsing technology that is appropriate for the phonological and phonetic domain.

11.5. Semantics and natural language understanding

The linguistic theory which has had the most direct observable effect on the actual design of natural language understanding systems is *Case grammar*. This is something of a paradox since it is probably fair to say that Case grammar is not considered by most linguists to be particularly influential as a semantic theory. The explanation is the different emphasis in semantic research in linguistics and natural language understanding. In linguistics the focus has been on *compositional* semantics, while the analysis of specific lexical items, other than the logical connectives, has been largely ignored. But in natural language understanding systems lexical semantics is of crucial importance. It is also desirable to have a theory which does not require the specification of detailed differences in meaning which the system will be unable to incorporate. Case grammar is a good fit in both respects. Lexical meaning, especially the meaning of verbs and prepositions, is among the main concerns of Case grammar. Moreover, Case grammar sidesteps the problem of semantic composition through the use of case *frames* which classify the relation between predicates, and it is noncommittal on complex issues such as the scope of quantifiers and intensional verbs. These features of Case grammar have given it a place in natural language processing, both as a basis for meaning representation and as a technique for performing semantic compatibility checks during parsing.

Fillmore's trend-setting article 'The case for case' (Fillmore 1968) has been the inspiration for much of the natural language processing work which is based on Case grammar. But an important separate tradition has been created by Schank and his colleagues with their research on *conceptual dependency theory* (Schank 1975), where case-like frames are used as the primary element in a formalism for knowledge representation. Systemic grammars (Halliday 1967), with their emphasis on the function of linguistic expressions in context and of a unified treatment of the syntactic and semantic aspects of language, have also appealed to designers of natural language understanding systems (cf. Winograd 1972, 1983).

Most linguistic semantic research is founded on mathematical logic, and a different tradition in natural language understanding has emanated from this work. There are two different approaches to building language understanding systems based on logic. In one type of system, the sentences are translated into formulas of logic, and logical inference procedures are used to draw conclusions on the basis of the information presented in them. The other approach is to use the syntax of a formal logical language as a basis for representing the meaning of sentences, but to give the resulting semantic representations of nonstandard (i.e. procedural) interpretation. The formulas which serve as meaning representations are not interpreted in terms of the standard semantics for the logical language. Executable procedures are instead associated with each of the predicates, connectives, and quantifier expressions in the language. For example, the sentence *Some integer less than 10 is a prime* is represented in the LUNAR meaning representation language as:

(1) (FOR SOME x / INTEGER : (LESSP X 10) ; (PRIME X))

Procedures are then defined which will determine whether PRIME is true of an object *x* and whether the LESSP relation holds between two objects *x* and *y*. FOR is also associated with a procedure, and SOME triggers the use of a certain enumeration function when the expression in (1) is evaluated.

The semantics for the logical language provides a sound grounding for the first approach, but the computational complexity of doing inferences in a full first-order logic is cause for worry. If a first-order formula is provable, there are algorithms which are guaranteed to find a proof, though this may take an exceedingly long time. But if a formula is not a theorem there is no decision procedure which is guaranteed to always inform us of this, regardless of how long we are willing to wait. An alternative is the use of a subset of first-order predicate calculus for which efficient proof procedures exist. One such subset is the *Horn-clauses* or the *definite clauses*, which has gained particular prominence with the advent of logic programming language PROLOG. But many systems follow the second approach and give the logical formulas a procedural interpretation. Both LUNAR and the CHAT-80 (Pereira 1983), which is PROLOG-based, fall in this group.

There are also systems which use meaning representations in the form of logical formulas as a step on the way to other types of output, e.g. queries in a standard query language. The GPSG inspired question-answering system described in Gawron *et al.* (1982) produces translations in first-order logic which are used to generate queries in a database-query language. This system is inspired by Montague grammar in the way translations for sentences are derived compositionally from the translations of its parts. Schubert & Pelletier (1982) and Rosenschein & Shieber (1982) describe a similar approach, though their goal is the derivation of logical formulas rather than database queries.

Montague's semantic theory (1970) is based on higher-order intensional logic (IL). Due to the complexity of the mapping between the surface syntactic form of utterances and their first-order semantic representation, linguists have tended to use logics such as IL which are more expressive and which have a more flexible syntax than first-order predicate calculus. But automatic deduction based on these systems is even less tractable than in first-order logic. Hobbs & Rosenschein (1978) and Gunji & Sondheimer (1979) consider interesting possibilities for the use of a possible-world-based model-theoretic semantics in the natural language understanding systems, but their initial enthusiasm has not been followed by actual implementations.[10]

The systems which are inspired by this direction of linguistic semantic research are usually not functional in the sense of providing information retrieval or storage capabilities. But several such implementations have proven to be useful for educational purposes and as tools in the development of natural language processing systems.

Friedman & Warren (1978) describe one such system intended for grammar development and grammar checking. Their program allows the user to define syntactic and semantic rules. A parser and semantic transducer is generated for the language described by the linguistic rules. Even relatively small grammars can exhibit complex interactions which give rise to unforeseen structural ambiguities and undesired readings. When the system is presented with sentences in this language it generates all syntactic and semantic analyses according to the grammar.

The recent surge in interest in syntactic parsers based on constraint-propagation techniques has also influenced the way in which semantic representations are recovered. Halvorsen (1983) extends constraint-based syntactic theory of lexical-functional grammar to include a model-theoretically interpretable semantics. This theory recognizes a level of semantic

---

[10] See Halvorsen (1986) for a survey of the impact of Montague grammar on natural language understanding.

representation which provides *descriptions* of classes of logical formulas in addition to (or instead of) the fully specified, unambiguous, expressions of the logical language. These techniques are also used in the approach developed in Fenstad *et al.* (in press) which integrates constraint-based grammar formalisms with situation semantics (Barwise & Perry 1983). Situation semantics provides an interesting alternative foundation for natural language understanding systems since it tackles two central problems head on: the context dependency of interpretation and the partiality of information.

The new semantic composition techniques developed in linguistic semantics suggest the possibility of more accurate language understanding systems with broader coverage of constructions, but the fulfillment of this promise is dependent on more efficient or more tightly controlled inference mechanisms.

11.6. Text-to-speech conversion (speech synthesis)

Perhaps the most impressive examples of commercially available linguistic technology can be found in the speech domain. Especially in the area of speech synthesis and text-to-speech conversion, linguistic theory and computational development have been well synchronized. Systems are now available which can convert unrestricted text (in English, French, Swedish, Spanish, and some other languages) to highly intelligible – if not natural sounding – speech, and this process takes place in real time on inexpensive equipment.

Several linguistic theories have contributed to the possibility of text-to-speech conversion. First, speech synthesis presupposes a theory of speech production. Some synthesizers (e.g. Flanagan, Ishizaka, & Shipley 1975) are based on an articulatory model, but currently the most successful systems (such as the one described in Klatt 1980 and its descendants) are formant synthesizers which are derived from the acoustic theory of speech production as presented in Fant (1960). Second, text-to-speech conversion relies heavily on morphophonemic, phonological, and prosodic rules, since it is not feasible to record in advance all morphological variants of a stem and all their contextually conditioned pronunciations.

Unfortunately, the exploitation of linguistic knowledge in speech synthesis systems has to be somewhat indirect, since a text-to-speech device requires a specification of the correspondences between *letters* and sounds, while phonological theory is concerned with the recovery of the sound structure of language without any particular interest in the facts of spelling. In text-to-speech conversion, letter-to-sound rules specify what sound or sound sequence a letter or letter sequence in the word corresponds to. Once the word is converted by rule to a sequence of allophone specifications, the allophones are synthesized, i.e. they are not just played back but are recreated from a symbolic representation by means of an LPC (linear-predictive coding) synthesizer.[11]

Much remains to be done before text-to-speech synthesis systems reach the stage where they can be mistaken for human speakers and thus pass the 'Turing-test'. But interestingly, at least for the time being the main limiting factor for improvement of the quality of text-to-speech conversion is not hardware or digital audio synthesis technology. Major advances are dependent on the availability of explicit linguistic rules for allophonic variation and prosody and efficient implementations of these in synthesis devices. The error rate in pronunciation could also be reduced if parsers capable of providing real-time category disambiguation could be integrated in text-to-speech systems (cf. the stress in examples such as *éxport* (n.) vs. *expórt* (v.)).

11.7. Speech recognition

Speech recognition is the problem of identifying the segments, words, or phrases in spoken utterances. It is currently an extremely active field of research spurred on by advances in linguistics and computer science as well as by the allure of many, and potentially extremely profitable, prospects for application. But we can be less sure of steady advances in speech recognition than in synthesis. Specialization of general-purpose pattern-matching techniques has made it possible to automatically recognize an increasing number of isolated words (~1000), but more powerful, and yet unknown, techniques are necessary to recognize ordinary connected speech.

Recognition of a limited vocabulary of isolated words is usually accomplished with a 'template-based' technique. This requires that samples of all the words which are to be recognized are recorded and analyzed in advance. There are several problems with this approach, in addition to the inherent restriction on the size of the vocabulary and the inconvenience of having to first record all words or phrases that are to be recognized. These problems have their root in the ubiquitous *variation* which characterizes normal speech. The same phrase pronounced by one and the same speaker at different times has different acoustic properties. And the same phrase pronounced by different speakers, even if they speak the same dialect, differ widely. The situation gets even more complicated when we take into consideration dialect variation and nonlinguistic factors such as noise. The problem is that the distance metrics can not distinguish between linguistically

---

[11] Bristow (1984) gives a tutorial introduction to different aspects of speech synthesis technology, including linear-predictive coding.

predictable variation in the pronunciation of a sound or a word (as in allophonic variation or variation due to dialect differences) and the variation which serves to distinguish one word from another. One can not make the computation of the distance metric sensitive to allophonic vs. phonemic differences.

The most ambitious project in speech recognition and understanding of spoken language was the ARPA Speech Understanding Project in the mid 1970s (Klatt 1977). A number of interesting systems grew out of this effort including HARPY and HEARSAY at Carnegie-Mellon University, and HWIM (Hear What I Mean) at BBN Laboratories.

HARPY exhibited the best performance when the project was concluded in 1976. HARPY accepted connected speech with a vocabulary of 1011 words from five different speakers after a moderate amount of training for each speaker. The sentences which the system was able to recognize pertained to a restricted task (document retrieval), but perhaps the most telling restriction was that only sentences generated by a highly restricted finite state grammar could be used.

Though the other systems did not quite match HARPY's performance, some of them, e.g. HEARSAY and HWIM, are important for many of their design features and in particular for the contribution they made to the study of different control structures for natural language processing systems with multiple modules. HEARSAY introduced a model for control in which autonomous modules for syntax, semantics, acoustics, etc. post their results in a data structure, the *blackboard*, where they are accessible by all the other modules. HWIM used a superordinate *control strategy* which facilitated experimentation with a number of different control structures.

At the present time a more balanced picture has replaced the view, prevalent during the ARPA Speech Understanding Project, that the acoustic signal is impoverished and that speech recognition is impossible without constant support from semantics, syntax and pragmatics. This is evidenced by the increased effort at culling detailed information out of the acoustic signal, which, together with higher-level information, can give clues about the identity of segments and the location of boundaries.

11.8. Machine translation

Machine translation has recently enjoyed increasing attention and advances as progress in semantic, syntactic, and morphological processing, as well as more powerful computers, have made the dream of automatically translating texts from one language to another seem more realistic.[12] The early approach

---

[12] *Computational Linguistics*, Vol. 11, issues 1 and 2 are devoted to a survey of past and present machine translation projects.

of considering translation as a problem of code-breaking was soon abandoned as the special properties of the linguistic 'code' came to be more widely recognized. A redefinition of the subject matter has also taken place. Many now aim to provide tools for the human translator (machine-aided translation, MAT). But there is now also a resurgence in work on fully automatic translation (MT).

Some of the relevant parameters of an MT system are whether it makes use of an *interlingua*, and whether the translation is *direct* or *indirect*. For systems that are geared to handle several language pairs, such as EUROTRA (King 1982), indirect translation can achieve savings in the effort required to write analysis and generation routines. On this approach the analysis of the source language proceeds independently of what the target language is, and the generation of the target language is not influenced by what source language was used. Systems that use an interlingua represent all synonymous sentences identically, regardless of the source or target language. Direct translation does not necessarily imply the use of an interlingua, since direct translation systems may use a *transfer* module which maps between abstract source and target language representations.

MT systems have not been quick to reflect changes in linguistic theory, but this situation may be changing. EUROTRA has adopted a grammar formalism that is heavily influenced by current base-generated approaches to syntax with GPSG and LFG as the most obvious sources of inspiration. EUROTRA also represents a departure from tradition by opting for a modular design where the statement of linguistic generalizations (i.e. the grammar) is separated from the specification of the parsing and generation algorithms. Another interesting convergence between linguistic theory and MT is Nishida's (1982, 1983) use of intensional logic as an intermediate representation in English-to-Japanese translation.

11.9. Conclusion

Natural language processing has a short history. What started out with string manipulation now includes ambitious attempts at simulation of complex linguistic behavior. Yet, it is only during the last 5–10 years that computation has become a concern of linguists to the extent that significant new developments in linguistic theory are informed by knowledge of their computational ramifications. As this trend continues, and linguistic science is reshaped by the growing understanding of cognitive processes which flows from joint work in artificial intelligence, cognitive psychology, and linguistics, computer applications of linguistic theory will also improve in quality and increase in number.

REFERENCES

Aho, A. V. & Ullman, J. D. 1972. *The theory of parsing, translation, and compiling*. Vol. 1: *Parsing*. Englewood Cliffs: Prentice-Hall.
Bach, E. & Harms, R. (eds.) 1968. *Universals in linguistic theory*. New York: Holt, Rinehart & Winston.
Bar, A. & Feigenbaum, E. A. 1981. *The handbook of artificial intelligence*. Los Alto: William Kaufman Inc.
Bar-Hillel, Y. 1971. Some reflections on the present outlook for high-quality machine translation. In W. P. Lehman & R. Stachowitz (eds.) *Feasibility study on fully automatic high-quality translation*. RADC-TR-71-295. Linguistics Research Center, University of Texas, Austin.
Barwise, J. & Perry, J. 1983. *Situations and attitudes*. Cambridge, MA: Bradford Books.
Bresnan, J. (ed.) 1982. *The mental representation of grammatical relations*. Cambridge, MA: MIT Press.
Bresnan, J., Kaplan, R., Peters, S. & Zaenen, A. 1982. Cross-serial dependencies in Dutch. *Linguistic Inquiry* 13: 613–36.
Bristow, G. (ed.) 1984. *Electronic speech synthesis*. New York: McGraw-Hill.
Čapek, K. 1920. *Rossum's Universal Robot*.
Carbonell, J. G. & Hayes, P. J. 1983. Recovery strategies for parsing extragrammatical language. *American Journal of Computational Linguistics* 9: 123–46.
Chomsky, N. 1959. On certain formal properties of grammars. *Information and Control* 2,2: 137-67.
Chomsky, N. 1963. Formal properties of grammars. In R. D. Luce, R. R. Bush & E. Galanter (eds.) *Handbook of mathematical psychology* 2. New York: Wiley.
Chomsky, N. 1977. Conditions on rules of grammar. In N. Chomsky *Essays on form and interpretation*. New York: North-Holland.
Church, K. 1980. On memory limitations in natural language processing. MIT/LCS-TR-245 and Indiana Linguistics Club.
Culy, C. 1985. The complexity of the vocabulary of Bambara. *Linguistics and Philosophy* 8: 345–52.
Earley, J. 1970. An efficient context-free parsing. *CACM* 6: 451–5.
Fant, C. G. M. 1960. *Acoustic theory of speech production*. The Hague: Mouton.
Fenstad, J. E., Halvorsen, P.-Kr., Langholm, T. & van Benthem, J. In press. *Situations, language and logic*. Dordrecht: Reidel.
Fillmore, C. 1968. The case for case. In Bach & Harms (1968).
Flanagan, J. L., Ishizaka, K. & Shipley, K. L. 1975. Synthesis of speech from a dynamic model of the vocal cords and vocal tract. *Bell System Technical Journal* 54: 485–506.
Floyd, R. W. 1964. The syntax of programming languages – a survey. *IEEE Transactions on Electronic Computers*, 13: 346–53.
Ford, M., Bresnan, J. & Kaplan, R. 1982. A competence-based theory of syntactic closure. In Bresnan (1982).
Friedman, J. & Warren, D. 1978. A parsing method for Montague grammar. *Linguistics and Philosophy* 2: 347–72.
Gawron, M. J., King, J. Lamping, J., Loebner, E. E. *et al.* 1982. *Processing English with a generalized phrase structure grammar*. Computer Science Laboratory Technical Note Series, Hewlett-Packard, Palo Alto.
Gazdar, G., Klein, E., Pullum, G. K. & Sag, I. A. 1985. *Generalized phrase structure grammar*. London: Blackwell.
Gordon, M. J. C. 1979. *The denotational description of programming languages*. New York: Springer.
Gunji, T. & Sondheimer, N. 1979. The mutual relevance of model-theoretic semantics and artificial intelligence. ms.
Halliday, M. K. 1967. Notes on transitivity and theme. *Journal of Linguistics* 3: 199–244, 4: 179–215.
Halvorsen, P.-Kr. 1983. Semantics for lexical-functional grammar. *Linguistic Inquiry* 14: 4.

Halvorsen, P.-Kr. 1986. Montague grammar and natural language understanding. *Computational Intelligence* 2: 54–62.

Hobbs, J. & Rosenschein, S. 1978. Making computational sense of Montague's intensional logic. *Artificial Intelligence* 9: 287–306.

Irons, E. T. 1961. An error correcting parse algorithm. *Communications of the ACM*. 6: 669–73.

Jensen, K., Heidorn, G. E., Miller, L. A. & Ravin, Y. 1983. Parse fitting and prose fixing: getting a hold on ill-formedness. *American Journal of Computational Linguistics* 9: 147–76.

Kaplan, R. 1972. Augmented transition networks as psychological models of sentence comprehension. *Artificial Intelligence* 3: 77–100.

Kaplan, R. 1973. A general syntactic processor. In R. Rustin (ed.) *Natural language processing*. New York: Algorithmics Press.

Kaplan, R. & Bresnan, J. 1982. Lexical-functional grammar: a formal system for grammatical representation. In Bresnan (1982).

Kay, M. 1967. *Experiments with a powerful parser*. Santa Monica: The Rand Corp., RM-5452-PR.

Kay, M. 1978. Functional grammar. In *Proceedings of the Fifth Annual Meeting of the Berkeley Linguistics Society*, University of California, Berkeley.

King, M. 1982. EUROTRA: an attempt to achieve multilingual MT. In V. Lawson (ed.) *Practical experience of machine translation*. Amsterdam: North-Holland.

Klatt, D. H. 1977. Review of the ARPA speech understanding project. *Journal of the Acoustical Society of America* 62: 1345–66.

Klatt, D. H. 1980. Software for a cascade/parallel formant synthesizer. *Journal of the Acoustical Society of America* 67: 971–95.

Marcus, M. 1980. *A theory of syntactic recognition for natural language*. Cambridge, MA: MIT Press.

Montague, R. 1970. Universal grammar. *Theoria* 36: 373–98. Reprinted in R. Thomason (ed.) *Formal philosophy. Selected papers of Richard Montague*. New Haven: Yale University Press.

National Research Council. 1966. *Language and machines: computers in translation and linguistics*. Publication 1416, National Academy of Sciences, National Research Council, Washington.

Nishida, T. 1982. An English–Japanese machine translation system based on formal semantics of natural language. In *Proceedings of the Ninth International Conference on Computational Linguistics (COLING 82)*. Amsterdam: North-Holland.

Nishida, T. 1983. Studies on the application of formal semantics to English–Japanese machine translation. Doctoral dissertation, Department of Information Science, Kyoto University.

Pereira, F. 1983. *Logic for natural language analysis*. SRI Technical Note 275 national, Menlo Park.

Pereira, F. & Warren, D. H. 1980. Definite clause grammars for language analysis – a survey of the formalism and a comparison with augmented transition networks. *Artificial Intelligence* 13: 231–78.

Peters, S. & Ritchie, R. W. 1973. On the generative power of transformational grammars. *Information Sciences* 6: 49–83.

Petrick, S. 1973. Transformational analysis. In R. Rustin (ed.) *Natural language processing*. New York: Algorithmics Press.

Rosenschein, S. J. & Shieber, S. 1982. Translating English into logical form. In *Proceedings of the 20th Annual Meeting of the Association for Computational Linguistics*.

Ruffino, J. R. 1982. Coping with machine translation. In V. Lawson (ed.) *Practical experience of machine translation*. Amsterdam: North-Holland.

Schank, R. 1975. *Conceptual information processing*. New York: North-Holland.

Schubert, L. & Pelletier, J. 1982. From English to logic: context-free computation of 'conventional' logical translation. *American Journal of Computational Linguistics* 8: 27–44.

Scott, D. 1976. Data types as lattices. *SIAM Journal of Computing* 5, 3.

Shieber, S. 1985. Evidence against the context-freeness of natural language. *Linguistics and Philosophy* 8: 333–44.

Shieber, S., Uszkoreit, H., Pereira, F. *et al.* 1983. The formalism and implementation of PATR-II. In B. Grosz *et al. Research on interactive acquisition and use of knowledge*. SRI final report 1894.

Wanner, E. & Maratsos, N. 1978. An ATN approach to comprehension. In J. Bresnan, M. Halle & G. Miller (eds.) *Linguistic theory and psychological reality*. Cambridge, MA: MIT Press.

Weischedel, R. M. & Sondheimer, N. K. 1983. Meta-rules as a basis for processing ill-formed output. *American Journal of Computational Linguistics* 9: 161–77.

Weizenbaum, J. 1976. *Computer power and human reason. From judgement to calculation*. San Fransisco: W. H. Freeman & Co.

Winograd, T. 1972. *Understanding natural language*. New York: Academic Press.

Winograd, T. 1983. *Language as a cognitive process*. Vol. 1: *Syntax*. Reading, MA: Addison-Wesley.

Woods, W. 1970. Transition network grammars for natural language analysis. *Communications of the ACM* 13: 591–602.

Woods, W. 1977. *Semantics and quantification in natural language question answering*. Report 3687. Cambridge, MA: Bolt, Beranek & Newman.

Woods, W., Kaplan, R. M., & Nash-Webber, B. 1972. *The lunar sciences natural language information system: final report*. BBN Report 2378. Cambridge, MA: Bolt, Beranek, & Newman Inc.

12 Metrics and phonological theory*

Bruce Hayes

12.1. Background

The field of metrics studies how conventionalized rhythmic patterns are manifested by phonological material in verse. Metrics and phonology are closely related fields whose interaction is yielding increasingly important results. This chapter outlines some of these findings, as well as directions for future research.

First, a caveat concerning what this chapter is *not* about. Metrics is only part of the larger field of poetics, which studies literature from the structural viewpoint adopted in linguistics. Excellent introductions to poetics may be found in Jakobson (1960) and Kiparsky (1973). I will also bypass work on metrics that is not focussed on the link to linguistic structure and to phonology in particular. The annotated bibliography of Brogan (1980) is recommended as a guide to such work.

A good place to start is to establish what questions linguists should try to answer in studying metrics; this defines the basic research strategy. To my mind the most compelling proposal has been the 'generative metrics' originated in the 1960s by Halle and Keyser (cf. Halle & Keyser 1969; Keyser 1969; and especially Halle & Keyser 1971). Generative metrics focusses on the problem of *well-formedness*. We assume that a meter is an abstract rhythmic form, internalized by those who command the relevant metrical tradition. Participants in a tradition share a tacit set of rules which determine which phonological sequences of their language constitute well-formed instantiations of a meter. Such sequences are termed *metrical*, while sequences excluded by the rules are termed *unmetrical*.

Consider an example. The English iambic pentameter can be represented roughly as a sequence of ten beats, alternatingly weak and strong: *w s w s w s w s w s*. The line by Shakespeare under (1a) would count as a metrical

* I would like to thank Matthew Chen, Morris Halle, Michael Hammond, Patricia Keating, S. Jay Keyser, Betty Jane Schlerman, and Moira Yip for helpful comments on an earlier version of this chapter. Responsibility for errors is my own.

instantiation of this meter in English, whereas (1b) would count as unmetrical.

(1) a. Beshréw that héart that mákes my héart to gróan   (Son. 133)[1]
          w s w s   w   s   w s w s
      b. *Then beshréw it, it provókes gróans dáily   (construct)
          w   s w s w   s w   s   w s

Metricality is typically gradient: among the metrical lines, some are more canonical manifestations of the meter than others. For example, line (2), although hardly unusual for Shakespeare, is clearly a more complex instantiation of the iambic pentameter than (1a):

(2) Príson my héart in thy stéel bósom's wárd   (Son. 133)
      w s w s   w s w   s w   s

Halle & Keyser thus assume a 'complexity metric,' which is a set of rules determining listeners' judgements of how far a line deviates from the ideal.

From this perspective, the initial goal of metrics is to discover the rules that govern the metricality and complexity of verse in the metrical traditions of the world. Note that these rules, like purely linguistic rules, will normally be unconscious; poets often cannot explicitly state rules that they observe rigorously in their verse. Accordingly, generative metrists use as data actual corpora of verse. If a given phonologically normal sequence never appears in the corpus lined up with the meter in a particular way, it is assumed that that alignment is unmetrical.

Just as in linguistics proper, the attempt to write metrical rules explicitly has yielded interesting results. The rules underlying the world's metrical systems show a remarkable variety, richness, and intricacy. To give an idea of the kinds of system that have been investigated, I will summarize three rule systems that have been discussed in the literature. For reasons of length, the summaries are greatly oversimplified and in no way substitute for the original work.

I. *English iambic pentameter*, as composed by Shakespeare. I follow here Kiparsky (1975, 1977), who draws on work by Halle and Keyser, Magnuson and Ryder (1970, 1971), and others.

The abstract rhythmic pattern can be expressed using the tree notation of metrical phonology, as shown in Figure 1. The tree specifies that the pentameter pattern consists of five feet, each containing a weak followed by a strong position. The feet are grouped into cola, with the rightmost foot of each colon the strongest. A line consists of a weak two-foot colon followed by a strong three-foot colon.

[1] Abbreviations for Shakespeare titles follow Spevack (1973: xii). Text and line numbers are from the Riverside edition (Evans 1974).

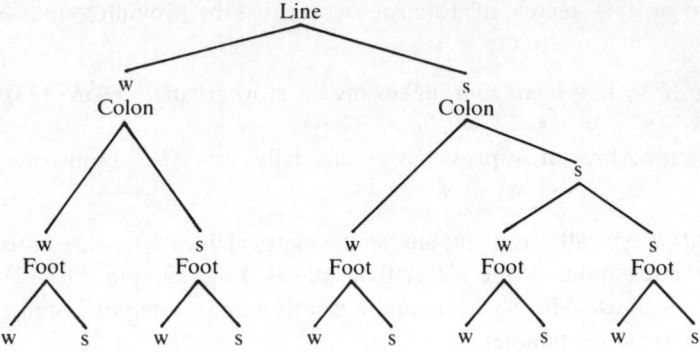

Figure 1. Rhythmic pattern for the English iambic pentameter

The 'correspondence rules' that determine when a line is metrical are as follows.

(3)   *Syllable count*: Syllables correspond one-to-one with terminal nodes of the metrical pattern.

That is, pentameters have ten syllables. I ignore the numerous rules that allow exceptions to this.

(4)   *Phrasing*: Line boundaries must coincide with phonological phrase boundaries.

(5)   *Rules governing stress*
       a. The '*Monosyllable Rule*'
          A stressed syllable must occupy *s* position unless:
             (i) it consists of a single, monosyllabic word; or
             (ii) it immediately follows a phonological phrase boundary.
       b. At the right edge of a phonological phrase, the sequence
          stressless–stressed must occupy *ws* position.

These rules admit as metrical canonical lines like (1). However, they permit Shakespeare a great deal of flexibility in writing lines that do not so directly reflect the rhythmic pattern. In the following lines, relevant phrase boundaries are marked with [/].

(6)   a. When to the séssions of *swéet* sílent thóught   (Son. 30)
             w   s   w s w   s   w   s w   s
       b. Or how *háps* it I séek not to advánce   (1H6 3.1.31)
             w   s   w   s w s   w   sw   s
       c. Resémbling stróng *yóuth*/in his míddle áge   (Son. 7)
             w s   w   s   w   s w   s w s

    d. To sée thy Antony/*máking* his péace   (JC 3.1.197)
       W S   W S W S W S   W   S

In (6a), the stress on *sweet* is mismatched, but the line is metrical because *sweet* is monosyllabic (5a.i). Line (6b) is metrical for the same reason. In (6c), *youth* bears a mismatched phrase-final stress, but the line is not ruled out by (5b), because *youth* is preceded by a stressed syllable. In (6d), the stressed syllable of *making* would violate the Monosyllable Rule, except that it immediately follows a phrase boundary (5a.ii).

Lines like those of (6) are not at all uncommon in Shakespeare. But lines that violate the rules of (5) are essentially missing from the corpus. This holds true even for lines that superficially sound much like the metrical lines of (6):

(7)   a. *When in the cóurse of *seréne* sílent thóught   (construct)
         W S   W S   W SW   SW   S
    b. * As it *háppens* I séek not to advánce   (construct)
         W S W   S W S   W SW   S
    c. *Resémbling *a yóuth*/in his míddle áge   (construct)
        W S   W   S W   S W   S W S
    d. *To sée that Brútus/is *máking* his péace   (construct)
        W S   W   SW S   W S   W   S

Thus while lines (7a) and (7b) have the same stress patterns as (6a) and (6b), they are excluded by the Monosyllable Rule. In (7c), the sequence *a youth* violates rule (5b). Line (7d) violates the Monosyllable Rule as, unlike in (6d), the word *making* does not follow a phrase boundary.

The size of the Shakespeare corpus is such that the absence of lines like those of (7) cannot be accidental. The rules of (5) must approximate the tacit principles Shakespeare used in deciding what lines 'sounded right' as iambic pentameters.

Further evidence in support of this comes from other poets. Kiparsky (1977) has shown that various English poets differ substantially in the rule systems that govern their metrical practice. The differences are far greater than what might be expected, given the similar overall 'feel' of the verse. Thus, for example, Shakespeare and Milton each wrote lines that would count as unmetrical in the other's system. Cases of this sort again suggest that the absence of lines in the Shakespeare corpus that violate Shakespeare's rules cannot be an accident.

The rules that govern complexity in Shakespeare (degree of divergence from the ideal among metrical lines) should also be mentioned. For present purposes we can simply say the following: a line is complex to the extent that its stressed syllables fail to occupy *s* position and its *s* positions fail to be occupied by stressed syllables. Later on I will discuss other 'complexity rules' in Shakespeare, which motivate the hierarchical structure of Figure 1.

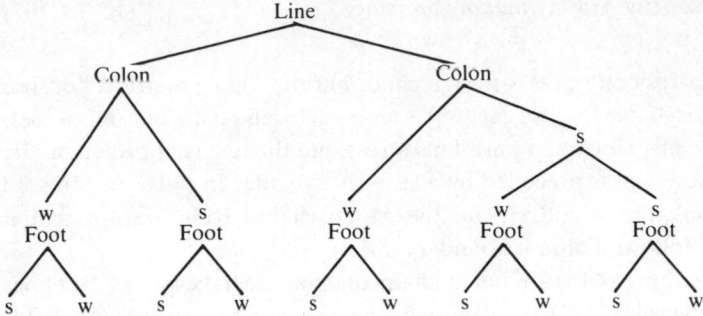

Figure 2. Rhythmic pattern for the Serbo-Croatian epic decasyllable

II. *The Serbo-Croatian epic decasyllable.* This meter was used in oral poetry: the epic verse composed spontaneously by Serbian *guslars*. The following account is based on work of Jakobson (1933, 1952).

The metrical pattern for this verse is hierarchical in nature. Each line consists of five trochaic feet, grouped into cola containing two and three feet respectively (see Figure 2). Observe that this pattern is quite similar to the one used by Shakespeare. However, as the correspondence rules involved are completely different, the outward form of the verse differs drastically from English. In particular, stress plays only a minor role, and the major constraints are placed on word boundary location and syllable quantity.

(8) *Rules governing word boundary placement*
   a. A phonological word boundary occurs obligatorily at the end of each colon.
   b. Colon-final feet may not include a word boundary.

(9) *Rules governing syllable quantity*
   a. If the ninth position is filled by an accented syllable, that syllable must be heavy.
   b. If the seventh or eighth position is filled by an accented syllable, that syllable must be light.[2]

Examples of lines observing the above rules are as follows. [/] indicates colon boundary, length is indicated by [:], and other diacritics denote various tonal accents.

(10) Stèva:n ùsta / iz šàtora svôga   Stevan rose from his tent,
      Pa pìrfati: / žĭcu telefó:na   gripped the telephone wire;

---

[2] According to Jakobson, all nonfinal syllables are open, at least in the style of speech used for verse recitation. Hence 'heavy syllable' here is equivalent to 'long-voweled syllable.'

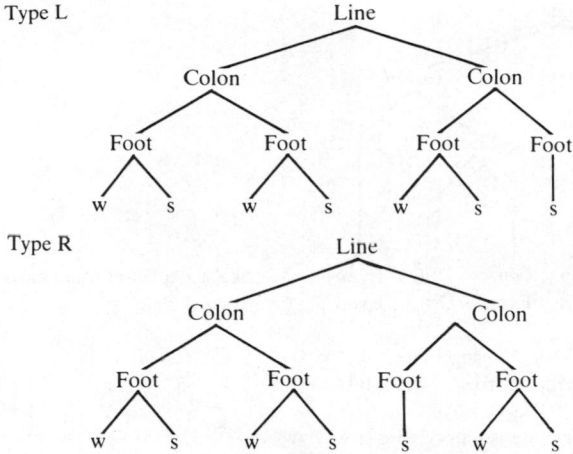

Figure 3. Rhythmic patterns for Chinese regulated verse

> Vî:če Stěva:n / svòje brigadí:re   Stevan called his brigadiers
> I nàniže / dòle oficí:re   and his junior officers.

> (guslar Radovan Ilić, heroic song on the battle of Dobrudža (1916))

The rules of (8)–(9) are iron-clad rules governing metricality. In addition, Jakobson noted the following rules governing complexity. (a) Stress tends to fall in metrically strong positions. (b) Syntactic breaks tend to coincide with line boundaries; failing that, they normally coincide with colon boundaries; failing that, they virtually always coincide with foot boundaries. (c) The quantitative restrictions of (9) are adhered to in unaccented syllables, though not as strictly as in accented syllables.

III. *Chinese regulated verse* (Chen 1979, 1980; Yip 1980, 1984). Here, there are two basic metrical patterns, which always co-occur in a quatrain (see Figure 3). The second colon is left-branching in Type L, right-branching in Type R. The patterns are deployed by the following principles. First, a quatrain consists of two couplets, one containing Type L lines, the other containing Type R lines. Each foot of each line is assigned to one of two tonal classes, comprising the 'even' tones and the 'oblique' tones, following a scheme outlined in Chen (1979). The rather complex pattern that results is overtly realized by a simple correspondence rule: the strongest syllable of a foot must bear a tone belonging to the tonal class of its foot. Figure 4 contains an example of a line that obeys this rule.

There are also rules governing complexity. First, the weak syllable of a foot, as well as the strong one, ordinarily bears a tone appropriate to the tonal class of the foot. This happens, for example, in two of the three disyllabic feet in Figure 4. Second, the phrasal structure of a line is ordinarily isomorphic to

225

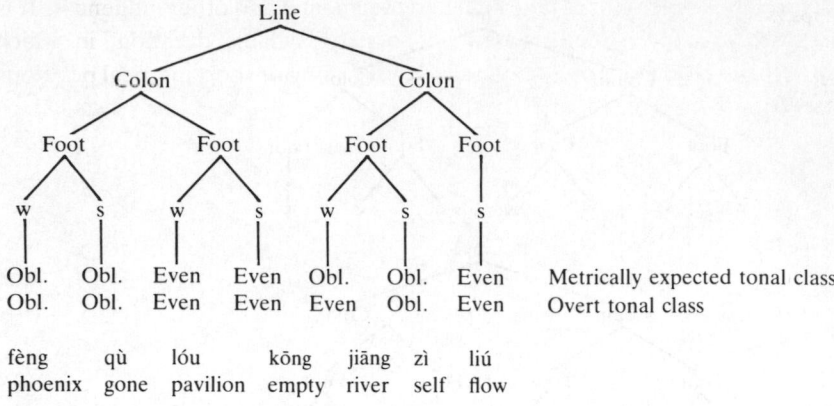

Obl.	Obl.	Even	Even	Obl.	Obl.	Even	Metrically expected tonal class
Obl.	Obl.	Even	Even	Even	Obl.	Even	Overt tonal class

fèng	qù	lóu	kōng	jiāng	zì	liú
phoenix	gone	pavilion	empty	river	self	flow

'The phoenix is gone, the pavilion is empty; the river flows on'

Figure 4. A scanned line of Chinese regulated verse

the line's metrical structure. In fact, severe violations of the latter rule, with extreme disagreement of phrasing and meter, are close to unmetrical. The only mismatch in Figure 4 occurs in the second colon, where *zì líu* 'self flow' is a mismatched phrase.

The three examples I have just presented only hint at the great variety found in the metrical systems of the world. In particular, the richness of phenomena found in prosodic phonology is matched by a parallel richness in how prosodic elements are deployed in meter. Only recently has it become possible to consider seriously what general principles might underlie the world's metrical systems. The possibility of truly explanatory work arises both from greater descriptive knowledge of metrical rules, and from recent advances in phonological theory which have proven directly applicable to metrics. In what follows, I will describe some areas in which metrics and phonology have aided each other's progress, and suggest glimpses of where a theory of universal metrics might ultimately lie.

12.2. Phonemic representation

A good place to start is with a basic assumption of phonology: that in the phonological system speech sounds are fundamentally *categories*, specified as distinct from each other, but lacking in quantitative detail until the very end of a derivation. This assumption is crucial to all theoretical work in phonology. As Jakobson (1933) pointed out, the evidence of metrics confirms it empirically. In all languages, metrical rules refer to phonological categories rather than to their overt physical manifestations.

Here is one of Jakobson's examples. In all languages, syllables vary in their phonetic length, as determined by segmental and other influences. It is easy to imagine a meter based on phonetic syllable duration, in which syllables would gravitate statistically towards long or short metrical positions depending on their phonetic length. But no such meter exists; instead, we find numerous 'durational' meters that rely on a *categorical* opposition. In these real-life quantitative meters, the language in question has a phonemic vowel length contrast, which forms the basis of a distinction between heavy and light syllables (see below), which in turn are matched against long and short metrical positions.

Jakobson's (1933) claims go beyond just limiting metrical relevance to phonological categories; he further suggested that only those categorical distinctions that are *phonemic in the language in question* may play a role in the metrics of that language. Taken in the strictest sense, this cannot be true, as stress is involved in the metrics of several languages that have predictable stress, such as Latin and French. But as a tendency it is undeniable, and helps account for why the metrics of a language is determined to a large extent by its phonology.

Kiparsky (1973) offers a variant on Jakobson's theme: if we think of a meter as a rhythmic repetition of linguistic sames, we can ask what subset of logically possible 'sames' can actually count as the same for metrical purposes. Kiparsky's answer is that the linguistic sames of verse are to be identified with the linguistic sames provided under universal grammar. For example, universal grammar permits phonological rules that count the number of syllables in a word, but apparently not rules that count the number of segments. The same holds true for rules of metrics. Similarly, the schemata that govern possible reduplication rules in phonology appear to be the same as the schemata that determine possible alliteration rules in metrics. If Kiparsky's thesis is right, then metrics can provide additional tests for proposals concerning the universally determined limits of linguistic competence.

12.3. Phonological derivations

The research program of generative phonology in the 1950s and 1960s was in part dedicated to showing that words are often phonemically represented in a highly abstract form, far removed from the phonetic surface. In large part, the evidence for this was that abstract representations permitted accounts of complex surface patterns using a small number of rules. However, phonologists also sought 'external evidence' (cf. Kenstowicz & Kisseberth 1979: ch. 5) to corroborate the conclusions arrived at with purely linguistic data. Data from metrical systems have played an important role here. The crucial cases have been those in which phonological material must be scanned, not according to its surface form, but according to its abstract underlying representation.

Consider a simple case from English. It can be argued that the final phonetic [m̩] in words like *spasm*, *orgasm*, and *syllogism* is underlyingly nonsyllabic /m/, and is vocalized on the surface due to the following rule:

(11) m → [+syllabic]/C—#

The arguments are as follows. (1) The nonsyllabic /m/ always shows up before vowel-initial suffixes (*spasmodic*, *orgasmic*, etc.). (2) *sm*# words are surface exceptions to a general rule (see Schane 1972 and later work) requiring that the rightmost nonfinal stressed syllable of a stem bear the main stress; compare exceptional *enthúsiàsm* with regular *enthùsiástic*. If /m/ is nonsyllabic at the time this rule applies, then *enthúsiàsm* will receive the correct stress contour in the same way as words like *enthúsiàst*. (3) *sm*# words always violate a general rule of Post-Stress Destressing (Chomsky & Halle 1968; Hayes 1982), which removes weak stress from nonfinal syllables when it immediately follows strong stress, as in *sénsory* from /sénsòry/ (cf. *aúditòry*). This rule never applies in words like *báptìsm*, *phántàsm*, *sárcàsm*, suggesting again that vocalization of /m/ is a late process.

On these grounds, then, it is arguable that word-final postconsonantal [m̩] in English is underlyingly nonsyllabic. It is thus interesting to note (Kiparsky 1975) that most English poets treat final [zm] as if it did not form a syllable:

(12) a. In the dark backward and *abysm* of time?
        w   s w   s   w   s w s Ø w s   (Shakes., Tmp. 1.2.50)
        Where it draws blood, no *cataplasm* so rare   (Ham. 4.7.143)
      b. To all Baptíz'd: to his great *Baptism* flock'd
                              (Milton, *Paradise Regained* 1.21)
        Their *Idolisms*, Traditions, Paradoxes?   (PR 4.234)
      c. Or under *chasms* unfathomable ever   (Shelley, Witch of Atlas 42.3)
        Whose shrieks and *spasms* and tears they may enjoy?   (Hellas 243)
      d. To bury in its *chasm* a crime like this   (Longfellow, Torquemada)

This is a straightforward example of what has been widely observed in other metrical systems: that the phonological representation scanned is one in which some or all of the phonological rules are 'undone.' Parallel examples have been found in Latvian (Zeps 1963, 1969, 1973), Old Norse (Anderson 1973), Turkish (Malone 1982), Vedic Sanskrit (Kiparsky 1972; see also Hock 1980), Old Irish (Malone 1984), Sephardic Hebrew (Malone 1983), and Finnish (Kiparsky 1968). The last of these is perhaps the most remarkable; Kiparsky shows that the Finnish national epic, the *Kalevala*, is written in a meter which requires that the phonology be 'undone' down to an astonishing depth. He further argues that this cannot be due to mere convention, that is, to an artificial invocation by poets of the historical scansions of the relevant words.

12.4. **Hierarchical structure in phonology**

The last decade has seen a thorough rethinking of what phonological representations look like. The theory proposed in *The sound pattern of English* (Chomsky & Halle 1968) invoked an extremely impoverished form of representation, consisting of linear strings of segments and boundaries, represented as feature bundles. The formal simplicity of this system was in itself a virtue, but ultimately proved a handicap to the understanding of complex phonological phenomena. The drastic enrichments proposed over the last ten years to correct this have gone in two directions.

In *autosegmental* theory, the phonological features are split up into parallel tiers. The tiers form quasi-independent sequences, each responsible for only a subset of the phonetic properties of an utterance. The segments of each tier are aligned in time using association lines, which denote simultaneity.

The other main strand of research is called (unfortunately for our purposes) *Metrical* theory. As the potential for confusion is large, I will distinguish phonological Metrical theory from the theory of poetic metrics by capitalizing the former. Metrical theory in phonology is concerned with phonological hierarchies; that is, with the organization of segments into syllables, syllables into feet, and so on into higher-level structure.

It can be argued that the empirical domains of autosegmental and Metrical theories are largely disjoint (cf. Anderson 1982). Autosegmentalism treats the disposition of phonetic properties in time, in areas like tone, nasal spreading, vowel harmony, contour segments, and the like. In Metrical theory, the phonetic properties of segments are largely irrelevant; we are concerned instead with the hierarchical relations of segments to each other. These involve syllable structure, phrasing, and stress. The latter is viewed in Metrical theory as embodying the rhythmic structure of a phonological representation.[3]

The way in which rules of metrics refer to the subdomains of phonology is partly predictable. Metrical rules may be divided into two distinct categories, which I will call *correspondence rules* and *identity rules*. All the rules discussed so far are correspondence rules: they determine when linguistic material is properly aligned with an abstract metrical template. Identity rules require that one part of the linguistic representation of a poem be identical or

---

[3] See, however, Halle & Vergnaud (1987), who argue that stress embodies both Metrical and autosegmental aspects.

similar to another part; these include rules for rhyme, assonance, alliteration, and the like.

It appears that correspondence rules refer only to Metrical representations; that is, they ignore the phonetic content of segments and are concerned only with their hierarchical relationships. Thus, while it is easy to imagine a meter which requires that syllables alternatingly contain front and back vowels, no such meter appears to exist. A survey of the basic verse types confirms the Metrical basis for correspondence rules. In quantitative meters, the phonologically relevant distinction is between heavy and light syllables, clearly an aspect of syllable structure (see below). Stressed-based verse, as in English, refers to the Metrical stress representation of an utterance. Verse based on boundary placement (e.g. the Serbo-Croatian meter noted above) appears also to refer to a Metrical hierarchy, as I will argue below.

The only possible recalcitrant case here involves tonal verse, as in Chinese. Although tones are in a sense 'prosodic,' they clearly embody specific phonetic substance. However, the rules for Chinese verse proposed by Chen (1979) show that the tonal patterns are largely disposed so as to meet an identity requirement, that of rhyme, rather than a correspondence requirement. Further, Yip (1984) argues that the tones were historically superimposed on an earlier nontonal metrical system that was extremely similar to the later tonal verse in all other respects.

For the sake of parallelism it would be nice to be able to say that the second class of metrical rules, those enforcing identity, refer only to autosegmental representations. Too little is known here, however, about either the metrical facts or the relevant aspects of autosegmental theory. We must clearly allow Metrical phonology to determine the phonological locations subject to identity requirements, as the syllables that rhyme and alliterate are usually stressed syllables.

With this general background, I will now consider three areas of Metrical phonology and their interrelation with metrics.

12.4.1. Syllable structure

Research on hierarchical syllable structure has centered on a number of areas; of these, the most significant for metrics has been the theory of 'syllable weight.'

Syllable weight plays a role in many phonological rules, but is most directly relevant to stress placement. Typological study of the world's stress rules shows that they normally refer only to a small fraction of the information available in the phonological string. In particular, stress rules either simply count syllables (for example, in assigning stress to the penultimate syllable), or they make a distinction of syllable weight, dividing the syllables of a language into heavy and light classes. The stress rule of Latin is a canonical example of this type; it assigns stress to the penult if it is 'heavy;' otherwise to the antepenult. (If a word lacks sufficient syllables to conform to this rule, stress is placed as far as possible to the left.) In the data of (13), I represent length as gemination.

(13) a. *Light syllables in Latin*: V, CV, CCV
          cf. áe.*o*.lus, com.pó.*ne*.re, mé.*tri*.cus, with antepenultimate
          stress
      b. *Heavy syllables in Latin*: VV, CVV, CCVV; VC, CVC, CCVC
          cf. hi.*áa*.tus, re.*fée*.cit, re.*plée*.tus
          co.*ác*.too, con.*tín*.git, re.*prés*.see, with penultimate stress

Comparison of (13a) and (13b) demonstrates an interesting fact: adding consonants to the end of a syllable (or lengthening the vowel) adds to its weight, whereas adding consonants to the beginning of a syllable does not. This is a general observation, which holds for numerous languages not related to Latin.

There are a number of ways to account for this formally. To my mind the most convincing is a proposal of McCarthy (1979) that the syllable universally consists of two primary constituents which, following earlier work, he calls the *Onset* and the *Rhyme*. The Rhyme contains the vowel plus any following consonants, and constitutes the 'prosodically active' portion of the syllable. The Onset contains all prevocalic consonants, and is prosodically inert. As the representations below show, a heavy syllable in the traditional sense can be characterized as having a branching Rhyme.

(14) a. Light   b. Heavy

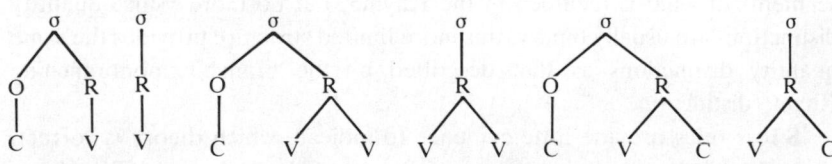

Numerous stress rules refer to the distinction between branching and non-branching Rhymes; see Hayes (1980) for a survey. The Rhyme constituent also allows for coherent expression of a number of phonological universals. For example, in many languages vowel length is in a trading relationship with the number of consonants following the vowel within the syllable; if short vowels can be followed by *n* consonants, then long vowels may only be followed by *n−1*. Such trading relationships never occur between vowel length and the syllable-initial cluster. The generalization is that languages typically impose a maximum on the length of the Rhyme, not on the syllable as a whole.

The evidence from metrics strongly supports the existence of the Rhyme: to my knowledge, all metrical systems that employ an opposition between long and short syllables use the distinction between branching and non-branching Rhymes; i.e. the traditional heavy–light distinction. I illustrate this with a scansion of the first line of Virgil's *Aeneid*, written in the Latin quantitative dactylic hexameter. /–/ and /˘/ represent long and short metrical positions, respectively.

(15) Arma virumque canō Trōiae quī prīmus ab ōris
    ar ma wi rum kʷe ka noo troo yai kʷii prii mu sa boo ris (syllables)
    ar a i um e a oo oo ai ii ii u a oo is   (Rhymes)

                                                      (meter)

The range of quantitative metrics is impressive. Languages which have at least partly quantitative meter, and which use the branching vs. nonbranching Rhyme distinction, include Latin, Greek, Sanskrit, Hindi, Arabic, Hausa, Persian, Old Norse, Finnish, Hungarian, Malayalam, and Serbo-Croatian. Kiparsky (forthcoming) argues that the badly misunderstood 'sprung rhythm' meter of Gerard Manley Hopkins is based in part on quantity. The quantitative system Hopkins uses invokes the characteristic embellishments English phonology adds to the basic heavy–light distinction (Hayes 1982).

Metrics can provide evidence to decide between rival hypotheses concerning how quantity is best represented in syllable structure. Clements & Keyser (1983) have suggested that the Rhyme constituent can be dispensed with, to be replaced by a Nucleus. The Nucleus would consist of the first two segments of what is included in the Rhyme, but no more. Since quantity distinctions are usually binary, this more limited structure provides the same quantity distinctions as that described by the branching/nonbranching Rhyme distinction.

Stress rules provide little evidence to indicate which theory is correct. However, the quantitative meter of Persian (Elwell-Sutton 1976; Hayes 1979; Heny 1981) is more illuminating. In Persian metrics, syllables are classified into three quantities, as follows:

(16)
Type	Membership	Scansion in meter
Short	CV, V	˘
Long	CVC, VC, CVV, VV	– or ˘ ˘
Overlong	CVCC, VCC, CVVC, VVC	– ˘

The generalization underlying the system should be apparent: every segment in a Rhyme corresponds either to a single short metrical position or to half of a long one. Thus in an overlong syllable, even the final consonant is prosodically active.

The latter fact provides some support for the proposal of a Rhyme constituent. The Nucleus theory would incorrectly assign the prosodically active second consonant of an overlong syllable the same status as a prosodically inert syllable-initial consonant, as (17) shows.

(17)   *Short*   *Long*   *Overlong*

	Short	Long	Overlong
Number of segments in Rhyme:	1	2	3
Number of segments in Nucleus:	1	2	2

In other words, the Nucleus theory wrongly predicts that adding a consonant to the right of the Nucleus should have effects no different from adding a consonant to the left. In so far as the two pattern differently, we have an argument to favor the Rhyme theory of syllable constituency.

2.4.2. Metrical stress theory

Under the Metrical theory of stress (Liberman & Prince 1977; Selkirk 1980a; Hayes 1980; Prince 1983), stress is regarded as the rhythmic structure of an utterance, embodying *relative* contrasts of prominence, rather than a local phonetic property of vowels. In particular, stress is not viewed as an *n*-valued distinctive feature, as was proposed in *SPE*. Figure 5 depicts both the Metrical and the linear stress representations for a line of verse. The *w*'s and *s*'s are to be interpreted as a relation of relative w(eakness) to s(trength), defined on sister nodes.

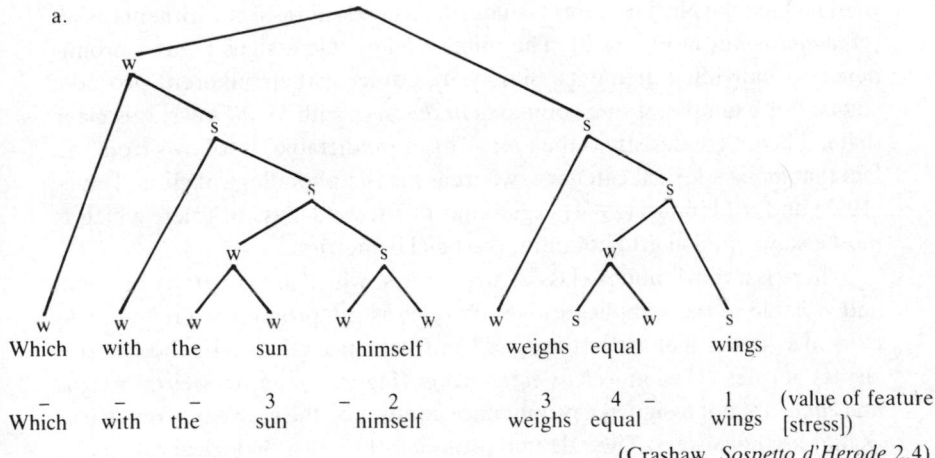

(Crashaw, *Sospetto d'Herode* 2.4)

Figure 5. Metrical vs. linear representations for stress

Work in metrics, notably Kiparsky (1977), strongly supports the Metrical theory. In particular, while metrical rules very frequently refer to the *relative* strength of neighboring syllables, they never refer crucially to a particular numerical level of stress, as the *SPE* theory would predict. Kiparsky demonstrates that his earlier work on metrics (1975) was seriously hampered precisely because of its use of *SPE*-style stress representations rather than Metrical theory.

While the notion of Metrical stress theory seems well-motivated in general, there remains considerable debate over the specifics of the theory and how to express them formally. Hayes (1983) argues that empirical improvements over Kiparsky's results can be obtained if the metrical rules refer not directly to trees, but to the Metrical 'grid' representations which Liberman & Prince (1977) originally proposed as a means of interpreting trees. At the same time, it was proposed in purely phonological work (Prince 1983; Selkirk 1984) to dismiss trees altogether, using grids as the sole means of representing stress. In my view, the most promising kind of representation would be a hybrid combining both tree and grid information (see Hammond 1984; Halle & Vergnaud 1987 for specific proposals). However, the issue remains open.

Metrical evidence can help to resolve this question, as the writing of metrical rules requires a precise and explicit characterization of the 'levels of stress' available in a language (Hayes 1983; Schlerman 1984). In addition, it is possible to outline some more general aspects of a Metrical stress theory that are demanded by the metrical data.

Phrasal stress rules appear to fall into two major types. One assigns a binary prominence relation between sister constituents. For English, such rules include the Nuclear Stress Rule, which labels phrasal constituents as *ws* (cf. *èqual wíngs* in Figure 5). The other kind of rule assigns greater prominence to individual elements, simply by virtue of their inherent prosodic status. For example, if one compares *in the trées* with *in tall trées*, it is clear that *tall* bears greater stress than *the*. This is predictable; it follows from the fact that *tall* is a lexical category, whereas *the* is a phonological clitic. Hayes (1983) and Schlerman (1984) argue that this second class of rules, which is most easily stated in grid notation, is crucial in metrics.

There is a third, minor class of stress rules, which are generally optional and variable in their application. Such rules assign prominence relations to pairs of syllables that are not assigned a prominence relation by the first two classes of rules. Thus in *weighs equal wings* (Figure 5) the stresses on *weighs* and *equal* are not assigned a prominence contour by the Nuclear Stress Rule, as they are not sisters. The rule that promotes the stress on lexical categories applies to both words; thus there is no firm prominence relation between the two. Accordingly, it is possible to assign greater stress to either one, as in *wèighs equal wíngs* or *weighs èqual wíngs*. (See Hayes 1984a; Selkirk 1984; Giegerich 1985 for accounts of the relevant rule.) Not surprisingly, it is this third class of prominence relations that are least relevant to meter; they scan much more freely than other sequences.

The upshot of this discussion is as follows. Rather than providing a single, unitary numerical stress contour to phrases, as the *SPE* system does, Metrical theory factors phrasal stress assignment into several distinct rules. This factoring out is empirically confirmed by the varying amounts of influence each rule has on scansion. While this generalization cannot decide between most current competing versions of Metrical theory, it does argue that the Metrical approach constitutes progress over earlier models.

2.4.3. Phonological phrasing: the *prosodic hierarchy*

Another use of Metrical structure in phonology has involved specifying *rule domains*. Many phonological rules apply across word boundaries; of these, a large fraction are constrained to apply only within certain phrasal domains. For example, the English Rhythm Rule (the rule that derives *thìrteen mén* from *thirtèen mén*) generally applies only when the secondary stress that is shifted leftward and the primary stress that induces the shift both occur within the same close-knit phrasal unit. Thus, while the stress on *Mississippi* readily shifts leftward in *Mìssissippi múd*, it cannot shift in **The governor of Mìssissippi vétoed it*.

Let us refer to the set of phrasal sequences within which a rule R may apply as the *bounding domain* for R. One may then ask what the basis of bounding domains is across languages. The obvious answer, of course, is that bounding domains are syntactic constituents. But in the languages that have been carefully studied, this turns out to be incorrect – cf. Clements (1978), Nespor & Vogel (1982), Odden (1984), McHugh (1987), and other work.

The most adequate theory of bounding domains, in my opinion, is that proposed in recent work by Selkirk (1978, 1980b, 1981) and Nespor & Vogel (1982). Under this theory, phrasal phonology is governed by an independent constituent structure, called the *prosodic hierarchy*, which is derived by rule from syntactic structure but is not identical to it. The rules that derive the prosodic hierarchy vary across languages, though the variation appears to fall within universally determined limits; see Hayes (forthcoming) for a survey.

The most salient aspect of the prosodic hierarchy is that it is *strictly layered*. This means that the topmost labeled constituents have as their daughters only constituents of the second highest type; which have as their daughters only constituents of the third highest type; and so on, down to individual words. Strict layering clearly cannot be a property of syntactic structure, which is normally self-embedded. To give an example, the syntac-

a.

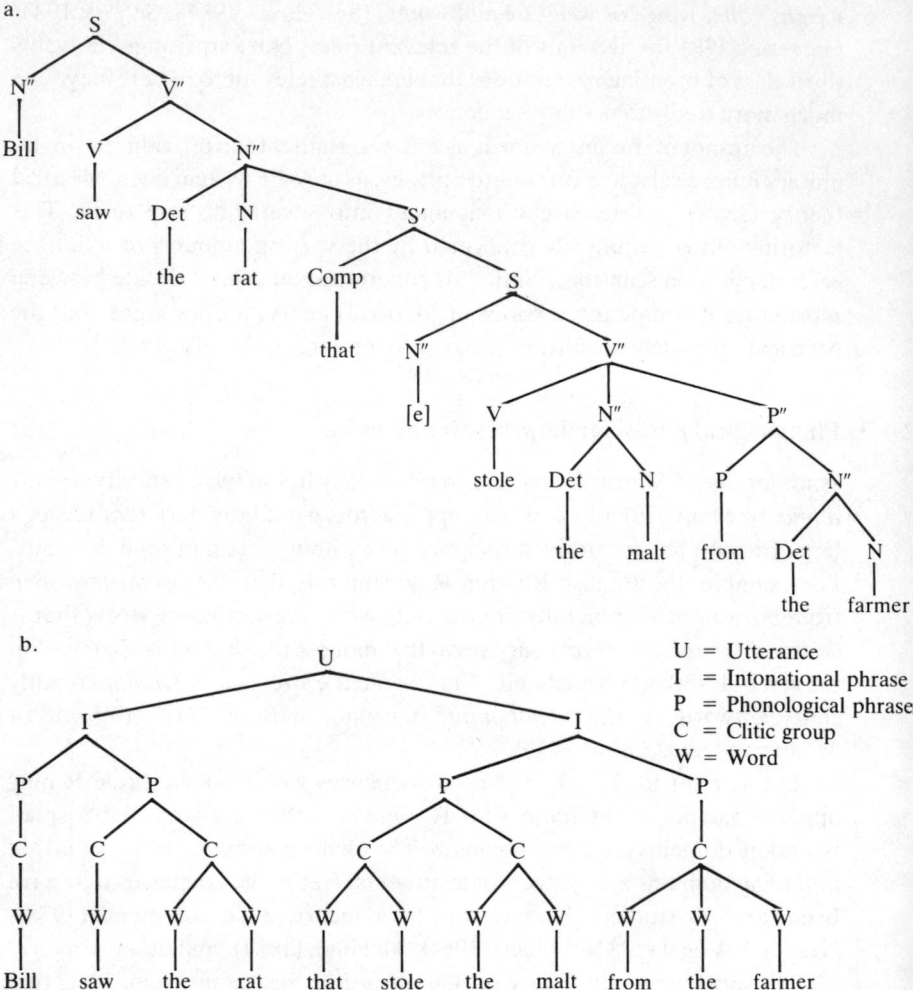

b.

Figure 6. The syntactic structure and prosodic hierarchy of a sentence

tic structure depicted schematically in Figure 6a can be argued to give rise to the prosodic hierarchy of Figure 6b.

The strongest evidence for strict layering concerns the relationship among phonological rules of the same language: if rule A refers to one bounding domain and rule B to another, then the two domains never overlap; one domain must form subconstituents of the other. If the only possible bounding domains of rules are categories in a strictly layered hierarchy, this is what we predict.

In addition, sometimes several rules of the same language make reference to the same rather idiosyncratic phrasal domain. If the domain is defined by the rules constructing the prosodic hierarchy, then we can capture the generalization in a single statement, rather than repeating the idiosyncratic domain in the structural description of every rule that refers to it.

Phonological rules make reference to the prosodic hierarchy in two ways. Most typically, a category of the hierarchy serves as the bounding domain of a rule. Thus the Rhythm Rule normally applies only if the focus and trigger lie within the same *phonological phrase*, as defined in the rules proposed by Nespor & Vogel (1982). In addition, phonological rules sometimes refer directly to the edges of a domain. Thus in Chi-Mwi:ni (Kisseberth & Abasheikh 1974; Hayes forthcoming), there is a rule that specifies the rightmost vowel in every phonological phrase as short.

The evidence gathered so far from metrics (cf. Dillon 1977; Devine & Stephens 1984; Hayes forthcoming) supports the prosodic hierarchy theory. Metrical rules are highly sensitive to the phrasings of the hierarchy, and they seem to refer to the hierarchy in just the same ways as phonological rules: they can be bounded within a particular domain, or can refer to particular phrase edges.

The 'Monosyllable Rule' for Shakespeare described above in (5) is a simple example of a bounded rule in metrics. If we refer to the prosodic hierarchy, the rule may be expressed in a very simple way: we require that any rising or falling stress contour on adjacent syllables must match the meter perfectly, with the proviso that the rule is word bounded. The rule thus can only 'see' stress sequences that occur within polysyllabic words. This is illustrated by the following scansions.

(18)   a. *Obeys the Monosyllable Rule*
         Plúck the kéen téeth from the fíerce tíger's jáws.

         w   s   w   s   w   sw   s w   s

                                             (Shakespeare, Son. 19)

         Sequences where the Monosyllable Rule can apply:
         [tíger's]
         s w

      b. *Violates the Monosyllable Rule*
         *Plúck imménse téeth from enráged tígers' jáws.   (Kiparsky 1975)
         w   s   w   s   w   sw   s w   s
         Sequences where the Monosyllable Rule can apply:
         *[imménse], *[enráged], [tígers']
         s   w   s w   s w

A remarkable consequence of this rule, discovered by Magnuson & Ryder (1970), is the counterintuitive scansion it requires for compounds that have the stress pattern *x́–x̀ x*, as in *grándfàther*, *lóve-làcking*. Because the

Monosyllable Rule only 'sees' one half of the compound at a time, and the monosyllabic first member will be properly scanned in any event, Shakespeare places these compounds in metrical *wsw* position, thus making their strongest stress metrically weak:

(19) a. How much *sált wàter* thrown away in waste   (Rom. 2.3.71)
          w   s   w   sw   s   w   s   w   s

      b. As this *fóre-spùrrer* comes before his lord   (MV 2.9.95)

      c. And looking on it with *láck-lùstre* eye   (AYL 2.7.21)

    The word is a salient unit on the prosodic hierarchy, governing numerous phonological rules. Not surprisingly, versions of the Monosyllable Rule are widespread in metrics, governing the verse of many English poets, as well as most of Russian (Žirmunskij 1966), German (Bjorklund 1978), and Dutch (Koster 1983) verse.

    As mentioned earlier, metrical rules, like phonological rules, often refer to the edges of units on the prosodic hierarchy. A typical pattern here is that rules requiring especially strict correspondence of meter and line apply at the right edges of units, while rules assigning extra freedom of scansion apply at the left edges. Here is an example: in Milton, the right edges of high-ranking phrases normally do not contain rising disyllabic stress contours that go against the meter (Buss 1974; Kiparsky 1977). The rarity of such cases depends on the rank of the phrase in question on the prosodic hierarchy. Thus if the phrase is a phonological phrase, exceptions are moderately rare; they occur in only 64 of the 12,500 lines in *Paradise Lost* and *Paradise Regained*. If the phrase ranks higher, as an intonational phrase, the exceptions are much rarer; there are only eight examples. If the phrase is a full utterance, the constraint becomes categorical, and no examples at all occur.

(20) a. *Mismatched rising sequences, right edge of phonological phrase (64 lines)*
        To *gìve Líght* on the Earth; and it was so   (*Paradise Lost* 7.345)
        w   s   w   s   w   s   w   s   w   s
        The *fùll bláze* of thy beams, and through a cloud   (PL 3.378)
        w   s   w   s   w   s   w   s   w   s

      b. *Mismatched rising sequences, right edge of intonational phrase (8 lines)*
        Round he surveys, and *wèll míght*, where he stood   (PL 3.555)
        s   w   sw   s   w   s   w   s   w
        Behold mee then, mee *for hím*, life for life   (PL 3.236)
        w   s   w   s   w   sw   s   w   s

c. *Mismatched rising sequences, right edge of utterance (no examples)*

*To *give líght*. And God saw that it was good   (construct)
   w s w   s   w   s   w s w   s

As can be seen, the frequency of lines diminishes as the rank of the relevant category rises. This is what we would logically expect in a strictly layered hierarchy: every right edge of a high-ranking category is necessarily the right edge of all lower-ranking categories at the same time.[4]

At left edges, the opposite pattern holds: the higher the category, the more freedom is provided for 'inversions' and the like; see Hayes (1983, forthcoming) for examples. In general, the ways in which metrical rules refer to the hierarchy appear to validate a general principle suggested by Kiparsky (1968): metrically speaking, beginnings tend to be free, endings strict.

The theory of the prosodic hierarchy is still in a very tentative state; much research will be needed to verify and improve it. I foresee that the evidence from metrics will be very useful in this task. At least for English, it seems that the evidence from metrics is clearer and easier to interpret than the available phonological evidence.

12.5. Rhythmic hierarchies

Kiparsky (1977) suggested that the kind of hierarchical structure posited in Metrical phonology might be suitable for describing the underlying patterns of meters. Subsequent research has supported this proposal. In particular, both the prominence relations (the sw labeling) and the bracketing structure of Metrical trees are empirically validated by their phonological correlates in verse. To see this, consider the metrical pattern for Longfellow's *Song of Hiawatha*, as I have analyzed it in Hayes (forthcoming) (see Figure 7). The pattern is a trochaic tetrameter: the four feet are grouped into two cola labeled *ws*, with the line as a whole labeled *ws* as well.

Evidence for the pattern comes from a number of sources. First, word boundaries coincide with foot boundaries with greater than chance frequency; that is, they tend to fall before strong positions, whereas in Longfellow's iambic verse they fall more often before weak positions. Second, the predominant syntactic pattern of a line matches the colon bracketing; one finds many lines like *Hiawatha! Hiawatha!* but few lines like *Never, Hiawatha, never!* The third kind of evidence is obtained from the

---

[4] I have oversimplified the argument somewhat, since to make a true comparison one must control for the overall frequencies of phonological phrase, intonational phrase, and utterance breaks within lines. With this taken into account, one still finds large frequency differences. For example, mismatched phonological phrase endings are about four times as common relative to their overall frequency as mismatched intonational phrase endings; the difference is statistically significant.

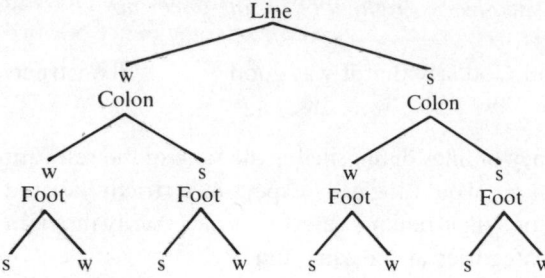

Figure 7. The meter of *Hiawatha*

methods of the Russian school of metrics (Bailey 1975; Tarlinskaja 1976; Smith 1980). These metrists often compile 'stress profiles,' which measure the frequency with which each position in a line is filled by a stress. A stress profile for *Hiawatha* roughly matches the abstract stress contour of Figure 7 if the pattern is interpreted by the normal conventions for Metrical trees.

(21) *Stress profile for* Hiawatha, *Book XIII (235 lines)*

Position:	1	2	3	4	5	6	7	8
% Stressed:	53.2	1.7	85.5	5.5	68.5	0.4	100	0.9

Observe that the seventh, strongest position of the meter is obligatorily filled with stress, a generalization which holds true for the entire poem.

The existence of hierarchical grouping has long been debated in the metrical literature, particularly in regard to whether feet exist. It is agreed that the foot is sensible as a purely theoretical notion, in that it expresses the inherent periodicity of verse. As Chatman (1965:116) says, 'It is simpler to assume that the series - - - - - - - - - - consists of five recurrences of one event, - - , than that it constitutes some single homogeneous event.' However, numerous metrists (including Chatman) have denied the significance of this, claiming that there is no evidence for feet in the verse itself (see also Jespersen 1933; Bailey 1975; Attridge 1982).

This widespread disbelief in hierarchical grouping stems in part from a too narrow database. It is true that many English poets, for example Shakespeare, show no tendency to place word boundaries in positions coinciding with foot boundaries. But nothing says that poets *have* to make the two line up; indeed, critics intuit such a lineup to be banal. The real point is that it would be difficult to explain the word boundary placement of other poets (like Longfellow) *without* positing feet. (See Jakobson 1974:120–2 for a similar contrast in Czech verse.) In addition, opponents of the foot have not taken into account various other kinds of more subtle evidence for bracketing; cf. the arguments for feet in Kiparsky (1977), Youmans (forthcoming), and Tarlinskaja (1984). Finally, and most important, there exist metrical traditions (e.g. Finnish, Serbo-Croatian, Latvian) where coincidence of word and foot boundaries is an essential ingredient of metrical well-formedness. These cases strongly validate the foot (and hierarchical structure in general) as a theoretical concept.

Some of the most interesting recent work in metrics has striven for a general theory of hierarchical metrical patterns; cf. the work of Kiparsky (1977), Piera (1980), Stein & Gil (1980), and Prince (forthcoming). I will review two specific proposals here.

Kiparsky (1977) and Prince (forthcoming) argue that the inventory of possible foot structures is limited by the following constraint: any branching node that is internal to a foot (Prince's 'subdivided metrical position') must be labeled *sw*. If we assume binary branching, this constraint limits the inventory of ternary feet to the configurations of (22), and excludes the logically possible structures of (23).

(22) *Possible ternary feet*

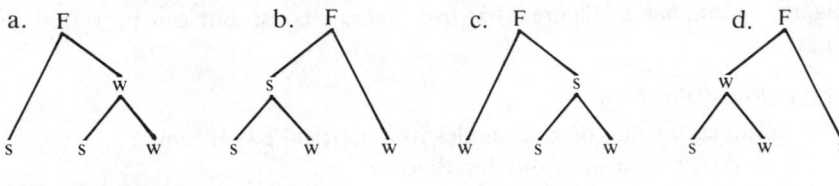

(23) *Impossible ternary feet*

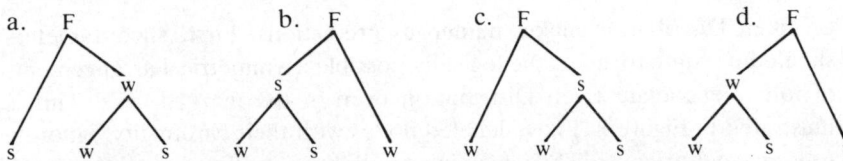

To the extent that the foot trees are empirically distinguishable, it appears that all and only those feet meeting the sw constraint are used in actual meters. For example, all known anapestic verse observes the pattern of (22d), which contains a secondary strong position foot initially, thus allowing lines like (24a). No anapestic verse gives the foot-medial position secondary prominence, as would be required by (23d), or makes both the first and second positions weak, as (23c) would require. The lines of (24b,c) illustrate what verse in these nonexistent meters would sound like.

(24) *Anapestic meters*
    a. Possible: (22d)
        I have known *nòble héarts* and great souls in thy sons

                              (Byron, *The Irish Avatar* 110)

  b. Impossible: (23d)
      *I have known *devòut héarts* and great souls in thy sons

                                                            (construct)
  c. Impossible: (23c)
      (24a) is ill-formed, and would have to be replaced by
      I have known *of the héarts* and great souls in thy sons

                                                            (construct)

Prince (forthcoming) also applies the *sw* law to a completely different area, the quantitative meters of Classical Arabic. The analysis he proposes is remarkable in its abstractness and in the hidden connections it reveals in the system.

Piera (1980) has made an important proposal for characterizing the inventory of possible metrical patterns. He argues that all meters must meet a requirement of symmetry called *Even Distribution*. This can be defined briefly as follows. Let the *cardinality* of a metrical constituent be the maximum path length from its root to a terminal node. For example, the cardinality of the ternary feet of (22)–(23) is three, and the cardinality of iambic pentameter (Figure 1) is five. Piera's constraint can be stated as follows:

(25) *Even Distribution*
      The cardinality of sister nodes in a metrical pattern must:
      a. differ by at most one (marked case);
      b. be equal (unmarked case).

Even Distribution makes numerous predictions. First, all tetrameters should be symmetrical, as the logically possible asymmetrical arrangements of four feet violate Even Distribution even in the marked case. This is illustrated in Figure 8. I have labeled nodes with their cardinality, ignoring foot-internal structure. The remaining possibilities are the mirror images of b and c in Figure 8, and are also excluded.

The facts confirm this prediction of symmetry. Thus Persian tetrameters, but not trimeters, may have a midline caesura. The usual phrasing of the line

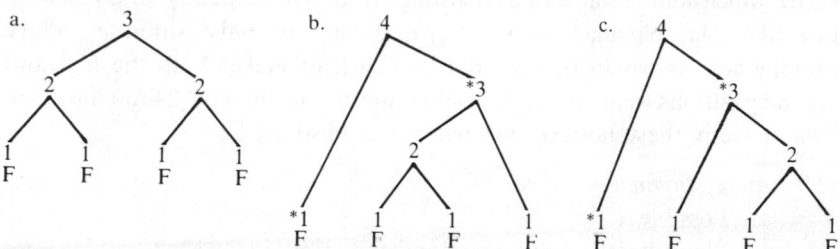

Figure 8. Even distribution in tetrameters

reinforces the symmetrical 2+2 scheme for tetrameters in English, Finnish (Kiparsky 1968), Spanish (Piera 1980), Chinese (Yip 1984), Serbo-Croatian (Jakobson 1952), and other languages. The stress profiles of tetrameters often show stress peaks in the two colon-final feet (Bailey 1975; Tarlinskaja 1976), again reinforcing symmetry.

Exactly the same reasoning predicts correctly that no foot pattern may contain one strong and three weak positions; there is no way such a foot can be bracketed to satisfy Even Distribution.

In pentameters, the unmarked provision of even distribution is unsatisfiable. The marked provision is met by two basic structures:

(26)   a. *2+3 pentameter*   b. *3+2 pentameter*

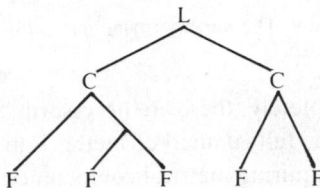

Piera (1980) convincingly argues that in Spanish, the two structures can be freely mixed in the same poem. He proposes that the basic pattern for pentameter is normally just a linear sequence of five feet, and that the general principle of Even Distribution freely provides the two options. In other pentameter traditions, only the 2+3 structure is available (cf. Serbo-Croatian decasyllables, Renaissance English verse, Chinese (Yip 1984), and some Romance verse forms). Piera suggests that 2+3 is the unmarked bracketing, and relates this claim to the general rhythmic principle that longer elements are placed after shorter ones (cf. Allen 1973:119–20).

Piera's ideas can help account for some of the diachronic shifts that have been observed in the metrical practice of Shakespeare. As Shakespeare's career evolved, he gradually carried out the following changes. First, the second most frequently stressed position in the line (after the main peak in position ten) shifts from position four to position six (Tarlinskaja 1983, 198–). Further, the second most frequent location of phonological phrase breaks (after line boundary) shifts from just after position four to just after position six (Oras 1960). Both changes reflect a shift from the unmarked 2+3 structure towards the more sophisticated 3+2. The shifted colon boundary behaves like a pale version of a line boundary, attracting both stress and phrase breaks.

Recall that 2+3 is the 'unmarked case' only in the context of the pentameter, which inherently cannot achieve strict Even Distribution. The truly unmarked case is found only in meters that satisfy the constraint

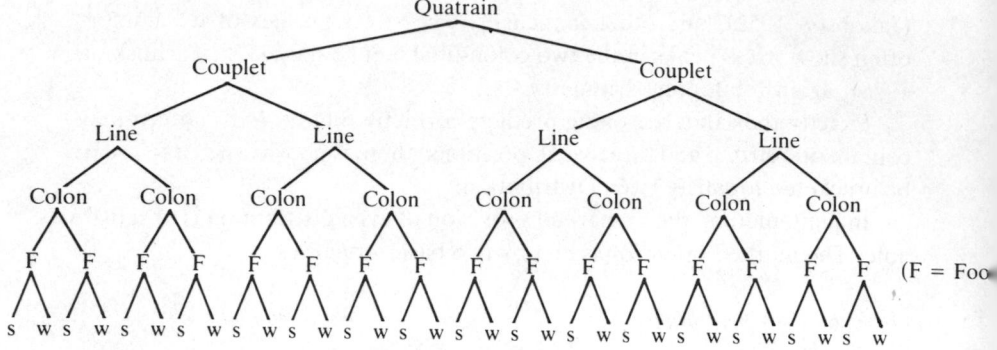

Figure 9. The nursery rhyme quatrain

completely; these are necessarily based on powers of two. A plausible place to find fully unmarked meters is in verse intended for those in the early stages of acquiring metrical competence – that is, in nursery rhymes. The work of Burling (1966) is striking in this regard. Burling collected nursery rhymes from a wide variety of unrelated languages, and discovered that they all fit a common rhythmic archetype. The lines of this archetype have four feet, and from syntactic evidence appear to be divided into two-foot cola. Lines are grouped by both rhyme and syntax into couplets, and the couplets pair off into quatrains. Thus in English we have:

(27) Péter, Péter, / púmpkin eáter,
      Hád a wífe and / cóuldn't kéep her,

      Pút her ín a / púmpkin shéll, (and)
      Thére he képt her / véry wéll.

This pattern clearly reflects Even Distribution, carried through in the most thorough possible way. The full metrical pattern of a quatrain (see Figure 9) pairs symmetrical constituents to a substantial depth of embedding. Burling found similar patterns in Chinese, Bengkulu, Cairene Arabic, Yoruba, Serrano, Trukese, and Ponapeian.

Further support for Even Distribution in children's verse comes from 'silent feet'. These occur at the edge of what appear superficially to be three-beat lines, as in (28):

(28) Híckory, díckory, dóck, Ø
      The móuse ran úp the clóck. Ø
      The clóck struck óne, the móuse ran dówn,
      Híckory, díckory, dóck. Ø

The existence of these silent feet is most strongly supported by recitation: an obligatory pause signals the missing foot. A recitation that simply followed the inherent linguistic rhythm would be non-idiomatic. Further evidence for silent beats is pointed out in Attridge (1982), Hayes (1984b), and Stein & Gil (1980).

Silent feet occur only in tetrameter verse, where they permit the strictest version of Even Distribution to be satisfied. I take this as significant evidence in favor of Even Distribution; readers presumably only insert 'fictional' pauses when an overriding general principle tells them that pauses are to be expected. The widespread linguistic distribution of tetrameter rhythm and silent beats in children's verse argues that Even Distribution may be an innate principle of unmarked rhythmic form.

The study of metrical patterns is a very early stage, though I think it shows great promise. One implication for phonological theory appears already to have emerged from this work: rhythmic structure in the general sense embodies not just a pattern of relative prominence, but also a grouping of rhythmic elements into constituent structure. The Metrical theory of stress currently faces a controversy over precisely this issue; cf. 12.4.2. If stress is the linguistic instantiation of rhythmic structure, then the clear example of rhythm in meter suggests that linguistic stress should involve constituency as well. In my view, this agrees with what the purely phonological evidence would indicate.

12.6. Conclusion: the content of universal metrics

Generative metrics has patterned its long-term goals after those of generative linguistics: we wish first to provide adequate factual coverage of individual metrical systems; then psychologically valid accounts of the rules that underlie these systems; and finally a statement of the universal principles on which all metrical systems are founded. In other words, we seek observational, descriptive, and explanatory adequacy. Interesting accounts of these goals as they relate to metrics may be found in Piera (1980) and Gil & Shoshany (forthcoming).

I would conjecture, however, that explanatory adequacy for metrical theory will involve a rather different kind of answer than what emerges from linguistics proper. In particular, I suspect that there may be no such field as 'universal metrics' *per se*. I base my conjecture on the vastly differing importance of linguistic and metrical competence for human beings. Chomsky (1980) has argued that true linguistic capacity is unique to humans; that we possess a specialized 'mental organ' dedicated to linguistic knowledge and processing. It is not obvious that the selective advantage provided by our linguistic abilities is also conferred by the ability to compose or appreciate metrical verse.

It seems more likely that metrical ability is an overlaid function, tapping into both linguistic competence and 'rhythmic competence.' Our understanding of the latter is less developed than our knowledge of linguistics, but it is clear that such a mental domain must exist, given the wide variety of things people do in regular rhythms. There are clearly general principles that govern rhythmic activity, among them (a) the tendency of rhythmic beats towards isochrony; (b) the existence of hierarchy, with stronger beats spaced at wider intervals; (c) the iambic/trochaic law: iambic, but not trochaic units tend to be reinforced with durational contrast. These principles govern other activities beyond verse, and arguably have direct effects in phonology itself (Hayes 1984a, 1985; Selkirk 1984).

The one aspect of metrics that may initially seem purely 'metrical' is the notion of correspondence; the task of determining a well-formed mapping between distinct rhythmic structures. But even this may reflect an ability that is more general; for example, Liberman (1975) suggests that the alignment of intonational contours with varying texts forms essentially a task of matching up two independent rhythmic structures.

If this conjecture concerning universal metrics is right, then two things follow. First, metrists should be wary of putative metrical principles stated in a way that is extremely specific to metrics. Such principles are unlikely to be sufficiently general. Second, if universal metrics is indeed derivable entirely from principles of other domains, then it can serve as very direct evidence for what those principles are. As research continues, both phonologists and psychologists of rhythm should find the results of metrics to be of increasing relevance and importance to their own work.

REFERENCES

Allen, W. S. 1973. *Accent and rhythm*. Cambridge: Cambridge University Press.
Anderson, S. 1973. U-umlaut and Skaldic verse. In S. Anderson & P. Kiparsky (eds.) *A festschrift for Morris Halle*. New York: Holt, Rinehart & Winston.
Anderson, S. 1982. Differences in rule type and their structural basis. In H. van der Hulst & N. Smith (eds.) *The structure of phonological representations (part II)*. Dordrecht: Foris.
Attridge, D. 1982. *The rhythms of English poetry*. London: Longman.
Bailey, J. 1975. *Toward a statistical analysis of English verse*. Lisse: Peter de Ridder Press.
Bjorklund, B. 1978. *A study in comparative prosody: German and English iambic pentameter*. Stuttgart: Verlag Hans-Dieter Heinz.
Brogan, T. 1980. *English versification 1570–1980: a reference guide with a global appendix*. Baltimore: Johns Hopkins University Press.
Burling, R. 1966. The metrics of children's verse: a cross-linguistic study. *American Anthropologist* 68: 1418–41.
Buss, K. 1974. Stress placement in Milton's verse: implications for the Halle–Keyser theory of English iambic pentameter. Doctoral dissertation, Brandeis University.
Chatman, S. 1965. *A theory of meter*. The Hague: Mouton.
Chen, M. 1979. Metrical structure: evidence from Chinese poetry. *Linguistic Inquiry* 10: 371–420.

Chen, M. 1980. The primacy of rhythm in verse. *Journal of Chinese Linguistics* 8: 15–41.

Chomsky, N. 1980. *Rules and representations*. New York: Columbia University Press.

Chomsky, N. & Halle, M. 1968. *The sound pattern of English*. New York: Harper & Row.

Clements, G. N. 1978. Tone and syntax in Ewe. In D. Napoli (ed.) *Elements of tone, stress, and intonation*. Washington: Georgetown University Press.

Clements, G. N. & Keyser, S. J. 1983. *CV phonology: a generative theory of the syllable*. Cambridge, MA: MIT Press.

Devine, A. & Stephens, L. 1984. *Language and metre: resolution, Porson's bridge, and their prosodic basis*. Chico: Scholars Press.

Dillon, G. L. 1977. Kames and Kiparsky on syntactic boundaries. *Language and Style* 10: 16–22.

Elwell-Sutton, L. P. 1976. *The Persian meters*. Cambridge: Cambridge University Press.

Evans, B. 1974. *The Riverside Shakespeare*. Boston: Houghton Mifflin Co.

Giegerich, H. 1985. *Metrical phonology and phonological structure: German and English*. Cambridge: Cambridge University Press.

Gil, D. & Shoshany, R. Forthcoming. On the nature of prosodic competence. Dept. of Linguistics, Tel Aviv University. ms.

Halle, M. & Keyser, S. J. 1969. Chaucer and the study of prosody. *College English* 28: 187–219.

Halle, M. & Keyser, S. J. 1971. *English stress: its form, its growth, and its role in verse*. New York: Harper & Row.

Halle, M. & Vergnaud, J. -R. 1987. Stress and the cycle. *Linguistic Inquiry* 18: 45–84.

Hammond, M. 1984. Constraining metrical theory: a modular theory of rhythm and destressing. Doctoral dissertation, UCLA, Los Angeles, Calif. Distributed by Indiana University Linguistics Club.

Hayes, B. 1979. The rhythmic structure of Persian verse. *Edebiyāt* 4: 193–242.

Hayes, B. 1980. *A metrical theory of stress rules*. Doctoral dissertation, MIT. Published 1985, New York: Garland.

Hayes, B. 1982. Extrametricality and English stress. *Linguistic Inquiry* 13: 227–76.

Hayes, B. 1983. A grid-based theory of English meter. *Linguistic Inquiry* 14: 357–93.

Hayes, B. 1984a. The phonology of rhythm in English. *Linguistic Inquiry* 15: 33–74.

Hayes, B. 1984b. Review of Attridge (1982). *Language* 60: 914–23.

Hayes, B. 1985. Iambic and trochaic rhythm in stress rules. In M. Niepokuj, M. VanClay, V. Nikiforidou & D. Feder (eds.) *BLS* 11.

Hayes, B. Forthcoming. The prosodic hierarchy in meter. In Kiparsky & Youmans (forthcoming).

Heny, J. 1981. Rhythmic elements in Persian poetry. Doctoral dissertation, University of Pennsylvania.

Hock, H. H. 1980. Archaisms, morphophonemic metrics, or variable rules in the Rig-Veda? *Studies in the Linguistic Sciences* 10,1: 59–69. Urbana: Dept. of Linguistics, University of Illinois.

Jakobson, R. 1933. Über den Versbau der serbokroatischen Volksepen. *Archives néerlandaises de phonétique expérimentale* 7–9: 44–53. Reprinted in Jakobson (1966).

Jakobson, R. 1952. Slavic epic verse: studies in comparative metrics. *Oxford Slavonic papers* 3: 21–66. Reprinted in Jakobson (1966).

Jakobson, R. 1960. Linguistics and poetics. In T. Sebeok (ed.) *Style in language*. Cambridge, MA: MIT Press.

Jakobson, R. 1966. *Selected writings IV: Slavic epic studies*. The Hague: Mouton.

Jakobson, R. 1974. *Über den tschechischen Vers*. Konstanz: Verlag K. Presse. German translation of the combined text of *O češskom stiche* (Berlin, 1923) and *Základy českého verše* (Prague, 1926).

Jespersen, O. 1933. Notes on metre. *Linguistica*. Copenhagen: Levin & Munksgaard.

Kenstowicz, M. & Kisseberth, C. 1979. *Generative phonology: description and theory*. New York: Academic Press.

Keyser, S. J. 1969. Old English prosody. *College English* 30: 331–56.

Kiparsky, P. 1968. Metrics and morphophonemics in the *Kalevala*. In C. Gribble (ed.) *Studies presented to Professor Roman Jakobson by his students*. Cambridge, MA: Slavica.

Kiparsky, P. 1972. Metrics and morphophonemics in the *Rigveda*. In M. Brame (ed.) *Contributions to generative phonology*. Austin: University of Texas Press.

Kiparsky, P. 1973. The role of linguistics in a theory of poetry. *Daedalus* 102: 231–45.

Kiparsky, P. 1975. Stress, syntax, and meter. *Language* 51: 576–616.
Kiparsky, P. 1977. The rhythmic structure of English verse. *Linguistic Inquiry* 8: 189–247.
Kiparsky, P. Forthcoming. Sprung rhythm. In Kiparsky & Youmans (forthcoming).
Kiparsky, P. & Youmans, G. Forthcoming. *Rhythm and meter*. Orlando: Academic Press.
Kisseberth, C. & Abasheikh, M. 1974. Vowel length in Chi-Mwi:ni – a case study of the role of grammar in phonology. In A. Bruck, R. Fox, & M. LaGaly (eds.) *Papers from the parasession on natural phonology*. Chicago: Chicago Linguistic Society.
Koster, J. 1983. Untitled ms., Vakgroep Algemene Literatuurwetenschap, Rijksuniversiteit te Leiden, The Netherlands.
Liberman, M. 1975. The intonational system of English. Doctoral dissertation, MIT. Distributed by the Indiana University Linguistics Club.
Liberman, M. & A. Prince 1977. On stress and linguistic rhythm. *Linguistic Inquiry* 8: 249–336.
Magnuson, K. & Ryder, F. 1970. The study of English prosody: an alternative proposal. *College English* 31: 789–820.
Magnuson, K. & Ryder, F. 1971. Second thoughts on English prosody. *College English* 33: 198–216.
Malone, J. 1982. Generative phonology and Turkish rhyme. *Linguistic Inquiry* 13: 550–3.
Malone, J. 1983. Generative phonology and the metrical behavior of *U-* 'and' in the Hebrew poetry of medieval Spain. *Journal of the American Oriental Society* 103: 369–81.
Malone, J. 1984. Generative phonology and Early Irish alliteration. Dept. of Linguistics, Barnard College, New York. ms.
McCarthy, J. 1979. On stress and syllabification. *Linguistic Inquiry* 10: 443–66.
McHugh, B. 1987. Syntactic structure, empty categories and phrasal phonology in Chaga. In D. Odden (ed.) *Current approaches to African linguistics, vol. 4*. Dordrecht: Foris.
Nespor, M. & Vogel I. 1982. Prosodic domains of external sandhi rules. In H. van der Hulst & N. Smith (eds.) *The structure of phonological representations, part I*. Dordrecht: Foris.
Odden, D. 1984. The phrasal phonology of Kimatuumbi. Dept. of Linguistics, Yale University. ms.
Oras, A. 1960. *Pause patterns in Elizabethan and Jacobean drama: an experiment in prosody*. Gainesville: University of Florida Press.
Piera, C. 1980. Spanish verse and the theory of meter. Doctoral dissertation, UCLA.
Prince, A. 1983. Relating to the grid. *Linguistic Inquiry* 14: 19–100.
Prince, A. Forthcoming. Metrical forms. In Kiparsky & Youmans (forthcoming).
Schane, S. 1972. Noncyclic English word stress. Dept. of Linguistics, University of California, San Diego. ms.
Schlerman, B. 1984. The meters of John Webster. Doctoral dissertation, University of Massachusetts, Amherst. Available from the University of Massachusetts Graduate Linguistics Student Association.
Selkirk, E. 1978. On prosodic structure and its relation to syntactic structure. In T. Fretheim (ed.) *Nordic prosody II*. Trondheim: TAPIR.
Selkirk, E. 1980a. The role of prosodic categories in English word stress. *Linguistic Inquiry* 11: 563–605.
Selkirk, E. 1980b. Prosodic domains in phonology: Sanskrit revisited. In M. Aronoff & M.-L. Kean (eds.) *Juncture*. Saratoga: Anma Libri.
Selkirk, E. 1981. On the nature of phonological representation. In J. Anderson, J. Laver & T. Myers (eds.) *The cognitive representation of speech*. Amsterdam: North-Holland.
Selkirk, E. 1984. *Phonology and syntax: the relation between sound and structure*. Cambridge MA: MIT Press.
Smith, G. S. 1980. *Metre, rhythm, stanza, rhyme*. Russian poetics in translation 7. Oxford: Holdan Books.
Spevack, M. 1973. *The Harvard concordance to Shakespeare*. Cambridge, MA: Belknap Press of Harvard University Press.
Stein, D. & Gil, D. 1980. Prosodic structures and prosodic markers. *Theoretical Linguistics* 7: 173–240.
Tarlinskaja, M. 1976. *English verse: theory and history*. The Hague: Mouton.
Tarlinskaja, M. 1983. Evolution of Shakespeare's metrical style. *Poetics* 12: 567–87.
Tarlinskaja, M. 1984. Rhythm–morphology–syntax–rhythm. *Style* 18: 1–26.

248

Tarlinskaja, M. 198–. Shakespeare's verse: iambic pentameter and the poet's idiosyncrasies. Unniversity of Washington, Seattle. ms.

Yip, M. 1980. The metrical structure of regulated verse. *Journal of Chinese Linguistics* 8: 107–25.

Yip, M. 1984. The development of Chinese verse: a metrical analysis. In M. Aronoff & R. T. Oehrle (eds.) *Language sound structure: studies in phonology presented to Morris Halle by his teacher and students*. Cambridge, MA: MIT Press.

Youmans, G. Forthcoming. Milton's meter. In Kiparsky & Youmans (forthcoming).

Zeps, V. 1963. On the meter of the so-called trochaic Latvian folk songs. *International Journal of Slavic Linguistics and Poetics* 7: 123–8.

Zeps, V. 1969. The meter of the Latvian folk dactyl. *Celi* 14: 45–7.

Zeps, V. 1973. Latvian folk meters and styles. In S. Anderson & P. Kiparsky (eds.) *A festschrift for Morris Halle*. New York: Holt, Rinehart & Winston.

Žirmunskij, V. 1966. *Introduction to metrics*. The Hague: Mouton.

13 Grammatical theory and signed languages

Carol A. Padden

13.0. Introduction

Speculation about signed languages is as old as theories about human language in general. In Plato's *The Cratylus* (368 BC), Socrates muses on the relationship between names and forms, and considers the case of those who are deaf and their manner of naming:

> *Socrates*: And here I will ask you a question: suppose that we had no voice nor tongue, and wanted to indicate objects to one another, should we not, like the deaf and dumb, make signs with the hands, and head and the rest of the body?
>
> *Hermogenes*: There would be no choice, Socrates.
>
> *Socrates*: We should imitate the nature of the thing, the elevation of our hands to heaven would mean lightness and upwardness; downwardness would be expressed by letting them drop to the ground; if we were describing the running of a horse, or any other animal, we should make our bodies and their gestures as like as we could to them. (Jowett 1953)

Over the centuries, various hypotheses have been put forward about signed languages and how they compare to oral languages. Many, like Plato, have been struck by the unique form of signed languages; lacking the familiar elements of speech and relying on the mode typically used for gesture, the overriding impression of signs is that they are largely analogic and have little segmentable content. Socrates warns Hermogenes that 'imitation' such as vocal mimicking of animals and the like cannot be considered 'naming', but he leaves open the question of whether the gestures of the 'deaf and dumb' are imitative or linguistic. Others, such as Leonard Bloomfield, have been more firm in their conclusions, arguing that gestures of 'deaf-mutes' are like those of Neapolitans and monks bound by vows of silence; they are secondary to speech, and ultimately analyzed as accompaniments to speech (Bloomfield 1933:39).

Over the last quarter of a century, new descriptions of signed languages have emerged, forcing a re-evaluation not only of signed languages but of many of our more persistent beliefs about human languages as well. One major contribution to altering our views of human languages has been the formulation of signed languages in terms of grammars.

Indigenous signed languages, i.e. naturally developed signed languages existing over generations of Deaf[1] signers are quite widespread, with reports of independent signed languages in various parts of the world (see Ahlgren & Bergman 1980; Kyle & Woll 1983; Stokoe & Volterra 1985). One of the more extensively investigated signed languages, American Sign Language (hereafter ASL) is used as a primary mode of communication by Deaf individuals in the United States and parts of Canada. Limited contact between separate areas of the United States has resulted in distinct varieties of ASL, including one used by many southern black Deaf signers. Geography and other forms of isolation in North America are responsible for distinct signed languages including French Canadian Sign Language, Alaskan Native Sign Language, and Nova Scotia Sign Language. ASL and French Sign Language are historically related, having shared key educators who introduced French Sign Language to schools for young Deaf children in America (Lane 1984), but British Sign Language, in contrast, is not related to ASL, due to a history of little contact between signers of the two countries.

The fact of the modality difference, that signed languages employ the hands, face, and body, rather than the vocal tract as articulators, suggests that oral and signed languages are vastly different from one another. The differences, it was thought, could be found in the structure of signed languages. Signed languages would lack certain properties shared by grammars of oral languages, and thus support a privileged speech–language association. But the task of identifying these differences and representing them in an explicit way turned out to be more difficult than first thought. In areas where investigators suspected possible differences, they were forced to conclude that the differences were misleading, and the similarities in structure and organization of oral and signed languages were profound. While it might appear that the unusual resources of signed languages would make possible certain forms, they have been demonstrated to be highly constrained following general restrictions on structure and organization proposed for oral languages. A review of these arguments appears below in section 13.1.

While the general picture thus far suggests much in common with oral languages, an explicit account of a number of areas of signed language structure remains incomplete. One area concerns the sublexical representation (hereafter, 'phonology') of signs discussed in section 13.2. below.

[1] I adopt here a recent device used in social sciences for identifying one subclass of all deaf individuals: those who use signed language as a primary means of communication. The capital in *Deaf* is used to refer to members of this subclass.

From the time of William Stokoe's early description of ASL structure in 1960, one of the more difficult issues in constructing a grammar of ASL has been how to segment the sign and represent dependencies between segments. Section 13.2. below discusses various proposals concerning the structure of the sign and how these proposals have, in part, been influenced by changes and developments in theories of oral language phonology and morphology. Another intriguing yet little understood area of signed language structure concerns the role of space in signed language grammar. In addition to the articulators of the hands, face, body, and head, the dimension of the space in front of the signer's body plays a role in the forms of signs and sign sentences. This is discussed briefly in section 13.3.

The goal of constructing grammars of signed languages allows us to understand structural properties of signed languages, but also enables comparison of oral and signed languages. As grammars of signed languages become more detailed and extensive, it will become possible to specifically compare, for example, phonologies of oral and signed languages and to determine how they differ, if indeed they do. Basic questions concerning how to segment the sign force us to address traditional approaches to segmentation of the speech signal and consider on what set of assumptions these approaches depend. By its nature and the challenges signed languages offer to grammatical theory, fundamental questions in analysis of oral languages must be addressed.

13.1. Structure of signed languages

13.1.1. Phonology

The notion that signs are global unanalyzable units was challenged by Stokoe's (1960) first description of sign structure. In what turned out to be a crucial first step toward representing sublexical structure in ASL, Stokoe argued that signs were not each novel creations, but rather, combinations of particular values of what he called 'aspects': the hand configuration of the sign, its place of articulation at some point on or near the signer's body, and the movement of the sign. The set of possible hand configuration values or 'primes' (Klima, Bellugi *et al.* 1979), place of articulation primes and movement primes in ASL is drawn from a limited inventory, determined on the basis of their recurrence across signs. From analyses of other signed languages, including Chinese Sign Language (Klima, Bellugi *et al.* 1979), it has been shown that the set of possible elements, including hand configuration, movement, and location, vary from one signed language to another.

In his description of ASL signs which employ two hands (as opposed to those which use one hand) Battison (1974) proposed conditions on co-occurring sublexical elements. One such condition, which he called the 'symmetry condition', disallows two-handed signs in which the two hands are specified for the same movement (and lack contact with each other), but have different hand configurations. The condition specifies that when both hands move independently, they must have the same hand configuration. Battison's observation concerned the more gross aspects of the sign, i.e. the patterning of the two hands with respect to one another. Except for a few other restrictions proposed by Klima, Bellugi *et al.* (1979) and Wilbur (1979), there was a remarkable paucity of conditions restricting combinations of sublexical units in signed language. This was at first puzzling, but was later discovered to be a descriptive problem: the internal structure of the sign had been insufficiently analyzed.

More recently, Supalla (1982) has argued that, contrary to early descriptions of motion in signs, which emphasized movement as a single unit, movement is segmentable into smaller units. In his detailed analysis of movement in a subclass of ASL signs, Supalla describes movement as consisting of ordered combinations of at least one movement 'root' and other movement elements. The number of possible movement elements and their possible combinations is highly restricted. Supalla describes the remaining aspects of the sign, e.g. hand configuration, orientation of the palm, as co-occurring with movement roots. Liddell (1984a) has likewise argued for sequentiality in ASL signs, stating in more explicit ways the representation of internal sign structure and dependencies between segments within signs.

Additionally, Liddell has proposed that formal representations of signs include not only manual activity, but also co-occurring facial and larger body movement. These nonmanual behaviors have been identified as adverbs and syntactic markers of various types, and are associated with specific sign segments.

Padden & Perlmutter (1987) examine phonological rule interaction in ASL and demonstrate a pattern which follows that proposed for oral language phonology (e.g. Kiparsky 1982). They state the conditions on a rule of derivational morphology in ASL, the 'characteristic adjective rule' (Klima, Bellugi *et al.* 1979) which takes as inputs one-handed adjectives and produces two-handed adjective outputs which have 'alternating' movement, a form in which the two hands alternate the same movement. Adjectives which are already two-handed are not affected with respect to alternating movement in the characteristic adjective form. They argue that the interaction of this rule and another rule, first described by Battison (1974), which Padden & Perlmutter call 'weak drop', shows the need for a postlexical, phonological component.

Weak drop has as input two-handed signs, and as output, one-handed signs where the nondominant, or weak hand (left hand for right-handed signers, and right hand for left-handed signers) is no longer present. They demonstrate that weak drop must be prevented from applying before the characteristic adjective rule since allowing it to do so would produce an incorrect form; i.e. if weak drop applies to a two-handed adjective, making it one-handed, and then the characteristic adjective rule applied, the output would be an ungrammatical two-handed alternating sign. The correct form is a two-handed, non-alternating sign. Weak drop must be prevented from applying until all lexical rules have applied.

Padden & Perlmutter propose another rule which introduces another possible two-handed form, one in which the weak hand loses movement, but retains all other features. 'Weak freeze', as this rule is called, must also be prevented from applying before lexical rules have applied. The interaction of weak drop and weak freeze with lexical rules in ASL supports positing a post-lexical phonological component in ASL. This type of evidence demonstrates that although signed languages employ unusual articulators, possible forms are constrained by the same rule interactions proposed for oral languages.

13.1.2. **Morphology**

ASL is perhaps most interesting for its unusually rich morphology. Verbal morphology, in particular, is highly complex. Three major classes of ASL verbs have been identified on the basis of which affixes may attach to them (Padden to appear). One class of verbs, called 'plain' verbs, permit only aspect inflections. Numerous aspect inflections have been described by Fischer (1973) and Klima, Bellugi *et al.* (1979), including affixes for 'iterative' ('again and again'), 'continuous' ('for a long time'), and others. A second class, 'inflecting' verbs, permit aspect, person and number inflections. Within this class, some verbs mark for person and number of the subject and object while others mark for only subject or only object (Fischer & Gough 1978; Supalla 1982; Padden 1983). A third class of verbs, including 'verbs of motion and location' (Supalla 1982, 1985) do not inflect for person, number, or aspect, but have unusually complex morphology, allowing long sequences of verb roots to which various affixes may be attached, including markers for noun class. The complexity of the morphology of the latter class of verbs has been compared to complex agglutinative morphological structures in oral languages (Supalla 1982; McDonald 1983).

Predicate adjectives in ASL likewise inflect for aspect. Klima, Bellugi *et al.* (1979) list at least eight different aspect inflections, including 'resultative' ('to become') and 'intensive' ('very'). Bergman (1983) and Brennan (1983) have described aspect marking on verbs and adjectives in Swedish Sign Language and British Sign Language, respectively. Nouns in ASL do not mark for case, but may take number affixes (Supalla & Newport 1978).

Derivational processes deriving nouns (Supalla & Newport 1978; Klima, Bellugi *et al*. 1979), adjectives (Klima, Bellugi *et al*. 1979), and verbs (Supalla & Newport 1978; Supalla 1982) have been described. The organization of derivational and inflectional morphemes in signed languages follow those proposed for oral languages. Newport (1981) demonstrates that in ASL, as in oral languages, inflectional morphemes cannot appear 'inside of' derivational morphemes (i.e. following Aronoff 1976, derivational rules must apply before inflectional rules). Wilbur, Klima & Bellugi (1983) likewise note this generalization, and demonstrate with various derivational and inflectional processes in ASL, that the forms follow those proposed by Selkirk (1982) for word formation in natural languages: derivational affixes attach to either roots or words (i.e. entire signs), while inflectional affixes attach only to words.

Baker (1976), Coulter (1979), and Liddell (1980) have described adverbs and adjectives which have the form of specific and characteristic facial configurations which co-occur with manual signs of certain word classes. That these facial configurations are indeed lexical and not intonational or expressive elements is demonstrated by the fact that facial adverbs, for example, can only co-occur (i.e. are simultaneously expressed) with manual verbs or adjectives, and not with signs of other word classes, e.g. nouns. Use of a facial adverb concurrently with a noun sign is judged as unacceptable (Padden to appear). Facial adverbs have also been reported for Swedish Sign Language (Bergman 1983).

13.2. The phonological representation

.2.1. The structure of the sign

The overriding issue in signed language phonology has been how to segment the sign. Analysis of the speech signal, by contrast, has long been guided by a traditional distinction between the consonant–vowel sequence and other aspects of the vocal signal such as tone, stress, pitch, and nasality. The different properties of the segmental and suprasegmental levels in oral languages have been documented in the literature, and various proposals have dealt with the representation of the different levels; but in the case of signed languages, the issue of whether there are levels, and what these levels may be, lacks the same tradition. Faced with the unusual dynamic visual array of the signed signal, the challenge for investigators of signed languages has been to identify the means by which phonological units are described, their levels, and how to determine their structure.

The traditional analysis, i.e. prior to 1960, viewed signs as global, unanalyzable entities whose forms are determined by the requirements of representing some visible feature of the referent. Stokoe's unique proposal (1960) turned out to be a basic insight: signs can be segmented into three 'aspects': the hand configuration, its place of articulation (position) and the motion of the sign. He claimed (1960:40) that: 'Like consonant and vowel, the aspects [of] position, configuration and motion may only be described in terms of contrast with each other.' Each aspect permitted a limited number of values, determined on the basis of recurrence across signs. In a later work (Stokoe, Croneberg & Casterline 1965), he listed a vocabulary of 2000 signs described according to combinations selected from 19 hand configuration primes, 12 place of articulation primes, and 24 movement primes.

Stokoe further stated that the comparison to consonants and vowels, however, could not be extended to the ordering of these aspects with respect to each other. Stokoe proposed that while in oral languages consonants and vowels are sequentially organized, in signed languages these aspects are 'simultaneously produced,' or no sequential order could be determined for them. But on closer examination, as others have pointed out (Liddell 1984), Stokoe's notation system, either intentionally or not, subtly showed an asymmetry in how the aspects were ordered with respect to each other. In particular, Stokoe sometimes used two or more movement primes ordered in sequence while other primes remained constant, or either in notation or description, noted that handshapes and locations changed during the execution of the sign. In other words, Stokoe recognized that at least some elements of signs had to be ordered sequentially, even if the execution appears 'simultaneous.'

Stokoe's observation regarding the degree of simultaneity in the sign signal was further expanded by others (Klima, Bellugi et al. 1979; Wilbur 1979; Siple 1982), who suggested that the simultaneous organization of units was possibly unique to signed languages, and an effect of the visual modality on the linguistic signal. Although they made note of portions of the signal which were sequentially organized, the fact of simultaneity appeared to be the most compelling distinction between oral and signed languages. These conclusions were in part guided by traditional analyses of English phonology in which simple linear types of structures were proposed to account for sound structure.

More recently, investigators of signed languages have begun to re-examine sign structure and have incorporated more sequentiality in their descriptions. These recent investigations have likewise benefited from a change in phonological theory toward more complex, hierarchical structures. Supalla (1982), for one, approached the question of phonological structure in ASL by focussing on a subclass of morphologically complex signs which he called 'verbs of motion and location.' These signs are marked by an unusual property not shared by other ASL signs: each phonological unit is also a morpheme. In other words, like phonemes, the minimal distinctive units of these signs cannot be further analyzed, but unlike phonemes and like morphemes, the units are also minimal units of meaning. Thus, as Supalla argued, whatever structure he proposed for the morphology of this subclass of signs would also constitute its phonological structure. That is, the organization of morphemes with respect to each other within the sign would likewise constitute their organization in phonological structure.

Supalla analyzed movement in these signs as made up of ordered combinations of one or more of a limited number of possible movement roots. Each movement root is a predicate of either existence, motion, or location. Attached to the movement root is a set of articulator morphemes involving other aspects of the visual signal including the signer's hands, body, and surrounding space. A sign meaning a vehicle traveling along a path, turning and then traveling on another path would be analyzed as having a sequence of three movement roots: a linear root, a midpivot root and then another linear root. The hand configuration and orientation of the hand remain constant throughout the sign, and are represented in Supalla's analysis as noun class and orientation affixes. The hand configuration is the noun class marker for 'land-bound vehicle,' and the orientation of the handshape indicates its form: it is upright. Thus, a verb of motion or location is made up of a multi-morphemic complex of at least one movement root and a set of affixes including noun agreement and orientation affixes.

This detailed analysis has allowed us to examine the sequential nature of movement, and how the sign can be decomposed into elements arranged either in sequence or simultaneously with sequential elements. Although Supalla largely restricted his analysis to the subclass of verbs of motion and location in ASL, it is clear that the same basic insights could be applied to the analysis of other vocabulary in ASL. A number of proposals have recently emerged as revisions of previous analyses of phonological structure in ASL signs. Liddell (1984a) and Sandler (1986a,b) draw from recent insights concerning multilinear phonological structure, including autosegmental phonology (e.g. Goldsmith 1979).

In Liddell and Johnson's analysis (Johnson & Liddell 1984; Liddell 1984a), signs are analyzed as sequences of M (movement) and H (hold) segments which they describe as comparable to vowel and consonant segments in terms of being two distinct segments, each with different properties. An M segment involves some basic change in form, e.g. a change in location or orientation, while H segments are relatively steady-state. In addition, an articulatory bundle of all other nonmovement features, including hand configuration, orientation, and location are associated to the M–H tier by autosegmental association rules. A monomorphemic sign such as THINK[2], which involves an approach to the forehead and then contact, is analyzed as

257

having two segments: MH. Other aspects of the sign, that it employs the index finger hand configuration, and a certain orientation of the hand, appear in vertically organized 'articulatory bundles' associated with the segmental tier. The analysis proposes that of the various aspects, movement determines segmental structure, and other features are organized simultaneously with respect to these segments. The formalism in this way attempts to represent both sequential (the M–H level) and simultaneous elements of the sign signal.

Sandler (1986a,b) has likewise applied the autosegmental framework to the internal analysis of signs but she segments the sign differently. Instead of a skeletal M-H tier, Sandler proposes that the segments are movements (M) and locations (L) and that those aspects of the sign which Liddell and Johnson call 'holds,' are specified as part of the (L)ocation segment. In addition, Sandler isolates hand configuration as a separate tier apart from hand movement.

The detail of this formalism allows us to ask specific questions about the representation of ASL phonology in terms of tiers, among them: how many tiers are needed to account for phonological structure in signs and what is represented on each tier?

Using a different approach, Wilbur (1982) accounts for sequentially and simultaneously organized movement units within the framework of a hierarchical syllable model such as that proposed by Cairns & Feinstein for English (1982). Movement which involves a trajectory, or 'path' movement, is described at the level of the syllable and 'local' movement, or movement internal to the hand, at the level of the nucleus of the syllable.

Finally, what these proposals ultimately address is the issue of the phonetic and the phonological description in signed languages. Investigators of oral languages have relied on a long history of analysis concerning how to determine which aspects of the oral signal are linguistically relevant and which are not. In signed languages, however, the task is relatively new. Some have argued that not all M segments in Liddell & Johnson's analysis of certain signs should be linguistically relevant, i.e. a phonological description would exclude some movements within the sign as 'transitions' to linguistically relevant movements (Perlmutter 1986; Sandler 1986b; Wilbur 1986). In another example, Padden & Perlmutter (1987) raise a number of issues concerning representation of one-handed and two-handed signs in ASL. In the case of two-handed signs where the hands are moving simultaneously, should their phonological description involve a representation for each hand,

---

[2] I use here standard notational conventions for ASL: a sign is represented by its English gloss in capital letters, e.g. THINK. A sign requiring a gloss of more than one English word is represented by capitalized words joined by hyhens, e.g. DOESN'T-MATTER. No structural or semantic comparisons to English should be inferred from this notational system.

that is, should each hand in a two-handed sign be represented as if it were a one-handed sign? Padden & Perlmutter argue that such a representation would have unsatisfactory results for a class of two-handed signs where the hands alternate in movement. In these signs, they argue that the alternating movement is a global property of the two hands together and cannot be represented as a feature of either hand. Resolving issues such as these crucially involve distinguishing between the phonetic and the phonological in ASL signs.

3.2.2. Morphology

Root forms in ASL may take a number of different affixes, and as in the case of ASL phonology, morphemic elements may be organized either sequentially or in layered co-occurring forms. Thus, the kinds of questions concerning how to represent simultaneously and sequentially organized elements of ASL phonology apply to its morphology as well.

In his description of verbs of motion and location in ASL, Supalla (1982) proposed a distinction between two classes of signs in ASL: the 'productive' lexicon and the 'frozen' lexicon. The distinction attempts to capture differences in basic morphological structure as well as differences in combinatory properties. The productive lexicon, including verbs of motion and location, is made up of signs formed from roots which cannot stand alone and must be combined with affixes. For example, in the verb of motion, VEHICLE-TURN, there are three roots in sequence, a linear root, a midpivot root and another linear root. These roots are each combined with classifiers agreeing in noun class 'vehicle' and noun placement, or the positioning of the hand in space, among other affixes. The unusual property of signs such as these is their potential for long strings of roots, each with a different set of affixes, creating enormously complex sequences. Another root could be added to VEHICLE-TURN, for example, creating yet another form: say another midpivot root was added following the second linear root, the form would become: VEHICLE-TURNS;MOVES-STRAIGHT; TURNS.

Within the productive lexicon, Supalla draws a structural distinction between roots and affixes. One or more roots are possible, but they are always sequential. Affixes do not appear in sequence with roots, but are always attached to, i.e. are simultaneous with, roots. Thus, in Supalla's analysis, roots are sequentially organized, while affixes co-occur with roots.

The frozen lexicon, on the other hand, is not formed from the types of root and affix combinations that characterize the productive lexicon. In the frozen lexicon, the hand configuration is not a morpheme, but simply a

259

phonological element. Signs in the frozen lexicon may take a number of derivational and inflectional affixes and as Klima, Bellugi *et al.* (1979) observe, derivational and inflectional processes in ASL do not involve simple sequential attachment of affixes, but involve an overall dynamic change that superimposes specific contours on classes of signs. The question facing investigators of ASL and other signed languages is how to represent the phonological form of this complex morphology.

Inflectional affixes mark the categories of person, number and aspect. One class of person inflections is characterized by attaching some spatial (place of articulation) point to either end of a linear movement. For example, the person-inflected form of GIVE, say: $_a$GIVE$_b{}^3$ ('he/she/it gives to he/she/it') begins at a point, *a*, on one side of the signer's body and moves in a linear path toward another point, *b*.

Person affixes may combine with affixes for number and aspect; number and aspect affixes each have their own characteristic movements. A verb inflected for person and number will have both the spatial point and the characteristic movements of the number and aspect affixes. Number inflections include: the singular inflection, with a single linear path movement; dual, which has two linear paths; multiple ('them') with a single sweeping horizontal arc movement; and others, each with a distinct set of movement features; reciprocal, exhaustive ('each'), allocative determinate ('selected ones'), allocative indeterminate ('any'), apportionative internal ('distribution within a group'), seriated external ('distributed members of a class') (Klima, Bellugi *et al.* 1979). Aspect inflections are characterized by the addition of distinct movement contours, including circular, elliptical, and linear movement with various dynamic features, including acceleration, holds, tenseness, and laxness. The continuative aspect, for example, ('for a long time') generally has a lax elliptical motion (Fischer 1975; Klima, Bellugi *et al.* 1979).

Liddell (1984b) and Johnson & Liddell (1984) propose that the types of analyses used for nonconcatenative morphology in Semitic languages (McCarthy 1981) may be fruitful for inflectional morphology in ASL. In Liddell's description of one stem–inflection pattern in ASL, the unrealized-inceptive aspect, the stem and the inflection are on separate tiers which are then associated. In this representation, the inflection consists of a 'segmental frame' which is filled out by certain features from the stem. Autosegmental spreading completes the association between the two.

In addition to the types of inflections described above, Klima, Bellugi *et al.* (1979), Supalla & Newport (1978), and Newport (1981) have noted

---

[3] Agreement and locative markers on verbs are represented by subscripts. Subject agreement markers are represented by a subscript before the gloss, and object markers after the gloss. In spatial verbs where there is a linear movement between two points, the first point is represented by a subscript before the gloss, and the end point, after the gloss. These are purely notational inventions and should not be used to suggest structural properties of ASL.

complex forms in ASL where more than one, in fact as many as three or four, inflections are added to a verb stem. In these forms, the inflections are embedded within each other. For example, the number inflection, 'exhaustive' ('to each') can be ordered two ways with respect to another aspect inflection, 'iterative' ('again and again'): either first exhaustive and then iterative, or first iterative and then exhaustive. Using brackets, the two possibilities can be represented as:

[[[Stem] exhaustive] iterative]
[[[Stem] iterative] exhaustive]

With the verb GIVE, the meanings would be, in the first bracketed example: 'give again and again to each' and in the second: 'give to each, that act of giving occurring again and again.'

With three inflections, another set of possible orders creates yet more complex forms. An adequate phonological representation of the morphology of ASL and other signed languages will need to represent the intricate mapping of forms such as these stems with multiple inflections.

13.3. The role of space in signed languages

In addition to the articulators (the hands, body, head, and facial musculature), signed languages employ another unusual resource, the area or space around the signer's body. Certain affixes and pronouns in ASL involve locating, or orienting the sign toward some point in the space around the signer's body. Two verb classes in ASL, 'inflecting' and 'spatial' verbs, have affixes whose phonological forms involve some spatial location near the signer's body. While the syntactic behavior of these affixes is not unusual, i.e. they are person and locative affixes, their phonological forms require specification of some spatial point. In this sense then, 'space' in ASL is not solely a semantic entity, as in various notions of semantic space or 'mental spaces' (e.g. Fauconnier 1985), but an actual element in the form of particular lexical items. Given that possible spatial points are theoretically infinite, the question facing investigators is how forms such as these should be represented in a grammar.

As described in 13.2.2, in certain inflecting verbs which mark for person and number of the subject and object, the subject affix involves a location at the beginning of a linear movement to another point where the object is specified. If, for example, a subject pronominal index appears in a sentence with an inflecting verb like GIVE, the spatial location of the pronoun must be the same as the spatial location of the subject affix, e.g. $_a$INDEX $_a$GIVE$_b$, but not: *$_b$INDEX $_a$GIVE$_c$.

Padden (to appear) notes key differences in how spatial and inflecting verbs exploit the spatial dimension. Spatial verbs also may involve movement in a linear motion from one point to another, but crucially, do not inflect for person and number. A spatial verb nearly identical to $GIVE$ above, TO-$HAND$-$OVER$ is a good example of the contrast between spatial and inflecting verbs. The sign, $_a TO$-$HAND$-$OVER_b$, 'handed over from here to there' has no person agreement, only two locative affixes marking locations a, b. Because the beginning point of the linear movement is a locative affix, the spatial location of the subject pronominal index may be different from that of the locative affix: $_b INDEX$ $_a TO$-$HAND$-$OVER_c$.

In discourse, the general interpretive rule for the unmarked case states that coreferential nominals have the same spatial point. However, under certain conditions, coreferential nominals may have different spatial points. As an example of the complex ways different spatial points are used in signed languages, Padden (to appear) describes a phenomenon in ASL called 'locus shifting.' In (1) below, the subject pronoun and subject agreement affix have the same spatial location, a, and they are coreferential. (Note: the subscripts, $i, j, k, \ldots$ are used to denote coreference, i.e. nominals which appear in the translation with same subscripts are coreferential.)

(1) $_a INDEX$ $_a GIVE_c$, $_a INFORM_c$ GOOD.
       'She$_i$ gave it to him and (she$_i$) told him it was good'

As mentioned earlier, if different spatial points were used for the pronouns and agreement affixes in sentences such as (1), only non-coreferential readings would be possible.

However, in certain two-sentence sequences like (2) below which contains a spatial verb, $PERSON$-$WALK$, coreferential nominals can have different locus positions. Specifically, the locations of the two subject pronouns in the two sentences are different although they are coreferential. In (2), the subject pronoun appeared in position a, but in the second sentence, location of the coreferential pronoun shifted to the position of the end point of the verb, b. As such, the locus position of the subject has 'shifted' from the beginning point of the verb to the position of the end point.

(2) $_a INDEX_b PERSON$-$WALK$-TO_c, STOP, THINK-ABOUT. $_c INDEX$ DECIDE WAIT.
       'She$_i$ walked over there, stopped and thought a bit, then she$_i$ decided to wait there'

A number of conditions apply to constrain locus shifting in ASL. First, while subjects of intransitive clauses shift (2), subjects of *transitive* clauses cannot, as (3) demonstrates, but direct objects of ditransitive clauses can, as in (4):

(3)　BOOK $_a$INDEX $_a$GIVE$_b$. $_b$INDEX WANT BOOK.
　　　*'She$_i$ gave him the book. (Now) she wants it back'
　　　'She$_i$ gave him the book. He$_j$ wants it back'

(4)　BOOK $_a$INDEX $_a$GIVE$_b$. $_c$INDEX SHOULD $_b$TAKE
　　　'She$_i$ gave him$_j$ the book$_k$. He$_l$ ought to get it$_k$ from him$_j$'

But when certain other discourse contexts are examined, it can be seen that stating coreference conditions on shifted nominals is complex. If the nominal appears in a sentence with a negative, modal, or aspect marker, there is no locus shifting. In certain other contexts, either the non-shifted or shifted location can be used, the difference indicating a subtle difference in time, i.e. this individual at the point prior to the action indicated by the verb, or this individual at the point following the action indicated by the verb. In (5) below, the pronoun form for MAN may refer to either point *a* or *b*, with a slight difference in meaning. $_a$INDEX indicates the point to boarding the vehicle, while $_b$INDEX indicates some permanent characteristic of the individual.

(5)　TWO-US TALK, FINISH MAN $_a$GET-INTO
　　　$_a$VEHICLE-MOVE$_b$.
　　　$_a$INDEX NICE MAN.
　　　$_b$INDEX NICE MAN.
　　　'We talked for a while and then the guy$_i$ got onto the bus and left.
　　　'He$_i$ was a nice man'
　　　'He$_i$ is a nice man'

Among the many questions investigators have about structures such as these is the question of where in the grammar the spatial points of pronouns and affixes are specified. An unlikely solution is one where each possible form of pronoun and affix with its spatial point is listed in the lexicon, which would then result in a lexicon with an infinite number of possible pronouns and affixes. Lillo-Martin & Klima (1986) have suggested that there be only one pronoun entry in the lexicon, unspecified for spatial location, and that interpretation of spatial points be carried out by a discourse representation component.

Another question for those investigating semantic structure in ASL is whether there is a correspondence between semantic space and the physical manifestation of space in syntax and discourse in ASL (e.g. Friedman 1975; Gee & Kegl 1982). While it would be attractive to imagine a language where the semantic component has a direct analog in spatial organization, detailed grammars are needed for discussions of correspondences such as these.

263

13.4. **Summary**

Constructing grammars of signed languages allows us not only to represent signed languages in explicit ways, but also to test the applicability of grammatical theory to a natural language in another modality. Early descriptions of sign structure emphasized the complexity of its co-occurring structures and suggested that such structures may be unique to signed languages. But as phonological theory turned to the problem of describing oral languages with co-occurring elements, particularly tonal languages, the unusual features of the sign became more ordinary in comparison.

The possibility that modality may influence language structure has guided many investigations of sign structure, but the evidence thus far has demonstrated that similar structures can be posited for both types of languages. Investigations in the area of signed language phonology and the role of space in grammars of signed languages may yet reveal possible differences, since these are areas where modality may play a crucial role. However, arguments for differences between oral and signed languages will crucially depend on having detailed grammars to compare.

REFERENCES

Ahlgren, I. & Bergman, B. (eds.) 1980. *Papers from the First International Symposium on Sign Language Research*. Stockholm: The Swedish National Association of the Deaf.

Aronoff, M. 1976. *Word formation in generative grammar*. Cambridge, MA: MIT Press.

Baker, C. 1976. What's not on the other hand in ASL. *CLS* 12.

Battison, R. 1974. Phonological deletion in ASL. *Sign Language Studies* 5: 1–19.

Bergman, B. 1983. Verbs and adjectives: morphological processes in Swedish Sign Language. In Kyle & Woll (1983).

Bloomfield, L. 1933. *Language*. New York: Henry Holt. Reprinted (1961) by Holt, Rinehart & Winston.

Brennan, M. 1983. Marking time in British Sign Language. In Kyle & Woll (1983).

Cairns, C. & Feinstein, M. 1982. Markedness and the theory of syllable structure. *Linguistic Inquiry* 13: 193–225.

Coulter, G. 1979. ASL typology. Doctoral dissertation, University of California, San Diego.

Fauconnier, G. 1985. *Mental spaces: aspects of meaning construction in natural language*. Cambridge, MA: MIT Press.

Fischer, S. 1973. Two processes of reduplication in the American Sign Language. *Foundations of Language* 9: 469–80.

Fischer, S. 1975. Influences on word order change in ASL. In C. Li & S. Thompson (eds.) *Word order and word order change*. Austin: University of Texas Press.

Fischer, S. & Gough, B. 1978. Verbs in ASL. *Sign Language Studies* 18: 17–48.

Friedman, L. 1975. Space, time and person reference in ASL. *Language* 51: 940–61.

Gee, J. & Kegl, J. 1982. Semantic perspicuity and the locative hypothesis: implications for acquisition. *Journal of Education* 164, 2: 185–209.

Goldsmith, J. 1979. The aims of autosegmental phonology. In D. Dinnsen (ed.) *Current approaches to phonological theory*. Bloomington: Indiana University Press.

Johnson, R. & Liddell, S. 1984. Structural diversity in the ASL lexicon. Washington: Gallaudet College. ms.

Jowett, B. 1953. Translation of *The dialogues of Plato*. Oxford: The Clarendon Press.

Kiparsky, P. 1982. Lexical morphology and phonology. In S. Yang (ed.) *Linguistics in the morning calm*. Seoul: Hanshin.

Klima, E. & Bellugi, U. 1979. (With R. Battison, P. Boyes-Braem, S. Fischer, N. Frishberg, H. Lane, E. Lentz, D. Newkirk, E. Newport, C. Pedersen & P. Siple.) *The signs of language*. Cambridge, MA: Harvard University Press.

Kyle, J. & Woll, B. (eds.) 1983. *Language in sign: an international perspective on sign language*. Beckenham: Croom Helm.

Lane, H. 1984. *When the mind hears*. New York: Random House.

Liddell, S. 1980. *ASL syntax*. The Hague: Mouton.

Liddell, S. 1984a. THINK and BELIEVE: sequentiality in ASL. *Language* 60: 372–99.

Liddell, S. 1984b. Unrealized-inceptive aspect in ASL: feature insertion in syllabic frames. *CLS* 20.

Lillo-Martin, D. & Klima, E. 1986. Pointing out differences: ASL pronouns in syntactic theory. Paper presented at the Conference on Theoretical Issues in Sign Language Research, Rochester, New York.

McCarthy, J. 1981. A prosodic theory of nonconcatenative morphology. *Linguistic Inquiry* 12: 373–418.

McDonald, B. 1983. Levels of analysis in sign language research. In Kyle & Woll (1983).

Newport, E. 1981. Constraints on structure: evidence from ASL and language learning. In W. Collins (ed.) *Minnesota symposia on child psychology* 14. Hillsdale: Erlbaum.

Padden, C. 1981. Some arguments for syntactic patterning in ASL. *Sign Language Studies* 32: 239–59.

Padden, C. To appear. *Interaction of morphology and syntax in ASL*. Garland Outstanding Dissertations in Linguistics, series IV. New York: Garland.

Padden, C. & Perlmutter, D. 1987. ASL and the architecture of phonological theory. *Natural Language and Linguistic Theory*.

Perlmutter, D. 1986. The inadequacy of WYSIWYG representations in ASL phonology. Paper presented at The Conference on Theoretical Issues in Sign Language Research, Rochester, New York.

Sandler, W. 1986a. Aspectual inflections and the hand tier model of ASL phonology. Paper presented at the Conference on Theoretical Issues in Sign Language Research, Rochester, New York.

Sandler, W. 1986b. The spreading hand autosegment of ASL. *Sign Language Studies* 50: 1–28.

Selkirk, E. 1982. *The syntax of words. Linguistic Inquiry Monograph* 7.

Siple, P. (ed.) 1978. *Understanding language through sign language research*. New York: Academic Press.

Siple, P. 1982. Signed language and linguistic theory. In L. Obler & L. Menn (eds.) *Exceptional language and linguistics*. New York: Academic Press.

Sorensen, R. 1980. Rhythyms, 'intonation' and sentence markers in Danish Sign Language. In Ahlgren & Bergman (1980).

Stokoe, W. 1960. Sign language structure: an outline of the visual communication systems of the American Deaf. *Studies in Linguistics, Occasional Papers* 8. University of Buffalo.

Stokoe, W., Croneberg, C. & Casterline, D. 1965. *A dictionary of ASL on linguistic principles*. Washington: Gallaudet College Press. Reprinted (1976) Silver Spring: Linstok Press.

Stokoe, W. & Volterra, V. (eds.) 1985. *Proceedings of the Third International Symposium on Sign Language Research*. Silver Spring: Linstok Press.

Supalla, T. 1982. The acquisition of verbs of motion and location in ASL. Doctoral dissertation, University of California, San Diego.

Supalla, T. 1985. The classifier system in ASL. In C. Craig (ed.) *Noun classification and categorization*. Philadelphia: Benjamins North America.

Supalla, T. & Newport, E. 1978. How many seats in a chair? The derivation of nouns and verbs in ASL. In Siple (1978).

Wilbur, R. 1979. *ASL and sign systems*. Baltimore: University Park Press.

Wilbur, R. 1982. A multi-tiered theory of syllable structure for ASL. Paper presented at the Annual Meeting of the Linguistic Society of America, San Diego.

Wilbur, R. 1986. Why syllables? Paper presented at The Conference on Theoretical Issues in Sign Language Research, Rochester, New York.

Wilbur, R., Klima, E. & Bellugi, U. 1983. Roots: the search for origins of signs in ASL. *CSL* 19: 314–36.

14 The linguistic status of creole languages: two perspectives

The linguistic status of creole languages is such a controversial issue that it seems reasonable to devote two contributions to the topic in this volume. While both take for granted the basic conceptions of generative grammar, they could not differ more in their conclusions. Derek Bickerton, in his 'Creole languages and the bioprogram' (Chapter 14.I), develops further the hypothesis with which he has long been associated, namely that creoles provide the most direct window possible into the properties of universal grammar. For Bickerton, such languages point directly to our biological capacity to recreate language should the normal generation-to-generation means for doing so break down. Pieter Muysken's 'Are creoles a special type of language?' (Chapter 14.II), however, questions whether the notion 'creole language' is anything more than a sociological epiphenomenon, devoid of special significance to grammatical theory. In Chapter 14.III, 'A dialogue concerning the linguistic status of creole languages,' Bickerton and Muysken engage in a spirited confrontation, challenging the conclusions of each other's chapters.

Frederick J. Newmeyer

14.I Creole languages and the bioprogram*

Derek Bickerton

14.I.1. The historical context of creole languages

There are two ways in which new languages may arise: one gradual, one catastrophic. The former, probably the better known of the two, involves the progressive divergence of related dialects, a process which most frequently arises when two or more populations of speakers become isolated from one another. Such situations came about, for example, with dialects of Latin after the collapse of the Roman Empire, and with dialects of Polynesian after the diaspora that populated the islands of the Eastern and Southern Pacific. After a number of centuries, processes of lexical and morphological change and decay and the emergence of syntactic and phonological innovations may render such dialects mutually unintelligible; these processes may, of course, be intensified and speeded up by language contact with unrelated groups. At some hard-to-determine point, we may conclude that the dialects are dialects no longer, but distinct languages.

In the present chapter I shall have nothing to say about language formation of this kind, which appears to obey no particular laws and to be largely at the mercy of historical accident. Instead, I shall concentrate on the catastrophic way, one in which new languages are produced *ab ovo* within the space of, at most, one or two generations. This process is of interest not merely in its own right, but for the light that it can shed on the nature of language in general. However, the reader should be warned that the account to be given here does not represent a consensus view; indeed, the issues involved are and always have been so controversial that no consensus could possibly be arrived at.[1] The most that can be said is that it is an account based on some eighteen years of inquiry, and a broad range of data supports it.

In brief, new languages may come into existence whenever historical

* The research on which this chapter is based was supported in part by National Science Foundation Grant No. BNS83-00351, for which grateful acknowledgement is hereby made.
[1] I shall not here attempt to survey or discuss the various theories that have been offered as explanations of the language-forming process, since this could only serve to confuse the nonspecialist reader. For an overview and critical discussion of these theories, see Bickerton (1977a).

circumstances cause an originally multilingual group to partially or wholly abandon its ancestral languages but do not provide that group with ready access to an already existing language. Historically, such circumstances seem to have come about in the course of European colonial adventures; even a new language largely derived from Arabic (Ki-Nubi – see Nhial 1975; Mahmud 1979; Owens 1980; Heine 1982) resulted indirectly from British imperial policy in Uganda and the Southern Sudan. Traditionally, the overall process has been broken into two halves, usually referred to as 'pidginization' and 'creolization' (see Hall 1966 and much subsequent work). However, these terms have been used with so many different shades of meaning that it is no longer clear whether they clarify or merely obscure and confuse what actually goes on in situations of this kind.

Historically, two types of event have set in motion the language-forming process. In the first, an outside group penetrates a multilingual area and forms associations with its peoples of a permanent or semi-permanent nature. In the second, which may follow directly on the first (as in West Africa) or occur quite independently (as in Hawaii), an outside group creates a new society by transporting people from several different areas, lacking any common language, to some uninhabited or underinhabited island or isolated coastal area. Two points should be emphasized here. First, there is no direct relationship between the events themselves and the linguistic processes involved; the former merely set the stage for the latter, which then proceed to evolve under their own laws.[2] Second, by the same token, the two types described do not necessarily exhaust the sets of possible circumstances which may have in the past, or may in the future, set in motion the language-forming process. All that is really required is that a multilingual group should need a common language but that access to an appropriate pre-existing language should be sharply restricted.

Granted these caveats, let us look a little more closely at the two types of situation, which I shall refer to as 'fort' and 'plantation' respectively. The fort situation is so called because the focus of it was usually one or a number of forts set up by Europeans in some non-European territory. In and around the fort there quickly sprang up a hybrid population consisting of European fathers, often partly indigenized in their customs, non-European mothers, and ethnically mixed children. Surrounding this core, and fading by imperceptible degrees into the general population, was a penumbra of servants, contract laborers, indigenous merchants, European-influenced chiefs, and so

---

[2] This is not to claim that such processes are totally independent of these and subsequent socio-historical developments. Clearly, such events as changes in the population balance or the substitution of one colonial overlord for another may have far-reaching consequences for the nature of a newly developed language. However, simplistic equations of 'language and society' make it necessary to emphasize that while different linguistic processes may be triggered by extralinguistic causes, the processes themselves are completely autonomous.

on – a society that had become economically dependent on the European presence, and some of whose members preferred to identify with it rather than with the local traditional society. These symbiotic relationships between Europeans and non-Europeans have been most insightfully treated by Rodney (1970) from a historical viewpoint and by Hancock (1972, 1985) from a linguistic one.

The plantation situation arose mainly in connection with the highly labor-intensive sugar industry, for which manpower was recruited on a worldwide basis (but mainly from West Africa, and through the slave trade). As a result, there developed a number of small, rigidly stratified societies, consisting of a European elite and a non-European majority in which manual laborers predominated (for a vivid, if impressionistic, view of such societies, see Patterson 1967). Although fort and plantation situations differed socially in a variety of ways, there was probably little essential difference in the linguistic processes which were set in motion by them (one must say 'probably' because the language-forming situation has never been observed directly; any account of it, including the present one, can only be based on a mixture of linguistic reconstruction, historical evidence, and commonsense assumptions about human behavior).

Under normal circumstances, strangers who lack a common language will, if their contact is to be more than fleeting, try to learn one another's languages. There is little doubt that speakers in the fort and plantation situations did this and, in the earliest stages of such situations, may even have done so with some degree of success. For, in those early stages, conditions for second language learning were far from unfavorable; indeed, there were factors present which gave the wives of European *lançados*,[3] and the first slaves to reach Caribbean and other plantation colonies, opportunities of achieving a reasonable second language fluency in the target language – opportunities of which they doubtless availed themselves to the extent of their varying capacities, interests, and motivations.

In both situations, the numbers initially involved were quite small. In the fort situation, the intimacy of the household environment offered generous opportunities for linguistic interaction. In the plantation situation, intimacy was generally less, but to outweigh this, Europeans initially outnumbered non-Europeans in every case of which there is historical record – an almost inevitable state of affairs, given that setting up the infrastructure of a new colony required skills that only European artisans could provide and protection that only European soldiers could reliably furnish.

We need not assume that the second language learning that took place in

---

[3] The term *lançado* for an expatriate European in West Africa is Portuguese, but there were *lançados* from every country that traded in Africa; Hancock (1985) provides extensive documentation for the English *lançado* community in Guinea.

such situations was unidirectional. In the fort situation, many Europeans must have learned, to a greater or less extent, one or more African languages. In the plantation situation, however, the fact that Europeans were unquestionably in charge from the beginning, and the diversity of the languages spoken by the labor force, must have discouraged any attempt at second language learning by Europeans. In any case, no new language arose from such attempts in either situation; we shall therefore concern ourselves only with the attempts of non-Europeans to acquire a European language (or Arabic, in the case of Uganda and the Sudan).

However, conditions favorable to learning by non-Europeans did not persist for long. In both situations developments took place that led almost inevitably to a dilution of the original clear model. In the fort situation, the second-language version of the European language that served as a medium of communication in many *lançado* households must have been quickly, if incompletely, picked up by clients and dependents of the European community (who would find it of use both as a means of communication with Europeans and as a *lingua franca* in their own multilingual communities) and must have become more diluted the further it spread from those households. In the plantation situation, the preparatory phase of sugar colonization gave way, with varying degrees of rapidity, to the exploitative phase, in which all suitable (and much marginal) land was taken into production, requiring a rapid increase in the numbers of unskilled manual laborers; again, dilution of the original model must have resulted.

This picture of an initially strong model which weakened over time contrasts with the traditional concept of 'pidginization', which envisaged a somewhat abrupt contact between a small European minority and an overwhelming non-European majority, resulting in a restricted, but quite regular, 'pidgin language' (the latter subsequently 'expanding' as it nativized, and coming to constitute a creole language). But the 'dilution' picture is inescapable, given the work of Baker (Baker 1976, 1982; Baker & Corne 1982) on the populating of Mauritius, an island which (as shown in Bickerton 1984) was quite typical of plantation situations. It also serves to explain many otherwise puzzling data about the creole continua of Guyana, Jamaica and elsewhere, in which varieties located between the 'standard' and 'true creole' extremes show archaic English features such as preverbal *did* and *does* in affirmative (but not negative or interrogative) sentences. The most plausible source for such structures lies in the 'pleonastic' *did* and *does* common in early seventeenth-century English (and persisting later in some regional dialects). If the standard explanation of such intermediate varieties – that they were formed during 'decreolization' of an original monolithic creole (DeCamp 1971; Bickerton 1975, etc.) – is correct, then Caribbean speakers in the nineteenth or twentieth centuries must somehow have re-invented seventeenth-century structures. A much more plausible explanation is that the creole continuum came into existence 'backwards', so to speak – those varieties closest to English originating from the earliest contact, and those furthest from English, from the phase in which the original model was most drastically diluted by a massive and rapid increase in the non-European population.

The conventional wisdom that a creole was impossible without an antecedent pidgin had, of course, been challenged by Alleyne (1971) on quite different grounds. However, Alleyne never spelled out a clear and detailed alternative to Hall's 'pidgin–creole cycle' (Hall 1966), and indeed this would hardly have been possible before Baker's careful work on demographics. Moreover, there was no empirical basis on which to challenge the claim that a uniform, systematic pidgin was the immediate ancestor of a creole until work by the present author (Bickerton & Odo 1976; Bickerton 1977b) showed that the immediate ancestor of Hawaiian Creole English was both rudimentary in structure (or perhaps, not really structured at all – see Bickerton 1987) and highly variable. For some time, then, the lack of a coherent alternative to Hall's account left the field open for all kinds of conjecture, such as that West Africans in the Caribbean might simply have 'relexified' their native languages by superimposing European morphemes on their original syntax (Lefebvre 1985).[4]

In fact, what took place in both fort and plantation communities (as originally suggested in Bickerton 1977c) was second language learning with inadequate input – or rather, input that was perhaps adequate in the initial stages but became rapidly less adequate as the non-native speakers who utilized it increased enormously in numbers. One may continue to refer to this process as 'pidginization' only if it is clearly understood that its end product did not consist of a systematic but reduced 'pidgin' which would subsequently 'expand'. There is, as Alleyne (1980) has pointed out, no evidence for an antecedent 'pidgin stage' in the development of new languages, although there is, as we shall see, much evidence from those languages themselves that a sharp, and in some cases quite radical, reduction in the structural properties of the original target language was an essential prerequisite for new language formation.

As suggested above, the degree to which the target language was diluted in any particular case was a variable indirectly determined by a number of

---

[4] If they shared enough of a common language heritage to make this possible, one wonders why on earth they went to such lengths – why they did not simply retain their native language(s) for intergroup use, adopting a drastically reduced form of the European language for unavoidable contacts with their masters. While it is true that cases of what look like partial or complete relexification do exist – the *media lengua* of Peru (Muysken 1981), the Kupwar dialects (Gumperz & Wilson 1971), Anglo-Irish (Todd 1984), etc. – prerequisites for these seem to include prolonged bilingualism and/or the need to define a social group within a larger bilingual society. Neither element was present in plantation colonies.

factors. One of these was the length of the period from initial colonization to what Baker (1982) has called 'event one' – the point at which the non-European population exceeded the European; this might range from two years (in Surinam) to over fifty years (in Reunion). The longer such a period was, the greater (other things being equal) would be the chance that some properties of the target language would persist and become incorporated in the resultant new language. Other variables were the rapidity with which, and the extent to which, the non-European population outgrew the European population after 'event one'. It follows that new languages formed under the conditions described (which we may, with due caution, continue for convenience sake to describe as 'creoles') may in consequence be ranged along a continuum from the most radical (those which deviate most sharply from their original model) to cases where the question whether we are dealing with 'a true creole' or merely 'a dialect of the superstrate' may legitimately be asked (if, perhaps, never satisfactorily answered!). The linguist who is concerned with the nature of the human language faculty will be most interested in the more radical end of the continuum, those languages whose histories included an early 'event one', a rapid expansion to a predominantly non-European population, and other factors calculated to dilute the model language to the highest degree.

Note, however, that everything that has been said so far has concerned the behavior of adults in contact situations – whether those adults were the African wives of *lançados*, local traders or contracted servants in Africa, or members of one of the many cohorts of slaves introduced into the Caribbean and other areas. The whole dilution process that has been described was the work of adults. We assume that, at every stage of the process, children were born who then had to learn whatever was available at the level of dilution that the model language had reached. However, there is this difference between adults and children in the same situation. Adults, who already have at least one viable language each, will simply make the most of the imperfect instrument they are presented with, eking it out with nonlinguistic strategies and arbitrary fragments from their own linguistic experience (an experience that would assuredly differ, to a greater or less degree, from one adult to another). Children, with no prior language experience but with their native language capacity to guide them, will take that same input and make good any deficit between it and a natural language. Even if they are recipients of the truly degenerate input found at late stages of the dilution process, they will be able to mold it into a new and fully viable language. The type of input that a child received at the end of the dilution process and what that child then did with that input will form our topic for the remainder of this chapter.

14.1.2. **The lexical learning hypothesis**

First, however, we must briefly examine the grammatical model that will be assumed in what follows. It is a model for which the facts to be discussed provide strong evidence, although there is of course independent evidence from other areas (Borer 1983; Borer & Wexler 1984); it may be regarded as a more explicit model of what was suggested in Bickerton (1981).

According to this model, there is a single set of universal syntactic principles. These principles are absolute and do not undergo any form of variation, parametric or other.[5] We may assume that they are in some sense given by the neurological equipment of our species. However, syntactic principles cannot be instantiated without lexical material, so that any possessor of this system of principles must acquire a lexicon or remain speechless. But lexical entries, whether full words or inflectional morphemes, have properties of their own. These properties are not, in the main, arbitrary ones; we may assume that they are drawn from a universal inventory of properties (resembling somewhat the universal set of distinctive features in phonology) which also forms part of the genetic endowment of the species.[6]

It has long been remarked that creole grammars are in some elusive sense 'simpler' than the grammars of older languages. The present viewpoint accounts very naturally for this 'simplicity'. In older languages, the universally shared set of syntactic principles is added to, and complicated by, a wide range of lexical and morphological properties acquired from the universal inventory of possible properties as a result of millennia of diachronic change. But the process of dilution of the model language described above had, as one of its results, the loss of a large number of these properties. What presumably happened was the following: the first cohort in the processes described (immediate family in the fort situation, first shipload of slaves in the plantation situation) would acquire something less than a full European lexicon and, for any given lexical item that *was* acquired, would not necess-

---

[5] In this model, then, syntactic variation arises from one or two causes: (a) options left unspecified in the syntax, which are free options that may be randomly chosen; (b) lexical and morphological properties, which are drawn from a finite and universal list, which may contain a markedness component. Thus all parametric variation is in the lexicon.

[6] The form that such principles and properties might take to be truly universal raises some interesting questions. We may suppose that instead of, say, the three principles of binding as stated in Chomsky (1981), there is a single principle which says, roughly, *any referential element lacking independent reference is obligatorily bound by, or disjoint from, some specific antecedent(s) drawn from the universal inventory*. Then, the distribution of particular pronouns and anaphors could be captured by the definition of 'antecedent' in each case: for the so-called 'core' cases, 'may be bound by any higher argument in own clause' (for anaphors) and 'must be disjoint from all arguments in own clause' (for pronouns), while at the same time the eccentric behavior of anaphors like Korean *čaki* (O'Grady 1985) could be captured by the antecedent definition 'may be bound by highest 3rd person singular human NP in any clause of root sentence' (the existence of a hierarchy of NP positions in terms of argument and/or grammatical structure is assumed, naturally, to constitute part of the universal inventory: see Nishigauchi 1984; Bickerton 1985; Carrier-Duncan 1985; O'Grady 1985).

arily acquire it in its full range of meanings and its full range of grammatical functions. Since those ranges are determined by that item's properties, this is tantamount to saying that not all the properties of a given item would be acquired.

Subsequent slaves or more distantly connected fort personnel would acquire from the first cohort only a subset of the first cohort's (already limited) lexicon and only a subset of the subset of lexical and morphological properties of individual items acquired by the first cohort; yet they in their turn would serve as the only effective models for others. If such a process went on long enough and/or was severe enough in its nature (see Byrne 1987 for an account of the most severe among such cases, that of Saramaccan), what was left of the original target model would be little more than a handful of morphophonemic shapes. The loss of most items from the target lexicon would conspire with the loss of properties by individual items to bring about, in the hands of the first creole generation, semantic shifts and word-class changes which under normal conditions would take several centuries.

Consider, for example, Guyanese Creole (GC) lexical items such as *riič* and *tiiff* in (1) and (2) below:

(1) abi na go riič tunait
   'We won't arrive tonight'

(2) wa mek i tiif di moni?
   'Why did he steal the money?'

Riič clearly derives from English *reach*, but is now an intransitive verb, like *arrive*. *Arrive*, however, is not in the GC lexicon, presumably having been lost in the dilution process. In consequence, *riič* has been detransitized to fill the gap. (2) shows an even more radical word-class change; again, *steal* is not in the GC lexicon, another dilution loss, but here the recreation of the necessary verb from the English noun *thief* left a gap in the noun class which was immediately filled by the innovation *tiifman*, 'thief'.

In some cases, lexical and morphological losses during dilution could have still more far-reaching consequences. Saramaccan, in common with several other creoles, failed to retain: (a) *seem* or any other English or Portuguese raising predicate; (b) the copulative function of *be*, *ser* or *estar*; (c) the morphology that forms past participles in either language.[7] In consequence, all verbs in this language assign θ-roles to their subjects and there are no empty NP-slots to serve as landing-sites for NP-movement, hence no NP-movement (and in consequence, no structures such as passives which require

---

[7] Saramaccan (see Byrne 1985, 1987, for detailed description) is unique in having two superstrate languages, English and Portuguese. Note that although copulative functions are lost, copulative forms are preserved with new functions: *bin* (< English *been*) becomes an anterior marker; *ta* (< Portuguese *esta*) becomes a nonpunctual marker.

NP-movement for their generation; see Chomsky 1981). Thus failure to retain particular lexical items and the properties associated with them (such as *seem*'s property of assigning no θ-role to its subject) can affect not merely the sense and distribution of specific items, as in the cases illustrated in (1) and (2), but also the basic patterns of the grammar.

The central interest of the processes described above may be taken to be the following: how much of the lexicon and how many of its properties can be lost and still leave a viable language? Taking Saramaccan as perhaps the most extreme case, we observe that the loss can include all bound morphology, many free grammatical morphemes and even a large part of the referential vocabulary (intolerable gaps in the latter were filled by retentions from a large number of African languages, amounting to perhaps 50% of the total vocabulary, according to Price 1976). But the tendencies which culminated in Saramaccan may be seen, to a greater or less degree, in every creole language.

14.I.3. **Loss, retention, and reconstitution**

The grammatical morphology of the original target language was lost because the generation that fixed the original form of Saramaccan and similar radical creoles received an input already partially stripped of such morphology and one too impoverished for the original functions of surviving morphemes to be determined from it. In all probability, the target's bound morphology had been stripped even more thoroughly, since it would have given adult learners the additional problem of determining where morpheme boundaries lay, or even that there *were* morpheme boundaries. But what should concern us here are the reasons why some free grammatical morphemes were retained even through radical dilution of the target model, while other, apparently similar, ones disappeared.

A number of factors seem to have been involved in the loss of morphology. First, morphemes that had several allomorphs were unlikely to be retained. An obvious example is the French definite article with its gender-, number-, and phonologically determined allomorphs: *le*, *la*, *l'*, *les*. These survive only as intrinsic parts of content morphemes, e.g. Haitian *lamer* 'sea,' *lamer-la* 'the sea'; *zef* (< *les oeufs*) 'egg,' *zef-yo-a* (lit. 'egg-pluralizer-the') 'the eggs,' suggesting that such items, although technically free, were as opaque to speakers in the language-forming situation as were inflections. Similar variation in the Portuguese article system led to a similar loss of articles in the Portuguese-based creoles, except that here the morpheme boundaries seem not to have led to any segmentation problems. It is worth asking why this should be so.

The question leads us directly to a second factor: phonological salience.

The tendency throughout creoles was to reduce non-CV syllables to CV syllables. Thus initial unstressed vowels would be lost: GC *merika* 'America,' *naint* (< English *anoint*) 'to use oil or cream on the skin' etc.; final vowels would be added: Sranan *taki* 'talk,' *tifi* (< English *thief*) 'steal' etc.; and epenthetic vowels would be inserted: Hawaiian Creole English (HCE) *wolokeino* 'volcano,' *kakaroc* 'cockroach,' etc. Any sequence of sounds had more chance of being perceived and retained if its phonological structure already conformed or at least approximated to the canonical syllable – although of course it did not follow that its meaning or function would be preserved or that it would be morphologically analyzed the same way as in the source language.[8] Thus French *le* or *la* was much likelier to be incorporated into lexical items than Portuguese *a* or *o*, which would tend to go the way of the vowels in *America* or *anoint*. Even a question word (and, because of their high frequency and indispensability of function, question words were among the forms most resistant to the dilution process) could hardly survive if it diverged radically from CV structure. Thus French *où* 'where' survived only in one dialect of Haitian, and there only as a part of the form *witi* 'where?', a clear reflex of French *Où est-il?* 'Where is he/it?'; elsewhere, synthetic expressions such as *ki kote* or *ki bord* (lit. 'who side' or 'who edge') replaced it.

Considerations of syllabic structure conspired with levels of phonological markedness to select particular grammatical items from source languages where two forms were potentially in competition with one another. Take Saramaccan, which could potentially choose between English *with* and Portuguese *com* 'with'. The former has CVC structure and both its consonantal sounds are relatively marked in the Jakobsonian sense. The latter effectively has CV structure (speakers of most, if not all, varieties of Portuguese render the final nasal as vowel nasalization if they render it at all) and its initial segment is unmarked. It is thus easy to see why Saramaccan should have *ku* (< *com*) but no reflex of *with*.

However, even the factors of allomorphy, markedness and syllabicity cannot fully account for the particular selection of source-language morphemes which we find in creoles. Both English *for* and *by* are free of allomorphs, both have CV structure in r-less dialects; if the diphthong in *by* is more marked than the vowel of *for*, the initial segment of *for* is more marked than that of *by*. One might therefore predict that the forms would have an equal chance of transmission into creoles. In fact, all English-based creoles

---

[8] According to Corne (1983), an assumed analogy with Bantu class-prefixes explains why forms with incorporated articles are much commoner in the Indian Ocean creoles (which have a sizeable Bantu component in their substratum) than in, say, Haitian. This does not, however, explain why such forms exist in Haitian yet are absent from non-French creoles. Note that very similar problems of segmentation are confronted by children learning their first language, and are often solved in similar ways – see Peters 1983.

have a reflex of *for* (functioning as an irrealis complementizer or verb-like quasi-complementizer) and none (if we exclude acrolectal versions of decreolized creoles) has a reflex of *by*. A similar generalization can be made about French *pour* 'for' and *par* 'by,' or their Portuguese equivalents *para* and *por*. It is significant, as we shall see, that forms derived from *para* and *pour* have functions largely identical to those of forms derived from *for*, in particular the function of irrealis complementizer.

While some morphemes seem more robust than others that are phonologically similar to them, it remains true that almost any grammatical morpheme may disappear in the course of model dilution. However, all grammatical morphemes fall into two classes:

(3) morphemes that, if lost, will not be reconstituted;

(4) morphemes that, if lost, must be reconstituted.

In other words, if a new language is to constitute an adequate native language there are certain minimal grammatical functions that must be discharged regardless of whether morphemes with appropriate functions are available from the source language; if they are not available, lexical forms will be recruited for these functions. Grammatical morphemes in class (4) include those listed under (5):

(5) a. articles
   b. tense/aspect/modality forms
   c. question words
   d. a pluralizer
   e. pronouns for all persons and numbers
   f. forms to mark oblique cases
   g. a general locative preposition
   h. an irrealis complementizer
   i. a relativizing particle
   j. reflexives and reciprocals

Grammatical morphemes in class (3) include those listed under (6):

(6) a. gender agreement (never retained)
   b. number agreement (never retained)
   c. bound verbal morphology, tense or participial, etc. (almost never retained)
   d. derivational morphology (almost never retained)
   e. pronoun case and gender forms (seldom retained)
   f. most prepositions

Probably the most interesting cases are those in which the original grammatical morpheme(s) in one of the subsystems of (5) disappeared in the contact situation and had to be replaced. Presumably, the single universal syntax requires some minimal set of grammatical morphemes for the discharge of the functions that it stipulates. If these are lost, replacements are recruited from a limited set of lexical items. The fact that, across creoles, similar lexical items with similar properties are recruited suggests that there must be markedness in the inventory of (possible) lexical properties and that creoles select unmarked options – but this possibility requires more extensive study.

One problem with this proposal is that, while all languages have tense/aspect/modality forms, pluralizers, question words, pronouns, etc., not all languages have articles or irrealis complementizers; it is thus unclear why universal syntax would require creoles to have them. Moreover, even if all these grammatical forms *did* have to be present, it would remain unclear what factors determined their nature. For instance, in some languages (e.g. English) some question words (e.g. *who?*, *which?*) are homophonous with relativizers; yet if a creole relativizer is recreated rather than retained, it is never homophonous with any question word in that creole.[9] Similarly, the particular types of tense, modality, and aspect expressed in creoles are far from the only ones found in languages generally.

With regard to articles, one might claim that while these are clearly not required by universal syntax, the latter might require every NP to carry some kind of specifier that would (alone or in combination with other factors) indicate its definiteness status: such a specifier could be a topic or non-topic marker or some other grammatical device, rather than an article. It might then be the case that creoles have articles (which *always* have to be reconstituted)[10] either because these are simpler to reconstitute than the allowable alternatives, or because they are more unmarked.[11] Some form of markedness hypothesis will surely be involved in accounting for the high degree of consistency in the creole system of tense, modality, and aspect: the categories anterior, irrealis, nonpunctual must in some sense be more natural than their alternatives. For instance, none of the superstrate and few of the substrate languages fail to make a past-nonpast distinction, thus the fact that

---

[9] One must beware of chance similarities here. Guyanese Creole (GC) has a relativizer *we* 'who, which' which might be thought to derive from English *where*. Perhaps it does, but it is still not homophonous with any GC question word, since GC *wisaid* or *wepaat* translates 'where?'

[10] The *di* or *da* articles found in all English creoles might seem to be counterexamples to this, but there is good reason to believe that they do not represent retentions. For instance, their distribution is baffling, if they do: 17 of the 30 English creoles dealt with in Hancock (in press) have *di* forms, yet the high-vowel allophone of English *the* which must then have served as model is far rarer in speech than its centralized alternate. Since, elsewhere, demonstratives constitute one of the commonest sources for articles, derivation from English *this* and *that* is much more plausible.

[11] I am assuming that among grammatical items there is some scale of markedness similar to Jakobsonian markedness in phonology, although what the physiological correlates of such a scale might be is, for the present, impossible to determine.

so few creoles make it can hardly be accounted for in terms of external influence.

One interesting question which has yet to be fully explored is whether the reconstitution of lost grammatical morphemes takes place immediately upon creole formation or is extended over a period of perhaps several generations. The timing of reconstitution may vary among the categories of (5). For instance, in HCE, a reconstituted article system, tense/modality/aspect system and irrealis complementizer are all firmly in place in the first generation; in other categories, retentions are present, with one exception: there is no HCE relativizing particle. Additional evidence that, if original relativizers are lost, they may be slow to reconstitute may be drawn from the optionality of the relativizing particle *di* in all positions in the most radical creole, Saramaccan (Byrne p.c.); historical textual evidence that *di* evolved relatively recently from *disi* 'this,' a nominal postmodifier optionally attached to relative clause heads; and the existence of zero relativizers in subject-relative positions in conservative dialects of Annobones, Guyanese Creole, Seychellois etc.

Further evidence may be drawn from reciprocals and reflexives. Evidence recently collected by Carden & Stewart (1985) suggests that Haitian originally had no distinct reflexive and that, accordingly, pronouns could be bound in their governing categories. Subsequently, systems based on the forms *tet-li* 'himself' (lit. 'head-his'), *ko-li* 'himself' (lit. 'body-his') and others came into existence, but with a good deal of instability. Similarly, reciprocals are expressed in a variety of different ways, depending largely on the verb involved:

(7) a. yo bat ansanm
      they fight together
      'They fought each other'
   b. yo   renmen
      they love
      'They loved each other'
   c. youn lave tet-lot
      one wash head-other
      'They washed each other'
   d. youn pale ak lot
      one speak with other
      'They talked to each other'

Guyanese Creole, Caboverdiense and Seychellois – three creoles as diverse as one could hope to find – have all evolved a reciprocal involving the word for 'friend,' yet apparently such forms are found nowhere else; while in Saramaccan, which has somehow retained (or else identically reconstituted) English reflexive forms, the latter also function as reciprocals.

Evidence such as that reviewed above might suggest that markedness extends *across* categories as well as *within* them – that one might be able to distinguish between forms that no language can possibly do without and forms that it is highly convenient to have, but which are not, strictly speaking, essential to a language. However, comparative analysis of creoles based on a retention vs. reconstitution approach is so novel that we should beware at this stage of imposing too much structure on what is known.

Moreover, in trying to determine which morphemes were reconstituted immediately and which subsequently, considerable caution is required in the interpretation of textual evidence. The fact that available texts or grammars may contain no cases of a given morpheme with a given function prior to some particular date cannot be interpreted as evidence that that morpheme lacked such a function prior to that date. Early texts are rare, often quite brief, often the work of non-native speakers; early grammars (or later ones for that matter) are always limited in their coverage and not always reliable in what they do cover. It is thus premature for Koopman & Lefebvre (1982) to decide, because of its mere absence from such sources, that Haitian *pu* as complementizer represents a recent innovation. Comparative data from other creoles and internal structural considerations (how, in the absence of *pu* as complementizer, did Haitian mark the distinction, otherwise universal in creoles, between realized and unrealized purpose and intention clauses?) suggest the contrary. The only way one can be reasonably sure that a morpheme was a later introduction or originally lacked a particular function is by finding in historical texts a sufficiently large number of cases in which modern rules would require the presence of that morpheme, but where it is in fact absent.

4.1.4. Conclusions

Although many details remain obscure, the bulk of the evidence supports the hypothesis that there are nonparametrized universal principles of syntax and that massive pruning of lexical properties from the original target languages is what gives rise to the particular instantiations of those principles that characterize creole languages. We have already referred to the general absence of NP-movement; also worth mentioning is the loss of case-marking prepositions, which in the more radical creoles entails the appearance of serial verb constructions for the marking of oblique cases. Another instance arises from the fact, also noted above, that creole relativizers and question words are frequently non-homophonous; where this is the case, the former are not *wh*-forms, pied-piping is impossible in relative clauses (but not necessarily in questions) and resumptive pronouns may accordingly be found in relativized participial phrases.

Indeed, contrary to what has often been suggested in the literature, the syntactic typology of catastrophically formed new languages is clear and unmistakable, the more so as one leans towards the more radical end of the continuum on which such languages are placed. All such languages in the plantation situation, and almost all in the fort situation, have extremely strict SVO word order, with subjects and direct objects marked positionally,[12] and oblique cases marked either with superstrate prepositions or (where these are lost) serial verbs. *Wh-* movement is present but NP-movement is absent or sharply limited in its scope. Participial or nominalized types of structure are virtually never found; even nonfinite structures are rare and, in the most radical case (Saramaccan) all but non-existent. The semantics of the various subsystems of grammatical morphemes are highly constant, and almost as constant are the etymologies of those morphemes: in almost all cases they are drawn from the superstrate language and usually the indefinite article will derive from the numeral 'one,' the definite article from a demonstrative, the anterior marker from a past form of the copula, the completive marker from a verb meaning 'to finish,' the nonpunctual marker from a verb of location, the irrealis marker from a verb meaning 'to go,' the irrealis complementizer from a preposition meaning 'for,' the pluralizer from the 3rd person plural pronoun; question words, if not retained from the superstrate, will consist of the superstrate form for 'who' or 'what' plus words for 'location,' 'time,' 'cause,' 'person,' and so on; and the invariant pronouns will generally be derived from accusative rather than nominative or genitive forms.

The consistency of this typology, despite the absence of any consistent empirical model for it, argues strongly that in addition to universal principles of syntax we must assume the existence of an unmarked set of grammatical options by which those principles can be realized, even if other, often more complex, options are unavailable to the learner due to the loss of grammatical morphology. These options would seem to include particular ways of marking the definiteness status of nouns, the tense, mood, and aspect of verbs, the reality status of complements, and the full range of *wh*-questions. In other words, the human species comes equipped not merely with a means for creating new languages but with the capacity to reconstitute language itself should the normal generation-to-generation transmission of input data be interrupted or distorted by extralinguistic forces. Since language is the defining characteristic of *homo sapiens*, this should not be viewed as in any

---

[12] The only exceptions appear to be among the Spanish creoles of the Philippines, fort creoles whose speakers are, without exception, also fluent in one or more of the Filipino languages, all of which are verb initial. In consequence, there has developed VSO order with an almost obligatory case marker for direct objects, *konel* (⟨Spanish *con el* 'with the').

way remarkable, but rather as the least we are entitled to expect from our biological heritage and from any well-ordered system of evolution.

REFERENCES

Alleyne, M. C. 1971. Acculturation and the cultural matrix of creolization. In Hymes (1971).
Alleyne, M. C. 1980. Introduction. In A. Valdman & A. Highfield (eds.) *Theoretical orientations in creole studies*. New York: Academic Press.
Baker, P. 1976. Towards a social history of Mauritian Creole. B. Phil. dissertation, University of York.
Baker, P. 1982. The contribution of non-Francophone immigrants to the lexicon of Mauritian Creole. Doctoral dissertation, University of London.
Baker, P. & Corne, C. 1982. *Isle de France Creole*. Ann Arbor: Karoma.
Bickerton, D. 1975. *Dynamics of a creole system*. Cambridge: Cambridge University Press.
Bickerton, D. 1977a. Pdigin and creole studies. *Annual Review of Anthropology* 5: 169–93.
Bickerton, D. 1977b. *Change and variation in Hawaiian English*. Vol. ii: *Creole syntax*. Final Report on NSF Grant No. GS-39748.
Bickerton 1977c. Pidginization and creolization: language acquisition and language universals. In A. Valdman (ed.) *Pidgin and creole linguistics*. Bloomington: University of Indiana Press.
Bickerton, D. 1981. *Roots of language*. Ann Arbor: Karoma.
Bickerton, D. 1984. Demographics and creole genesis. Paper presented at the Twelfth NWAVE Conference, University of Pennsylvania, October.
Bickerton, D. 1985. Binding and argument domains. Paper presented at WCCFL IV, UCLA, March.
Bickerton, D. 1987. A two stage model of the human language faculty. In S. Strauss (ed.), *Ontogeny, phylogeny, and historical development*. Norwood: Ablex.
Bickerton, D. & Odo, C. 1976. *Change and variation in Hawaiian English*. Vol. i: *General phonology and pidgin syntax*. Final Report on NSF Grant No. GS-39748.
Borer, H. 1983. *Parametric syntax*. Dordrecht: Foris.
Borer, H. & Wexler, K. 1984. The maturation of syntax. Paper presented at the Conference on Parameter-Setting, University of Massachusetts, Amherst, May.
Byrne, F. X. 1985. Verb serialization and sentential complementation in Saramaccan. Doctoral dissertation, University of Arizona.
Byrne, F. X. 1987. *Grammatical relations in a radical creole*. Amsterdam: Benjamins.
Carden, G. & Stewart, W. A. 1985. Binding theory and models of creolization. City University of New York. Mimeo.
Carrier-Duncan, J. 1985. Linking of thematic roles in derivational word formation. *Linguistic Inquiry* 16: 1–34.
Corne, C. 1983. Substratal reflections: the completive aspect and the distributive numerals in Isle de France Creole. *Te Reo* 26: 65–80.
Chomsky, N. 1981. *Lectures on government and binding*. Dordrecht: Foris.
DeCamp, D. 1971. Towards a generative analysis of a post-creole speech community. In Hymes (1971).
Gumperz, J. J. & Wilson, R. 1971. Convergence and creolization: a case from the Indo-Aryan-Dravidian border. In Hymes (1971).
Hall, R. A. Jr. 1966. *Pidgin and creole languages*. Ithaca: Cornell University Press.
Hancock, I. F. 1972. A domestic origin for the English-derived Atlantic creoles. *Florida FL Reporter* x: 1–2.
Hancock, I. F. 1985. The domestic hypothesis, diffusion and componentiality. Paper presented at the Amsterdam Workshop on Universals versus Substrata in Creole Origins, March.
Hancock, I. F. In press. A preliminary classification of the anglophone Atlantic creoles. In G. Gilbert (ed.) *Pidgin and creole languages: essays in memory of John E. Reinecke*. Honolulu: University of Hawaii Press.
Heine, B. 1982. *The Nubi language of Kibera: an Arabic creole*. Berlin: D. Reimer.

283

Hymes, D. (ed.) 1971. *Pidginization and creolization of languages*. Cambridge: Cambridge University Press.

Koopman, H. & Lefebvre, C. 1982. *Pu*: marqueur de mode, préposition et complementeur. In C. Lefebvre, H. Magloire-Holly & N. Piou (eds.) *Syntaxe de l'Haitien*. Ann Arbor: Karoma.

Lefebvre, C. 1985. Relexification in creole genesis revisited: the case of Haitian Creole. Paper presented at the Amsterdam Workshop on Universals versus Substrata in Creole Origins, March.

Mahmud, U. A. 1979. Variation and change in the aspectual system of Juba Arabic. Doctoral dissertation, Georgetown University.

Muysken, P. C. 1981. Halfway between Quechua and Spanish: the case for relexification. In A. Highfield & A. Valdman (eds.) *Historicity and variation in creole genesis*. Ann Arbor: Karoma.

Nhial, A. A. J. 1975. Ki-Nubi and Juba Arabic: a comparative study. In H. Bell & A. H. Hurreiz (eds.) *Directions in Sudanese linguistics and folklore*. Khartoum: University of Khartoum Press.

Nishigauchi, T. 1984. Control and the thematic domain. *Language* 60: 215–50.

O'Grady, W. 1985. The interpretation of Korean anaphora. University of Calgary. Mimeo.

Owens, J. 1980. Monogenesis, the universal and the particular in creole studies. *Anthropological Linguistics* 22: 97–117.

Patterson, O. 1967. *The sociology of slavery*. London: McGibbon & Key.

Peters, A. M. 1983. *The units of language acquisition*. Cambridge: Cambridge University Press.

Price, R. 1976. *The Guiana maroons: a historical and bibliographical introduction*. Baltimore: Johns Hopkins University Press.

Rodney, W. 1970. *A history of Guinea, 1500–1900*. Oxford: The Clarendon Press.

Todd, L. 1984. *Modern Englishes: pidgins and creoles*. Oxford: Blackwell.

4.II Are creoles a special type of language?

Pieter Muysken

4.II.0. Introduction

Why should there be a field of pidgin and creole language studies? Since the languages are not all genetically related, nor spoken in the same area, they must be considered to have something else in common in order to be meaningfully studied as a group. In the field there is an implicit assumption that the creole languages share some property that calls for an explanatory theory. What property this is depends on the theory concerned. Any of three properties are assumed to play a role (I will limit myself here to the creole languages, since pidgins raise a series of issues of their own):

(i)   Creole languages are assumed to be more *alike* than other languages.

(ii) Creole languages are assumed to be more *simple* than other languages.

(iii) Creole languages are assumed to have more *mixed* grammars than other languages.

These assumptions play a role in the various theories of creole origin in the field, theories which can be organized in terms of two dominant intellectual traditions: *historicism* and *romanticism*. The historicist tradition stresses the continuity of transmission of conventions and institutions, and the romanticist view stresses discontinuity and the intervention of (human) nature. Table 1 presents these theories, grouped as either romanticist or historicist, in relation to the three underlying assumptions of being alike, simple, and mixed. Before going on to discuss these properties in more detail, I will briefly sketch the nine theories listed in the table.

The *semantic transparency theory* is not a full-blown genesis theory, but simply claims that the structure of creole languages directly reflects universal semantic structures. The fact that they are alike, in this view, is due to the fact that the semantic structures are universal. They are simple because the

Pieter Muysken

Table 1. *Theories accounting for the supposed properties of the creole languages*

	Alike	Simple	Mixed
ROMANTICIST THEORIES			
Semantic transparency (Seuren 1983; Seuren & Wekker 1986)	x	x	
Imperfect second language learning (Andersen 1983)	(x)	x	
Baby talk (Naro 1978)	(x)	x	
Bioprogram (Bickerton 1981, 1984)	x	x	
Common social context (Sankoff 1980)	x	(x)	
HISTORICIST THEORIES			
Afro-genesis (Alleyne 1981)	x		x
Portuguese monogenesis (Whinnom 1965)	x	(x)	x
Atlantic mono-source (Hancock 1986)	x		
Regional European variety (Bosman 1923; Raidt 1983)	(x)	(x)	

semantic structures involved fairly directly map onto surface structures, without a very complex transformational derivation.

In the *imperfect second language learning theory*, creoles are the crystalization of some stage in the developmental sequence. The speakers of the proto-creole simply did not have sufficient access to the model, and had to make up an approximative system. In this view, the fact that creoles are simple is due to the simplification inherent in the second language learning process. For some adherents of this view, the creole languages are also similar, and this similarity is due to universal properties of the learning process.

The *baby talk theory* is similar to the imperfect second language learning theory in postulating that creoles are frozen stages in the second language learning sequence. The difference lies in the fact that in the baby talk theory the responsibility for the simplification is shifted from the learners to the speakers of European languages, who provide a simplified model. The similarity between creoles would be due, in this view, to universal properties of the simplified input.

The *bioprogram theory* claims that creoles are inventions of the children growing up on the newly formed plantations. Around them they only heard

286

pidgins spoken, without enough structure to function as natural languages, and they used their own innate linguistic capacities to transform the pidgin input from their parents into a fully fledged language. Creole languages are similar because the innate linguistic capacity applied is universal, and they are simple because it reflects the most basic language structures.

The *common social context theory*, finally, among the 'romanticist' approaches, adopts a strictly functional perspective: the slave plantations imposed similar communicative requirements on the slaves, newly arrived and without a common language, in many cases. The commonality of the communicative requirements led to the formation of a series of fairly similar makeshift communicative systems, which then stabilized and became creoles.

The *Afro-genesis model* really deals only with the creole languages spoken in the Atlantic region (West Africa and the Caribbean) and postulates that these languages have emerged through the gradual transformation of the West African languages spoken by the slaves under influence of the European colonial languages. The similarity of the languages involved is due, in this model, to the fact that they share the same African language features, mixed together with features of European languages. To be fair to this model, I should add that similar explanations have been proposed for creoles in the Pacific and in other areas.

The *Portuguese monogenesis model* has undergone several modifications. Crucial to all of these is the existence of a trade language with a predominantly Portuguese lexicon, used in the fifteenth through seventeenth centuries by traders, slave raiders, and merchants from different countries throughout the then emerging Third World. The monogenesis theory holds that the slaves learned this language in the slave camps, trading forts, and slave ships of their early captivity, and then took this language, really no more than a jargon, with them to the plantations. The different creole languages as we know them are based on this jargon, but have replaced the Portuguese words by words from other European languages. The supposed similarity of the creole languages is due of course to the underlying Portuguese jargon, and their simplicity to the simplicity of this jargon. The creoles may be mixed, finally, because different colonial languages may have added structures to the Portuguese jargon, with the result that the present-day creole languages show some differences, as well as similarities.

The *Atlantic mono-source hypothesis* limits itself to the English-based creole languages of the Atlantic. Its central idea is that there was an English jargon or pidgin spoken along the coast of West Africa from which a wide range of English-based creoles were later derived. Clearly, common features of these creoles are then assumed to be due to this early pidgin.

The *regional European variety theory* holds that creoles essentially reflect nonstandard, dialectal features of the colonial languages, the result of migration by dialect speakers to the newly founded colonies, compounded by the existence of a strongly dialectal 'nautical language'. In this theory, similarities between creoles hold only for those derived from one colonial language; creoles may be simple because the nonstandard varieties were simpler than the written national standard.

In all these models or theories, notions such as 'alike', 'simple', and 'mixed' play a role. They are in fact taken for granted, assumed to be the thing to be explained, and therefore not called into question. The contribution that the study of creole languages can make, in my view, to grammatical theory is that it can help to elucidate the three concepts 'alike', 'simple', and 'mixed'. All three turn out, I think, to be relevant to the central concerns of modern grammatical theory. In order to see this, let us examine the concepts involved more closely. When we say that languages x and y are more alike than y and z, we are claiming in fact that in the total (abstract) variation space allowed for by the human language capacity x and y are closer than y and z. Consequently, the claim that the creole languages are more alike than other languages implies a clustering in the variation space. If we think of the variation space as defined by parameter theory (as in recent work by Chomsky and others), trying to develop a notion of 'alike' really boils down to developing a theory of parameters, parameters along which similarities and differences between natural languages can be defined.

Consider now the concept of simplicity. The idea that creole languages are simple has been taken to mean two things. On one level it has meant that creole languages do not have a rich morphology; on another, that the overall grammar of creole languages is less complex than that of other languages. Both interpretations are relevant to grammatical theory. The idea that absence of morphology is related to grammatical simplicity needs to be evaluated in the context of contemporary research into morphology–syntax interactions, and the grammatical status of inflection or INFL (Chomsky 1982; Rizzi 1982, and others) and of case marking (Stowell 1981). Even more importantly, the idea that the creole languages are not grammatically complex in general only makes sense if one has a theory of grammatical complexity to fall back on, and this brings in markedness theory. Consider next the notion of mixedness. Mixing implies that elements of one language are put together with elements of another one, and this in turn calls into question the cohesion of the grammatical systems involved. Recall Tesnière (1939) voicing the consensus on this issue: 'La miscibilité d'une langue est inverse à sa cohésion.' The tighter a particular subsystem (e.g. the vowel system, or the system of referential expressions) is organized, the less amenable it will to restructuring under borrowing. Tightness of organization in modern grammatical theory is conceptualized within modularity theory: the grammar is organized into a set of internally structured but externally independent modules, the interaction of which leads to the final grammatical output. For this reason, the notion of mixing is important: it forces us to think about which parts of the grammar are tightly organized, and hence about the notion of modularity. Tightness of organization or cohesion may have either a paradigmatic dimension, in terms of the hierarchical organization of feature systems, or a syntagmatic dimension, in terms perhaps of the notion of 'government' (Chomsky 1981) as a central principle of syntactic organization.

Keeping this in mind, then, the potential contribution of pidgin and creole studies to grammatical theory is clear. The whole idea of talking about the creole languages as a group presupposes that we have come to grips with one or more of the core notions of grammatical theory:

alike:	parameter theory
simple:	morphology–syntax interactions
	markedness theory
mixed:	modularity

Studying creole languages implies a constant confrontation with these notions, and helps one to develop a vocabulary to deal with them. In this paper I will look at empirical evidence for the three concepts mentioned, organizing the discussion as much as possible around one construction type: serial verbs. These have been discussed in several important recent contributions, including Bickerton (1981), Sebba (1986), and Byrne (1987), and are illustrative of the contribution that pidgins and creoles can make to grammatical theory.

I should be honest and say right out from the start that my own perception of the evidence from contemporary creole grammatical systems is that creoles may well share a number of typological properties, but that they are neither particularly simple nor unmarked. With respect to mixedness, things are not clear. It is not the final *result*, however, that is relevant to grammatical theory, but the *reasoning* required to arrive at a particular result.

.II.1. How similar are the creole languages?

At first sight, the creole languages are remarkably similar. The following examples, taken from different language groups and from different areas of the world, give an indication of this:

(1)　wanpela man i bin skulim mi long Tok Pisim　　　　　Tok Pisin
　　　one man PR ANT teach me in Tok Pisin
　　　'A man was teaching me Tok Pisin'

(2)   sõ mõ ka ta toka pálmu   Senegal Kriol
      one hand NEG HAB touch palm
      'One hand can't touch its palm'

(3)   m te pu bay lazã   Haitian
      I ANT MD give money
      'I had to give the money'

Examples such as these have features in common, as set out in (A)–(C) below.

(A)   *Word order*

It is remarkable that the large majority of the creole languages are strictly SVO. For the English and French creoles this is not so surprising, of course, given French and English SVO word order. For Portuguese- and Spanish-based creoles, with a lexifier language (the language that has provided most of the vocabulary) characterized by frequent VSO patterns, and for Dutch-based creoles, with a lexifier language characterized by underlying SOV coupled with a verb-fronting rule, some explanation is, however, called for.

Now one explanation might be that all the substrate languages involved, e.g. the West African languages originally spoken by the slaves that were transported to the Caribbean, are SVO languages. Recent work by Koopman (1984) and others suggests, however, that the underlying order of a number of West African languages may well be SOV, with a verb-fronting rule applying in almost all contexts. In addition, Smith, Robertson & Williamson (1987) have shown that one Caribbean creole language, Berbice Dutch (spoken in Guyana), is directly related to the completely SOV language Ijo, as well as being derived from an underlyingly SOV language, Dutch, and the result is still a straightforward SVO system:

(4)   ɛk wa jefi-a kali kali
      I ANT eat DUR little little
      'I was eating very little'

(B)   *Preverbal particles*

All the examples (1)–(4) include preverbal particles: In (1) we have a predicate marker *i* and an anterior marker *bin*; in (2) the negative element *ka* and the habitual marker *ta*; and in the Haitian example (3) the anterior marker *te* and the modal *pu*. In (4) we have the anterior marker *wa* and the durative suffix *-a*. Much work by creolists of various theoretical backgrounds has been dedicated to discovering the regularities in the preverbal particle system and *grosso modo* it boils down to something like the phrase structure rules in (5):

(5) a. S   → NP AUX VP
   b. AUX   → (negation)(predicate marker) tense, mood, aspect
   c. Tense   → anterior
    Mood   → irrealis
    Aspect   → perfective, progressive

Particularly (5c), and to a less extent (5b), have many exceptions, as pointed out in a number of recent articles and reviews of Bickerton (1981), a study in which preverbal particles play an important role in arguing that there are remarkable structural and semantic similarities among the creole languages. These similarities, in Bickerton's view, can only be due to innate linguistic capacities of the children who created the creoles on the basis of the pidgin input of their parents. Still, there is no doubt that the very existence and overall similarity of the preverbal particle systems needs to be explained by a theory of creole genesis.

(C) *Morphological simplicity*
Seen from the perspective of the European lexifier languages, the creole languages have very little inflectional morphology. This has led in the past to primarily negative characterizations of these languages: languages without properties x, y, and z. In (1)–(3) verbs have no tense and person marking, nouns lack case and number marking. Any number of the theories presented above can account for this feature of the creole languages, as the reader may wish to ascertain.

  A natural conclusion to draw from the absence of inflectional morphology is that it explains why there is no subject–verb inversion in the creole languages based on Portuguese and Spanish, and why subjects have to be obligatorily present even in these languages (Rizzi 1982). Compare (6a) with (6b) and (6c):

(6) a. e ta kome   Papiamentu
    he ASP eat
    'He is eating'
    (cf. Spanish *él está comiendo*)
   b. *ta kome
    ASP eat
    (cf. Spanish *está comiendo*)
   c. *ta kome maria
    ASP eat Maria
    (cf. Spanish *está comiendo María*)

This conclusion is only partially correct, however. It is not the absence of inflection, but rather the absence of pronominal features in the INFL node that accounts for the contrasts mentioned. This is clear from the data on Hawaiian English Creole given in Bickerton (1981). There is no inflection but there may be a pronominal element that is part of the preverbal particle cluster, and hence there is the possibility of inversion:

(7) a. sam gaiz samtaimz *dei* kam
     'Sometimes some guys come'

    b. difren bilifs *dei* get, sam gaiz
     'Some guys have different beliefs'

It remains to be seen to what extent other creoles present isolated instances of pronominal elements in INFL, allowing for pro-drop. Promising candidates are Tok Pisin and Papiamentu, where 1st and 2nd person pronouns sometimes appear to be part of the cluster of auxiliary particles. Hence the parameter of not allowing for pro-drop may not be completely general among the creole languages.

Having mentioned three properties that the creole languages share, we now turn to a feature in which we find large differences among creoles: serial verbs. Serial verb constructions are characterized, to put it in simple and perhaps provocative terms, by more than one verb per clause. Some examples:

(8) e-l-a *bula bay*   Papiamentu
     he ASP fly go
     'He flew away'

(9) li *pote* sa *bay* mo   Guyanais
     he bring that give me
     'He brought that for me'

(10) dɛm go in *tɛk* im *go* bak   Gullah
     they go and take him go back
     'They are going back with him'

In addition to the main content verb, another verb or set of verbs is used to mark an additional dimension of the predicate. In (11) I list some of the additional verbs found, together with the modification they bring about:

(11) *Locational*:   'come'   Direction towards
                        'go'   Direction away
                        'surround'   Around
                        'be'   Locative

     Argument: 'give NP'   Benefactive, dative
                        'take'   Instrumental, comitative, object
                        'say'   Finite complementizer

Degree:	'pass (NP)'	Comparative, 'too much'
	'suffice'	'Enough'
Aspectual:	'finish'	Perfective
	'return'	Iterative
	'be'	Locative, continuative

Other verbs are involved as well in individual languages, but the ones listed in (11) are the most important ones. Much more descriptive work is needed to determine which creole languages have which serial constructions. At present it seems that Haitian and the Surinam creoles Sranan and Saramaccan have the widest range of serial constructions. We can distinguish several semantic categories, as indicated in (11), and in addition there are a number of lexicalized combinations.

In contrast with the features of SVO word order, preverbal particles, and absence of inflection, the feature of serial verbs is not common to all creole languages. There are major differences between them in this respect, and at least three groups must be distinguished. I use the presence of the serial verb 'take', perhaps somewhat arbitrarily, as a diagnostic feature because this verb plays such a central role in the expression of grammatical relations:

(12) a. *Creoles with serial constructions, including 'take'*

Saramaccan

Sranan

Haitian

Krio

Gullah

Jamaican

Guyanais

b. *Creoles with serial constructions, but no 'take'*

Sao Tomé

Tok Pisin

Principe

Negerhollands

Papiamentu

c. *Creoles without serial verbs*

Philippine Creole Spanish

Hawaiian Creole English

Senegal Creole Portuguese

Mauritian Creole

Seychellois

Reunionais

This diversity poses considerable problems for the notion that all creole languages essentially share one grammar. Creolists have been aware of this, of course, attributing the diversity to any of three historical causes:

(a) Creoles were originally similar, but historical developments (particularly the type of colonial society and the proportion of different ethnic groups) have caused different degrees of deviation from the original basilect subsequent to the genesis of the creole languages.

(b) Creoles have been subject to different amounts of substratum influence, either because the slave populations were not equally homogeneous linguistically or because their numbers varied.

(c) The emerging creoles have been subject in different degrees to influences from the superstrate languages. In some early plantation societies there were a great many Europeans, in others very few.

There is no doubt that all these factors played a role, and a number of recent historical studies show the usefulness of careful documentation of the circumstances of creole genesis, but I very much doubt that we can explain away, in this fashion, the differences between the grammars of the different creoles.

Before turning to the notion of simplicity, I should mention one other difference between the grammars of the creole languages, a difference that has played a role in recent discussions about parameter theory: preposition-stranding (van Riemsdijk 1978; Kayne 1981). In fact, there turn out to be three types of creole languages with respect to stranding, as presented in (13):

(13) a. *Stranding allowed*:   Jamaican
                                         Krio
      b. *Stranding not allowed*:   Saramaccan
                                         Sranan
                                         Haitian
      c. *Stranding with trace spell-out*: Papiamentu

This is the same kind of parametric variation that we find among the European languages, and it is difficult to find an independent explanation for it. One could argue, for instance, that Jamaican allows stranding (the marked option?) under the influence of English, but the same could not hold for Krio. We return to preposition-stranding below.

14.II.2. **Are creole grammars simple?**

We will couch our discussion of simplicity in creole grammars by turning once again to serial verbs. How can we explain the presence of serial verbs in the creole languages? One type of answer lies in *category theory*. Serial verbs, such an answer might run, come in lieu of the use of prepositions; this category is absent since basic creoles only have nouns and verbs. A second type of answer lies in the theory of the *lexicon*: Serial verbs emerge because the basic creole verb is a two-place predicate, and some additional way is needed to mark grammatical relations. Let us look at both types of answer, discussed in Bickerton (1984), since both presuppose some kind of simplicity. Suppose we adopt the categorial features of Chomsky (1972), as in (14):

(14) a. Nouns $[+N, -V]$
       Verbs $[-N, +V]$
    b. Adjectives $[+N, +V]$
       Prepositions $[-N, -V]$

We have two basic maximally opposed categories, nouns and verbs, one mixed category, adjectives, and one neutral category, prepositions. A theory of markedness could make any one of three predictions, as set out in (a)–(c) below.

(a) A maximally unmarked system has just the opposed categories in (14a).
(b) The unmarked system has just the feature $[\pm N]$, resulting in a system such as (15):

(15) Nouns, adjectives $[+N]$
     Verbs, prepositions $[-N]$

(c) The unmarked system has just the feature $[\pm V]$, resulting in a system such as (16):

(16) Nouns, prepositions $[-V]$
     Verbs, adjectives $[+V]$

Creolists elaborating the notion of an unmarked category system will find little use for (15) and (16), since there are no obvious ways to relate nouns to either prepositions or adjectives. Superficially creole systems would be roughly as in (17):

(17) a. Verbs, adjectives, (prepositions)
    b. Nouns

Evidence for adjectives being a subclass of 'verbals' derives from their behavior in predicative constructions, as is shown in the following example from Saramaccan:

(18) a. a bi waka   'He walked/He had walked'
    b. a bi mangu   'He was thin/He had been thin'

While it is true that in Saramaccan adjectives of the class in (18) behave like verbs, there is a process of reduplication that creates true adjectives (Alleyne 1987), as in (19) and (20), if we take the presence of a copula to indicate that the complement is not a verb:

295

Table 2. *Basic prepositions in five creoles*

Haitian	Saramaccan	Krio	Principe	Negerhollands		
ak	ku	wit	ki	mit		'with'
na/kote	a		na	(n)a		'to'
na	a	na	na	(n)a		'in'
pa			po			'through'
su		pan				'on'
ka(y)	a	klos/to	na			'at'
pu	fu	fɔ	pa	fo		'for'
sã	sondo		si			'without'
žis	téé	ric	tɛ	tee		'until'

(19) di mii bunu   'The child is good'
       di mii de bunbunu   'The child is fine'

(20) a satu   'It has been salted'
       a de satusatu   'It is salty'

Sebba (1982) has argued for Sranan, as well, that adjectives need to be distinguished from verbs, even though they are superficially similar.

Let us now turn to the category of prepositions, more directly related to the issue of serial verbs. The hypothesis that serial verbs emerged because the creole languages had no category preposition in their initial stages will have to confront at least two objections. First, all creole languages, including those with extensive serialization, have the category preposition, as Table 2 demonstrates. These selective data show that even languages with extensive serialization possess a number of prepositions. Further research will reveal more prepositions, probably, since this is an under-researched area in creole linguistics. Thus it is not the absence of the category of preposition as such that gave rise to serial constructions.

The second objection to be made is that only a small number of serial verbs is used instead of prepositions, as our chart (11) illustrates. The use of serial verbs to mark aspect, degree, or location must have another source. Quite generally speaking, we find that the formal pattern of serialization is not linked to any specific semantic category, in the same way that the formal pattern of P+V phrase formation in Dutch (e.g. van Riemsdijk 1978) is involved both in marking grammatical relations, marking location, and lexical extension.

It should be noted that serial verbs have characteristics that differ from those of prepositions: they allow for stranding, and they can be involved in predicate cleft (cf. Jansen, Koopman & Muysken, 1978). Consider the contrasts in (21) and (22), taken from Sranan:

(21) a. *a   nefi san a e   koti a   brede *nanga* [e]
            the knife that he ASP cut   the bread with
            'The knife that he cuts the bread with'
      b. san   edgar *teki*.[e] koti a   brede
            what Edgar take   cut the bread
            'What did Edgar cut the bread with?'
      c. san   edgar *koti* [e]
            what Edgar cut
            'What did Edgar cut?'

The preposition *nanga* in (21a) cannot be stranded, while the serial verb *teki* in (21b) can; in this it is similar to an ordinary verb, as in (21c). Similarly, serial verbs can appear in predicate cleft constructions, (22b), just like ordinary verbs, (22c), while prepositions can't, (22a):

(22) a. *na *nanga* edgar koti a   brede *nanga* a   nefi
            be with Edgar cut the bread with   the knife
            'With the knife (really) Edgar cut the bread'
      b. na *teki* edgar *teki* a   nefi koti a   brede
            be take Edgar take the knife cut the bread
            'Really with the knife Edgar cut the bread'
      c. na *koti* edgar *koti* a   brede
            be cut Edgar cut the bread
            'Edgar really cut the bread'

Thus, grammatically serial verbs and prepositions are very different categories.

For these reasons, to explain the emergence of serial constructions by assuming that creoles have or had a much simpler category system, without prepositions, is not a promising line of research. The same holds for the idea that in the early creoles all verbs were simply two-place predicates, and that serialization is actually argument extension. The second objection to the absence of preposition hypothesis, that serial verbs are not only involved in argument extension, holds for this hypothesis as well, and furthermore, all creoles have double object constructions. Examples are given in (23):

(23) a. ham a   gi   de man si gout   Negerhollands
            he ASP give the man his gold
            'He gave the man his gold'
      b. mi ke   pindja i   wan soni   Saramaccan
            I want tell you one thing
            'I want to tell you something (in secret)'

297

c. bo a duna mi e buki   Papiamentu
   you ASP give me the book
   'You have given me the book'

d. mi soim yu banara bilong mi   Tok Pisin
   I show you bow PREP me
   'I show you my bow'

e. mõ pu deman mõ papa morso larzã   Seychellois
   I MOOD ask my father bit money
   'I shall ask my father for a little money'

f. li rakõte papa-li istwa sa-a   Haitian
   he tell father-he story this
   'He told his father this story'

All these examples show double object constructions, and on purpose I chose a number of them from languages of which the European lexifier language has no double object construction: Saramaccan and Papiamentu with a Portuguese lexical base, Haitian and Seychellois with a French lexical base. The inescapable conclusion is that creoles do have three-place predicates and this invalidates the possible explanation for the emergence of serial verbs.

In fact, Principe Portuguese Creole exhibits a contrast between the double object construction and the serial construction, as shown by Gunther (1973):

(24) pwé sa *dá* mínu dyó   /   *da* dyó *da* mínu
     father ASP give child money / . . . give money give child
     'Father gives the child money / . . . gives money for the child'

(25) n ka *futá* mwí   mε dyó   / . . . *futá* dyó   *da* mwí   mé
     I ASP steal mother my money / . . . steal money give mother my
     'I stole money from my mother / . . . stole money for my mother'

In the double object construction the meaning of the sentences depends on the semantics of the main verb, but when a serial verb is added, a specific interpretation associated with that verb is brought in.

Thus it seems that any explanation for the emergence of serial verbs that claims that they were called upon for a specific semantic function will not work. Can we find a more formal explanation, still maintaining the assumption that creole languages are simple in a theoretically interesting way? One way to explain the emergence of serial verbs would be to say that it is simply the optionality of the subject inside of S that would constitute a simplification, allowing for verb phrases to occur as constituents separate from any subject. The disadvantage of this is that it would be rather stipulative: why are subjects optional? Is the optionality of the subject a parameter in itself (the subject being optional being the unmarked option)? It seems to me that the second interpretation of simplicity that we have discussed could be promising: the formal separation of V and INFL in creoles may have as its effect that verbs no longer automatically have subject associated with them, since the subject is required by INFL rather than by the verb itself. This frees the verb phrase from its primary function (in nonserializing languages) of being the predicate of the subject, and allows for all kinds of other (secondary) predications: aspect marking, degree marking, marking of additional arguments and of additional locational information.

4.II.3. Are creole grammars mixed systems?

The idea that creole languages are mixed systems, resulting from the matching of an African, Oceanic, or Asian syntax with the lexicon of a European language is quite old. We find it in Schuchardt's (1921) study of Saramaccan, Turner's book on Gullah (1949), Comhaire-Sylvain's work on Haitian (1936), and more recently in Alleyne's work on the Caribbean English-based creoles (1981). The idea of a lexicon–syntax matching is as attractive as it is misguided, however. There is a host of grammatical differences between the creoles and the African etc. languages that they are related to. It must be a smaller set of features, then, that was incorporated into the creole languages.

To ascertain this set forces us, as well, to define the feature transferred in very precise grammatical terms. I will illustrate this with two grammatical phenomena: predicate cleft and serialization.

Predicate cleft was illustrated briefly in example (22) above: the main verb appears twice, in focus position and in its original position. This construction occurs in most, if not all, Caribbean and West African creoles, as well as in an important subset of the African languages. It does not occur in the Indian Ocean or Pacific creoles. This distribution makes it a promising candidate for postulating a substratum origin. There is considerable syntactic and semantic variation in this respect between the creole languages, however, which would need to be explained. Predicate cleft is interpreted as intensification of the action expressed by the fronted verb in some languages, and as focussing on that action in others. In addition, the locality restrictions vary considerably from creole to creole, as shown in (26):

(26) a. Unbounded predicate cleft (subject to island conditions) in African languages and Haitian (Piou 1982; Koopman 1984; Clements p.c.).
     b. Clause-bound predicate cleft in Papiamentu (Muysken 1978).
     c. Predicate cleft across one clause boundary in Sranan and Saramaccan (Sebba 1986; Byrne 1987).

The parameter-setting allowing for predicate cleft suggested by Koopman (1984) will only work effectively for (26a) and may not even carry over exactly to Haitian. The fact that predicate cleft in the Caribbean creoles may be a much more local phenomenon than in the African languages could point to a restriction on substratum influence that it can only involve local features. If this insight could be made precise, we would have a way of defining conditions on mixibility of components in terms of their locality.

Just as predicate clefts, serial verbs are a plausible candidate for substratum influence. They are a common feature of the Kwa family of West African languages, occur in most West African and Caribbean creoles, and they do not occur in the Indian Ocean and Pacific creoles, with one exception – Tok Pisin (and there it may be possible to claim substratum influence from Austronesian languages). Again, however, lexical variation with respect to serial verbs between the different creole languages makes it hard to define what exactly was transferred. If it is possible for VPs to occur as secondary predicates, dissociated from INFL, as suggested above, why can certain verbs participate in this feature but not others? If it was actually a property of lexical items, i.e. certain verbs, that was transferred, why do we have innovations in the New World in serial verb use, such as Saramaccan *poi* (from 'spoil') as a kind of degree marker with negative connotations? Similarly to predicate cleft in the creole languages, serialization is a local phenomenon in that it always involves an immediate government configuration, as in (27), a structural representation of the serial verbs in (8):

(27)

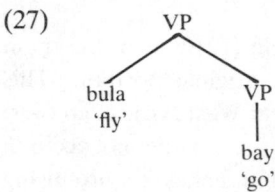

If we can think of serialization in the creoles as having resulted from language 'mixture', again we may consider it a local kind of mixture.

The substratum hypothesis has as much chance of being correct as any other hypothesis about creole genesis, but the very brief discussion of predicate cleft and serialization illustrates the kind of conceptual and empirical problems it still faces (in addition to those pointed out by critics of the substratum idea, such as Bickerton 1981). Still, the notion of mixture forces grammatical theorists to think very precisely about what a grammatical feature exactly is. To conclude, thinking of creole languages as alike, simple, and mixed is far from unproblematic. The very notion of a 'creole' language from the linguistic point of view tends to disappear if one looks closely; what we have is just a language.

REFERENCES

Alleyne, M. C. 1981. *Comparative Afro-American*. Ann Arbor: Karoma.
Alleyne, M. C. 1987. Studies in the structure of Saramaccan. *Caribbean Culture Studies* 2.
Andersen, R. W. (ed.) 1983. *Pidginization and creolization as language acquisition*. Rowley: Newbury House.
Bickerton, D. 1981. *Roots of language*. Ann Arbor: Karoma.
Bickerton, D. 1984. The language bioprogram hypothesis. *Behavioral and Brain Sciences* 7, 2: 173–221.
Bosman, D. B. 1923. *Oor die onstaan van Afrikaans*. Amsterdam: Swets & Zeitlinger.
Byrne, F. 1987. *Grammatical relations in a radical creole. Complementation in Saramaccan*. Amsterdam: Benjamins.
Chomsky, N. 1972. The Amherst lectures. ms.
Chomsky, N. 1981. *Lectures on government and binding*. Dordrecht: Foris.
Chomsky, N. 1982. *Some concepts and consequences of the theory of government and binding*. Cambridge: MIT Press.
Comhaire-Sylvain, S. 1936. *Le créole haitien: morphologie et syntaxe*. Port-au-Prince.
Gunther, W. 1973. *Das portugiesische Kreolisch der Ilha do Principe*. Marburger Studien zur Afrika- und Asienkunde A.2.
Hancock, I. 1986. The componential approach to creole genesis. In P. Muysken & N. Smith (eds.) *Substrata versus universals in creole genesis*. Amsterdam: Benjamins.
Jansen, B., Koopman, H. & Muysken, P. 1978. Serial verbs in the creole languages. *Amsterdam Creole Studies* II.
Kayne, R. 1981. On certain differences between French and English. *Linguistic Inquiry* 12: 349–71.
Koopman, H. 1984. *The syntax of verbs. Verb movement in Vata and in universal grammar*. Dordrecht: Foris.
Lefebvre, C. 1986. Relexification revisited: the case of Haitian. In P. Muysken & N. Smith (eds.) *Substrata versus universals in creole genesis*. Amsterdam: Benjamins.
Muysken, P. C. 1978. Three types of fronting in Papiamentu. In F. Jansen (ed.) *Studies on fronting*. Lisse: Peter de Ridder; distributed by Foris.
Naro, A. J. 1978. A study of the origins of pidginization. *Language* 54, 2: 314–47.
Piou, N. 1982. Le clivage du prédicat. In C. Lefebvre, H. Magloire-Holly & N. Piou (eds.) *Syntaxe de l'haitien*. Ann Arbor: Karoma.
Raidt, E. H. 1983. *Einfuhrung in Geschichte und Struktur des Afrikaans*. Darmstadt: Wissenschaftliche Buchgesellschaft.
Riemsdijk, H. C. van 1978. *A case study in syntactic markedness*. Dordrecht: Foris.
Rizzi, L. 1982. *Studies in Italian syntax*. Dordrecht: Foris.
Sankoff, G. 1980. *The social life of language*. Philadelphia: University of Pennsylvania Press.
Schuchardt, H. 1921. *Die Sprache der Saramakkaneger in Surinam*. Verhandelingen der Koninklijke Akademie van Wetenschappen te Amsterdam, NS 14, 6.
Sebba, M. 1982. Adjectives and comparatives in Sranan. *Amsterdam Creole Studies* IV.
Sebba, M. 1986. *The syntax of serial verbs. A study of Sranan and other creoles*. Amsterdam: Benjamins.
Seuren, P. M. 1983. The auxiliary system in Sranan. In F. Heny & B. Richards (eds.) *Linguistic categories: auxiliaries and related puzzles 2*. Dordrecht: Reidel.
Seuren, P. M. & Wekker, H. 1986. Semantic transparency as a factor in creole genesis. In P. Muysken & N. Smith (eds.) *Substrata versus universals in creole genesis*. Amsterdam: Benjamins.
Smith, N. S. H., Robertson, I. & Williamson, K. 1987. The Ijọ element in Berbice Dutch. *Language in Society* 16: 49–90.
Stowell, T. A. 1981. The origins of phrase structure. Doctoral dissertation, MIT.
Tesnière, L. 1939. Phonologie et mélange des languages. *Travaux du Cercle Linguistique de Prague* 8: 83–93.
Turner, L. D. 1949. *Africanisms in the Gullah dialect*. Chicago: University of Chicago Press.
Whinnom, K. 1965. The origin of European-based pidgins and creoles. *Orbis* 14: 509–27.

14.III A dialog concerning the linguistic status of creole languages

Derek Bickerton

In Pieter Muysken's stimulating, informative, and comprehensive overview of creole theories there are unfortunately one or two misinterpretations of my position. While I have claimed that creoles are more *alike* than other languages, and have suggested that they may be in some sense more *natural* than other languages, I don't think I have ever explicitly stated that they are more *simple*: the whole concept of simplicity in language is strewn with epistemological and other landmines, and should perhaps be avoided altogether.

Again, on a minor point of detail, it is not the case that 'around them, [first-generation creole children] only heard pidgin spoken.' Obviously, they also heard an indefinite number of ancestral languages; these, however, they ignored, precisely because the elaboration of the pidgin represented, to them, far less of a task than the learning of an ancestral language and the subsequent transfer of features from that language to the nascent creole. The nature of the bioprogram rendered input from other languages quite unnecessary for them.

In light of the approach sketched in the present chapter, two of Muysken's 'core notions', parameter theory and morphology–syntax interactions, simply fall together: parametric variation is relegated to the lexicon and the interaction between a variable morphology and invariant principles of syntax is what in fact produces the so-called 'parametric differences' among languages. As for markedness, it is no longer clear to me that this concept is helpful. Rather than claim that creoles have (largely) unmarked lexical and morphological properties, I think I would prefer to say simply that, due to the stripping process of pidginization, they inherit fewer such properties, and it is this paucity, rather than a particular (unmarked) type of property, that gives creole languages their high degree of similarity.

As for the differences between creoles that seem so salient to Muysken, these are predictable from the simple fact that (due to circumstances described above) the number of morphological items inherited by different creoles, and the number of original properties that these items retained, were both variables. It is no accident, for instance, that the creoles that have few or no serial constructions are those that inherited the largest amount of superstrate morphology, while the creoles with the most serial constructions are precisely those that inherited least morphology from their superstrates.

Muysken tackles, and predictably routs, the straw-man argument that preposition loss was the cause of verb serialization. But of course it was not only prepositions that were lost; complementizers, adverbs and members of other categories were lost too, and verbs were recruited to discharge the functions of these. Naturally, such verbs retained many of their verbal properties – in many cases they could be fronted, stranded and so on. There is nothing either surprising or contrary to the present position in the range of facts that Muysken points out.

But even in the specific case of the relationship between 'case-marking' serials and preposition loss, Muysken's main argument – that creoles often preserve the corresponding prepositions, and that therefore serial verbs did not have to be introduced for government or case-marking purposes – goes through only under the assumption that creole languages were homogenous from the beginning. But this assumption is counter to fact in most, perhaps all, cases. A variety of factors, including the early colonial demographics referred to above, a rigid system of social stratification, and the isolation of geographic regions and even single plantations from one another, produced in most cases a variety of dialects rather than a single homogenous creole. In some cases, these dialects leveled or merged; in others, e.g. Haiti, they remain fairly separate even today; in others, e.g. Guyana, they formed a stable continuum; in Surinan, they gave rise to several distinct languages.

What this means is that in many cases, dialects *without* preposition x (and thereby forced to develop serialization) existed alongside dialects *with* preposition x, and thus without serials. If these dialects subsequently merged, both expressions would continue to exist side by side in the same language. Such a development is clearly apparent in Saramaccan, with its joint stock of Portuguese and English lexical items. It is no accident that the instrumental (*ku*) preposition is from the Portuguese stock while the instrumental serial verb (*tei* 'take') is from the English stock. Clearly, the English-influenced members of the original Saramaccan population did not inherit a preposition (there is no reflex of *with* in the language) and therefore had to recruit an English verb to govern and case-mark nouns with instrumental θ-roles; however, the Portuguese-influenced contingent did inherit the appropriate preposition, and therefore did not develop a Portuguese serial verb.

In other cases where instrumental prepositions and instrumental serials are found side by side, there are good reasons for supposing that the former was originally a comitative – for instance, Sranan *nanga*, which also appears as an NP (but never as an S) conjunction. Muysken's Table 2 will soon disabuse the reader of any suspicion that prepositions were inherited with their superstrate functions and properties intact. None of the equivalents of *to* can have a dative (or indeed any other than a locative) reading in any creole; few of the *for* equivalents will take a benefactive reading. On the other hand, equivalents to *to* and *in* have fallen together in at least four out of Muysken's five creoles (as well as in many he does not mention). Finally, one should note that only three out of eight basic prepositions (the ninth, *until*, is only a complementizer in most creoles) have reflexes in all five creoles. Certainly, as Muysken claims, prepositions constituted a class in all creoles, but that class was a severely defective one, and where particular prepositions were missing, verbs (the only other [−N] major category) were the only things that could be recruited to fill the gaps.

Since Muysken is very properly suspicious of the substratophile approach, he finds himself without any explanation of serial constructions. Indeed, his conclusion that 'the substratum hypothesis has as much chance of being correct as any other' seems strangely at odds with the material that he himself has surveyed. On the substratum side, as Muysken is fully aware, there is a dearth of hard facts and a singular lack of coherent argumentation. In contrast, the bioprogram hypothesis is backed by massive evidence from language acquisition and socio-historical data as well as from comparative creole studies; alone among the 'theories' (many hardly worthy of that name) that Muysken lists, it provides a coherent and self-consistent account of all aspects of the creolization process that fits both the creole data and what is known about how language in general is acquired and transmitted.

Pieter Muysken

The major innovation presented in Derek Bickerton's, in many ways lucid and insightful, paper is the attempt to embed the language bioprogram hypothesis as presented in Bickerton (1981, 1984) within the lexical learning hypothesis developed by Borer and Wexler at the University of California at Irvine. Quite independently of what we think about the latter approach to linguistic variation (my personal view is that its very simplicity holds promise, at least as a research program), Bickerton's adopting it raises a number of issues.

The first one is primarily methodological. The proposal is that we should look at three categories of morphemes in contemporary creoles:

(a) those maintained from the lexifier language in some form, e.g. Sranan *waka* from English *walk*;

(b) those that have been lost and not been reconstituted in the creole, e.g. English agentive *by*;

(c) those that have been lost and the meaning of which is expressed by some other element, e.g. the English complementizer *that*, which appears in Sranan as *taki* (from *talk*) as a factive complementizer and as *di* (from *disi* 'this') in relative clauses.

Now what morpheme falls into what category is not by itself revealing: a number of factors (frequency, morphophonemic simplicity, phonological saliency, phonological markedness, grammatical complexity, perhaps also semantic transparency) may intervene in retention or loss. What is claimed to be important is the distinction between (b) and (c), and the paper falls back on markedness theory, in combination with the idea of a single universal grammar (UG) contained in the lexical learning hypothesis, to explain why certain 'core' elements fall into (c) and others into (b).

What concerns me at this point is the assumption, implicit in this approach, that the vocabulary of the pidgin is a fairly simple function of the vocabulary of the lexifier language: if the latter has *n* words, the pidgin has simply a proper subset of those *n*. Perhaps the lexical entries have lost some of their features, but they are assumed to be basically the same lexical entries. This assumption runs counter to the possibility that what went on in the very early stages of language contact was massive restructuring of the vocabulary of the lexifier language. Restructuring could have come about through relexification or second language learning.

In relexification, the abstract properties of lexical entries of the native languages of the slaves are matched with phonological representations from the lexifier language (this possibility is rejected as relevant to pidginization by Bickerton, to be fair). In second language learning, the abstract properties of the lexical items of the lexifier language are simplified and reinterpreted.

In fact, the word *morpheme* is used ambiguously, both for the phonological form and for the abstract lexico-semantic-syntactic category or feature expressed by that form in the lexifier language. A more adequate classification would be something like:

(a) neither form nor content retained

(b) form retained, different content

(c) content retained, different form

(d) both form and content retained

From what we know of the evolution of pidgins, L2 learner systems, and creoles, there are many cases of (b) and (c), many of them documented by

Bickerton in earlier work. This makes it very difficult to find out from an inspection of the present-day creole lexicon what lexical items or morphemes the pidgin had or didn't have, as Bickerton proposes.

The other problem with linking the language bioprogram hypothesis directly to the lexical learning hypothesis is that the latter assumes an invariant UG and the former relies heavily on some notion of markedness. The main attraction of Bickerton's original idea was that it explains the observation that many creoles have very similar preverbal tense/mood/aspect particle systems, by assuming that these are unmarked in the AUX component of UG. Now within the notion of an invariant UG of Wexler & Borer there is no place for markedness in the syntax. There may be more or less marked sections of the lexicon, but that is it. Now it is hard to recapture Bickerton's original insight within a lexical account: what is particularly lexical about the notion of anterior tense? Perhaps the whole original notion that creoles are unmarked systems semantically was misguided, but so far it remains as the most substantial contribution of Bickerton to the field. Now there is no base for it.

These critical remarks notwithstanding, the focus on the creole lexicon in the present chapter is long overdue, and when used with caution will lead to exciting research.

Subject Index

Abnormal language acquisition 96–114
Accessibility, cognitive 153–5
Accessibility hierarchy (AH) 58
Accommodatory phenomena 121
Acquisition *see* First language acquisition, Second language acquisition, Abnormal language acquisition
Age-dependent variation in linguistic capacity 90–1
American Sign Language (ASL) 101, 113, 251–64: adjectives 254; adverbs 255; aspect inflection 254, 260; distinct movement contours 260; locus shifting 262–3; morphology 253–5, 257, 259–60; nouns 255; phonology 252–3, 255–9, 264; sequentiality 253; sublexical structure 252–3; verbs 254, 256–7, 259–61
Anaphora, first language acquisition and 45–6; quantifier binding and 155–7; relevance theory account of 153–5; second language acquisition of 58–60; Truth-conditional semantics and 142–7, 153–5; *see also* Pronouns 42–8, 58–60, 142–7, 153–7
Aphasia 76–81, 90, 118: agraphia 77; alexia 77; anomic 77, 83; apraxia 77; Broca's 76–80; conduction 77; global 79; linguistic analysis of 78–80; Wernicke's 76–81, 83
Applied linguistics 2, 198–216
Architectonic areas of brain 82, 88
Arcuate fasciculus 77
Articles: discourse analysis and 172–4
Artificial intelligence (AI) 202, 216
Aspects of the theory of syntax: language processing and 3, 4, 17
Audiolingual method 2
Augmented transition network (ATN) 206–9
Autism 103
Autonomy hypothesis 5–7, 20–6, 31–2
Autosegmental phonology 129–30, 229,
257–8; *see also* CV phonology, Suprasegmental features
Auxiliary in child language 36–7

Behaviorist psychology 1–2, 53
Binding 47–8, 60
Biological endowment for language 74–92
Bioprogram hypothesis *See* Creole languages
Bounding domain (phonology) 235
Brain structures and language 74–92
Broca's aphasia *See* Aphasia
Brodmann area 83

Case grammar 210–11
Categorical opposition 227
Causatives 37
C-command 43–6, 148: effects on acquisition process 43–5
Center-embeddings 7–8
Characteristic adjective rule (in ASL) 253–4
Child language *See* First language acquisition
Chinese regulated verse 225–6
Choline acetyltransferase 83
Chomsky-hierarchy 204
Cleft constructions: *dos* (in Yiddish) 169–71; *es* (in Yiddish) 169–71; *it* 169–71
Cloze procedure 23
Cognitive psychology 2, 16, 216
Competence 200–1: discourse and 164–79; linguistic 5–7, 122–5, 164–79; performance and 122–5, 200–1; pragmatic 166–7; speech error support for 122–36
Competing plan hypothesis 118–19
COMP-INFL parameter 61
Complements: head-direction and 58–9, 62–3; second language acquisition of 58–9, 62–3
Complementizers (COMP) 49n, 61, 79
Complexity metric 221

307

Name Index

Contents of Volumes I, III, and IV

Volume IV   Language: the socio-cultural context